HAVE FUN AT WORK
WILLIAM L. LIVINGSTON

HAVE FUN AT WORK
WILLIAM L. LIVINGSTON

HAVE FUN AT WORK

By William L. Livingston

Published by:

F.E.S. LTD. Publishing
Box 70, Bayside NY 11361 USA

First Printing 1988

Printed in the United States of America

Library of Congress Cataloging in Publication Data
Livingston, William L.

Have Fun At Work

1. Management, Principles of   2. Complex Problems   I Title

Library of Congress Catalog Card Number 88-81542

L53   658.404

ISBN 0-937063-05-3 softcover

F.E.S. LTD.
PUBLISHING
BOX 70 BAYSIDE N.Y. 11361

Unfun At Work

The monthly project review meeting has concluded and three of the workers who were in attendance have gathered in a quiet corner. The men are trying to score the presentations made by their managers.

"Hey, Joe, that was some crazy meeting," said Ace, "How could all those guys cover up like that, and keep straight faces? Everyone in the room knows the project is in big trouble, and yet they carried on like nothing was wrong. Did you hear Casella tell Simpson that the control console will be shipped next month? No way! I know Purchasing made them go out on competitive bid for the meters and the order hasn't made it through the accounting signoff steeplechase yet."

"Look Ace, it was the same blizzard conditions last month," responded Joe, "and it will be the same deep snow-job next month too. They put on the ritual meeting to keep the client paying the bills."

"For crying out loud," said Dan, "even an airhead could figure out something's wrong. The project is already a year late, and the latest budget to completion is more than we bid for the whole job at the start. If anything, there's more cover-up going on now than before."

Joe dropped something on the floor and spoke from behind the desk.

"Have you noticed, Dan," said Joe, "that this project is going down just like the last one we worked on? Remember the fire-fighting we had to do on the Astoria job when they finally admitted the computers weren't talking to each other? Same as now. It just doesn't make sense. The two customer organizations don't even know each other. Yet, there seems to be a pattern. This kind of junk went on all the time in the last company I worked for too, and it wasn't even in the same damn industry."

Joe stood up. "Hey, suppose it's us," he said. "Maybe we're too stupid to know how to handle these kinds of things. We must be doing something wrong. Somebody, somewhere must have worked out the answer to this situation. Tell you what. Let's put on a conference and invite everybody here. That way we can find out who has the answers and we can copy their approach. I can get the Engineering Society to sponsor a workshop on computer applications, and no one will be the wiser about our real intent. It will be a lot of sweat, but what do you say?"

"The idea stinks like work, Joe, but let's do it," offered Ace, "I've had it with wasting my time trying to get the bozos in engineering and operations to work together."

"It doesn't look like we're going to get any help from upstairs," Dan added. "The only thing they know how to do is ask for more reports. Every time I try to tell them about the problems down on the design floor, they recite Rule One: 'You get paid to solve problems, not complain about them.'"

The workshop notice went out all over the country to clients and competitors alike. The audience was too large to fit into the one auditorium, so the crowd was handled in three groups. For three days every related subject was covered and the discussions were put on tape. When the meetings were finally over, Dan, Joe and Ace met to summarize the findings.

"Now I know why they call it a workshop," cried Dan, "That pace just wore me out. I can't believe all the war stories I heard. What a mess!"

"Did you hear the racket at the party last night?" said Ace, "These guys were going bonkers hearing the same news coming out of each other. The one about automating the refinery in Texas was unbelievable."

Joe volunteered, "What have we done, unleashed the forces of evil? We went to all this trouble looking for answers and all we found was a bunch of poor slobs caught up in scenes worse than ours. And they were from everywhere and in everything!"

The discoveries that unfold before you in this book began for Dan and Ace and Joe when they had to return to their project empty-handed. Going home to the mess was a drag. The old feeling of helplessness was augmented by a new feeling of hopelessness. Without the "fix" they had hoped for, the project lumbered on in futility. The schedule slipped again, and again, and the costs continued out of control. No one said anything about the vital issues, and everyone acted as if everything was going to work out by itself. The client was continuing to let it all happen and gradually going bankrupt in the process. The lawyers were starting to swarm.

This is not a fun situation.

Foreword

First impressions can be deceiving. Cartoons and slang expressions can make for what appears to be a funny book. And what follows is, indeed, just that. But this is also a very serious book about a very serious topic: the seeming inability of our contemporary organizational structures to deal with complex technology. From the back rooms of the capitol to the boardrooms of Detroit, from space technology to nuclear power, from basic design to quality control, we seem to be awash in technological failures that upon investigation reveal no shortcomings in technology at all, but **repetitive organizational behavior patterns** of duplicity, coverup, failure to communicate, and outright stupidity, just to name a few.

The notion that this is a serious problem was perhaps at its most striking during the Challenger inquiry. It was suggested at that time that the problem was serious enough to warrant criminal charges based on the organizational behavior of the booster manufacturer. Fortunately or unfortunately, depending on your point of view, that did not come to pass. Nevertheless, the gauntlet has been thrown down and judicial thinking will have to grapple with management responsibility for organizational dysfunction, or what our author likes to call "only the most significant problem facing the human race."

Interestingly enough, judicial thinking in tort law is not entirely unprepared to deal with the central conceptual theme that runs through Livingston's work, i.e., negligence, although not named as such. Or to frame Livingston's issue in terms of the appropriate legal question, "What is the duty of care that a person (manager) of ordinary prudence would exercise under the same or similar circumstances."

English and American jurisprudence have grappled with this problem since the inception of that uniquely English phenomenon known as the Industrial Revolution. In a now-famous 1921 arbitration proceeding in England (the Polemis case, 3 K.B. 560 (C.A. 1921)), the court was faced with a stevedore who had negligently dropped a scaffold-board into the hold of a ship. Unknown to the stevedore or anyone else, the hold contained a high concentration of benzene vapors. An explosion followed. On final appeal, the King's Bench ruled that since **the act itself** was negligent, the fact that its exact operation (outcome) was not foreseen was immaterial, holding the defendant liable for damages. Thus did the concept of **foreseeability** find its way into our jurisprudence.

Not particularly satisfied with the Polemis ruling, no less a figure than Chief Justice Cardozo of the New York Supreme Court decided in 1928 that foreseeability was indeed the issue, but that it operated to limit liability. In Paulsgraf v. Long Island Railroad Co., 162 N.E. 99 (N.Y. 1928), Justice Cardozo was faced with a railroad porter, who, in assisting a passenger onto a train, accidentally dislodged a package containing unknown fireworks. The package fell under the wheels of the train. The resulting explosion caused a set of scales to fall on Mrs. Paulsgraf who was standing farther down the platform.

Unfortunately for Mrs. Paulsgraf, the Chief Justice ruled that the lack of foreseeability of her injuries from the falling package absolved the railroad. Imagine Mrs. Paulsgraf's frustration. Too bad her lawyer didn't base her suit on the railroad's duty of care to secure the scales, an issue not presented to Chief Justice Cardozo for decision. But that's another topic. Nevertheless, a rule of **"see no evil, expect no liability"** found its way into our jurisprudence.

The frustration of the Mrs. Paulsgrafs of this world was not to go without redress, however. It is that frustration that has arguably led to an entire new corpus of tort law called **strict product liability.** Simply stated, the law (Restatement Section Torts, sec. 402A) states that if a product placed into the stream of commerce injures a person or property, the manufacturer and seller are held strictly liable, i.e., they are liable for damages even though they were not negligent. Stated in Livingstonese, if an organization doesn't do its foreseeability homework, liability for damages caused by their products will ensue. Polemis lives!

It is from within this judicial tradition that Livingston's work should be read. When he speaks of the need to conduct interdisciplinary work to uncover the unintended functions that a control system **can exhibit,** he is talking foreseeability homework. When he speaks of organizational roadblocks, social controls, coverup, undiscussables, fuzzball eaters or whatever, he is addressing the failure of organization managers to exercise their duty of ordinary care.

Laugh at the cartoons and enjoy the book. But don't dismiss it. It is a very small judicial step from strict product liability to strict management liability. The foundation is laid. And when the inevitable courtroom drama unfolds, justice may be addressing not just ordinary but gross negligence, punitive damages, and better yet, the rather permeable membrane that separates tortious and criminal conduct. It is a very serious matter.

Daniel J. Shea, Jr.
South Texas College of Law
Houston, 1988

Contents

Illustrations, Charts & Diagrams

Preface

The goal of this book is to help workers, especially those who have been captured in the corporate zoo, to have fun on the job. As the horrible statistics of employee stress shout, most people are not enjoying the work scene. This prevalent situation is not caused by some inherent feature of the arrangement which, because change is impossible, must somehow be endured. It is due to ignorance.

The reader is warned about two necessary evils for removing the basic impediment of ignorance. The first is that you will have to think. Acquiring competence for having fun at work is work for the brain. The book is a kind of mental health spa to reduce stress, where the weight machine is replaced by a large conglomeration of concepts and evidence. The second cranial challenge is that the subject matter is presented as a buildup of connected packages. The prescription for having fun at work is presented only after the foundation network has been thoroughly prepared. If you want context, you will have to start from the beginning. This book is not a collection of stand-alone essays.

The good news is that you will be able to understand the long train of thought by reference to your own experience. This book is about things you already know, but seldom bring to your consciousness. Although the material presented is more taboo than an entire catalog of illegal subject matter, it breaks no law. The copyright was obtained out of habit, not because of any functional purpose. There is no danger that other writers will have the courage to criticize the source of their income. It takes some guts to read this book.

The book is for workers written by a worker who **has had it**. I get considerable satisfaction out of knowing the Establishment has banned the book. It makes us even. The first offering in the series, **The New Plague,** had management and professors at management training camps confused as to which parade I was marching in. This book removes all doubt in blunt fashion. It is simply impossible to have fun at work by following the dictates of the 'system.'

The layout of the book is designed for three kinds of workers. Those who read will find the language in the narrative story somewhat in excess of kindergarten level and they are rewarded with a rich array of case histories punctuated by "rules." For the legions who don't read, the same story is told in cartoons. All workers in between can try the plain-speak captions associated with the graphics. As a further convenience, the graphics were placed **verso,** or primarily on the left-hand page. The non-readers can thereby thumb through with one hand and never even have to look at all those intimidating polysyllabic phrases. The feature also eliminates tossing the book back and forth at the copy machine when all you want to reproduce are the cartoons.

Chapters 1 & 2 survey the ubiquitous wreckage coming off of the assembly line and present the array of non-contributory factors. The next two Chapters present the trigger condition and the process which produces the wreckage. The first four Chapters, then, are a set which describes WHAT happens. Chapter 5 introduces some concepts that are necessary to understand the WHY, which is covered in the next four Chapters. The topical content switches from the language of failure to the language of success at Chapter 10 and continues for another Chapter. The reason the book is banned by every sector of the Establishment, and a reason you will find quite understandable after reading it, is Chapter 12. It was written as something you could attach to your letter of resignation and save the trouble of burning a lot of bridges. The instruction manual for having fun at work is provided in Chapters 13 & 14. The last Chapter is a summary of tools and aids showing some of the ways each can be used.

The editor, designer and producer of this book was Carolyn Bonnie Crosby. All of the graphic material displays in whole or in part the benefits of her inspiration and effort, over a wide range of talents, and this book is a testament to her skills. Her contribution was essential to making the book happen, and it is thankfully acknowledged.

The major source of encouragement to explore the uncharted waters of organizational behavior came from the readers of **The New Plague.** Their response helped to separate the victims from their enemies and directed attention to the most fruitful places. Special people deserve special thanks: Mal Beaverstock, Leo Beltracchi, Robert Carroll, Ben Clymer, Bruce Fairchild, John Gabriel, Richard Gitlin, Acisclo Liquet, Robert Lundberg, Sean McClure, William Perry, Jim Peterson, Richard Riker, Don Schurman, Dan Shea, Dominick Sollecito, Mark Tagliamonte, and Paul Whelan.

It is one of the paradoxes in the behavior business that the closer you approach to truth about organizations, the more people are afraid to be associated with your activities. Thanks is tendered to the many full members of the Establishment who made it clear when I was getting close to 'home.' Their behavior is an indispensible aid to navigate me directly toward their vulnerabilities. It is only when the Establishment is indifferent that steering is guesswork.

William L. Livingston, III
Bayside, New York

HAVE FUN AT WORK
WILLIAM L. LIVINGSTON

Chapter One

Here, there, everywhere

The opening story of Dan, Ace and Joe is not a rare account. You can read one of the stream of letters about the same experience. The sample is placed in the back of the book for those who start from the finish. Discovery that things are not always sensible at work is a natural product of experience and personal injury. The pain builds when it is finally realized there is no place in the organization where such discoveries can be taken for a fair hearing - which then dawns little hope for correction.

We were convinced for years that the answer to big failures in large programs and projects must be around, somewhere. The search was eventually extended by a study of government projects of all kinds and sizes. The lowdown on various developments in the military, aerospace and commerce was first obtained through relatives, friends, association contacts, and extensive reading. One story led to another. More connections led to others. It is not difficult to find examples of big failures in government programs and projects. Just look.

Surely the government knows

We learned that the methodological Merlins of the government were able to foul up practically anything. The scenarios, all basically the same, started to become quite familiar. No correcting mechanism could be found. It was just more war stories. Thinking that the pandemic of project disasters might be a brainchild of the current administration, the US Navy was arbitrarily singled out for a review of its history with technology (the military keeps excellent records of their activities). We present a small sample of the continuing saga of this large, entrenched, antiquated organization in its typical dealings with a changing world in order to illustrate the persistent pattern of failure you can find anywhere. Just look.

In 1845, a civilian named Isambard Kingdom Brunel built a large iron-hulled commercial ship, driven by a screw propeller, called "Great Britain." This vessel could outrun any warship in service. By 1860, concerned that a Navy which couldn't keep up with merchant vessels would have little future, the British Royal Navy built the "H.M.S. Warrior." This battlewagon was a combined sail-steam design 425 feet long equipped with unheard-of firepower, which scared the rest of Europe and the United States right down to their shipyards.

The American answer to the "Warrior" was the "Wampanoag." Built in 1868, the "Wampanoag" was a man-of-war, totally steam powered, displacing 4,200 tons (the "Warrior" was over 9,000 tons). It featured a screw propeller 19 feet in diameter and an iron hull. A narrow beam and 355 feet of length allowed it to be the fastest ship in the world. Averaging over 17 knots, the "Wampanoag" rode well and was declared by the captain and the crew to be "perfect." Hardly a project disaster at that point, in two years the Navy turned the "Wampanoag" into a floating office permanently tied to a pier - their reasoning being that such vessels would change the status of jobs aboard ship and thereby alter the way the Navy conducts its business afloat. The decision to retreat to the status quo of sail power was made at the same time foreign nations adopted the steam-powered technology as standard.

More Conservative - More Waste

New technology and banks form a contradiction in terms. The treatment of every issue as one which can be fixed by throwing money at it is joined with a mindset which equates error to sin. The result is endless expense to save face, and endless disaster. Conservative corporations, like insurance companies, railroads, government bureaus, and universities, always provide the largest cases of failure for study. Their slogan, "We're no worse than the others," is the only released comment which is true.

The next noted Navy technology caper involved the aiming of guns. It was traditional practice to set the aim of the cannon when the ship was level and fire away. As the ship bounced around, of course, the aim of the guns bounced around also. The British gunners learned to change their technique and keep the cannon aim on target, letting the ship roll around as it would. This innovation meant that whenever the time was right to fire, the guns would be already aimed. A young US Navy observer was impressed with the great increase in gunnery effectiveness and encouraged the US Navy bureaucracy to follow suit. Finally, with the help of President T. Roosevelt, the Navy devised a test for the claims. A gun was mounted on a railroad flatcar and a target was established on a mechanism that went up and down to simulate the rolling sea. Gunners struggled without success to follow the bouncing target with the cannon fixed to the stationary flatcar and proved the idea was worthless.

Undaunted, the young sailor pointed out that on ship it is the target that stays fixed and the ship does the work of moving the cannons. All the gunner had to do was to help the gun stay in a fixed position relative to the target while the ship wobbled about. After much fuss, the real situation was tested and the scheme proven. The Navy responded to the success the same way it did to the "Wampanoag." Citing the precedent of the famous Naval victory in Manila Bay during the Spanish American War, the Navy saw no reason to change from the traditional gunnery procedure. It was years later before anyone checked the Manila Bay performance record. The Spanish were exposed to 9,500 cannon blasts in that "battle." Only 121 hit a target!

In more recent times, the 688-Class Fast Attack Submarine project continues the tradition. The trail, well covered in the media, continues with the submarine project overrun by billions of dollars, and a bail-out via Congress to the taxpayer. Years late, the product is ending up as a compromise with neither the speed nor the diving capability needed. The history of the Navy is filled with smaller and larger examples of the same process.

Boom!

On a scale of no interest to the media, the Navy is now in the process of "hardening" its shipboard electronics gear to take the shocks of battle. Test work shows that while the ship structure survives a blast as designed, communications gear does not. One of the gadgets that fails is the teletype machine. The Navy standard dates to pre-World War Two times, a noisy contraption featured in newsreels of that era. The manufacturer finally stopped production of the machines in 1970 and spare parts in 1976. At great expense, the Navy maintains repair facilities and has a crew going around from ship to ship adding braces and springs so that the archaic teletype machine can continue to operate in battle. Of no interest to the Navy, the Army developed a modern teletype already certified for Navy service that is smaller, better and shock-proof. This gadget can be ordered from the federal storehouse and installed for a tiny portion of the cost of backfitting fixes for the obsolete mechanical contraption. The Navy answer - "It's green and only grey can go on ship."

The mismatch of communications gear between and among the services is legendary. The call home from a Ma Bell telephone booth by a soldier in Granada to get the Navy to stop shelling his position (it worked!) is old hat. Too bad they didn't have better telephones in Vietnam and Korea where the same mismatch problem existed. Today finds the communications equipment far more sophisticated and the problems far worse. What remains constant is the lack of any plans specifically designed to remedy the situation. The Navy is a level above the rest of the defense Establishment on the almighty organization chart, by tradition, and intentionally uses a special communications format to mark its lofty territory in the hierarchy. If the Army were to change over to the Navy system, the Navy would soon adopt another - damn the cost.

Last resort

Once we had our government survey completed, things looked no better for finding the "fix." We studied an institution we thought beyond the taint of what was becoming, in our minds, a planetary plague. **"Banks** don't make mistakes," we thought. "Banks could never stay in business if they handled their affairs like the government." We were wrong.

Connections were established to the financial world to learn how super-conservative, risk-averse organizations move their high technology projects along. It was a little harder to break the ice, but soon the tales, were pouring in. Except for the amounts wasted, the banks outdid the government. The only disparity noted was that the bank messes, unlike the government fiascoes, seldom made it to the newspaper. There was no **weltanschauung** at the banks. The tales from insurance companies, stock brokers and big bankers were identical. Except perhaps for more impressive camouflage, it was the government all over again. Eventually, through endless error with the given party line (the framework against which we judged our actions) the programs injected into our crania by school and corporation were discredited and erased. It was time for more study and a lot of looking around with minds less cluttered by party-line baggage. We had plenty of clues from experience. The formation of a new mental model repertoire of reality began.

The common, identical character of the situations meant they must spring from the same basic phenomena. The discovery that the mess is a "natural phenomenon" led to the first book about the problem, **The New Plague.** Its title was given in recognition of the ubiquity of the mess and its capacity for carnage. As luck would have it, the title was superseded by the AIDS epidemic (the misbehavior of the health care dynasty provides yet another raft of insights to failure in the 'system').

Response from readers of **The New Plague** has filled our library of horror stories to the rafters. Episodes have emerged involving industries from aluminum to zinc. One major Wall Street broker has provided over thirty documented cases of disaster projects, some still in progress. When the material is presented at conventions, unsolicited war stories pour in for weeks afterwards. Pent-up frustrations gush forth with case histories of disaster that stagger the imagination. Where once we plundered the landscape to find relevant examples of the species, we now dig foxholes to escape the barrage. Where once we found a shop with a nest of thirty, for instance, we would check the scene out at another shop for verification. Now we don't even ask. If it's at the broker, it's at the bank, and the insurance company, and the accountant and ...

What fun is this?

There are a lot of people caught up in the global mess. **They are not having fun at work.** They do not go off to labor the daily grind on level ground - they are cast in a muddy hole and not by their own choosing. Without a compensating mechanism, the bad situations soon lead to human stress and the statistics on work-related psychological stress are frightening. The segment of the U.S. health care empire that deals with the **effects** of stress is an industry larger than General Motors. About half of all non-wellness today is related to human stress. The big producer of human stress, by far, is the corporate scene. Few escape. That such a terrible price should be paid so regularly by civilized man without question, is a clear warning to show respect for the nature of the problem. The largest causes of death (over one-fourth) to young adults are suicide and homicide. The trend for the stress business is up.

Aspects of the work situation which are associated with the experience of stress have a lot to do with the 'impossible' demands made by the monster mess factory. Stress is an individual **psychological** state resulting from your internal self-appraisal of your ability to deal with the external scene. When you recognize you are not maintaining the relationship you want with the environment (psycho-social and physical), the price is poor health of the brain and the body. This condition is not happy, not good, and we label it "Unfun."

Unfun is unavoidable when your mental models are in conflict with the realities and the constraints of the work scene, some of which are unnecessary, some stupid. It is your own evaluative process that imbues the situational encounters at work with 'meaning.' The basic job demands are amplified by constraints to your response options and your coping resources are greatly influenced by the support (or lack thereof) you get from others as well as your past batting averages. While the equations of stress may be hard to understand, stress is easy to recognize when you have it.

RULE - Work scene stress needs your support.

We are programmed with a set of instructions inherited from the very ancient past which is mingled with another set inserted by the Establishment. This fundamental amalgam of values orders our life and the actions we take are referred against this standard. Studies made in the last decade show that over 70% of the subconscious programmed instructions are, in some way or another, **harmful** to their owner. We call these instructions for failure the Bad Seventies. When we order our lives with our genetic inheritance and our indoctrinations, without critical and conscious self-analysis, we are asking for big trouble.

Where's the fun?

The fun will begin as soon as we get rid of Unfun - which is kind of fun too. Assaulting Unfun consists of adjusting **to** the situation and adjusting **of** the situation. We will be advocating strategies of both kinds which, unfortunately, will require some demolition of your cherished beliefs (in the Bad Seventies category). The wrong mental reference models in your head which impale you with unwarranted stress must be replaced with wisdom more appropriate to the realities of modern times. A supermarket of tools will be provided both for altering situations, and to increase your capabilities to cope with what can not be changed.

The first priority in the assault on Unfun is to gain understanding of what is going on in the global mess factory. The purpose for this knowledge is to reframe your mental models about the "demands" of work. That is the shortest way up out of the Big Muddy to level ground. Unfun has got to go. This book contains the elixirs which dissolve Unfun generators, and you will find the recipes and tools for having fun at work by **making** work fun. But, like any strong medicine, at first it is going to hurt. To learn how to **have fun at work** is going to fry your brain. That's right, a book about having fun at work begins by doing violence to your instincts and perceptions. We started by giving you a hint of how primordial and extensive this problem is in order to keep your expectations for a quick fix in check.

The Big Muddy

Join the corporation and slide into their muck of old policies. Get brainwashed and outfitted with old tools and methods for facing big, new and scary problems. Be socially controlled to fail. Welcome to the Big Muddy.

The size and durability of the Unfun scene is awesome. No matter how many stories about respectable paranoia arrive in the daily mail, we remain astonished that a problem so huge and so widespread could flourish in so-called civilized society. We hope to transmit awareness and appreciation of this global psychosis to you. Don't think that the widespread wreckage and wholesale carnage is the result of a simple misunderstanding. Don't think that civilized society operates on the basis of rational self-interest and that, in time, justice will be done. Areas of such significance to your personal well-being should not be entrusted to institutions with such a terrible track record.

As we said, the first problem area is your current mental model repertoire of reality. It is smack in the way of learning. If you hang on to your counter-productive programs and treat this work as additive rather than as substitute material, you are going to get nowhere. The Bad Seventies must be erased and replaced. You really didn't think it was going to be easy, did you?

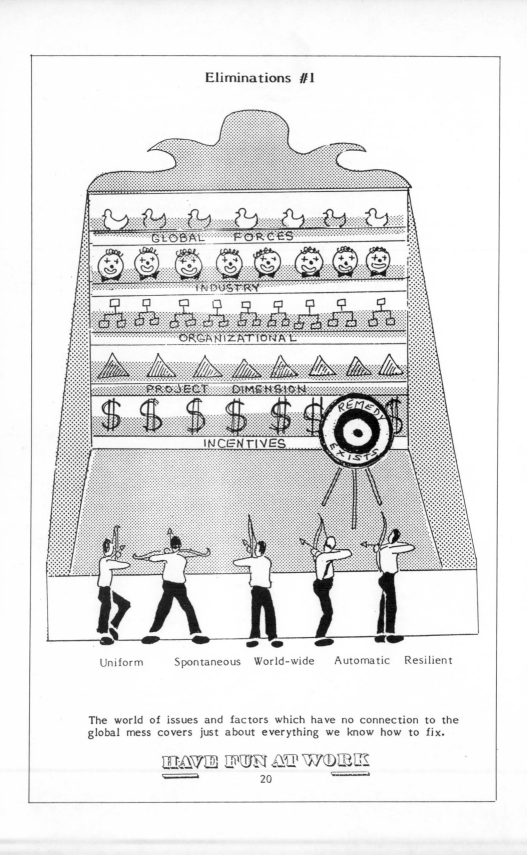

The world of issues and factors which have no connection to the global mess covers just about everything we know how to fix.

HAVE FUN AT WORK

Chapter Two

The Power of Negative Thinking

In the face of all the evidence, it was still hard to believe that the appalling scenes we had experienced were part of a global preoccupation. The best approach we found to get rid of our intuitive denials of plain truth and the Bad Seventies (everything we had been taught at school was at stake) was to take the facts and, rather than **guess** at an answer, eliminate what could **not** be the answer. It was a significant plus for learning and the basis of a profound lesson in humility. For the first time we started avoiding some of the many blind alleys and brick walls - none of which we had managed to dodge in the tumultuous past thrashing around in the big, black Muddy.

Accepting that the mess process is **counterintuitive** is the initial ante for understanding. If you hang on to your instincts, you just go through your own junk yard programs again (More - More, Better - Better, Faster - Faster). Those models, the Bad Seventies, whether you like the idea or not, are directly connected to the prevailing situation. If you can't bear to examine your encrusted beliefs, think of the whole affair as a cosmic practical joke - on you.

RULE - The natural process of forming a belief prefers myths to truth.

The telltale wreckage

We define a "mess" as a disaster project, a horror show, a war story or a botch job - in other words, an activity that has run amok in **great** disparity to original expectations. Big overruns of budget, large slippage in schedule, and a poorly performing product are some features of the project wreckage that elect the endeavor to the Hall of Shame. What makes your work Unfun and the project a disaster is that failure and the incredible waste, animate and inanimate, **are unnecessary.**

Project outcome classifications are relative to those who are involved in them and do not necessarily involve big dollars. New York City closes down its largest ice rink for repairs, which can easily be completed during a summer, and spends decades and millions of dollars to prove to a deprived public that it can't be done. The hospital can automate its billing process and lose track of medicines for the patients. The school can equip its students with computers and graduate a class composed mainly of illiterates. The manufacturing plant can install the latest robots in its production line and go out of business. A disaster project upsets the lives of many people during its run, and everyone afterwards.

RULE - If the situation gets happier when you run the film backwards, you're in the Big Muddy.

Beginning the process of elimination

Much can be learned about the "mess machine" without having the answer book. Whatever it is, it is everywhere and in all the flavors. It is also certain that the FDA-approved list of cures for the mess is pure quack medicine. Loosen the soil around those deeply-rooted mental models. It's time to start yanking the Bad Seventies out. Don't worry, you will still have plenty of brain programs left to function. You already know how little you need of those to get over at work.

POSIWID: The Purpose Of a System Is What It Does

The purpose of this corporation is to produce wheels, of which no two are round or alike, and to generate as much human debris as possible in the process. They are good at what they do and they thank you for your support.

Mental models drive actions and actions drive to the 'truth and consequences' of the grand conclusion. If the wreckage keeps piling up while the mental models stay the same, the solution activities unleashed (obviously) are not related to the problem. Practices cause situations and produce outcomes. The first program erasure recommended is the dogma to believe the hype before viewing the object. **Replace** that counterproductive fallacy with a priceless contribution from Stafford Beer - "The purpose of a system is what it does" (POSIWID). The process of elimination is POSIWID in action.

The mess-producing activities are spontaneous, automatic and uniform. These facts mean that the how-to instructions for producing the wreckage are in place and ready.to go - just like the law of gravity for matter found anywhere in the universe. There is no planning session, no collusion, no exchange of control signal information. Institutions do not set up formal training classes to show their members how to manufacture disaster. There is no need. From the first moments of the initiating condition on to the end, the blueprint to ruin is instantly and impulsively enacted - in any language.

RULE - In a contest between emotion and intellect, bet on emotion.

The fact that the mess is so widespread is key to identifying what are non-factors. For openers, the mess flourishes independently of culture, political system and education. The mess can't be driven by differences in language, law, technology, business, commerce, industry or folklore. The process that generates the mess is so identical from case to case and culture to culture that most of the differences we might prefer to exist - don't. **Erase.**

We would very much like to think that the USA "system" is better than the Russian "system" and that the excellence advantage is reflected, accordingly, in results. One such expectation is that fewer large-scale disasters would be generated. Unfortunately, the differences between the Three Mile Island and Chernobyl catastrophes, we shudder to admit, are merely in the extent of the damage - not in the government-sponsored process that caused them. To ensure strategic crippling of the US space program, the organizational zoo that produced the "Challenger" tragedy was the only beneficiary in the post-mortem revisions. To think that the Communists have cornered the market on bureaucratic suffocation is to ignore the voluminous, inglorious history of world governments. **Erase** the idea.

Also excused from culpability are individuals. Any federation in the business of supplying trained soldiers to cause the global mess would possess the biggest army on earth. Even small armies are difficult to hide. While individuals are certainly the engine for turning the mess machinery, **particular** individuals are not. Just like flocks of geese flying in Vee formation (shoot half and the Vee survives intact), mixing the roster has no effect on the overall situation. However painful to admit, this corollary also excludes differences in management. **Erase.**

RULE - In a screwed-up situation, turnover is not related to turnaround.

There is no way the mess can be so global and be caused by these factors. Go ahead and try them out, make your day.

Since the list of subjects that can not be causes of the mess contains many that our instincts would like to deny, the list itself is a great locator of the Bad Seventies that have to go. We are accustomed to placing blame on individuals. It is socially popular that management is "ultimately responsible" for failure. Our troubles (stress) are always caused by "Them." Unfortunately, the energy spent in affixing blame in these areas is wasted and diversionary. Any possible cause that can be openly discussed in social propriety, almost by definition, can not be relevent. If it were, we wouldn't have the mess. **Erase.**

There is a shopping list of incentives (published by management schools), that is supposed to motivate executives of organizations. The quantified promise of growth and profits is supposed to pull in a positive direction and the measurable drains of poor quality and decreasing market share are supposed to push away from a negative direction. Although often cited as necessary and sufficient inspiration for remedy, the practice of developing such incentives is a colossal waste of time. **Erase.**

The universality and spontaneity of the mess inexorably eliminate factor after factor until the only remaining places left to look for clues, as to the causes, are in the nature of the thing being messed up and the process by which the mess is achieved. Accordingly, the list of possible relevant factors has been reduced further by analyzing projects that produce the characteristic wreckage.

More unrelated factors

Three striking conclusions emerge when disaster projects are studied in depth and without passion. First, the outcome has absolutely nothing to do with a deficiency in technology. The "Challenger" booster seal failure, for instance, was not due to a lack of effective sealing methods for those tough conditions of pressure and temperature. Searching the debris for clues never finds a lack of enough solutions to solve the problem. Usually one finds the opposite. It is rare to find a participant in the mess project who connects even part of the mess to a shortage in technology. Although the technical fix is the remedy of preference (it avoids the social taboos), no one really expects the monster to go away after the "fix" is applied. It doesn't. **Erase** technology.

The second remarkable factor that emerges from an examination of the history of horror projects is that failure is unrelated to calendar time. Of course there wasn't enough time allotted to the project in the first cycle. But in hindsight there certainly was enough by the time the fourth circuit around the mess track was made. Looking back at a project floundering for years, no participant thinks that time was a critical factor in getting the job done. As the saying goes, "There is never enough time to do the job right, but always enough time to do it over." Like the case of inter-service communications among the military, time is an embarrassment of riches. As time goes on and the global mess gets worse rather than better, it becomes more obvious that time is an independent variable. **Erase** time.

The third conspicuous non-factor is resources. The amount of money spent in generating wreckage is awesome. To be sure, the original budget was insufficient to complete the project, but one could hardly blame "cheap" after it has been exceeded by a multiple of five. Once the total costs are piled upon the table, no one thinks it should have taken so much. If resources have any correlation to the mess at all, it is negative. That is, the more money that is thrown at a project, the more it will cost to produce the disaster and camouflage the fact. Heavy funding of a defective process does not improve the process, it just makes a higher heap of rubble (Parkinson's first law). **Erase.**

The Five Year Rule

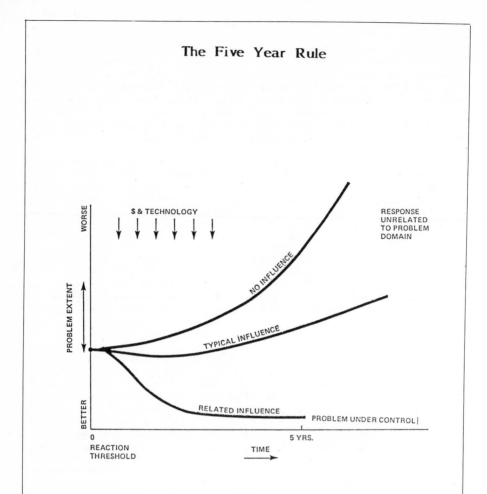

The rule clock starts when money and technology are thrown at a problem. If they are related to the problem, it will be in a maintenance mode within five years. Great projects like the man-on-the-moon, the atomic bomb, and the Panama Canal are notable examples in this group. When what is being done has no connection to the problem, the problem gets worse with time. Examples include illegal drugs, organized crime, political corruption, toxic waste disposal, Ethiopian famines, health care costs, and education. The World Bank has 6,000 employees spending billions of dollars in misguided attempts to help the needy and human suffering increases. Typically, there is a slight initial effect from the attention of money and science which soon evaporates as the core issues, unaddressed, take their toll. There is no natural compensating mechanism.

A painful, well-publicized example. is supplied by the education industry. Thinking that money would solve the mess as promised by the educators, the USA doubled per pupil spending over the 1960 levels. The budget for education even exceeds that for the Department of Defense. For this extra expense, SAT scores are down 20% in the same period along with a reduced sense of student well-being. The only increases produced by the additional money have been in delinquency and dropouts. Government programs to help the poor and disadvantaged follow the same path. The solution activities sanctioned by the institutions are simply not related to the problem domain.

RULE - When the remedies are unrelated to the malady, large doses only make more malady.

One of many suites of cases that illustrate the irrelevancy of all three project dimensions has to do with the development of computerized data bases for application to practical problems. One example in that suite relates to the development of data bases of materials for use in computer-aided design (CAD). Since the first attempts over ten years ago, over one hundred materials data base projects have been launched around the world. These projects have been disasters which fall into two categories - those that have limited use in a narrow area and those that don't work at all. Not only have ten years and millions of dollars gone by the board, but nothing is being learned from the failures. This is not an unusual case.

It is a massive blow to the Bad Seventies of conditioned perceptions when the factors of time, money and technology are taken out of the picture. We can not gain from looking for causes or remedies in those "acceptable" places. We privately sense that the wreckage must be connected to the practices, but we have no socially-safe avenue for problems that cannot be disposed of with a little more time or money or technology. If such are the only remedies allowed, we face, with Pogo, an "insurmountable opportunity." Invariably, the effort to solve the puzzle with more of the standard, sanctioned corrections only makes matters worse - a feature recognized in the Rogovin report on Three Mile Island and the Rogers report on the "Challenger." disaster.

So now we know why the mess is so common: the solution-activities directed to operate on the problem (and presumably solve it) are unrelated to it. The Harvard Business Review of today preaches management practices no different than it promoted twenty years ago. The one article it will never print is the one connecting its instructions to the endless wreckage. No wonder the mess thrives.

The mess process is not something that is exhibited piecemeal or in gradual increments. It is either florid or it is absent. This snap-action characteristic is another clue to the hidden culprits. The great diversity of projects that take the swift dive into the great dry pool have no common inanimate item. There is no gearbox, e.g., which is used in all ill-fated projects that suddenly flies apart. Oh, that it was so! **Erase.**

Looking at the residuals

So the mess is universal, automatic and spontaneous, on/off, resilient and detectable in large and small domains alike. This far about 50% of your cherished beliefs should have bitten the dust. Time, technology and money are gone. Inanimate matter as an entire class is gone. Human matter, regarding the attributes of global diversity, is gone. (How could the mess be so global if it **was** influenced by differences in people and their cultures?) Incentives programmed by the Establishment are gone, and what a diversion they are!

Uniform   Spontaneous   World-wide   Automatic   Resilient

It's bad enough that the description of the problem is wrong, without knowing that effective solutions exist too. Remedies are as deliberately ignored as the eliminated factors are pursued.

HAVE FUN AT WORK

We also know that the global mess has neither a simple cause nor a quick fix. We went through them all. It is not just a case of pointing out the situation to officials and letting them take over from there. Neither the problem nor its recognition are new. The literature is filled with learned, on-target criticisms and counsel. While we have a different way of expressing the relevant knowledge, there is little in the process of elimination that is original discovery. A long history of elucidation and warning, plenty of wreckage to illustrate the point, but society has shown indifference. That has been noted too. **Erase.**

It is essential to appreciate that remedies to address the core issues are known and they have been demonstrated. There have been many distinguished champions of the cures. The methods of success which avoid the mess altogether have been set down in print and made available to the public. Not only is it unnecessary to support the mess factory, but the path of success is quite happy and fun. Unfortunately, advocating corrections to the calamitous course taken by the human herd has proven to be a hazardous occupation. On-target advocates are only punished. **Erase.**

Since inanimate objects are out, the only residue is the animate. The only common creature in the residuum is man. Since the great variety of man has been shot down, the only area left is the shared fundamentals. The fundamental parts that don't vary include denial of feedback (connecting the wreckage back to the practices which caused it), rejection of a proven solution, and persecution of the advocates of viable remedy.

The ultimate problem

Some mess. There is no greater problem facing humanity. This problem is also between you and fun at work. To **have fun at work** you must understand the man-made monster malady. It is the fundamental driving force behind most of the silly job situations that otherwise rational people create for themselves at work with manic determination. When you know the rationale behind the irrational deeds, you have acquired a basic tool for having fun at work.

It is not fun to examine long-held mental models. After all, 30% of them are still your chums. The discrimination of bad from good is not always an error-free affair. Mental value systems are hard to erase, even when you want to. We rely upon our intuitions and instincts to navigate through life and they are not easily questioned. Thinking is labor of the highest difficulty and the most unpopular sport in the world.

The only ointment we can prescribe is to take your time. We sure took ours. The necessity for every one of these requisite "erasures" can be confirmed by your own experiences and examinations. We can help guide your scalpel to the bad cranial tissue, but only you can perform the surgery. Take a moment and try looking at this from our perspective. If we wrote a joke book about the work place, how long would the fun last? How long do you laugh at any joke? Writing a comic book would be easy, but it would also be a cop-out. We have learned how to **have fun at work** and identified the necessary knowledge and skills. We will try to build your competence in the least painful way and as quickly as possible. Now get yourself into the mental model operating room, Doctor, and get it over with.

The on/off switch for the mess factory is flipped to "on" by a distinguishable threshold situation. The next Chapter will zero in on the common circumstances that set the mess production line in motion.

29

The Unfun Trigger

It's easy to recognize problems that are not routine. As foreign material, non-routine fuzzballs are loaded onto the corporate catapult, the spring-loaded trap is sprung, and away go the fuzzballs to elsewhere. Fuzzballs are too complex for Routineland. They take care of those big-space matters upstairs. Sure They do.

HAVE FUN AT WORK

Chapter Three

The trigger that flips the switch

The search for the Unfun trigger mechanism was long and arduous. We kept trying the wrong things and looking in the wrong places - like management libraries. We were thwarted by conditioned notions of "standard" motivators like greed, avarice and power, as dramatized on TV. Only by firsthand experience with failure did we learn that none of the standard, tangible incentives were tripwires. When we finally had our brains kicked in enough times, the dawn of discovery began. It was not a very professional procedure to uncover what, in hindsight, is now patently obvious.

It is the degree of **complexity** in the subject matter that determines whether or not there will be a mess. If complexity is sufficiently high to flip the switch, hang on to your hat. If complexity is below the threshold setting, there will be no mess. That's it. **Replace.**

Literature abounds with the perennial ills of government, finance, medicine, industry, education, etc., but few observers have made the connection to essential complexity. Usually the descriptions are tangled in the tree of specific details about the application. Once the connection to complexity is made, however, the great forest of equivalent messes becomes apparent.

When the association to intrinsic complexity becomes a working mental model for reference, half of the confusion evaporates immediately. When you hear, e.g., about physicists anxious to learn string theory (which unifies the knowledge about matter) who then run away in droves when they find out the theory works in ten-dimensional space, **it makes sense.**

Complexity is a world of interlocking relationships, like a ball wound from motley pieces of string. It is impossible to extract one string without moving every other one in the fuzzy matrix. Most large problems today are complex fuzzball-type problems. Some large problems are more difficult than they are complex, while others are complex only by intervention and accident.

RULE - The situations YOU have to face are complex. Those faced by others are simple.

Researchers (with their mental models based upon the simpler times of past centuries), have been trained to learn about things by holding all variables in their experiment constant but one. Since the big fuzzball problems of society don't fit that mold, and since they are so dynamic and interconnected that alteration of one factor immediately acts on many others, the entire class of problems is ignored by the scientific community. Now, the fact that the investigation of complex problems is evaded by the very institutions entrusted to do so, **makes sense.** Before going any further, a working definition of complexity is in order.

Human Coping Limits

Single Problem Bigger
Than Human Capacity

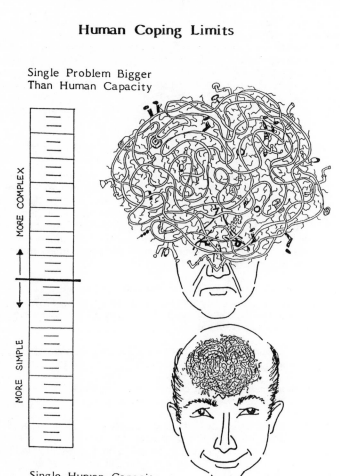

Single Human Capacity
Bigger Than Problem

There are two limiting conditions in our cranial cellular congress to cope with reality. The brain capacity to process information is finite, and the machinery with which to do it is not a conscious unity. When the space requirements of problems fit the network there, things go well. When they don't, things go to Hell.

Complexity

For all the Unfun that it creates, **complexity** is a term that is seldom considered by itself as a concept. Complex issues are a turnoff (stressed thinking) equivalent to social leprosy. It's bad enough to bring up complicated subjects (try talking about plasma physics at the next church social), to discuss complexity as a topic itself is to invite ostracism. Personal bells may ring when complications set in on a particular matter, but the concept of complication itself is left dangling. "I'll know it when I see it," is a typical response to the complexity topic. Complexity is so unpopular and discussed so rarely that it is difficult to obtain many points of view.

The abstract notion of complexity is imbued with human perceptions of reality. Each of us has a nebulous line inscribed upon our instincts, inherited and acquired, that separates things we consider to be simple from things that we sense are not simple. The sense for complexity is tied to our perceptions of control, or more precisely, our lack of control. According to our working definition, a thing is complex when it exceeds the capacity of an individual to understand it sufficiently to develop comfortable, effective control - regardless of the resources placed at his disposal. In terms of Unfun, we call a thing complex when we perceive an imbalance between what we think the situation requires of us and what we think we can handle.

RULE - If you think you can't cope, you can't.

Our instincts about control are usually pretty good. At least we know when we feel comfortable about being in control and when we don't. The discernment of complexity ties well into the reality of what it takes to be in control. Control ties into how many things, and what kinds of things, have to be controlled. Accordingly, the impression of complexity can be ascertained by categorizing and counting the elements that make up genuine control. Inherent complexity includes a selection from the following:

- Many unfamiliar, new elements
- Many parts, many dissimilar parts
- Many relationships between parts, many kinds of relationships
- Many technologies, crafts, skills, disciplines, arts
- Many departments, many organizations, many regulators
- Long time exposures, changing conditions, shaky assumptions
- Large risks, large consequences, large staffs
- Political controversy, conflicting objectives
- Big dollars, long time to recover investments
- Many solutions, many constraints, many requirements

The more characteristics from this list possessed by an issue, the more likely the issue will be perceived as complex (beyond any **one individual** to be in control). A nuclear power plant project, for example, contains all of the elements. The shameful history of human endeavors in that enterprise speaks for itself.

Complexity is not a one-dimensional quantity. Man is able to handle difficulty in a single dimension quite well as some of his remarkable work in physics, biology and mathematics can attest. As we reserve the word here, **complexity** has many dimensions and forms a "space." Some problems occupy a space that can fit inside of a man's head. We call those simple problems. Complex problems fill large spaces and compared to a man's head are spaced-out. The mathematician who improves the equations of ballistics can very well panic

Simple or Complex?

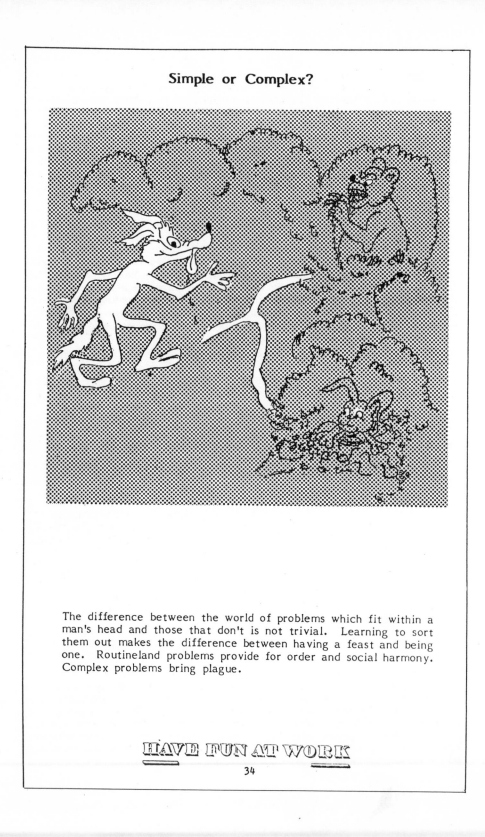

The difference between the world of problems which fit within a man's head and those that don't is not trivial. Learning to sort them out makes the difference between having a feast and being one. Routineland problems provide for order and social harmony. Complex problems bring plague.

at the thought of dealing with the Pentagon to gain military acceptance. Even adding a single dimension, such as many departments, greatly increases the complexity space, like adding a corner to the Pentagon (hexing the Pentagon?).

RULE - It's too complicated to think about complexity.

The notion of "being in control" can be measured. Each of us has finite channel capacities as to how much information we can handle. We can only **do** so much at a time and in a time. When you are fully occupied in coping with Unfun, you are not, at the same time, available to learn something - something that may well be critical to controlling the situation. We have limits in cognitive processing rate abilities. The first trip to Disney World usually fills the cognitive processing bucket in a few hours. It takes time to transfer short-term memory into long-term memory.

There is just **so much** that we can understand and keep on active cognition pertaining to a problem situation. Being in control always involves cognitive appraisal. For complex matters, appraisal requires extensive information processing capacities. This assignment usually overloads the designated appraiser. In those situations, decision-making is seldom rational. It flows from the most minimal and biased processing of piecemeal knowledge. Insufficient information is inadequately analyzed. Only one of a number of possible solutions is generated and considered. A single solution is commissioned without evaluation of its impact and no learning occurs as a result of the experience. Welcome to Mess City.

RULE - Typical decision-making is an ad hoc process using intuition in place of rational faculties - no matter how much time is available.

When decisions are being made without command of all the necessary knowledge and baseline data (in one brain) essential for objectively evaluating all possible solutions, control has been lost. When perceived, loss of control is the engine for Unfun. The affinity is now made between the capability to **have fun at work** and learning how to better cope with complexity.

Some matters, like ball bearings, are much simpler as a solution than they are in manufacture. Others, like the Space Shuttle software, are very complicated as a product (one million lines of code) and 99% of the cost goes into testing it. Computer chips are made more complicated by the need for a self-test window that leaves only 70% of the chip available for application work. There are many breeds of complexity and not all are readily apparent. Depending upon the scope of the application, any material object can be as complicated as you wish.

Man and his complexity fetish

Our definition of complexity has been made in human terms. That is, what makes a matter simple or complex is not just a measure of innate properties of the thing itself. Complexity is also in the mind of the beholder. Things that men call complex have always been around. While the technical features of intrinsic problem complexity will be addressed throughout this book, human perceptions of complex problems have proven to be critically more important in the process of getting complex problems solved. The human reaction to the term **complexity** is so negative that we have adopted the term **fuzzball** as a substitute. For some reason fuzzballs don't seem to be as intimidating. A fuzzball problem is a complex problem. It has fuzzy edges and lots of fuzzy, stringy touching parts all wrapped up together in a fuzzy non-symmetrical lump.

35

Simple vs Complex Projects

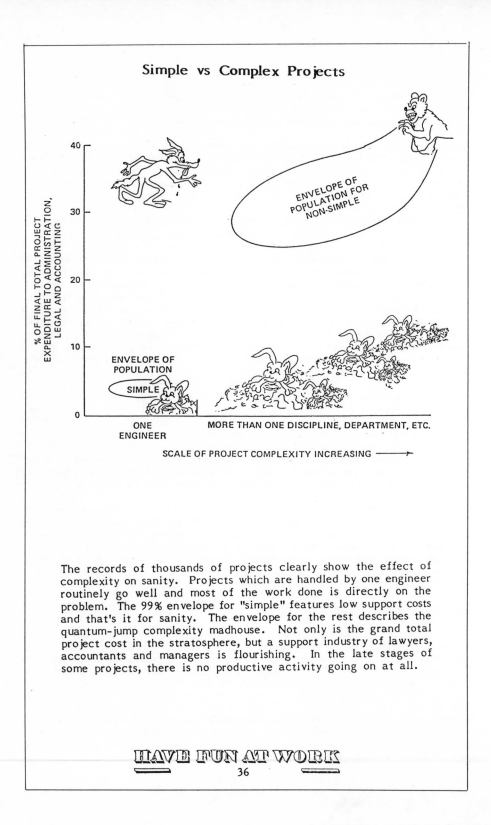

The records of thousands of projects clearly show the effect of complexity on sanity. Projects which are handled by one engineer routinely go well and most of the work done is directly on the problem. The 99% envelope for "simple" features low support costs and that's it for sanity. The envelope for the rest describes the quantum-jump complexity madhouse. Not only is the grand total project cost in the stratosphere, but a support industry of lawyers, accountants and managers is flourishing. In the late stages of some projects, there is no productive activity going on at all.

Complex problems do not fit our inculcated mental models of reality, so, like the officials we have entrusted to deal with our large collective problems, we run away and search for issues that do fit. This evasion, however, does nothing to help solve our most needy issues (like worker stress). **Erase** your ill-founded fears of complexity. Learning about how to deal with complex matters is going to set you well ahead of the pack. A working grasp of **any** complex matter (like your organization) is nothing but an investment of time and labor. Understanding complexity is not a construction with profound or peculiar difficulty. You do not have to possess prodigious mental capacities. You can do it.

The Zone of Indifference

The necessary and sufficient complexity threshold that trips the switch for a block change in human behavior is a mismatch between the space occupied by the problem and the space capacity of **a** man. In a given situation, a man starts with his pre-developed capacity for control of familiar matters. If the problem to be faced fits within that capacity and his mental models, there are excellent prospects for a solution. Every man also has a band of tolerance for issues that don't quite fit his routine, where the chances of success are also quite high. The Zone of Indifference (ZOI) is the limited space between the demonstrated capacities (where you know he is indifferent) and the point of increased novelty where he suddenly is no longer indifferent. That is, if you present a man with a problem which fits within his ZOI, he is unperturbed by the situation and will proceed to solve the problem just as he would any other problem within his ZOI. However, if the problem exceeds the ZOI of the man, for whatever reason, it's a whole new ball game. There is no graceful degradation. Mental model madness has been released. The situation blows up.

It is important to recognize the phenomenon of threshold, what we call crossing the ZOI border. It is quite common in animate behaviors. The organization shows no change as complications to routine life build. The variable 'complexity' can spend an appreciable amount of time not varying (oh, the good old days). When some definite value of complexity is exceeded, however, the temporary and conditional coupling to dysfunction snaps into place.

Everyone has a finite ZOI. Organizations and nations have a finite ZOI. Complexity is an index for measuring the human ZOI that can be used to obtain an improved perspective on how humanity has fared over its past. The boundaries of the Zone of Indifference are marked in the course of daily living by noting the responses made by people to calls for action. Sometimes you will find the ZOI posted on the wall. "This is not Burger King" is a popular workplace decoration.

The ZOI is an economical expression for an intra-psychic adjustment to stress perceived. The everyday reactions witnessed above represent efforts to adjust the situation from potentially stressful back to comfortable levels. Both levels are guaged on an intuitive basis. It is rare to find someone who reacts to an exceeded ZOI at work by calmly trying to adjust himself to the situation. In contrast, it is common for the same individuals to thoughtfully adjust to real world demands when acting alone.

RULE - The expression "We really would like to help you" is always followed by the word "but."

The Zone of Indifference
and
Indicators of Complexity Perceived

- That's not my/our work.
- They do that over in the _____ department.
- You should be working over in the _____ department.
- No one told us to start.
- The Doctor didn't prescribe it.
- I don't care if they do cancel the order.
- You want it, when?
- The responsibility should be shared.
- You're not on the distribution list.
- This authorization is no good.
- They don't make that part anymore.
- Those items should go to _____.
- Everyone needs to sign off on the documents
- We don't use that information here.
- We don't do that with/to _____.
- I can't take it any more.
- That's a problem for management to handle.
- You've got to be kidding.
- Who sent you here?
- It's too close to our coffee break.
- We never pay any attention to that buzzer.
- We always put the cart first.
- That's never been our responsibility.
- You didn't ask for that part.

- Do you want paper or do you want code?
- This is not Burger King. You do not get it your way.
- We're too busy on other work to do that.
- That is a vendor-supplied item.
- That work hasn't been assigned yet
- We don't work for you.
- Any answer would be misleading.
- The client wants it that way.
- Never mind the problem, how did you find it?
- It has already been shipped.
- We don't sign off until they have signed off.
- No one told us to stop.
- Where is your _____ form?
- We never put out the list in that order.
- I have no idea where you should go.
- Did you try the shipping department?
- Our department doesn't do that kind of work.
- We never said we were going to provide that piece.
- If it doesn't fit, its not our problem. It's what was ordered.
- I know that's better, but ...

Sampler of historical collisions with the Zone of Indifference

Russia has been faced with ZOI-exceeding situations for centuries. In 1903, a member of the Czar's court provided an insider's view of the prevailing organizational setting - "This insane regime. This tangle of cowardice, blindness, craftiness and stupidity. Ruled by a sovereign with the sole aim to preserve intact the absolute monarchy bequeathed to him by his father." This aim was set upon by many complications of an increasingly turbulent world, but it was not modified. When told of the annihilation of the Russian fleet at Tsushima, the Czar went back to playing tennis. When informed of the German preparations for war, Nicholas, bored with such extraneous news, responded with "God's will be done." The German avalanche into an unprepared Russia forced a panic mobilization of soldiers. Having to face the bedlam of mobilization and the excellent prospects of being killed, the soldiers soon turned the indoctrination centers into a mass of vodka-laden drunks. This debacle was followed by a hastily-enacted prohibition of alcohol, a state monopoly. This simple move promptly cut off a third of the income to the government. In one stroke Russia entered the record books as the only country which, in time of war, renounced the principal source of its revenue. It was a great way to start off World War I - in the Big Muddy.

Not to be outdone, a brilliant way to follow that act was conjured up by an American enterprise. In 1917, one week after the October Bolshevik uprising, the First National City Bank of New York opened its first office in Moscow. Ignoring the fundamental changes that launched the recent war and convinced that the uprising was just a flash in the pan, the bank plunged heavily into Czarist bonds.

While violent changes in Russian government continued for decades, its reaction to a violation of the ZOI remained the same. Rather than the Czar, it was Stalin who, with stultifying stubbornness, refused to believe the stream of reports about the massed forces of Germany once again at the Russian borders. It was a great way to start off World War II. Not to be outdone, the USA entered the same war in the same way. General Billy Mitchell went on public record in the 1930s with his forecast of a Japanese attack on Pearl Harbor. Same ZOI.

RULE - When everyone thinks the same, no one has to think.

In technical matters the ZOI provides a benchmark. The Ming dynasty proclaimed there would be no new technology in a law which specified death as the punishment for any apprehended inventor. The gun first found its military use in 1346 at the battle of Crecy. In England, it was another 250 years before the gun displaced the long bow as the basic weapon for the infantry. When Bell demonstrated his telephone to president Rutherford B. Hayes, the president commented - "That's an amazing invention, but who would ever want to use one of them?" When he went to the Western Union Telegraph Co, Bell's father-in-law offered to sell all the patents cheap. Western Union's president showed the man and his offer the door with "We have no use for an electrical toy." Years later, Western Union lost a patent infringement suit with a settlement that froze them out of the telephone business to this day. An employee of Hewlett-Packard, who had rigged an electronic gadget on his own time, was told "Thanks for the offer to market your product but get lost." Steve Wozniak did and co-founded Apple Computer Inc. There are tons of the same story behind Xerox and Polaroid.

One array of political ZOIs that will have their thresholds mauled in the next few years relates to the USA garbage/trash fiasco. Accumulating like the refuse itself, the complexity of the multi-dimensional problem is deliciously rich. The law-passing phase has been over for ten years and the problem, of course, grows larger. As established methods of rubbish disposal expire, the ZOI of millions will be clobbered. Trash is real and apolitical. It will have the last word. The Zone of Indifference is part of the landscape of human mental models and complexity is the instrument by which it is surveyed. We hope you are making good progress in shedding your Bad Seventies. It's time to start your ZOI-stretching exercises.

RULE - There is no problem known that can not be solved by a nation which already knows how to dispose of its wastes without objection from the people.

The price of Unfun

With a world supplying an endless stream of case histories, it would be easy to write a large book on nothing but the mess pandemic. The reason for emphasis on the wreckage is to help you understand why getting rid of Unfun generators is necessary to **have fun at work.** Most workers in dystopia have a tangle of resentments that mature into low self-esteem. Adjusting to the tedious tragedy gets smack in the way of having fun.

For the mess it generates with complexity, human society (this means you) pays a staggering price for supporting Unfun City. The numbers are incredible, unless somebody can appreciate a growing stack of currency that represents about half of the GNP of the world. The bill is paid every day to several accounts.

The first invoice is from the Personnel department. Human lives are wasted, crippled and destroyed in the mess. Failed projects take many people over the falls with them. Time wasted is unrecoverable. The loss in control over one's actions is a serious personal issue. Careers of frustration take their toll in mental and physical disorders. Many participants know instinctively that the mess is unnecessary, but they don't know what they can do in safety to alter the outcomes. It is the inherent conflict between knowing the lunacy is going on and the futility of an attempt to stop it that causes the well-known linkage between the mess of complex projects and personnel problems. Definitely not fun.

During decades in complex project environments, we have seen friends and associates lost to the contradiction between needs for personal growth and corporate demands for social dependency. The correlation of health to organizational dysfunction is so strong and so easy to measure that it is an undiscussable issue. Reputable medical firms in this field knowingly treat only the effects rather than the causes - and that too is an "undiscussable." Preferring to spend a dollar for treatment to a penny for vaccine (the annual bill for **direct** costs has been estimated at $150 billion), society pays a gargantuan price in human misery without a murmur. Real people die in these messes.

RULE - Human suffering has never been a factor of influence to the corporate decision-making process.

A physician named Ignaz Semmelweiss faced a typical 12% maternity-ward death rate in his Vienna clinic. In desperation, he decided to clean up the rooms and the hands of the attending physicians with carbolic acid in a bold attempt to reduce the carnage. In one year (1848), the new procedure had reduced the death rate to 1%. In retaliation he .was dismissed from the hospital in 1849. Going on to Budapest, he repeated the performance with dramatic success. After publishing his findings, he was thrown out of medicine, and died soon after in an insane asylum. It was 40 years and a Joseph Lister before disinfectants were accepted in maternity hospitals. During those 40 years, millions of lives were unnecessarily lost.

RULE - Adjusting to the diseases of a sick organization will not make you well.

Another invoice is from the Treasury department. The 1986 bill for the unnecessary waste of resources, published as $869 billion, is mind-boggling. Picking on government programs as examples of fiscal insanity is so obvious it qualifies as un-sportsmanlike conduct. A rundown of industries in turbulence, such as steel and computers, will provide all the evidence required. It's so systemic, we no longer flinch upon hearing the numbers. Everyone knows.

One rationalization we sometimes encounter is that the waste aids employment, and well it might. In view of the damage done to self-image and the associated complications, however, it seems like a high price for regular wages. It also would be far more civilized to stop the waste and direct the savings to more worthwhile causes. We have yet to find virtue in the mountains of wreckage. In this game there are only losers.

The French were hosts and victims of one of the most stupid forms of battle ever concocted by the military: trench warfare. Following World War I, France spent several billions of dollars (Depression era dollars it could ill afford) to build the Maginot line just in case the lunacy of World War I came around again. Instead, the French got World War II and the Maginot line was home to their enemy in a week. The price in human agony for that project was charged to the personnel account.

RULE - Spending money on unrelated remedies can even buy poverty.

Yet another invoice comes from Corporate Development. The heap of resources and humanity associated with the mess, doesn't solve the problem. While the original problem continues, usually getting worse rather than better, new complex problems emerge. In the process, sooner or later, the organization must face extinction. Society may soon find out what lawyers do when there is nothing left but lawyers.

The growing effect of Establishment lawyers, regulators, accountants, bankers and insurance underwriters, who work together to protect their turf and their piece of the action, has been to take elegantly simple projects, like hydroelectric dams, and make them fail. This is accomplished by injecting so many non-technical constraints and complexities, that when it finally becomes time to dig dirt, the dam organization is a tower of Babel. Towers of Babel are facilities that consume, rather than generate, power. The time is gone and the money has been siphoned to the many arrangers. When large engineering projects, like the Golden Gate Bridge, were tackled in the past, the money was gathered first and given over to the project engineer, since he was solely responsible, to spend as he saw fit. Now, such projects are directed by consortiums of technical illiterates, none of whom is responsible for anything -

The problem has been presented and the wreckage surveyed. The starting condition which leads to the wreckage, complexity, has been identified and discussed. Next, the trigger situation will be traced all the way to the debris. As you suspect, it is the path of least organizational resistance.

including the disaster which their own system, devised for their personal benefit, has guaranteed for the project.

RULE - No technology is so simple that can it can not be rendered unmanageably complex by the Establishment.

The 1987 rate of corporate failures in the USA is over 60,000 per year, up 600% in 5 years. Not all of these are young, small or stupid companies. Included are giants of the past and high technology outfits that were very profitable just two years ago. Corporate takeovers of failed stars, like Peoples Express, conceal an even larger extinction rate of corporations and the attendant waste of money and lives involved in the process. The principal reason a good many of these corporations go belly up is the failure with complexity.

While it is easy to tally what is being lost, plus or minus a trillion dollars or two, we are at a loss to sum what is being gained. We see no visible exchange of money or lives for matter. POSIWID shows that espoused values like health, wealth, dignity and survival don't rank very high in the social totem pole. But what are the dominant, and apparently unconscious priorities? What is the value structure that humanity covets so desperately as to pay such a price year in and year out? Whatever it is that extorts this price, its power to govern human behavior should have your respect and your attention. It certainly commands ours.

RULE - The Establishment does not understand technology.

Moving on towards fun at work

No organization can control change in the real world environment. No nation can act alone. Changes in parts of the global fuzzball ripple all over and upset the transaction equilibrium. We have looked at the bottom line and surveyed the wreckage. We know they make a mess. The link between the results (wreckage) and the cause (situational complexity) has been made. With this background, the time has come to discuss the **what** that transpires in between. The next Chapter will present the Universal Scenario, the stock play that drives us from the trigger-event opening to the junk-yard finale in such inelegant style.

NOTICE - If you are content with failure, read no further.

While organizations go to considerable lengths to ignore non-routine matters and put them off as long as possible, the tough problems get worse with time (the USA garbage scene is a classic example). When the issue can be avoided no further, the threshold is breached and action comes in a rush. We know the flurry of activity is not in implementing a strategic, innovative plan for resolving the persistent complexity.

43

Formerly Spaghetti

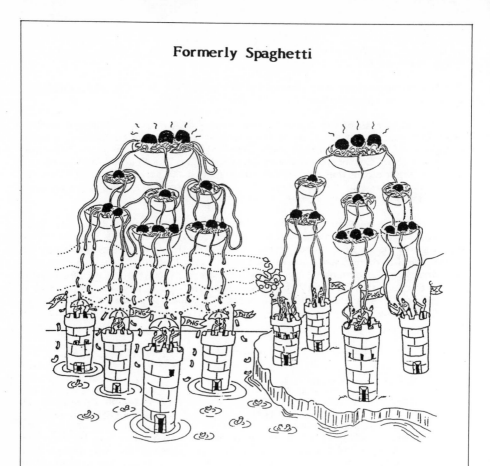

In quiet times, the organization is connected from the top to the bottom via spaghetti-like channels of communication. Even if the chatter contains noise, at least there is a connection. When the trans-departmental fuzzball problem comes crashing through the corporation, lines of communication are blown up by the workers. Spaghetti is transformed into macaroni and all messages fall by gravity to the moat.

Chapter Four

The Universal Scenario

"To have doubted one's own first principles is the mark of a civilized man."

                                        Oliver Wendell Holmes, Jr.

The Grammar of failure

The yellow brick road that connects the complexity threshold (ZOI) starting gate tripwire to the great burial mounds for project wreckage is called the Universal Scenario. The ubiquitous stock play is a reflection of innate human behavior regulated by the institutional setting. The drama is called universal because it's everywhere and it is called a scenario because regardless of who has which parts, it's always played the same.

Man behaves according to sets of rules and priorities embedded in deeply subconscious programs. The set which governs him facing a situation as a private citizen is dramatically different than the value system in control when he is functioning as a member of an organization. To join an organization is to grant an unconditional surrender of your option space. The right of the organization to constrict your behavior and limit your freedoms for action is a basic social assumption.

The naturally wide diversity of individuals is regulated by the organization to achieve predictable responses to recurrent business events. In a very real sense, people are thereby "standardized." Many people call the social brainwashing process legitimate activity, some don't. When functionally-equivalent situations are exposed to "standardized" people, standard reactions are produced. These equivalencies form well-defined behavioral patterns that can be easily recognized if they occur again.

RULE - To have fun at work temporarily suspend your belief in miracles.

The concoction of corporate culture, whatever its fragrance, contains the properties of self-locking and breeding. Once organizational practices congeal, they lock-in and become inaccessible to the factors that would "uncongeal" them. Once routines solidify into dogma, the herd mentality breeds like an avalanche. For as long as the conditions which shaped the developing culture remain steadfast, the self-locking and breeding properties are of little concern. Work may be some fun or it may be boring, but at least it is rational and efficient.

The luxury of steadfast cultural consistency in today's times is, at best, fleeting. Walter Cronkite is on TV narrating films of the devastating Kamikaze raids on the US Naval forces off Okinawa in 1945. The fiery scenes of sinking aircraft carriers are interrupted by a commercial - for the latest luxury cars from Tokyo. The Kamikaze effectiveness show is immediately followed by another series describing the war in Europe. Cronkite is covering the battle for Berlin and the bitter fighting in the rubble is interrupted for another commercial - the

FUZZBALL

The inseparable social-technical combination

HAVE FUN AT WORK

ultimate experience of Mercedes. These kinds of social model flip-flops make one pause to consider the strategic rationale of their source. Instability is the mother of the Universal Scenario and it is regular fare.

RULE - The only nations that do not prosper after a war with the USA are called the victors.

The Universal Scenario is a concatenation of distinctive behavioral patterns triggered by a threshold-crossing disturbance to organizational stability. Few have avoided participating at some time or another in the production itself. Based upon your own experience, prepare to resonate with most, if not all, of the associated situations. We adopt code words for the parts of the play as an introduction to the language of failure. Learning the vocabulary is a fun move.

To be or not to be, that is the question

Because of the phenomenon of threshold, not every project follows the yellow brick road to disaster. Only sufficiently fuzzball (complex) projects do. The following checklists are a job performance aid (JPA) for sizing up the prospects on a particular case. In practice, there are no borderline situations. You are either safely in routine-procedure land or you are neck-deep in the Big Muddy. All projects, facilities and organizations are an inseparable combination of a technical system and a social system. First, the technical system indices.

- Are there more than two technologies or disciplines involved?
- Can the technologies change much during the project?
- Will the solution system require a lot of maintenance?
- Is the **real** problem poorly understood by the project officials?
- Will standard technical practices be used?
- Any new or unfamiliar technologies involved?
- Are there more than two adequate solutions?
- Is the project time frame more than two years?

More than one "yes" answer to the questions on the technical system checklist is qualification enough for you to proceed to its companion, the inseparable ever-involved social system.

- Is the organization large (>250 persons)
- Is the organization over five years old?
- Is the project controversial?
- Are there more than three departments involved?
- Will standard corporate procedures be used?
- **Is prime project responsibility distributed?**
- Is project control assumed by professional officials?
- Any built-in adversarial relationships?
- Are there more than two organizations involved?
- Many lawyers, bankers, regulators, insurers, consultants?

Any four or more "yes" answers to the social system list, cuts the tie-down rope and catapults the project on to the yellow brick road. There are no intermediate stops. It is an all-or-nothing proposition. The underlying mapping principle for the route of the yellow brick road is that it follows the path of least organizational resistance. For routine matters it leads to glory. For non-routine, fuzzy undertakings, it leads straight to Hell.

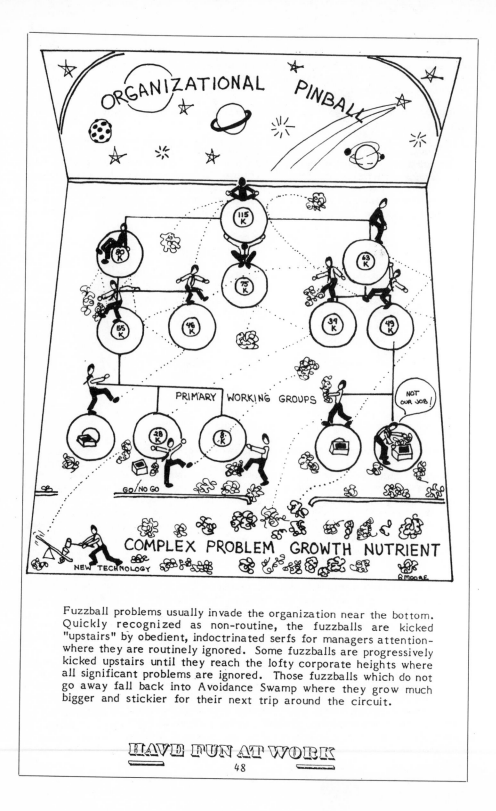

Fuzzball problems usually invade the organization near the bottom. Quickly recognized as non-routine, the fuzzballs are kicked "upstairs" by obedient, indoctrinated serfs for managers attention—where they are routinely ignored. Some fuzzballs are progressively kicked upstairs until they reach the lofty corporate heights where all significant problems are ignored. Those fuzzballs which do not go away fall back into Avoidance Swamp where they grow much bigger and stickier for their next trip around the circuit.

HAVE FUN AT WORK

RULE - The path of least organizational resistance is a two-lane highway composed of the path of most immediate benefit joined to the path of least consequential pressure.

The complexity play

The Universal Scenario consists of several scripts linked together in a protocol forming the path of least resistance through the organization. The situation generated by the first script triggers the lines for the next scene which produces another situation that triggers the next scene and so on. Neutral holo-phrases like "Feeding Frenzy" provide a vocabulary for fun discussions of these normally sensitive matters (failure) among associates. The vocabulary and set of concepts for failure are suitable for representing a great spectrum of real-world situations.

RULE - It is much easier to give up good habits than bad routines.

It is a play in two acts. No written scripts or rehearsals are necessary. The scenes and their sequence in the Universal Scenario are shown below.

Ready, Fire, Aim - Act 1, scene 1
The Feeding Frenzy - Act 1, scene 2
Party Time and Disconnect - Act 1, scene 3
Error, Distance and Camouflage - Act 2, scene 1
Growth of Error and Camouflage Squared - Act 2, scene 2
End-of-Project-Mismatch-Discovery - Act 2, scene 3
Run, Break and Fix - Act 2, scene 4 **or**
Recycle - back to Act 1, scene 1

Ready, fire, aim

The Universal Scenario begins with the fuzzball problem, which has been bouncing around for some time in the lower echelons of the organization. Unaware of the threshold nature of the affair, a series of small concessions to delay carries the situation, unnoticed, over the brink. The play is set into motion when the decision is finally made to launch a direct effort to solve the problem. Getting "Ready" is accomplished through avoidance, neglect and a futile hope that the problem will go away by itself. During the "Ready" phase, in spite of increased church attendance, the original problem grows to alarming proportions. The waste disposal debacle is one display sample of the popular Ostrich Syndrome. Eventually the threshold tripwire is crossed and the dam blows up.

More fuzzballs: the Japanese challenge to Detroit by building quality automobiles to capture market share is another example of the Ostrich Syndrome. Going unanswered for many years after the strategy of quality was first introduced by Deming, an American, the Japanese became entrenched before any thoughts of change were heard from Detroit. Deming was driven out of Michigan long before he went with his innovation to Tokyo.

RULE - The only condition necessary for management to provide stress at work is for the workery to do nothing.

As the curtain opens on the first scene in Act 1, the long-delayed decision has just been made by the powers that be to address the thorny problem. The plot begins with the gut-feeling that the problem is 'large' (which means the problem is bigger and messier than anyone wants to call his own). The inherent

The Feeding Frenzy

Simple problems fit the existing work cells and are consumed as fast as they form. Complex problems, since they don't fit the organization, are disregarded until they reach crisis proportions. When the fuzzball is finally released for solution, it still doesn't fit. The feeding frenzy is promptly staged to butcher and distribute the fuzzball carcass until the illusion is created that the problem has been matched to the institution. Sharp teeth are guided in the slaughter only by the cries of organizational distress. Project failure has not been left to chance.

complexity is outstanding and too important to be ignored. Facing up to the complexity, in this switched-state, is precisely what is avoided by the organization. The coverup for the perception of 'largeness' is the distribution of responsibility for the endeavour. There is no talk of a single home of accountability. That plum is saved for simple problems. Largeness, unfortunately, does not invalidate the principles.

Using the latest automated technique, provided by lawyers, accountants, consultants, insurers, regulators and bankers, the singular problem responsibility is loaded into a blunderbuss and blasted at the organizational chart. Boom! Pellets of accountability strike at random and all at once. The Wheel Division will cover anything to be made out of rubber. The Chemical Division will handle anything fabricated out of soybeans. The Accounting Department will be responsible for issuing all specifications. Assembly is to be the charge of the Aerospace Group and installation will be managed by the Shipyard. The disintegration of responsibility is a precautionary measure, unconsciously made, that takes out an executive insurance policy for salary-continuation in case things go berserk. In practice, the only thing this policy insures is that the project will screw itself right into the ground. Self-fulfilled prophecy.

The "Aim"ing maneuver, saved until last, is crushed in the mob scene rushing to the Feeding Frenzy, the very next scene. The quiet voice of reason is drowned-out by the din of the stampede. Nothing in the Universal Scenario is more energetic than the Feeding Frenzy. It adds a lot of excitement to the show.

The Feeding Frenzy

Act I Scene 2 is the Rush to Reductionism - the Feeding Frenzy. William Wordsworth described the frenzy with "We murder to dissect." The furious activity is all over in a short time and few outsiders are aware of the event. The Feeding Frenzy begins soon after the resources cannon is fired when the nebulous complexity called the problem/mission is dropped into the alerted organization. It is a hot potato and it is 'large.' There is no time for problem definition. There is only time to get a piece of the action before all the fresh money has been distributed.

As "the purpose of a system is what it does," then the function of the Feeding Frenzy is to take a problem that is not understood and grind it into organizational components that are. The procedure avoids the immediate necessity of confronting the complexity of the problem. That crucial task is aborted to an uncoordinated collection of organizational compartments, which are regularly encountered anyway as part of normal business. Decisions are made by gut reaction and then defended as if they were sent up by The Creator.

RULE - There are many sides to a decision, until you take one.

For any problem, simple or complex, there are countless solutions, each with multitudes of proponents (e.g., computerize, subcontract or use robots). Not all solution promoters are equal. The complex problem, by definition, is larger far beyond what any one solution element (shark) can swallow. As soon as the problem carcass is dropped into institutional waters, the competitive frenzy begins.

RULE - When dialogue is controlled by the most clever tongues rather than the most appropriate solutions, what you fear is what you get.

Party Time

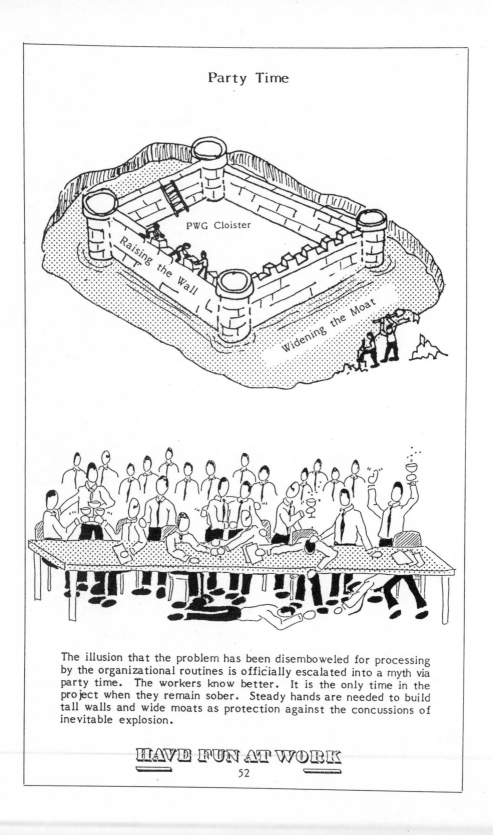

The illusion that the problem has been disemboweled for processing by the organizational routines is officially escalated into a myth via party time. The workers know better. It is the only time in the project when they remain sober. Steady hands are needed to build tall walls and wide moats as protection against the concussions of inevitable explosion.

HAVE FUN AT WORK

The shark attack is a wild affair. Solutioneers close in, ripping off the largest chunks they can hold. Solutions swallow other solutions. In short order, like the Potsdam conference in which lots were cast for conquered land, there is nothing left of the problem but a vague notion, soon forgotten, of what it may have been. Right after the Feeding Frenzy there is a deafening silence as organizational life appears to return to normal. Sometimes there can be a hierarchical set of feeding frenzies once a big prize (larger than a department) is brought back from the kill into the home organization (e.g., Star Wars research).

Through the Feeding Frenzy we learn that Primary Working Groups (PWGs) are entirely capable of communicating with others. Group rules make a provision for the bedlam of the frenzy as the members are expected to use whatever means are necessary to bring home the spoils. It is even possible to have convergent teamwork among diverse groups. It is possible to have a coordinated, integrated activity among strangers. It all happens in the Feeding Frenzy, naturally.

RULE - The world of solutions is always larger than the world of the specification.

The intelligence of the problem structure (people network, processes, and technology), however, cannot be arbitrarily dispersed and simultaneously retained. Unfortunately, and inevitably, the sharks disintegrate the wrong problem (the real problem is still unknown). This is because the archaic boundaries of the solution elements never fit the cleavage lines of the problem (department X is making nuts with left hand threads and department Y is making bolts with right hand threads). The decomposition fracture lines shatter unified characteristics into oblivion. Problem pieces, all sixes and sevens, fall through the cracks and get lost. The critical essence of the problem cannot be reconstructed from the pieces strewn about the organization. No one knows and no one is tasked to care. The undefined problem now resides dismembered in separate undefined receptacles. The largest is named 'overlooked.' In spite of the fact that project failure has not been left to chance, the stage is now set for Party Time.

Party Time and Disconnect

In complex projects there is an afterglow of the Feeding Frenzy we call Party Time. It is Act I scene 3, a time of relief from the anxiety of complexity on-the-loose (the leaders of Congress toast passage of the tax simplification act). Officials who supported the frenzy travel about and enjoy the delights of life during this honeymoon phase. The workers (that's you) are anxiously busy in their lairs. No one knows what is happening in the other foxholes and it doesn't matter. Everything is vague and intergroup communication is happy with unimportant matters. No party-goers will be workers (that's still you) and none of the managers will be around when it is time to search for the guilty. Party Time is where the political ability to make midcourse corrections is dissipated. Party Time may be fun for the officials but it certainly is no fun for you. It is when projects are complex, that ordinary, established methods reveal their destructive power.

RULE - The higher the spirits of management, the less they are aware of what is going on.

During Party Time the working groups each realize that no one is in control of the project (control, along with the problem, was never defined in the first place) and they silently disconnect from one another. With all of the loose ends

Error, Camouflage & Shrinkage to the SOE

Feeding Frenzy

Post Party Time Shrinkage

E.O.P.M.D.

EVERYTHING IS ON PLAN!

SQUARE PEG GROUP

Error & Camouflage

The real Span Of Effectiveness (SOE) of an agency has no relationship to its advertising or to the kind of work it will agree to undertake. The more the project is disintegrated, the more it becomes out of control. At the same time, the scopes quietly narrow back towards the center of the agency's true SOE. Fine granulation of the wrong problem coupled with work in isolated cells forms a guarantee of undetected error. Small errors lock in and breed more errors. Errors grow so large they must be camouflaged to avoid detection. Scopes creep toward the vanishing point of the sanctioned routine. Disintegration takes its toll.

left dangling by the insensate frenzy, the first group task in the project is to retrench group positions to a sphere of domain over which the group knows it can exercise rational control. That domain, as delineated by the organization, is quite small and well short of the illusions created during the Feeding Frenzy. The suspense builds as to what will take place when the parties are over. End of Act I.

Error, Distance and Camouflage

During Party time the workery was busy raising walls and digging moats. The first scene in Act II starts with building the errors which are inherent in the independent, uncoordinated efforts. It can't miss. All the initial project efforts of the worker bees have been devoted to ordering the wrong parts and to concealing that fact. Without fanfare, the scopes of work have been quietly retrenched inside of fortress walls. Errors in communication and performance are hidden through a variety of covers. During "Camouflage" all sorts of nervous behavior, typically related to style rather than subject content, is exhibited. Camouflage is mutually condoned and reinforced as an alternative to discussing the vital issue of independent, uncoordinated activities (i.e., the project is out of control). Nevertheless, strain continues to build and automatic defense mechanisms take charge. The project is on tenterhooks. It is Stress City.

RULE - When you don't know who is coordinating the "solutions," no one is.

Because of the self-locking property, now developed, any attempts at coordination and integration are doomed. The project **plan** definition can be no better than the **problem** definition. No thought about going back and correcting that monstrous oversight is allowed. For each primary working group (now a full-blown cloistered fortress), project responsibilities are limited, and they are still shrinking. Officials managing the total project are actually playing in a sandbox of camouflage and progress reports glissade ever further from the truth. Regardless of its popularity, camouflage fools few. It amounts to a game of mutual undiscussables, a game where there are only losers. The camouflage pattern has no correcting mechanism and the stage is all set for Escalation. Welcome to Viet Nam.

Compounding of error

The Escalation scene follows when the counterproductive mechanisms are in place and breeding over a long period of time. The working cloisters continue to go about their business (like bankers laundering money for the Mob) in isolation. No one dares to look at the integration laterally or to admit knowing that the scope of supply each agency is actually going to deliver is now quite a bit different and smaller than what was promised at the conveniently-forgotten Feeding Frenzy. Each group heaves its intermediate products "over-the-wall" to another walled group. Without question the packages are opened, altered to suit, translated, inflated, repackaged and lobbed over the transom to the next cloister. There is no possibility that the assembled pieces will fit and resolve the problem. Communication is loaded with noise and fidelity-destroying mechanisms that turn routine messages into fantasy.

RULE - It is the genius of management which keeps the workery from questioning the inequity of the "system."

The Facade of Futile Feigned Faith (F4)

- Let's give the "new" organization time to work.
- The new policy should solve the problem.
- The project manager has just been made an assistant VP.
- We are confident that these adjustments will work.
- Things should start to look better next month.
- The vendor says it will be fixed in the next revision.
- We have added two more assistant project managers.
- We are going to install a more powerful computer.
- The new software will be put on line next week.
- The boss just called for a big project review meeting.
- We're sending the key men off to management school.
- We see some signs that things are turning around.
- There is plenty of safety factor built into the seals.
- We have developed a new training program.
- The boss himself is going to take charge.
- It just needs more time to straighten itself out.
- If we all work together, we can make the schedule.
- We're going to increase computer memory.
- Today we start mandatory overtime, seven days a week.
- Corporate is coming out with a new policy.
- We have hired a consultant with a great track record.
- The last meeting really cleared up the misunderstandings.
- We are suing the vendor for non-compliance to the specification.

There is no shortage of optimism when it comes to defending entrenched practices. Since the only tolerable condition is status quo, a favorable light is put on every detail in the unfolding disaster. Getting rid of the bad apples changes nothing.

HAVE FUN AT WORK

As the project careens forward and error builds, the working groups distance themselves ever farther from each other while devoting considerable energy to hide that fact. Each primary working group desperately wants to be left alone to do its thing and reduce its stress (adjusting of the situation vs adjusting to the situation). Camouflage is now a peckish way of life and there is no going back. Accordingly, the act of camouflaging itself must be camouflaged (camouflage squared). Early in this stage the participants start their just-in-case (JIC) files. Later on in the scene the cover-your-ass (CYA) and Pearl Harbor (PH) files appear. The sure behavioral signs are listed below.

- Adversarial relationships between developer and user
- Uncertainty, mistrust, avoidance, persistent conflict
- Face saving, blind conformity, demands for loyalty
- Intergroup rivalry, inter-organizational competition
- Invalid, asymmetrical information for important issues
- Increased secrecy, increased parochial interests, myopia
- Ineffective management decisions, abulia

One feature of the Escalation script is a popular, general-purpose behavioral pattern we call the facade of futile feigned faith (F4). It is an embodiment of the social doctrine of eternal optimism in the "system," like teaching one's grandmother to suck eggs. Child of the path of least organizational noise, F4 gains another increment of time with the horrible, but familiar scene. No matter that the project boat is plowing towards disaster, completely out of control. There is hope that the latest rearrangement of deck chairs will catch the wind and steer the ship away from its collision course with the iceberg. It is the halftime sermon by the coach of the Vienna Choir Boys' football team, behind 220 to nothing, claiming that by giving a little more effort (110% is the usual goal) they will yet be able to prevail over the Washington Redskins. The only thing accomplished is to increase the agony. Everyone left in the boys' locker room is going to end up in the hospital with his team-mates, and they know it. There are many everyday examples of the facade of futile feigned faith (F4):

As the project achieves a momentum towards disaster that is then perceived to be beyond the influence of the people who, in fact, **are** the project, hope is displaced by despair - another self-locking property. Many who correctly understand that the mess is a man-made affair also believe that it is necessary. As long as the disaster outcome is accepted as inevitable, it is guaranteed. During the Camouflage phase, the project is inaccessible to reason. Any accurate forecaster, who speaks up out of concern for the future of the project, will cause a work interruption while he is tracked down and obliterated by the very people he is trying to help.

RULE - Sick projects breed sick people.

When managers start to purl about form rather than content, project waste is at its peak. Work stops while the cloisters (working groups) elevate the transoms - some observers call it cementing broken glass to the top of the wall. Thus reinforced, error can continue to compound. All attempts to prevent the wreckage backfire. Changing managers changes nothing. Adding officials makes things worse. Like the icy Challenger all tanked up on the launch pad, the fireworks are now in place for public display of the disaster.

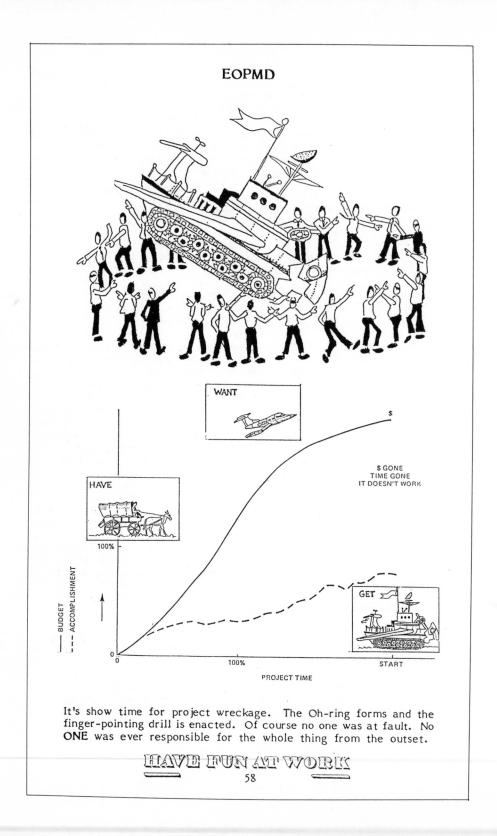

EOPMD

It's show time for project wreckage. The Oh-ring forms and the finger-pointing drill is enacted. Of course no one was at fault. No **ONE** was ever responsible for the whole thing from the outset.

HAVE FUN AT WORK

58

End-Of-Project Mismatch Discovery

When some event, like the failure to complete the system on the tenth schedule extension, tears away the camouflage, it triggers End-of-Project Mismatch Discovery. This term is bulky and we resort to its acronym, EOPMD. This late stage of the project is when all of the fragments of development are finally assembled. It is here that the mismatch between expectations and reality becomes painfully apparent. It is time to catch a Tartar. Of course, most of the issues highlighted in EOPMD are based upon information that was available long before the parts came together. Camouflage has taken its toll. The money is gone, the time is gone, and the thing doesn't work. The telltale indicators of impending EOPMD are shown below.

- Remanagement and management by crisis
- Task force firefighting
- Search for acceptable recipients of blame
- Diversionary publicity, shredding of the records
- High turnover of technical leaders
- Hiring of consultants, increase in support staff, committees
- Frequent rescheduling, end date even later than worst case

EOPMD can be frantic. The news of the particulars, now public, spreads like wildfire. It is payoff time for the fragmentation and scattering of project responsibility that was contrived at the start. Searches are hurriedly made through the carefully preserved Pearl Harbor files to show that it wasn't anyone's fault. As planned, there is no one to blame. Each agent reviews the limited scope assigned and points the finger at another agent who failed to deliver on some intersecting aspect, thus preventing accomplishment of the assignment. Scattering of responsibility works every time (to fill its own prophecy). There may be a ritual sacrifice of some temple priests, but golden parachutes cushion the fall.

RULE - When the mess hits the fan, make sure you left a year ago.

As an example of dispersed responsibility at EOPMD, look at the extended mess with the liability insurance fiasco, an obvious, clear-cut social system disgrace. No one could possibly believe that there is any merit to shutting down a society because of risk. We owe our very existence to a series of risk-takers and accidents. But because the responsibility for this particular debacle is scattered among many vested and entrenched entities, the Establishment is unable to mobilize an effective assault on the lunacy. We see the insurance juggernaut point at the legal profession (to name only two of the players) and we get confused in aiming our anger. The outrage diffused, the town pool is closed without a whimper. A cold snap in Southern California takes the lives of many homeless unfortunates while spacious, heated public buildings remain closed in deference to insurance premiums. Medical malpractice is an illustration of this merry-go-round.

> In some states... the doctors are having a harder time with the patients in the courts than they had with them in the sick rooms... Unless something shall be done... to protect the practitioners from lawyers, surgery and kindred branches of medicine must soon come to an end. It is costing doctors more to defend lawsuits against them for alleged malpractice than they make by the profession.

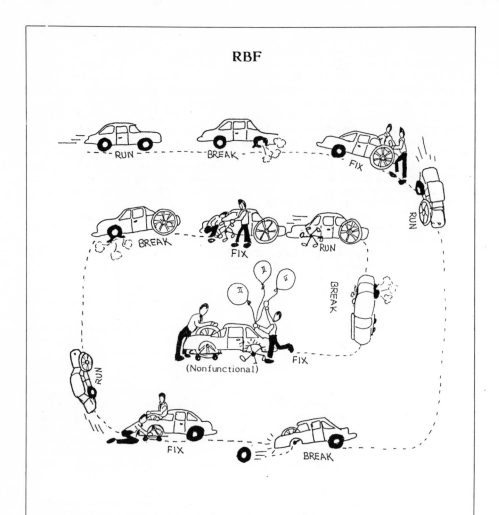

Finding the particular mismatches and oversights after the thing
has been installed is for the birds, the birds of Pray. Long cycle
RBF is the worst possible project practice and an embarrassment to
the designing profession. Short cycle RBF is the stuff of great
projects. All learning is from error and learning builds knowledge.
Designing on knowledge makes marvelous, durable systems. At the
elemental level, short cycle RBF is none other than the quality-
circle on the production floor. All it takes to guarantee long cycle
RBF is to demand error-free performance. The energy that should
go into the project goal goes instead to camouflage of the inherent
error in reaching it. Fools!

These words appeared in the **Medical Herald** in 1879. The sanctioned practice to avoid responsibility through granulation and dispersion is having a long and very expensive run. No matter the price, we never demand that a whole complex problem have a central responsibility. It is a super error. **Erase.**

Run, Break and Fix

The alternative to a repeat performance of the Universal Scenario is the turn-over of the fruits of the mess to the Operations Department. This action begins the era labeled as Run, Break and Fix (RBF). In RBF, the thing is run, it breaks down and the damage is fixed. Operations professionals are only too happy to continue the RBF cycle. Their peculiar culture is to reinforce the pattern. Operations personnel do not want to get involved in the design any more than the designers want them to. But Operations is never at fault for RBF. A hostage management explains the invoice through corporate spokespersons as the cost is passed on to you (after the "Challenger" catastrophe, the budget for the Shuttle program is increased).

Run, Break and Fix is the fundamental principle of Operations. It is an effect of the Universal Scenario. The same policy is in force in every industry. In a new facility, the operating organization detaches from the central office. Departmental "walls" are quickly erected on site. It soon becomes a closed-loop community, wherein the attention is focused inward toward conducting inter-departmental tournaments. There is no natural correcting mechanism.

Recycle

In many cases the assembled system does not solve the problem by such a wide margin that (Boom!) the play is repeated, without pity, using a different cast of players. Counter-intuitive, but true. Of course, the outcome of Round Two is exactly the same as Round One. There are some florid cases where the cycle has been repeated several times in the same organization. Often, the new problems that are introduced by the "fix" make the original problem look tame. It is an endless minuet, a perpetual disposal of resources.

In Recycle, the project disaster just manufactured becomes a nonoccurrence. Then, since it "never happened," there is no reason to change the entrenched process that produced the wreckage. The new crew convinces itself that the failure was caused by a lack of skill in arranging and implementing established practices, or names any one of the factors eliminated here earlier, like time, money, or the wrong specific individuals. Through added emphasis on the sanctioned fundamentals, it is believed, a successful outcome can be deliberately achieved. It is the confidence of dolts. Without feedback, there can be no correction.

RULE - There is no project disaster, it bears repeating, that can't be repeated.

The Universal Scenario

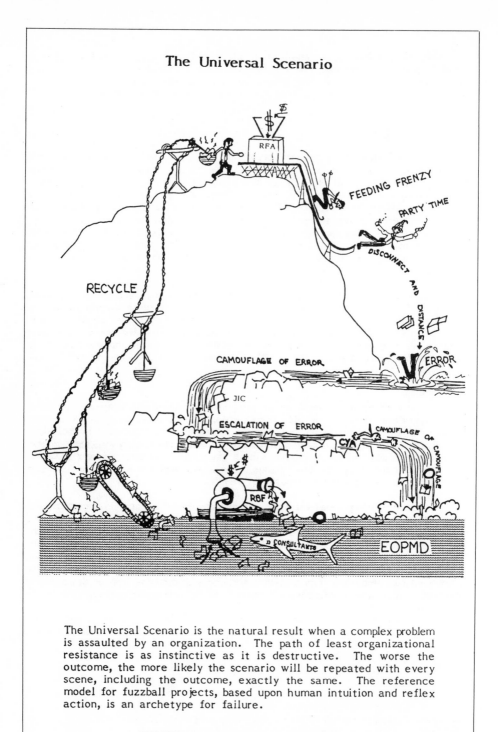

The Universal Scenario is the natural result when a complex problem is assaulted by an organization. The path of least organizational resistance is as instinctive as it is destructive. The worse the outcome, the more likely the scenario will be repeated with every scene, including the outcome, exactly the same. The reference model for fuzzball projects, based upon human intuition and reflex action, is an archetype for failure.

HAVE FUN AT WORK

You may have seen, in your travels through Dystopia, a very popular worker-office wall decoration describing common project phases. This folk wisdom is presented below together with our corresponding stages:

Uncritical acceptance .... Ready, Fire, Aim
Wild enthusiasm .... The Feeding Frenzy and Party Time
Dejected disillusionment .... Disconnect & Distance and Camouflage
Total confusion .... Compounding of Error
Search for the guilty .... Impending EOPMD
Punishment of the innocent .... EOPMD
Promotion of the non-participants .... Recycle

It seldom occurs to the pundits that the same sign is on display around the world - put up by brother victims of the Universal Scenario in widely separated human endeavors. Some of the inbuilt programing has managed to collect itself into the object of humor. The sign sells well, we are told, in 32 languages.

Summary of the What

The real problem has been disintegrated. A wrong replacement has been fractured into solution elements that don't fit together and are seldom even related to the problem at all (a particular quirk of the computer solution swarm). The "solution" fragments are developed in isolated, cloister fortresses. The agents of error collaborate to conceal the collective mismatch until assembly time. There can be no uncertainty about the outcome. Innocents are sent to Coventry. The fancy excuses emitted, of which society has an endless supply for all occasions, fool no one. Much critical feedback intelligence, however, is discarded and the cycle is regenerated intact.

It's a Track A world

The Universal Scenario is enacted by the standard-design organization doing the standard activities on a non-standard matter. Our shortspeak code for the established 'natural' situation is the expression **Track A.** It is the basic fabric of the world Establishment.

Track A problems are simple, recurrent problems. They are efficiently handled by Track A organizations using Track A practices. To encourage Track A practices, and discourage non-Track A practices, institutions have established a Track A environment and formed Track A doctrines. Track A schools, (and there are only Track A schools) dutifully inculcate a Track A mindset. Track A has locked-in on the global stage, inaccessible to the factors that would upstage it. It is accepted, reinforced and defended. No other issue in the spectrum of civilized man, as history well documents, has caused more carnage.

RULE - The Establishment has always chosen destruction before giving up any acquired advantage.

Legacy of the Universal Scenario

The Universal Scenario is the centerpiece of a hierarchy of distinctive behavioral patterns, all related to complex problems. While the Universal Scenario is the fundamental script directly causing project wreckage in a confrontation with complexity, the wholesale failure of organizations to solve solvable complex problems and the paranoid reluctance to apply lessons-learned from their failures sends repercussions in all directions.

Loss of Control

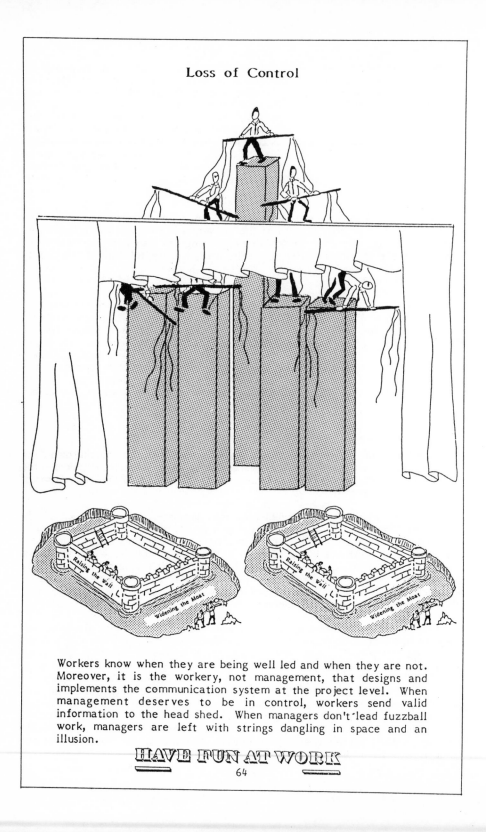

Workers know when they are being well led and when they are not. Moreover, it is the workery, not management, that designs and implements the communication system at the project level. When management deserves to be in control, workers send valid information to the head shed. When managers don't lead fuzzball work, managers are left with strings dangling in space and an illusion.

HAVE FUN AT WORK

Repetitive failure with complexity can modulate into an organizational norm. The impalpable acceptance of project failures in one organization can infect an entire industry to the point where failure becomes the standard. It happens all the time. For instance, a disastrous attempt at modernizing one steel mill can paralyze the efforts at another. Collectively, the steel industry can hand over its market to nations which have been better able to cope with the needs of productivity improvement. There is a recent case in Indiana where a steel mill completed its modernization project on the very day it closed its doors for good. Work with the computer world, which infects everything it touches with a mess, shows the commonality of principles across industries.

RULE - Practice in making disasters makes them perfectly disastrous.

Higher levels in the hierarchy of behavioral patterns wait for messes to appear before they emerge. For instance, a large hospital has at least as many complex-problem messes going on at once as it has departments (they call it unit modernization). The pedantic hospital administration reacts in a behavioral pattern for the epidemic of messes unlike the one employed when there was only one or two cases. Likewise, the agencies that administer groups of hospitals have a different script for the situation where most of their clients are in a mess, than they show when an exceptional case has erupted. This reaction feeds back to influence the behavior of their constituent hospitals and, in the case of high mess ratios, always impacts in a counterproductive direction.

RULE - An organization of sheep begets an administration of wolves.

To illustrate, it is normal practical practice to disregard selected hospital policy and procedures, and there are many ways to cover the tracks. As the situation is common to the industry, regulators adjust to the norm and become content to spend their energies getting more regulations put on the books. The hospitals soon learn there is no real enforcement. The discrepancies escalate. This whirls back to the regulators and goes on to more laws as a defense for potential criticism. Enter the occasional whistleblower to activate the "regulation" system, loaded with the goods on a particular hospital, and a defensive script is enacted. The regulators simply exterminate the whistleblower. His lifeless body is then placed on display as a reminder for those who may have similar thoughts about moral responsibility and meeting their sworn oaths. In the place of the word "hospital," other words such as "stock broker," "nuclear power plant," "justice system," or "school" can be substituted.

When dozens and dozens of messes in various stages along the Universal Scenario are all going on at once, the institutional response is to shift the measures of productivity from objective to comparative forms. We are told, as a justification for endless disaster, that the situation is no different over at the competition. We know that high mobility of personnel guarantees that the competition will also fail. There is a perceptible cultural shift to organize for failure as the norm. As long as the money doesn't run out, the culture of failure is a guaranteed winner. With practices and procedures in place to deal with failure as a regular, recurrent condition, it is a simple matter to torpedo any potential success, for which the organization is ill-prepared, and convert it into a mess, for which it is ready to handle as routine business.

RULE - Orgman only honors conformists and retired innovators.

The journey to disaster from the start to the finish is now complete. What triggers the global mess (2) has been described with the gory details along the trail of least organizational resistance to the chamber of horrors result (1). What happens (3) is well known and can be checked by reference to your own experience. In case you have led a sheltered life, you will find the bibliography well stocked with literature about the mess. The same show has been staged for thousands of years.

HAVE FUN AT WORK

The behavior pattern includes knowledge disavowal of any problems (e.g., corporate performance is a model for the industry), placement of the discussion of problems into supreme taboo, and retreat to the familiarity of failure. Corpologic reasons that since there are no problems, there is no need to entertain thoughts of a solution. Since there is a residue of traditional markets, there is no need to discuss developments in the outside world. Only talk about the status quo is permitted.

The buck rises

The collective effects of industries in a tailspin of failure to cope with complexity (agriculture, electronics, steel, automotive, etc.) show up in amplified form to trigger a well-known and well-documented pattern of government machinations in foreign and domestic affairs. When things are going up, government cruises along with "if it ain't broke, don't fix it." When things are grim, there is a williwaw of shortsighted, counterproductive responses. Nothing the government is empowered to do has the slightest effect upon the root cause of the dilemmas faced. Governing agencies have the same ridiculous relationship with complexity as the governed. When the government can only deal with effects rather than causes, the basic problem, like the mountain of rubbish to be disposed, grows.

Usually the process ends in war, as it has several times in this century. The benefit of war is that the side which loses gets smarter (new) institutions. Our concern is that the ancient remedy for displacing the adamantine institution is still in use, while the implements associated with that expedient, like atomic bombs, have achieved the power to destroy humanity altogether.

RULE - If social lessons were learned from technological innovations, the Department of Defense would be the smallest agency in Government.

At the top of the complexity hierarchy are behavioral patterns (such as Afghanistanism) which emerge in response to a society of self-obsoleted institutions. These reactions, all flowing from the same instincts, lead to tariffs, common markets, alliances and conflict. Like all encounters with complexity, there is no natural correcting mechanism. Observe the trigger conditions and watch the circus march down the yellow brick road on cue. The lessons of 1914 led to the lessons of 1939 which led to the lessons of 1952 followed by the lessons of 1964 ...

RULE - All actions taken by an institution that knows it can't handle complexity will increase the severity and frequency of complexities it must confront.

Recognizing the language of failure is the first step to **have fun at work.** Use the new frame of reference to see what is going on in your own world. Think about how widespread it all is. "They" are not picking on you, but acting impulsively and predictably. You can chart the course. To know is to grow. It is, in the final analysis, an extraterrestrial joke.

Before going on to the WHY of the global mess, some vocabulary in the language of success is necessary. The understanding of WHY needs to have sight of the beacon of success as well as the lighthouse of failure. It is the comparison to **both** landmarks that locates our position.

Sailing to Success Harbor

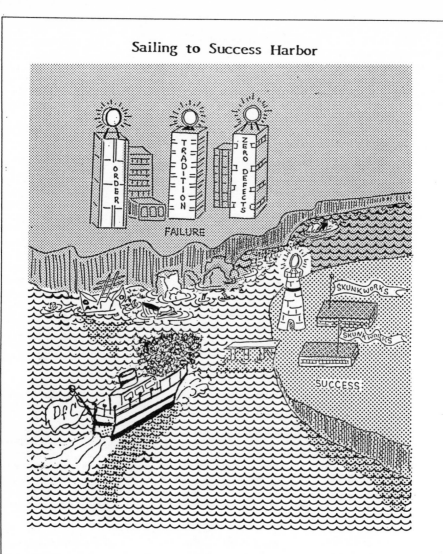

The human reference model for survival, evolved for the savannah, is now a template for organizational extinction. Using proven failure references exclusively as a beacon to navigate projects can only lead to another addition for Davy Jones' Locker. To succeed, a success reference is essential for navigation, since the route is narrow and passes around many hazards. The natural straight line of human instinct is the shortest path to disaster.

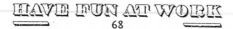

Chapter Five

A Beginning Vocabulary For Success

The basic course of failure has been traversed. We have seen that when the largeness of a multidimensional (complex) problem exceeds cognitive trigger limit values of the individual, the Universal Scenario of the organization springs to life. Through time and the instinctive, but counterproductive script, the calamitous outcome is assured. The enduring mess with complexity continues, not because remedies to the situation are unknown, but in spite of them. Preparation for **Why** needs the context that the ridiculous mess is quite unnecessary. This Chapter will introduce some conceptual building blocks for a success vocabulary.

RULE - Any official denial by the firm confirms the worst suspicions of the workery.

Now that many of your Bad Seventies, those counterproductive mental models, are crumbling, it is time to think about some worthwhile replacements. Once the language of failure is inserted in one corner of your cranium it should be complemented with the language of success in the other. If you have good reference models of failure and good reference models of success, you can better dimension "reality." You can not only locate your position, but you can chart a deliberate course of action. With good bracketing reference models, all the important questions can be decided **by counting. Replace.**

The requisite success process is so seldom employed that a common semantic language has never been developed. A decent vocabulary for success has not been necessary because the established reference models are all failure-oriented. Over the years we have assembled a "language" of success, not as a goal but as a necessity. While we would never try to defend the particular choice of vocabulary, the **concept** of a central success reference is not negotiable.

RULE - School lied: success does not come from appearing to have avoided failure.

Success talk begins and ends with structure

Tools for handling large-space problems include several good mathematical techniques for processing data and algorithms for highlighting relationships among different kinds of data (in some ways the "artificial" intelligence industry is based upon systems practices). These tools enable the technical solution of system problems which greatly exceed the cognitive limitations of an individual to understand by intuitive methods. Man invents systems to deal with chaos.

Systems work (solving complex problems) is working with **structures.** Structures organize, contain and convey content. Systems with a great many elements can be described by few structures - few enough to be comprehensible. Systems tools do not by themselves guarantee a solution.

Complex problems always involve systems, and almost all systems are complex. Solving a complex problem is done through the design of appropriate mechanisms which control aspects of the problem. For instance, getting to the moon was a complexity of considerable proportions. The goal was achieved through developing an array of interrelated technical and social systems that were capable, together, of doing it. You should learn about **systems** but don't flaunt the vocabulary in public. Carrying the same social stigma as complexity, people who traffic in systems are compared unfavorably to Atilla the Hun.

Unfortunately, "system" has become too popular a word to be useful in a precise sense. It shows up in too many places with customized, and usually inconsistent meanings. For example, "system" is often used in the computer industry to denote some combination of hardware and software in an application. However, when a computer user asks for a systems engineer, he only wants someone to change the printer ribbon. Most people use the term "system" to conceal their ignorance about the subject.

The spotlight on solving complex problems illuminates twenty established branches of science at work, in universities around the world, refining logical tools which are especially adapted to help solve fuzzball (complex) dilemmas. These are the sciences for systems. The analytical toolbox for coping with the objective side of complexity, such as Shannon's work on communications, is in great shape and has been for some time. Note that the existence of the toolbox, widely known, has failed to provide the slightest deterrent to the enactment of the Universal Scenario. **Erase** the lack-of-cure notion.

The total failure of the systems sciences, like Operations Research and Cybernetics, to make any noticeable dent on the growing pile of complexity woe, **makes sense.** These wide-span generalist cults are guilty of the very pathologies they decry in "hard" disciplines and they run with equal speed away from rich, real-world problems. Unavoidable complexities, like waste disposal management, are dismissed as chaotic or insensible. While each advocate is right within his own bough of science, and can readily provide excuses acceptable to his peers, not one guild dares take on whole problems in the trenches. This situation is common and it provides additional insight to the nature of the enduring problem. Few organizations, for example, are more rigidly coupled to the status quo of decades past than the Futures Societies.

Systems IS Complexity

In order to deal with the great variety of systems, animate and inanimate, a framework is used where they can be ordered, related and understood. This framework is interested in ways that a system functions (behaves), not so much in what the system does, but what it is **capable** of doing (all possible behaviors). The properties we ascribe to systems, such as fast and safe, are really describing behavior.

RULE - A well-structured problem is already half solved.

We use the notion of "system" as it pertains to tangible matters which have distinguishable pieces and parts in some kind of relationship to each other. That is, relationships exist (often very complicated ones) between the whole system and its parts. Systems are subject to controlling factors and no factor can pass from part to part with insignificance. This definition of "system" can be used at different levels: systems can be subsystems to parent systems. For instance, a whole automobile can be viewed as a system. A car can also be an element in a system of highways which are in turn part of the national transportation system. The automobile consists of connected systems itself, such as the electrical, braking, and heating systems. (For decades, at our peril, car engineers neglected to include the driver "system" as part of the design.)

A working system description is a tabulation of related variables, vectors and trajectories that **have** to be taken into account in order to develop useful knowledge about the system. To define a collection of related parts as a system, it must also have defined boundaries. The arbitrary boundaries between the system and its environs don't have to be solid walls, but every penetration to the outside world must be identified. The comprehensive definition of boundaries is a craft in itself. In solving a complex problem, a loosely defined system is an instrument of **terror**.

In practice, we view a system as a bounded collection of elements, attributes of elements, and relationships among elements and their attributes. Both attributes and relationships are characterized by measurable functions called variables. Coupling relationships add to the complexity the same as the tangible entities connected. At any point in time the state of the system is the set of numerical values held by its variables within the system "space." It is the same space as used earlier in the discussion about complexity. The process of keeping the values of designated variables within specified limits, called homeostasis, is error-controlled negative feedback, the basic mechanism of control in all systems, natural or man-made, animate or inanimate.

RULE - Feedback is a better buddy than a dog, which is the best friend known to man.

While it is common to think of system as a single network, it is helpful to conceptualize system as two "separate" subsystems joined together. One subsystem is the aggregation of mechanisms directly involved in the **productive** process, like the engine and transmission in your car. The other subsystem is the conglomerate of mechanisms that **control** the purposive subsystem to stay within desired boundaries, like brakes and steering. In order to achieve "system," the control subsystem is joined to the production subsystem. This definition allows us to zero in on each of these subsystems as necessary without confusion with the other (makes the job easier to understand).

The first step in dealing with a fuzzy problem, and one we are using here to transfer **have fun at work** knowledge to you, is to let the core matter simmer while the **context** of the fuzzball is defined and described. Always begin a task by placing the scope in the higher-order world of which it is a part. They always give it to you wrongly-defined anyway. Thus, by the time you get the detailed instructions for having fun at work, the foundation for this weird competency will have been provided. In that way, you will be able to meet new and unexpected situations with some degree of resiliency.

Structural tools that apply to **all** systems increase **variety** in your complexity coping mechanisms. Organizational behavior is a good example of a complicated system. We will be demonstrating the use of systems tools in this book to describe it. We can give you no greater gift to **have fun at work**.

71

System

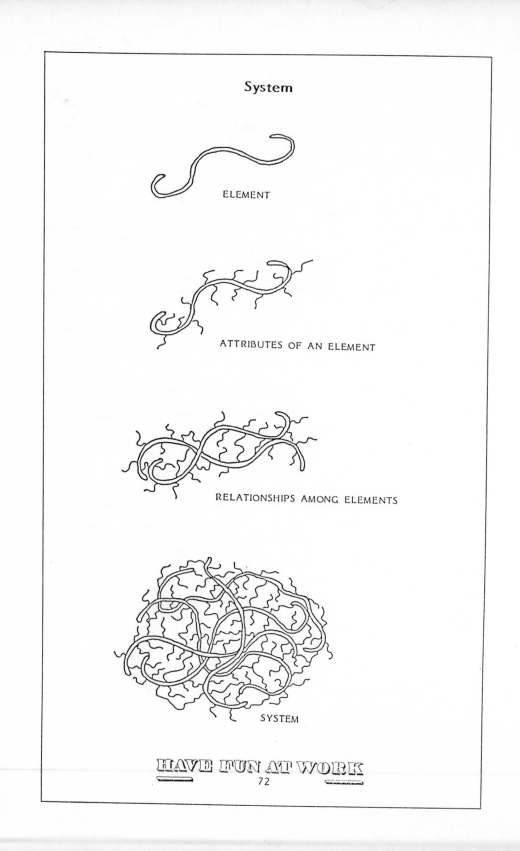

ELEMENT

ATTRIBUTES OF AN ELEMENT

RELATIONSHIPS AMONG ELEMENTS

SYSTEM

The coin of complex systems has two sides

The sanctioned side of solving a complex problem, i.e., working out the gears and wires of the system that does the defined job in an orderly manner, is well documented in the handbooks of systems. If only it was that simple, various system simplifications could be ordered and related, and there would be no mess to write about. The other side of the coin is the fact that the real **process** of solving a complex problem, and one that gives the organization a fit, is none other than the disorder of **innovation.**

More organizational tolerance to adjust exists for the routine problems, where it has little significance, than for the conditions of large complexities where innovation is a requisite. When the largeness-of-problem index crosses the threshold of the Zone of Indifference, the world of dystopia snaps-in to displace rational activity. This forms an immediate mismatch of capability demand (innovation) to capability supply (entrenched practices).

RULE - Innovation is not just the best thing for complexity, it is the only thing.

A complex problem, like hazardous waste disposal, persists unremedied for decades simply because it cannot be solved in terms that fit snugly into the machinery of prevailing society. The solution space permitted by the established order (which was solidified before this particular complexity was exhibited), does not include the domain of the problem.

To travel into new solution domains, those that may include the problem complexities in hand, is to explore, to create, to invent and to innovate. Innovation also means **making errors,** lots of them. Without innovation at the core of the solution activities and **fast-cycle feedback,** the complex problem is not going to be solved. The Establishment plainly demonstrates this with boring regularity.

Unlike analytical systems practices, the innovation process is virtually undocumented and undiscussed. The reigning Establishment has always used the media to control information about innovation and adaptation directed at the workers. Innovators and their disorderly processes are avoided, evaded, ridiculed, suppressed and rejected as social undesirables. The microscopic amounts of information about innovation that do sneak through media barriers are invariably prepared by certified members of the Establishment, who are neither innovators themselves nor bold enough to describe the real innovative process. Even when the **accomplishments** of innovation are correctly described, you can be sure that the description of the innovative process, if offered at all, will be a lie.

RULE - If it wasn't for the innovator, the Establishment would still be living in caves. Therefore, the Establishment treats innovators as sworn enemies.

It was an unknown innovator who started the process of human "civilization" itself. Since then, civilization has never made a single advance that wasn't directly attributable to the handiwork of a single innovator. The self-adopted role of the Establishment is to **hold** ground won by the innovators past (and long forgotten) and to persecute any and all who would practice the profession. You are informed by the media that some problems have gotten so large that only "departments" managed by the likes of Bell Labs and IBM can cope with them. This information is false. **Erase.**

Inversion

It is often thought that "Necessity is the Mother of Invention." Since effective remedies for complex problems are well known, they are often proposed by loyal Samaritans to help the organization in distress. When remedy can not make use of the standard, FDA-approved snake oils, the organization automatically repels the very remedial actions necessary to avoid progressive degeneration. Inverted logic flows from the rift between primitive instincts and reality. Good Samaritans become dead Samaritans.

HAVE FUN AT WORK

To cope with large-space problems, **Replace** that member of the Bad Seventies with a mental reference where innovation is the fundamental structure around which everything else must revolve. Fortunately, and in spite of being oppressed by social institutions which intentionally fail to inform youths about the source of their affluence, there **are** innovators and there **is** an innovative process. Together they make the critical coupling between the availability of objective systems methods and achieving remedy of a complex problem.

Complex systems technology in practice

The analytical tools for systems were well developed by the mid-1950s. A surge of interest in systems thinking by the government occurred during the 1970s when systems engineering was all the rage for large projects in aerospace and military gear (i.e., the "fix"). Military specifications and standards called for a big dose of systems work and much money was spent in the name of the systems approach. In a few years, the Army first noticed that less results were being obtained with higher expense, and that soon was the end of that. Today, for all practical purposes, systems science and systems engineering are dead issues. If any of their founders were alive and applied for membership today, they would be rejected.

RULE - The organization is always taken by surprise at any display of systems thinking and common sense.

The technology for systems, when coupled with innovation, has been successfully demonstrated in a variety of applications. The Manhattan Project is a notable example of innovation in solving the large, complex problem of building and delivering the first atomic bomb. That project violated every rule in the Establishment book (it was given license to do so) because it was the only way to beat the schedule for invading Japan. The Apollo Project was another exhibit of the innovative process joining with systems practices to solve an enormously complicated problem. Unfortunately, both areas have been eroded back into the mainstream of mediocrity.

On a smaller scale, the combination has been worked to deliver the personal computer, electric power, and the Polaroid camera. The Japanese used the dynamic duo to switch their polarity on product quality in just two decades (remember when "made in Japan" meant junk?). Demonstrations of solving complex problems go on all the time. It is always done in the same way with the same combination of systems technique and innovation (i.e., outside of the established rules where the solution space contains the problem space). In the great majority of complex problem cases, however, the proven process is avoided like a new plague.

Failure has gone to their heads

Ordinary logic would question the apparent contradiction of an Establishment punishing the very innovative process which provides its support and its luxuries. Common sense would wonder about an Establishment staying stuck in the muck of unresolved complexities while prohibiting the necessary work to drain the swamp. Plain reasoning would wince at the spectacle of organizations, in relentless pursuit of the impossible, diligently repeating their practices which have been proven, on every occasion, to fail. Go no further until you **replace** your "sensible" mental models with these counterintuitive ones. It is the only way you can **make sense** of the world around you.

RULE - Any time intuition is used in addressing a complex problem, the cause is lost.

When any organization acts to limit activities to a range that is harmful to itself in the prevailing circumstances, it will succumb. The more such an organization is exposed to threshold-exceeding complexities, the sooner it will perish. It is the "cool heads," not the hot ones, who push humanity towards the final precipice. As any creature has been endowed, you are a perceptual organ. Unfortunately, society has covered your windshield on the world with mud.· Stop often to clean your perceptual window so as to better see reality. That is how you avoid accidents.

Our preferred version of the innovative environment and the systems engineering process for solving complex problems is called the **Design for Complexity** (DfC). An introduction to the DfC is presented in a later Chapter. In implementation, the methodology is happy and enormously productive. Successful experience forms a most valuable reference model to compare what is done in normal practice when organizations confront non-routine matters. As much as organizations are shocked when systems practices and innovation are employed (their reference model is failure), we are shocked when they aren't. It is only when complexity is large that systems methods reveal their power. As mentioned before, there is no profound magic or special divine intervention necessary to understand and resolve the complex problem. It is basically an investment of time and labor. **Replace.**

Successful experience has answered another burning question about complexity. While it was known that complex problems could be solved that were beyond the capacity of an individual to comprehend, we did not know just how big a chunk of Complexity Mountain could be bitten off without severe indigestion. The happy answer is that very large, very complicated problems can indeed be solved with efficiency and fun. Only when the transformation between the normal mess and the DfC is seen first hand can the full potential of cooperative multidisciplined human endeavors be appreciated. It is fun at work.

RULE - The biggest boost to productivity is obtained by releasing the corporate "brakes" on innovation.

Every so often, as with the nonstop, two-person "Voyager" flight around the world, we get a glimpse of what can be accomplished. What few get a chance to see is the process behind those achievements. We never wonder why the feat had to be made by a small band of impoverished engineering mavericks instead of the hordes at Boeing. Did you wonder why the "Voyager" team publicly thanked the President of the United States for keeping the government out of its project?

Rejection in the face of success

In the continuing trail of elimination, the existence of a practical remedy must be added and re-added to the list. That is, the mess does not flourish because of a lack of suitable methodology, adequately demonstrated. **Erase.** The remedy is known and deliberately rejected. **You** figure it out.

The aversion of the Establishment to innovation and the technology for coping with complexity has been witnessed during incredible occasions when an institution deliberately turns its back on a demonstrated success and punishes the participants. A recent case involved the manufacture of computer hardware in France, where the plant had tried delegating autonomy and responsibility to workers for assembly, checkout and autographing entire systems. Productivity soared, quality soared and the workers became expert resources for designing the next generation of gear. The upshot of this popular success was a quick return to the assembly-line approach.

A frame manufacturing firm in Ohio decides to modernize its production line and coordinate manufacturing with the sales department. The maverick project is a blazing success and profits soar. Management, afraid of releasing authority to the workers, kills the living proof in the cradle.

An electronics firm in Arizona gets high on quality and achieves all the benefits promised by Juran and Deming. The facility becomes a showplace of the quality ethic. Victim of a takeover by a normal corporation, the new management wastes little time in restoring their own familiar brand of failure. In spite of a dramatic contrast in productivity, the quality ethic is marked "undiscussable."

Time to visit the **Why** department

The list of case histories grows like weeds. Between the daily newspaper and the TV, you don't even have to leave the living room to add to the collection. Your replaced mental models should start proving their worth in fresh insights, especially when you realize that all these mess situations, looked at by others as situation-unique affairs, are really the same. Knowledge of the "why" is important because it directs the design of principles to **have fun at work**. The "why" of the self-destructive madness, done in the holy name of survival, is a strange story. As usual, we start with a review of the underlying factors.

A complex problem, as defined, is beyond the scope or capacity of an individual to cope with all its details. Abandoning hope for the strategy of the hero (where is Superman when you need him, anyway?), the next human step up from individual man is a group. It is well established that groups of men can handle complex problems, like building the Panama Canal, which exceed individual capabilities. Bigger problems require lots of groups, usually with diverse skills. In human society, groups form or are found ensconced in organizations. It is very important to appreciate the inherent connection of complex system problem-solving to organizations. The coupling is critical.

When the context of problem-solving shifts from internal man to infernal organization, aspects are gained and aspects are lost. Crossing the threshold involves a lot of tradeoffs. What is gained is the **capability** to solve an otherwise unsolvable problem (with time and labor). What is lost is the freedom to use the requisite methods. Wow!

While system problems present themselves in a continuum of technical and organizational complexities, the associated human-powered methods of successful solution make a dramatic switch. That is, as a problem becomes incrementally more complex and suddenly leaves the domain of the individual, it is no longer the same problem to be solved. The technical component may be the same, but there are many more problem dimensions to be accommodated, and problem space explodes. This characteristic leap in issue complexity, because of a requisite

Linkage Escalation

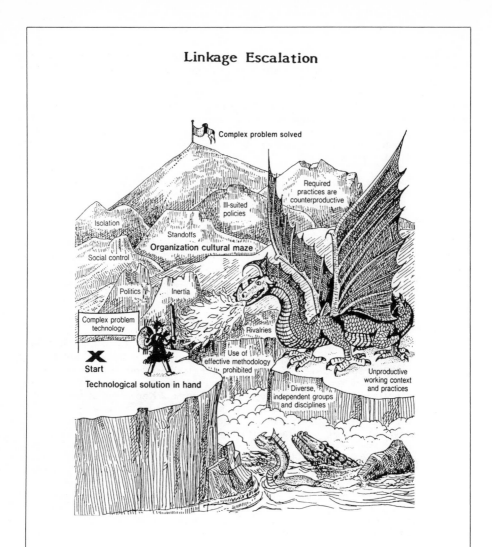

There are few complex problems of today which do not have satisfactory technical solutions. Rather than a final solution, technology is only a ticket to enter the organizational marathon obstacle course. Linkage to the social system escalates the problem to monstrous proportions. Making the technical problem look tame by comparison, the social system rarely has difficulty to prevent anyone finishing the gauntlet intact. Technical merit can not make it on its own.

entanglement with an organization, we call **linkage escalation.** It marks the transition from single to multiple man. Like any cataclysm, it is a most noteworthy event. It is the threshold switch.

RULE - Just when the problem gets to be too much to handle, in comes the organization to put any solution beyond reach.

It is necessary to distinguish simple problems from complex problems precisely because of great conflicts between the workable process for solving each respective class. Routine problems are solved by methods that are destructive to innovative procedures. The process used by a man to solve a man-size problem is unencumbered by many constraints that are fundamental to corporate life. Individual man has indeed brought some great boosts to civilization. In the two decades ending at 1910, while society was still predominantly agricultural, individual innovators brought atomic energy, radio, motion pictures, airplanes, X-rays, vacuum cleaners, air conditioning, permanent waves, helicopters, electric arc welding, and the mass production of automobiles into being. In the meantime, the Establishments of the world were preoccupied with preparations for the first World War.

The effects of suppressing innovation for solving complex problems can be seen in many places. For instance, there are intricate hobbies, such as building ship models, that find a high proportion of battered corporate veterans among the ranks. The over-qualified talent finds a needed release of its frustrations with linkage escalation on the job. There are many tough problems in constructing ships to small scale, but whatever skills a man can acquire and whatever solutions a man can conceive for the problems encountered, he is unconstrained in trying them out. He can fail with impunity, learn from his failures and tell anyone or no one. He doesn't have to worry about appearances or monthly reports. His product speaks for itself, by itself, occasionally with great eloquence.

Having fun at work is tied to increasing the variety of your coping mechanisms to deal with the variety of job situations that can not be avoided as well as those you elect to fashion. The key to it all is a working understanding of what makes Dystopia run. There are many more ways to be miserable at work than there are ways to be happy. You need good reference models to discriminate which is which. That's why the **why** story takes up four Chapters.

Origins

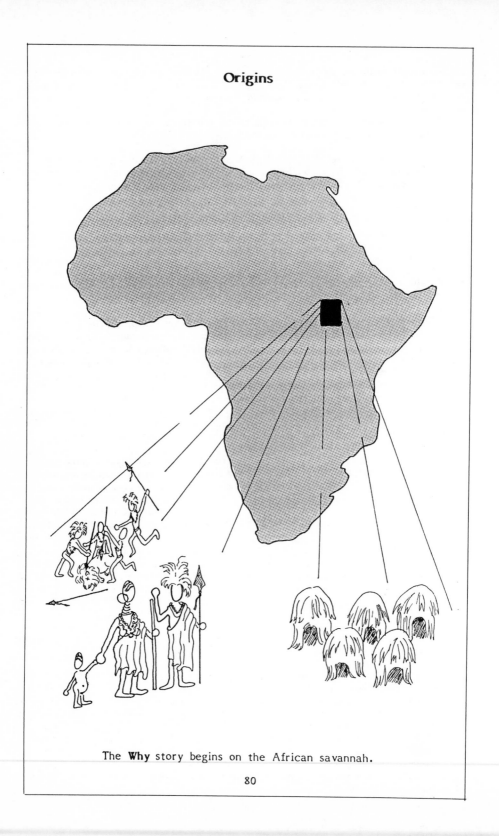

The **Why** story begins on the African savannah.

Chapter Six

"We can easily forgive a child who is afraid of the
dark; the real tragedy of life is when men are
afraid of the light."

Plato

The hidden enemy of fun at work

The relentless enactment of the Universal Scenario in the face of its
destructive madness is a testament to the higher order structure of human
values. The prime directives to the sanitarium up on the bridge of the ship are
engraved far down in the bilge of the subconscious, among the undiscussables.

No matter how diligent the attempt, complex matters are never solved
without free and open discussion of the important factors. When a problem fits
within a man's head, open communications among brain elements relating to the
problem can not be prevented. When many heads must be involved, each
containing a chunk of the matter, the need for unimpeded communication is
paramount. Organizations do the opposite, but that does not suspend the
necessity.

RULE - In a government agency, man controls man. In corporate life, the
reverse is true.

Accordingly, it's high time to get vital Why issues out on the table. How
can you **have fun at work** without understanding the most powerful forces that
dwell there? The energy behind the Universal Scenario, like atomic energy, can
be your servant genie or your dungeon master. Some unmarked directives you
must avoid, and some of these forces you can harness for your own purposes.

When we started the search into the vast library of illusions, myths, taboos
and undiscussables, the infallibility of institutions could only be doubted by
heretics. Now, the **fact** that organizations certainly will, in threshold-crossing
circumstances, act decisively against their own best interests can only be doubted
by an abandonment of reason. It is easy to show the **what** that organizations do
in converting a resolvable complex problem into a big mess - it can be witnessed
anywhere. Just look around. The big question is why. Why do they do it when
it is so exorbitant, so tragic and so unnecessary?

RULE - To understand the anatomy of organizational dysfunction, you must place
your rational faculties on holiday.

We know the answer to the **why** question is far from a simple one, like
jealousy. Over our many years of error, our why models have changed quite a
bit. Thanks to a bump in the right direction by John Warfield and Chris Argyris,
enough is known about the why to deliberately and systematically cause a success
which, left to the natural process, would be just another disaster. There is one
case, with which we were associated, that actually ran a side-by-side comparison
and paid many tens of million of dollars for the honor of sponsoring the
experiment. In fact, years later, the natural process version is still going around
and around the Universal Scenario (at last count, Recycle trip three). It looks
like perpetual motion.

RULE - If you perceive a situation only as Orgman sees it, you are less the representative of group-think than its victim.

There is a minimum set of knowledge about the Why required in order to build competence in having fun at work. The domain of the almighty technical fix, while impressive by itself, is no match when the vast social domain of the threshold-crossing problem is ignored. The connection of the mess to the organization (as the common denominator) requires a dispassionate overview. As a member of the guilty species, you must do your best to disqualify your inherent humanness in your observations of human nature. At least be aware of your prejudice and watch out for the mischief of your interpretations. Objectivity requires a strong will to be objective.

RULE - The only thing always well organized by an organization is hypocrisy.

Organizations are human social arrangements designed by human instinct, triggered when humans are exposed to certain situations. The instinctive design manual for concocting organizations is based upon conditions of stable tribal life on the East African savannah. Although the design manual was prepared over a million years ago, it has been genetically transmitted complete and unaltered. It is the only manual for organizational design supplied by the Master Architect. No updates.

You need to acquire an healthy appreciation for the long roots of instinct. In addition to being undiscussable, instincts in conflict with reality account for most of the behavior exhibited in organizational dystopia.

Appreciating the grip

In the early naive days, after the Universal Scenario pattern was first confirmed, we approached many messes-in-process and displayed the findings. The reaction was immediate recognition and acceptance of the fact that the participants were indeed enacting the ubiquitous play. At first we thought that awareness would lead the victims to some sort of remedial action to deflect the natural course of events. That strategy turned out to be another lesson in humility. Underestimating the tenacity of the grip of the organization on human behavior is, unfortunately, the rule rather than the exception. We now know that the most severe social punishments are displayed when we navigate closest to the truth about motivations. This discovery has developed into our most reliable indicator about instinctive behavior. We know of nothing in the spectrum of human nature that is more fiercely defended as rational than instinct, especially when it is obviously irrational.

RULE - Orgman is a sheep that turns into a wolf for conformity.

While daily life around the institution seems harmless enough, the organization can quickly turn into a factory of **terror** (always remember the threshold characteristics of lock-in and breeding). This behavioral stuff is nitro-glycerine. Learn to appreciate the power of instinctive social control over rational man. Treat it with utmost respect and you won't lose your head. Do your own experimentation in remote settings where you have nothing to lose. Having fun at work is the art of using this nitro for good causes and remaining intact to tell about your exploits.

The drive to ruin is so powerful that the Universal Scenario participants are helpless. As outsiders we can describe project past and project future in great detail, obtain unanimous agreement from the players as to the madness of the situation, and watch the show unfold, unmodified, on cue.   Normally, psychological filters (the Bad Seventies) make the dementia invisible. Compulsion without self-analysis will do it every time.

RULE - We are discouraged from learning too much about the behavior of Orgman.

Understanding basic elements of the organization

The knowledge that organizations are the basic vehicles of the Universal Scenario and the direct cause of the mess, is only an entrance fee to enter the murky underworld of Why they do it.   We start with some fundamental facts about organizations in general, only because the topics are so rarely discussed. For anything so important in the lives of people, it bears another note that the workings and influence of the dysfunctional organization on its members are socially undiscussable (mutinies will be severely punished).

"One needs to look near at hand to study men, but to study man one must look from afar."

Rousseau.

Technical literature on organizations can be classified into two categories- irrelevancies and lies. Most people who write books on these topics are salaried employees of particularly gruesome organizations called universities.   Their researchers who study organizations belong to a sprig of science, a guild within which they must confine their topical content and their language.   The fact of the published book itself testifies to the choice made by the academemicians between telling the truth about organizations, like their own (which knows full well it is a disgrace), and retaining employment. Regrettably, the same forces operate to release the truth from research about many other significant organizationally-sensitive subjects, such as mismanagement, ineffective government and employee stress.

RULE - Authority is harsh in direct proportion to its ignorance.

Organizations can be described from many directions.   In an input/output view, corporations are living organisms, consuming part of their environment in terms of men, machines, money, information and other entities. Organizations import materials, energy and information and export a transformation of them to the environment with, we expect, value added.

The bad news

Not many centuries ago, civilized man still thought that he was the grand center of the universe and substantially different from all other, "lower" forms. Perhaps such egocentric thinking felt good. The few who thought otherwise and spoke about it in public, however, were rewarded for their audacity with the dungeon.   The more modern man learns about the behavior of modern man in modern times, however, the less special he becomes. As the evidence rolls in, it becomes less and less surprising that man will commit such organizational atrocities. It becomes more and more amazing that man was able make it to the present at all.   To put it delicately, the enormous antiquity of institutional forms contains only primitive content.   First and foremost, humans are animals.

Closed Systems

Left to natural instincts, organizations function as closed systems. Acting as though the world ends where the walls begin, corporations are aggressively disinterested in changing environments. During stable times, the closed system mentality causes no harm. During turbulent times in the real-world loop, the closed system design is a prescription for disaster. Today, the only constant is the instinct to defend the status quo in the face of all realities. That's how species reach Extinctville.

RULE - Orgman defends his errors as if he is defending his life.

Each of us is a temporary, disposable container of genetic material, appearing as modular configurations of the nucleated cell. We are made of a microbial concoction of communities of bacteria evolved from the pre-biotic soup. Zoologically speaking, Homo Sapiens Sapiens (that's us, modern man) is genetically close to the African Apes. Man shares 97% of his genes with the gorilla and 98% of his genes with the chimpanzee, from whose class of primates the early forms of man branched off about five million years ago - before taxes. Chimpanzees branched off from the baboon about thirty million years ago. Like the design of your "new" car, all of man's physical parts were taken from the pre-existing stock room and are shared with animals of far older vintage.

You will have much better success understanding the behavior of man by starting from the ape end rather than from the so-called civilized end (the end that was hand-formed from intergalactic dust on the sixth day of creation, patterned after an image with impeccable credentials).

RULE - The more they learn about man, the more plausible his idiocy.

The brain of man is unique among the mental equipment of living creatures even as it retains a structural design and many features inherited from his ape ancestors. What survives the individual organism to transmit behavior is certain patterns of genes. In **every** creature, specific models and mechanisms are provided for a life of choosing between possibilities. Intellectual power is directly tied to the power of appropriate selection. Learning which choices are best to make is guided by instincts, and instincts are directed by genetics and the layout of the parts of the brain. For instance, the limbic part of the brain, which has not changed in over a million years, contains our instructions for social order. The brain is your primary means of survival.

The wiring plan of the brain does not provide an open infinity of unlimited capacities. Our brain is a compromise, not made by anybody we know on a first name basis, that allows us to be smart at some things and sets us up to be embarrassingly stupid in others. For instance, the small-brained chickadee is able to keep track of his caches of seeds, numbering in the hundreds, with great accuracy. Given the same task, man loses track of his warehouse locations when they number greater than twelve.

Behavior also can be shaped by social conditioning that has specialized for the tasks likely to be encountered. This plan works very well when the tasks actually encountered fit the molds. Cultural additions to what is inherited are very small and very slow. Survival depends upon stability, i.e., that the **scheme** for survival still works. The reason 99% of all the species that ever lived have become extinct, is that the fit of the survival scheme to the prevailing conditions has not been continuous.

RULE - Custom and habit are blind to both evil and good.

The instinct and compulsion chop shop

We have been given spare resources for translating our learning from thinking and experience into new programs that can complement or contradict our genetic inheritance. It is those reserves that we plead into action so you can learn how to **have fun at work.** Those resources, and only those resources, allow you to erase and replace your Bad Seventies mental models. Don't look for an

Human Brain Evolution

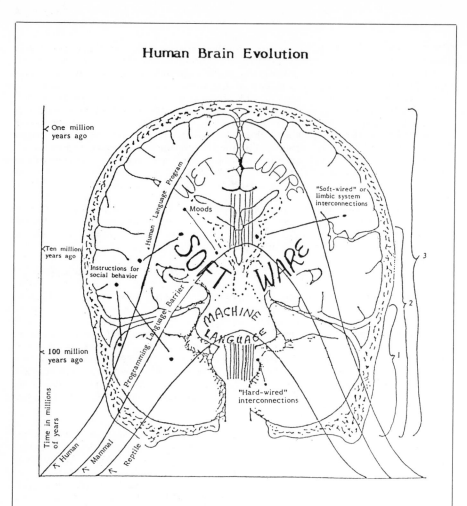

The human brain is a marvel of capacity and complexity. Seen looking towards the front of the head, above, physical developments are contrasted against the time scale at the left. The wetware which drives our social system behavior comes, unaltered, from the reptile brain (1) developed 100 million years ago. In the lower brain area reside such instincts as those for territory, shelter, hunting, homing, mating, breeding, social forms, the selection of leaders and other habits. The mammalian level, including the primitive cortex (2) indicates areas concerned with feelings, emotion, learning, adaptation and the expression of sensitivities. The large overbrain, programmed in human language a mere one million years ago (3) involves areas attributed to memory, foresight, symbolic language, conceptual thought and self-awareness. The ancient programs are written in a language our conscious intellect cannot transform. In addition to the vertical, there is also a left-right distinction: one side of the brain does a good job of assessing reality, while the other reshapes and interprets it according to rules science cannot yet understand.

easy way out. You are being spared much, even as it is. If a geneticist was given dictatorial powers over reproduction in order to improve human learning, he would not know how to begin. There is no expedient to avoid thinking. We tried every quick fix in the manual.

The brain organ is the written script of the programs that reference our lives as well as a repository of knowledge written in its own language. Living depends upon an incessant flow of information processed by the brain, whose arrangement provides the signs which constitute a code or language (software). The brain contains control mechanisms to maintain order. Order means constraints to thinking. Believe it.

RULE - When computers learn to cover up their limitations and their errors, the day of true artificial intelligence will have arrived.

Our actions are governed by mental programs that are modified by cultural conditioning (that's how about 50% of your software became bad). Human processing of information is done through this intricate set of plans which can think our thoughts. Significantly, many people are quite happy with the arrangement. They remain unaware that, for their own good, it is a most dangerous convenience.

RULE - When only successes can be discussed, none will occur.

Coping with modern life equipped with a value system created for conditions long vanished, we refer to this archaic standard in deciding our actions. This genetic compulsion is all the hook the organization needs to control your behavior. You need to understand how human nature bends you according to imperatives of the past so that you are conscious of the hook. It's there all right.

Biological drives run deep. The deeper they are, the more their power should be respected. We cannot separate what we think from how we think, and we cannot escape our limitations to thinking beyond the design of our thinking machinery. We take too much for granted.

There is no quality assurance (QA) on cranial software. There is no automatic upgrade program for obsolete, erroneous or now-dangerous instincts. Your information processing capacities can not be increased by adding another megaton hard drive. All the mental software you have been given to create new mental software to adapt to new situations, which is what intelligence is all about, is fixed and cannot be expanded. If you don't revise your concept of a problem **through error** with the old concept, then your only chance to be 'intelligent' just flew out the window. The social stigma of error, even though error is the only way we ever learn anything, is backwards.

RULE - When error is socially punished, the frequency and size of errors will increase without limit.

Where's the miracles?

Our mental software programs for social order reside in the small two-part limbic system. One part was lifted intact from the reptiles and the other was formed by pre-man apes over several million years of evolution. The large overbrain, which abruptly appeared, has been Homo Sapiens' continuous property for about half a million years. The big brain got big, not because the limbic system

87

and its cortex grew, but because the neocortex alone multiplied in size. The last incremental evolution of the brain, a slight expansion of the neocortex, occurred about fifty thousand years ago and another Sapiens was attached to our name tag.

After you mark the dawn of civilized man at about twelve thousand years past, do some arithmetic. Note that the large brain of man was around a mighty long time before it started showing off. That is, the facility for "intelligence" was around a long time without being put to much use to improve the lot of man. Current thinking suggests that the forces for social order, a program resident in reptile brain, were able to neutralize the power of the large addition to the brain until recent times. While social order got us here, it was the mortal enemy of civilization (innovation) from the start. It still is.

The social institutions of today take full credit for transmitting the culture of civilized man from one generation to the next. The subtle association with **providing** civilization, however, is an honor richly undeserved. From the big dawn until now, every single advance in civilization was made by an individual acting **outside** of the influence of social controls of the tribe.

RULE - General knowledge that it is the innovator who matters to humanity, not the Establishment which oppresses him, is the last thing the Establishment wants taught at school.

The ever-active mind of man has always had a great excess in capacity over that necessary to satisfy basic material needs. Suppressed by the social system for hundreds of thousands of years, the breakthrough finally came when an unknown maverick invented and promoted the bow and arrow. Now a man could provide for his family without participating in the tribal hunting band, where he had to follow rigid customs in order to obtain food. Breaking the bondage to social controls was necessary to start human civilization. That necessity has not changed either.

Man as a social animal

The genetic plan for the propagating man has always included living with others. The strategic advantage for continuing man in general has outweighed the many disadvantages of the tribe in particular. Living with other men automatically brings many problems that otherwise would not emerge. The space for individuality intrinsically conflicts with the social boundaries of the group. Wide-ranging personal capabilities may be proclaimed a virtue, but such encouragements are always conveyed with the conflicting signal that social independence will be discouraged. Nature has provided mechanisms especially adapted for the conflict, including the instinctive predisposition of a group member to place his needs for personal growth at a lower priority than the needs of the group for social order. Sometimes that's good news, sometimes that's very bad news.

By placing the goals of the tribe at a higher value than his own best interest, man automatically pledges allegiance to the whole spectrum of group processes that operate to attain those goals. Because the commitment is so instinctive, man never stops to examine consciously whether or not the ancient group processes still make sense for a particular situation. Those instincts came from an epoch when, for thousands of generations, the environment was stable.

RULE - The organizational rut is a coffin with its ends knocked out.

Prime directive

In order to drive down the yellow brick road oblivious to the mess being created, critical faculties, rational censors, filters, and barriers to lies must be suspended. When persons stage the play, the "person" is exactly the item which is bypassed. This herd-like behavior is the product of an underlying structure of rules, which we keep calling mental models, an unconscious possession. Man, as an active planner, decider and doer, continuously but subconsciously compares his actions to his rules (value system). When this comparison finds consonance, man finds tranquillity. When this comparison finds dissonance, man finds anxiety and everything stops until a balanced account is once again registered. One of the most common forms of counterproductive behavior in the Universal Scenario is driven by **cognitive dissonance.**

RULE - A person under the grip of cognitive dissonance can see anything he wants out of anything there is.

The Greeks distinguished between two kinds of rule-based behavior, **taxis** and **kosmos.** In taxis, the code of behavior has been overtly discussed, developed and set in place, usually documented as a policy. This is not to say that group policy is always followed, but at least it is materialized.

In kosmos, the code of conduct is not explicit. Even while the rules lie hidden in the unconscious mind, however, the conduct is predictable. It is likely that cognitive dissonance is guided by kosmos class rules contingent upon the environment. Nevertheless, the rules are coercive and strictly enforced.

A powerhouse motivator

The only requirement to activate the power of cognitive dissonance (it clobbers perceptions of reality) is that the individual must consider his action to be the result of his free choice. If the action decision is made by others, the results are not taken as a personal matter. We believe that the decision to join a group is held as a "free" choice and that the value system supplied by the group is thereby superimposed on the value system of the individual. In this way, the opportunities for cognitive dissonance and its attendant stress are greatly increased.

Man is driven to justify his decisions to act in harmony with his mental models, and he thereby becomes a slave to a built-in controlling overseer (another subconscious program). The overseer works to alter conscious experience. In times of turbulence, it is common to encounter information which is incongruous with that supplied by the group and become socially disorientated. Stress.

RULE - Only man, among all earth's creatures, is able to successfully lie to himself on a regular basis.

By adopting the value system of the group he joins, man is "socialized" and placed under group control. When stricken with cognitive dissonance, man is compelled to justify his association on any basis he can hallucinate. Cognitive dissonance can be used to induce people, who have been socially indoctrinated, to do things that are highly discrepant with their own attitudes. It is a form of learned helplessness to blind instincts and reflexes, as attitudes fall in line with the commitment to group rules.

Cognitive Dissonance

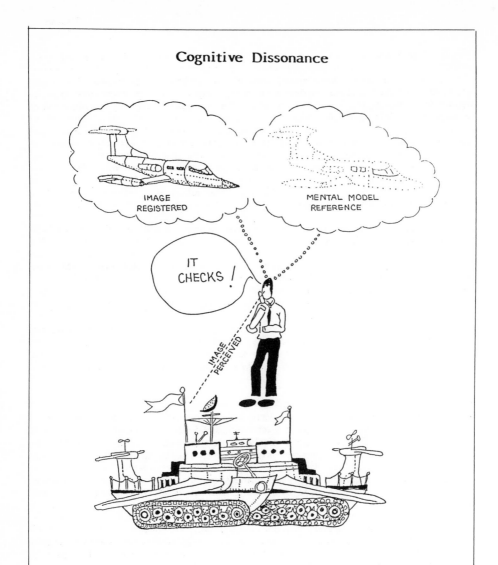

Ignorance of the illusion of conscious unity causes a lot of mischief. Rather than accept the fact of a wrong decision (cognitive dissonance hurts), one section of the brain translates reality to fit a model of the reality that would confirm a right decision. Such unauthorized tampering of sensor data has led more than one emperor to shed his clothes for parades in public. Not to be outdone by any garden-variety emperor, the public has often managed to view naked emperors and award them best-dressed honors. Perhaps the brain enjoys the scam to give the emperor a cold.

Raising these factors to your consciousness is essential for remaking your mental models. You have to protect yourself from the trap of cognitive dissonance. Change your mental model of what is "rational" about the organization. Remember, the forces of social control successfully kept the big brain gift from helping man to reach towards his human potential for over 400,000 years. This nature still thrives.

RULE - The corporation is a group that has taken the fair political process out of its politics.

Emphasizing the power of social control

The self role is always in conflict with the role imposed by the situation, and we have a constant reminder of its power where we work. Alexander Hamilton is buried in the yard of Trinity Church at Broadway and Rector in New York City and we see his tall white monument daily. We have been to the dueling grounds in New Jersey and watched parades from the marked spot in Weehawken where he was taken, mortally wounded, to die. We often wondered why it came to happen to a brilliant, educated man.

Before the duel with Aaron Burr (1804), Alexander spent a week arranging his affairs in preparation for death. One of his chores was to document the rationalization for his impending contest. He listed five reasons for declining the invitation to duel.

- On religious and moral grounds it is wrong to duel. "It would give me pain to be obliged to shed the blood of a fellow creature in a private combat forbidden by the laws."
- My wife and seven children are dependent on me.
- I am obliged to my creditors who, "by the forced sale of my property, may be in some degree sufferers."
- I feel no ill will toward Burr.
- I have much to lose and nothing to gain by this duel.

These seem like pretty good reasons, for a man of his intelligence, to eat a side order of crow and call the whole thing off. An immoral, sacrilegious, illegal, pointless risk to life, limb, and family without potential benefit has little to recommend it. Nevertheless, Hamilton went to his death, without hesitation, because "The ability to be in future useful, whether in resisting mischief or effecting good, in those crises of our public affairs, which seem likely to happen, would probably be inseparable from a conformity with public prejudice in this particular." Such is the power of social control to enforce prevailing social standards.

The history of dueling makes a good reference example showing how social norms can melt the good sense of rational man. Hamilton's case was certainly no exception. Dueling flourished for more than a thousand years. Challenges were seldom made for any but the most trivial reasons and, like the lawyer business of today, little value for either winner or loser was ever registered. Cardinal Richelieu (1638) had so many of his court staff lost to dueling that he instructed his army to attend the events, routinely congratulate the winners, gather all the participants and spectators at the dueling grounds, and put the lot to death.

RULE - Nothing compares to the power of social controls to influence human behavior.

91

Holding the reputation and social position of their members in their hands, groups dictate behavioral norms. Social control is the normalizing force for regulating behavior to conform, at least outwardly, to group standards (value system) and it is applied with religious conviction. The would-be violator of group rules has continually before him what will happen to him if he is found out. Unfun.

The organizational social element is an aggregation of individuals, mentioned earlier, called the Primary Working Group (PWG). This group, numbering less than ten, is the organization in miniature and controls more power to shape individual behavior than all the other organizational formats put together. Socially, PWGs are not very diverse and they meet situations in remarkably similar ways. The power of the PWG to influence the behavior of its members can not be exaggerated. Its arsenal of social control weaponry covers the spectrum of psychological and physical devices. The power has been measured many times in research experiments on behavior. The outcomes are always the same. Whether the experimental object is harmless or fatal, the power of the group is supreme.

RULE - Orgman regards company policy as a finished product.

Such research has shown how simple a matter it is to coerce a PWG member to report the wrong length of a line (which can be unambiguously measured) in order to conform with the other members acting a part in the experiment. This effect can be observed routinely in business meetings. We only get scared when a participant acts like he really believes the lies he is coerced to recite. Studies show that the 24,000,000 meetings held each working day in the USA are largely unproductive - a waste of time. Now, that **makes sense.**

In another eye-opening study, highly educated citizens were planted in a PWG environment where the confederates were systematically escalating torture on a complete stranger. There was no hesitancy in the action of the subjects to push the button for electrocution of the victim, whose only crime was to fail an exam in arithmetic. As interesting as the experiment itself was the reaction of the sponsoring Ivy-League institution: "Good research, but we strongly suggest you get into a different field of investigation." Since all of the players were members of the college staff (the exploits of the university as a dysfunctional organization are notorious), it was feared that the outside world might make a connection. Worse yet, someone might suggest acting on the evidence. It was no problem for the university to flex some social control muscle and scare the researchers into harmless activities. In practice it only takes a hint of punishment. Electrocutions are quite unnecessary. Forget about the fact that they had stumbled upon and measured one of the most important forces on earth. The research was terminated.

RULE - Never has the amount of human suffering ever been sufficient to influence the Establishment to change its course.

Behavioral norms

Like the organization, the dominant strategy of the PWG is to preserve its value system at all costs. Like the tribe on the savannah, PWG social control has no difficulty in masking out your eccentricities. No matter about the bow and arrow contraptions from the father of human civilization.

The underlying concept of group value systems is to insulate members from change. Since this idea lets them avoid the labor of thinking, most people are quite willing to ante up their individuality. Today, they pay much more than they appreciate. While the rules of behavior are designed to avoid uncertainty in predicting performance in routine situations, they form a bulwark against innovation. Precedents develop a sanctity, which places them, with other corporate pathologies, above criticism and justification. Feedback is suspended. Bad.

Because group idealogies are extremely resistant to change, non-routine situations become ZOI-crossing triggers for cognitive dissonance. Information is processed to reduce stress by fabricating narrow, self-affirming models of reality. There is no reason to adapt. Changes are delayed until the group is very much out of kilter with the environment. These long, adaptive lags set the stage for trauma and major catastrophes. For example, hospital regulations for pharmaceutical dose control of lethal drugs always lag until lives are lost. The blood bank refuses to screen for the AIDS virus until lives are lost. Standard, accepted business.

RULE - It is easy to be irresponsible when you are just one intermediate link in a long chain of action.

By definition, the complex problem is a new problem, and new means non-routine. Groups thereby do not view complexity from level ground, but from the dreaded pit of cognitive dissonance. When the sanctity of group doctrine is in danger, all members instinctively rally to its defense. There is no greater threat than having to re-establish your orientation to a group. Innovation means a large redistribution of social power. It all ties together. **Replace.**

The mature organization

Organizations, particularly in their bureaucratic forms, are the most efficient mechanisms ever created to handle routine chores. Each part of the man-made arrangement has a permanent, clearly defined role in a hierarchy of roles. The bureaucracy, mechanically executing orders according to established rules, is a splendid machine for making standardized decisions. Such organizations have won wars and provided an inexpensive automobile. When it is in harmony with its environment, the bureaucratic organization has no equal for cost-effective production. We call this arrangement Track A.

The success of the hierarchical organization is rigidly tied to the stability and continuity of the environment which gave it standing. All devices that provided the necessary flexibility to start the organization are soon jettisoned in the name of efficiency. With time, the organization becomes brittle and increasingly dependent upon an unchanging environment to maintain its useful stature. When the organization is no longer blessed with the suppleness of youth, a changed environment becomes a shattering event. These situations cause institutional cognitive dissonance and, unlike the individual and his PWG, there is no instinctive remedy.

RULE - No technical change is organizationally neutral.

When the organization remains glued in place as the world spins on to screw-in new challenges (problems), the forces of dissonance grow and grow and eventually the threshold is crossed. The practices of a lifetime, the very practices that made the organization succeed (and which have provided the most

The Zone of Indifference
and
Social Control

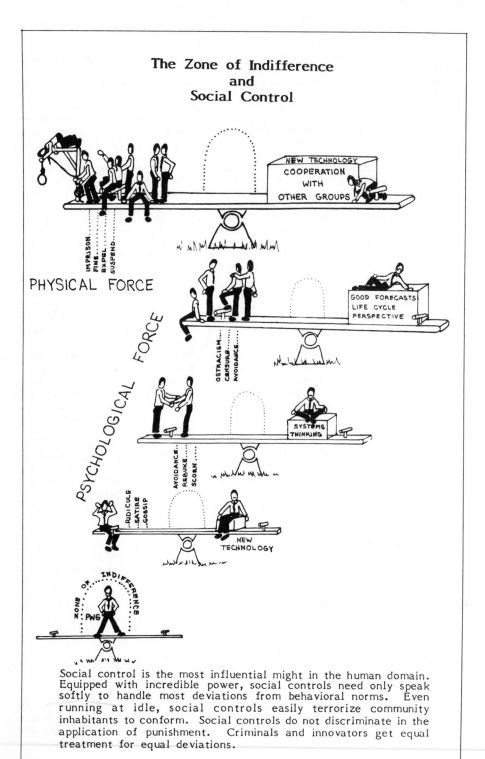

Social control is the most influential might in the human domain. Equipped with incredible power, social controls need only speak softly to handle most deviations from behavioral norms. Even running at idle, social controls easily terrorize community inhabitants to conform. Social controls do not discriminate in the application of punishment. Criminals and innovators get equal treatment for equal deviations.

examples of success), now become counterproductive. Policies that are no longer valid drive the organization in the direction of greater mismatch with the environment, a significant feature that will be covered more fully with the presentation of Livingston's Law.

This suicidal propensity has not escaped attention. It is difficult to find a book written within the last fifty years that has much good to say about contemporary institutions. The organizational record certainly substantiates these documented insights. When organizations are good, they are very, very good and when they are bad, they are horrid. To **have fun at work** you need to be able to discriminate the factors which build one apart from those which develop the other.

RULE - Nothing reinforces failure like failure in quantity.

Dystopia described

Often confusing causes with effects, organizational behavioralists have described the inherent limitations of an organization from several perspectives. The tirades blasted at thick corporate walls around the turn of the century remain valid today even though the organizations of that era have since chosen to perish. A selection from this bounty is provided below for your enlightenment and entertainment. **Replace.**

- Organizations hide behind an accepted fiction of unchallengeable wisdom. Their vested thoughtways lead them directly to ruin.

- New situations are met in a blind manner. The organization is armed only with precedents, a trained incapacity, and remains oblivious to the peculiar trying attributes of the situation. The goals of the organization are displaced by the goal to abide by the rule book.

- Momentum, not strategy, prevails. Momentum (towards ruin) is thereby reinforced and amplified.

- New situations demand precisely the kind of skills that traditional bureaucracies crush.

- Organizations covertly substitute simplistic and erroneous values for complex settings in an effort to deny the complexities.

- Organizations liberate from their members responsibility and an active choice for good.

- As organizations become more complicated they need a larger variety of possible actions to prevent dissolution. They do the opposite, increasing their fund of aggressiveness to defend what they have.

- Organizations reduce the worker to a docile and obedient drudge. Organization man can not conceive of any departure from the system. He is the creator and the creature, the originator and the ultimate victim.

- The Maginot Lines of institutions have been created by an illusion of invulnerability, collective rationalization, belief in inherent morality, self-censorship of deviants, shared illusion of unanimity, insulation from adverse information and social control on disagreeing members.

The Forbidden Zones

The instinctive structure for human organizations is an arrangement of cells in which independent tribal life can flourish, in conditions replicating the savannah. To keep order, taboos are enforced by fierce predators who patrol the tribal borders. No co-mingling or cooperative ventures are tolerated. Every cell must employ a unique language, unintelligible to the others.

HAVE FUN AT WORK

- Organizations convert our technical blessings into a curse. Specialization is necessary for the performance of particular departments and it is at the throat of achieving necessary coordination.

- A hierarchical, bureaucratized organization is grossly despotic. The management core of the organization controls the power to reward and penalize. The workers on these despotic islands have no protection from such tyranny. The political freedom afforded the citizens of the USA by the checks and balances of the Constitution can not be carried into the job.

- Individuals are constrained by the very organizations they form and they automatically accept the constraints. The organization denies choices outside of itself.

- Organization man is a human artifact achieving a small subset of his potential, his brain shrunken to meet the narrow requirements of the corporation. As the corporation grows older, the residue of life necessary to carry on becomes more minute and meaningless. Orgman is dead at 28, but he is not buried until he is 72.

- Organizations are hierarchical coalitions of cliques and cabals managing different kinds of information to achieve a variety of inconsistent goals.

- Hierarchies automatically develop restraints against free communications, especially criticism by subordinates against their superiors.

As illustrated above, man could not have contrived a more hostile environment for solving the complex problem than the traditional organization. We even use the same social machinery to settle affairs with our nuclear-equipped neighbors as we used when the only weapon available to both sides was a spear. No wonder we make a mess. Evolution should come with variable speed drive.

RULE - To be like the herd, forfeit your self.

Success is in the individual

The glory of the civilized age is a celebration of the individual, not the corporation. All incremental gains in civilization have been launched by an individual reaching out to his full genetic inheritance in spite of, not because of, the institution. The enemy of innovation, and the enemy of the very civilization that invention enables, is the organization. In the final analysis, all complex problems are solved by the "model" of the individual.

As the subject unfolds further in subsequent chapters, you will see more of the great deceptions and monster stupidities that abound when we take our ancient, primitive social machinery with the square wheels and enter it into the Indianapolis 500. When the earthly human population once again is confined to the East African savannah and consists only of isolated tribal groups, with less than 50 members each, who kill for a living, the instinctive organizational design we share today will be back in business.

Tidal Wave

Thousands upon thousands of human generations saw little change in man's world. Few people, no books, no technology, no organizations, and no civilization - the mass-produced model T of human DNA entirely suitable for survival. A tidal wave of sudden change is here and model T DNA is made out of rock. Witness the process of extinction.

HAVE FUN AT WORK

Chapter Seven

"The world that we have made as a result of the level of
thinking we have done thus far creates problems that we cannot solve
at the same level we created them."

Einstein

Solar System Sanitarium

Entire industries are being bombarded by new, challenging situations with
unprecedented frequency and severity. To cope with this technological version
of the Great Flood, however, the organization is saddled with a configuration
designed for the primeval East African savannah. It is an arrangement it loathes
to change. Even though the tribal tools and practices used for today's problems
are DNA legacies from an era where new problems were separated by thousands of
years, they are blindly applied with devout fervor.

With the exception of the hunt itself, communication within tribal groups
was controlled by folklore, custom and taboo. For the co-operative male hunting
band, which was framed to bring down game that was too much for one man to
handle, emphasis was placed on free communications, mutual assistance and trust.
With little time for confusion during the hazardous attacks, there was a lot of
practice, preparation and discussion. Until the invention of the bow and arrow,
man was dependent upon this arrangement for his survival. An organization is
not a separate entity from its members.

Man retains a strong instinct for co-operative male activity (male bonding is
a biological propensity) and he still practices his skills of power and finesse for
hunting (baseball, track, tennis, etc.). Hunting is the master plan of the human
species. In human communities, the male group is one of the least variable parts
and it helps provide continuity of cultural patterns. No one can fail to find male
hunting bands daily on TV, displaying their hunting prowess with clubs, balls and
ovate spheroids. Exploits of male hunting bands are exceeded in newspaper space
only by that allocated to advertising.

RULE - Never get between a man and his hunting band.

When tribes began to cultivate the land, they increased in size, and
complications came with the territory. With the success of agriculture,
communities grew still bigger, crossing dormant thresholds that snapped new
problems into place. With the village came great increases in communications
traffic and subdivisions of labor to create new dimensions to the task of
maintaining order. The cooperative hunting band form was not effective in
running every affair of the large village. The genetic answer to the dilemma was
the hierarchy. As community populations grew, the hierarchy spawned the
Establishment.

The idea of a hierarchical organizational structure, which limits
communications traffic to more tolerable levels (for an individual), has been the
standard for the last five thousand years. While early man could not do any
better than Orgman in solving the complex problems of today, he would do no
worse.

Progress is the rare exception, not the rule, among social communities. At least 95% of the known human story finds little development for conquering the environment, which included four ice ages. Between the last ice age and the start of recorded history, man innovated in tillage and raising stock. With his start in recording history itself, man began an unprecedented era of innovation frequency that, with a few notable ups and downs, is still accelerating. It was only in the last century that somebody got the inspiration to make right and left shoes.

RULE - The Establishment is quite capable of adjusting to any innovation, as long as changes only come spaced a thousand years apart.

While the evolutionary machinery runs at a very slow pace, the sudden avalanche of changes in so many dimensions of living has caught world societies with no instinctive methods of contention. The same measure of stress perceived by an individual at work applies to society as well. It is simply a running cognitive balance sheet between the known demands and the effectiveness of sanctioned processes in coping with those demands. Societies know full well when their institutional monuments are in over their heads.

Like you, the organization has two basic choices to reduce stress on its status quo. It can achieve balance by an adjustment **to** the situation (increase coping capabilities) or attempt an adjustment **of** the situation itself. Gut-reaction organizational processes always choose for an adjustment **of** the situation. The same institutions that throw big dollars at computerizing their obsolete manufacturing processes will not contribute one farthing for modernizing the archaic social processes wedded to the production line. And that, exactly, is how all living species become extinct.

Organizational stressors

Appreciating the quiescent history of community government (in contrasting light to the abrupt, massive changes going on) helps you to understand the origins of the havoc raised by the current organizational menagerie. We pound away at these themes because you must demolish your Bad Seventies before you can **have fun at work** and, if your reluctance to do so is like ours, you will need the aid of a sledgehammer.

RULE - An organization is a group of people united by a common delusion about its purpose.

The dimensions of organizational stress on today's menu include explosive growth in population, new technologies, information and specialization. With coping mechanisms evolved for 80,000 human generations based upon small changes every thousand years, truckloads of each stress dimension are now dumped on a single lifetime.

When humans started to record history, the world's population was less than 100 million, a value that was exceeded about the time of the Pharaohs. Over three thousand years later, after the Black Death had taken its toll, the planet's population was still below 200 million. While rapid growth followed the Bubonic plague, it took until 1850 to reach the first billion (one million thousands). Population spurts followed an increase in commerce, not technology. The next billion increase only took 80 years. On July 7, 1986, just 56 years after the 2 billion mark, the earth supported 5 billion living humans. Several estimates for the future call for more than 8 billion by the year 2020. Instinctive social forms were never designed to cope with the enormous complications associated with dense populations. Everything inter-tribal started by instinct always ends up in a war.

Until the industrial revolution, the only men who belonged to hierarchical bureaucracies were soldiers, a tiny segment of the population. Because it came first, much of what is known about organizational communications comes from measuring the military experience. The number of organizational forms has grown in step with the migration from the farm to the city and is compounded by the population explosion. Urban dwellers live in a spider web of organizations and are very confused whether they are spiders or meals. The unprecedented era of Organization Man as Everyman is well underway. Another complication.

RULE - If organizations retained the qualities they possessed when they were founded, there would be no need for bankruptcy laws.

For the first time in history, society is not stemming the tide of technical innovations. By not killing the inventors, as it always did before, the Establishment is far outclassed by the complex situations that now develop relentlessly. While technological innovation flourishes, institutional innovation commensurate to accommodate or regulate the expanding array of complexities is, of course, forbidden.

Science is producing new information at a rate which makes our technical libraries obsolete in less than a decade. The doubling rate of scientific knowledge is less than five years and accelerating (90% of all scientists who ever lived are alive today). The half-life of technical truths is 18 months and shrinking. Even if now is incorrectly called the Age of Information, one must still be impressed with the cosmic quantities. There are now over a hundred journals which do nothing but abstracts. Every day, 7,000 new technical articles are published totalling 100,000,000 pages a year. There are even journals that do abstracts of abstracts. Automation of knowledge has come to total bankruptcy, because to know more and more about less and less is, in the end, simply to know less and less. Meanwhile, the average number of pages read each year, per person, continues to decline.

There is little disagreement that the growth in society is locked in step with the growth of complex issues. As more and more complex matters emerge, the connection to failure becomes clear. It is not clear when the Establishment will learn how to deal with large-space problems. History is not very encouraging.

It is routine for the Establishment to handle complex matters by ignoring them. For instance, there are 7,000,000 known chemicals and 50,000 are commercially produced. Only 30% of those chemicals are classified as non-toxic. One thousand new chemicals join the commercial ranks every year. Some problems, like the oil tanker spills, go away. Other problems, like some agricultural chemicals, get worse in ways that are poorly understood. The rate of new materials being introduced to commerce precludes the usual slow process of learning about their properties in use through experience. Today, the life of the application often exceeds the time of the material's existence. Undaunted, we accumulate these chemicals in our garbage heaps so that rain can eventually carry them to our water supplies.

The atomic blast over Japan should have triggered great public interest in learning about this new energy source. Once proven to exist, there are many kinds of decisions to be made about how such an awesome power is going to be

Baby Fuzzball Maternity Ward

Complexity has a big future. Midget problems yield to dwarf solutions and seldom have any offspring at all. The solution of a simple problem has nice sharp edges. Large-space problems are prolific breeders. Solutions wedded to fuzzball problems beget large family trees of new infant fuzzballs. Often an embarrassment to their parents, suckling fuzzballs are temporarily concealed in a hidden nursery where they can grow into giants on a rich diet of denial, neglect and indifference. Sooner or later the babies become mature fuzzballs and are ejected from the orphanage to menace the project like their mothers. Like a swarm of locusts, fuzzball families consume everything in sight. All solutions produce new problems.

assimilated and used. When the public chose to avoid the effort to become informed about the technology of atomic energy, abandoning the responsibility to the "elite," a chain of events was set in motion that continues to cause considerable mischief.

It was a colossal mistake to trust the Establishment with managing an innovation which their representatives would not take the trouble to understand. Governments made many errors and still devote great resources to cover up that fact. Humanity is now only a few War Department miscues away from committing suicide. Sooner or later, the ability of society to succeed in spite of its gross incompetency with complexity will run out.

RULE - The Establishment carries the formula for its own destruction. The form lives on only through genetics.

Every generation in recorded history has left the landscape scarred with the evidence of power gained but not retained. We can see examples in the remains of the Pyramids, the Coliseum and the Parthenon (preferred by its current owner to be in ruins). Typically, when civilization variety grew to exceed the tolerance band (ZOI) of the social institutions in power, variety was reduced by force (e.g. the Spanish Inquisition) rather than accommodated by adjustments in those institutions. Societies never lack for rationalizations of their dirty deeds.

A scorecard on "Gut Reactions"

Current literature abounds with case histories showing the inherent limitations of the hierarchy. The largest corporate conglomerates regularly encounter troubles they cannot resolve. The lack of executive control is openly and correctly cited as a contributing factor. Rarely, however, is the organizational design identified as a culprit. When the CEO of a large conglomerate says he can't be expected to know what is going on in his organization, we think he is kidding.

Organizations develop new technology that complicates the environment in which they function. New solutions always bring new problems. Helping civilization spiral off into uncharted waters, the organization is itself faced with a wider variety of considerations in conducting its affairs from competing organizations. Institutions, burdened by mismatched design, are ill-equipped to cope with high rates of change and there is no instinctive mechanism provided for fixing itself except specialization which, uncompensated, only makes matters worse.

For example, in spite of elaborate paperwork, watchdog agencies and a huge auditing expense, the government reckons that its complex system of assuring prudent expenditures misses the goal by more than $100 billion a year in the Department of Defense alone. This is not a small mismatch that can be explained away as petty theft. That amount of embezzlement can only take place with the cooperation and knowledge of thousands (with top insecurity clearances). The offending organizations did not recruit hundreds of criminals to staff key positions. It is regular citizens, not felons, who violate their principles with such dependable regularity. Between genetics and social conditioning, something is lacking in our ability to transcend the intuitions our biology imposes on us.

Technology Bucket Brigade

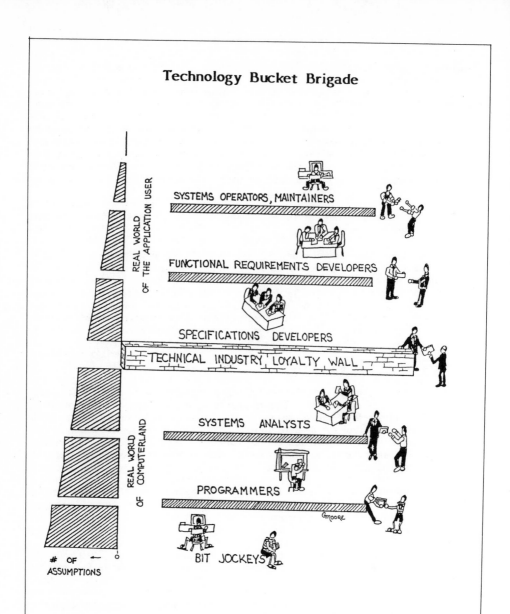

Solutions are directly chained to applications only in fantasy land. In truth, the association is nothing but a series of error-filled translations and assumptions which happen to be flying in close formation. Errors grow and accumulate in geometric proportions to the number of cells. In monster projects, like Star Wars, there are so many cells that error is the only truth to be found. The profuse breeding of specialization turns communication into a carrier of serious disease.

Ultimate defense

In their obedience to genetic programming, institutions act to ensure their private brand of order. The rules for order form a locked-in doctrine that protects against change. The protecting mechanisms are so powerful and instinctive that even catastrophic failure is insufficient incentive for revising doctrine. It is seldom appreciated that payoff events like Challenger and Chernobyl are natural, inevitable products of the organizational design itself. Few realize, even after it happens time and time again, that the organization's final choice before adapting to a changed world, is extinction.

The technical complexity of nuclear power and space travel was widely recognized as cosmic from the outset and, as such, automatically entrusted to a network of organizations. As we have learned, confederations of large organizations quickly and incorrectly atomize such complexity as well as their responsibility for regulation. The division of tasks and knowledge, through gut reaction, is ground so finely that wholesale translation errors in communication are guaranteed. It is not a master plan but a series of small reflex actions that forms the gigantic tower of Babel.

RULE - No single factor has caused more damage to the ability of man to solve his problems than the uncompensated proliferation of technical specialties.

While Babel takes its toll, the messes it generates are labeled as unfortunate technical glitches compounded by the regrettable performance of particular individuals. The only organizationally-acceptable reasons for tragedy are component failure, operator error and a horrible string of bad luck (acts of God). The design of the organization is never at fault.

Nothing is spared in organizational defense, the ultimate motivation. The amount of money spent on peripheral issues, while carefully avoiding the limelight on organizational matters, is without limit. The pleas of an observant Rogovin (TMI) or Feynman (Challenger) about institutional dysfunctions are dutifully ignored until they fade away. The organizational designs that lie at the root of the horrible problem survive intact, fully operational, to continue the process. All the conditions that caused the wreckage remain in place. Hierarchy preserved, Babel prevails. **Replace.**

RULE - Specialization prevents criticism.

While New York City, as an example, encourages eating and supports restaurants in great abundance, the City discourages rest rooms with fanatic zeal. The New York City Transit Authority, in loyal support of that policy, closed subway toilets twelve years ago. A concerned taxpayer, Mr. Oliver Leeds, brought suit against the Transit Authority to restore sanitary sanity to the subways in a progression of courts. Without hesitation, the Transit Authority spent more money to defend itself (successfully) than it did to pursue the corporations which supplied them million-dollar subway cars with doors that fly open when the train is moving, escalators that won't climb the stairs and elevators that haven't moved since they were installed. The courageous Mr. Leeds learned that while the Establishment has no mechanism for correcting the obvious, it has unlimited means to quiet the dissonance of truth. The subway rest rooms will remain closed.

RULE - One occasion exhibiting the collaboration of diverse organizational forces is the driving of project requirements to unreasonable levels.

Incremental Concessions

Small give-ups can lead to hitting the tripwires of great catapults that flip the world upside down. It is the principle behind the mousetrap. It works in man-size models too.

The hierarchical structure must, when thresholds of size and complexity are breached, create a Babel-like organization. To preserve the form and the dogma, the diversity of tongues is encouraged and reinforced rather than counterbalanced. The situation can only progressively degrade. And so it does. It is the process that takes an array of young organizations able to put a man on the moon ahead of schedule and, through time and oblivious to great new technology, prevents the same organizations from being able to repeat the performance.

Since the specialization of labor is done in small increments, few notice when significant thresholds have been crossed. One threshold that affects everyone is the unheralded transfer of responsibility, from The Doctor to you, for your wellness. At one time there was only one kind of doctor. When you took your problem to The Doctor, your problem became his problem. Your chance of survival may not have been too good, but at least every one knew who to blame for failure. A hundred years ago, the number of medical specialties could still be counted on your fingers. Even so, your problem was The Doctor's problem because you did your part by getting to his office, or, believe it or not, The Doctor came to your house.

Nothing remains today of that assumed relationship. Detection and diagnosis are **your** responsibility now. It is up to you to figure out, when you have a problem, which specialist to visit. If you choose wrong, doctors will tell you, don't blame The Doctor. How is the knee specialist supposed to know about your allergies? Doctors are no longer responsible for anything so huge as your health. If you don't know a lot about medicine, too bad. To be fair, one thing has remained constant for millenia. You have no control over the bill. They complained about that setup in Caesar's time too. In the USA, no part of medicine and no sector of the Establishment, including the government, has any control over the inexorable rise in health care costs. Ditto legal costs.

The incredible barrier to feedback

In spite of being contrary to the laws of nature, the Establishment fiercely resists any attempt to learn from its big mistakes. Nature's primary engine for adaptation of the species is negative feedback. The successes and failures of a living species system in the real world environment, at a slice in time, set the level of energy behind the driving force for change. For most species, change is the only constant and negative experience feedback drives their evolutionary adaptation.

Feedback is a fundamental regulating mechanism. As perceived stress is the error signal, showing a discrepancy between the desired condition and the actual, feedback of the results of actions taken is how skills at reducing stress are adapted. Taking the opposite tack for a moment, if the actions taken to decrease stress are ineffective, and feedback is disconnected, what device is going to improve the situation? It is psychological gridlock that can only get worse with time.

RULE - If any system, animate or inanimate, with its inherent strengths and weaknesses, stays rigidly the same under changing conditions over which it has no control, sooner or later it will be exposed to conditions that will do it in.

Linear Think

Linear think is the basic ingredient of corporate doctrines. The orders are to go forward and make another mess, never to stop and give thought to the connection between the wreckage strewn about and the practices which manufactured it. The natural reluctance to use the intellect is supplemented by institutional orders which forbid it.

HAVE FUN AT WORK

The critical role of the feedback process for survival has not been suspended for man. As mentioned earlier, when threshold values have not been crossed, organizations encourage suggestions for improvement of pieces and parts of their routine operations. Most regrettably, however, when the company has crossed the complexity threshold and flipped, the natural negative feedback process is forcefully and visibly blocked. That is, the more the organization needs the negative feedback process to help it stop manufacturing disasters, the more aggressively and overtly feedback is forbidden.

Organizations do not distinguish between good or bad experience in blocking feedback when there is risk, however slight, that there might be a mad dogma attack. Successful demonstrations of the innovative process are barred with the same dedication as lessons-learned from catastrophe. For instance, the solution of a complex problem always requires working outside of orthodox organizational boundaries and, since recognition would pose a threat to established corporate routines, a success is disavowed as an occurred event. Heroes that persist in demanding organizational adaptation to the process for success are soon eliminated.

Reference situations for feedback

In living with the Bad Seventies and not always knowing which instincts to trust, it is important to have good reference structures to determine your relative position. Checks and balances are necessary to sustain objectivity. The tolerance band for honest feedback is quite small and we use reference situations that cover both polar extremes. The reception for feedback about failure of the "system" forms one reference guidepost and the reception for feedback about success of a non-standard "system" bench-marks the other end.

The reference for failure lessons-learned is the accurate forecaster of disaster and post-tragedy whistleblower. Roger Boisjoly and the Challenger calamity present a recent benchmark situation that marks one pole. Boisjoly was rewarded for his heroic attempts to prevent the launch of Challenger by total ostracism and financial ruin. Where thousands from NASA and Morton Thiokol should have lined up in front of Boisjoly to express thanks for trying, only Sally Ride actually did so - and left NASA. Providing no funds to correct the known seal problem, Thiokol proudly informed its workers in writing that "We will dedicate all necessary resources to defend against Mr. Boisjoly's unsubstantiated allegations and ultimately to vindicate the Company and its employees." The reference here is that if your work project situation is really bad, forecasting disaster and its feedback will be met with savage retaliation. Just imagine the thousands who know Boisjoly was right permitting corporate mind control to abscond with their moral fibre.

The reference for success lessons-learned is the demonstration of accomplishment. Deming's situation will serve as a benchmark of success that is unlikely to be superceded for centuries. The quality way is so clearly superior that no justification is needed. Thanks to Deming, the Japanese are well on their way to owning Manhattan. Unlike the conspicuous punishment of the whistleblower, the successful innovator is castigated with violent indifference.

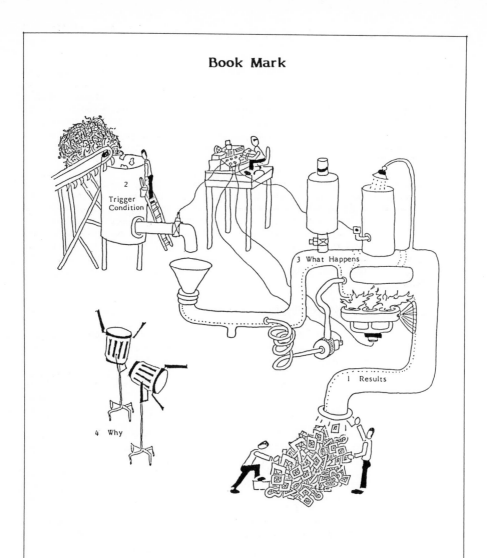

The why (4) for the what (3) has been introduced. This flow-chart appears later (page 180) as the cycle of control. Complexity overwhelms first the individual human capacities, and then those capacities of the organization designed exclusively for non-complex situations. Once the trigger conditions have been broached, the network of habits and customs takes control of the project and, in a series of short-sighted maneuvers, sends the project over the falls. The corrective virtues of lessons-learned and applied are submerged under the additional sin of blocking negative feedback.
And the beat goes on ...

If your work project situation is really great, feedback will be met with apathy. Only if you persist in the feedback of success will you receive harsh punishments. Just imagine the millions who know Deming is right permitting corporate mind control to imprison their good senses.

RULE - Suppress any tendency to engage in direct feedback on very bad or very good situations.

All organizations have their mavericks who find it necessary to conspire against norms in order to solve problems, and they play a critical role in sustaining the corporation. Rules of conduct have escape clauses and allow excuses for certain individual deviations. The maverick is permitted to operate at a limited distance outside of organization walls simply because the maverick is able to get jobs accomplished that can not be done within the confines of the rigid corporate doctrine.

The maverick is always very productive (a maverick who isn't is called a former employee). The price of this "freedom" is the withholding of normal rewards. Mavericks are never paid what they are worth - by plan. The organization knows full well who their mavericks are and how they are treated. The message to the non-mavericks is "be a maverick if you must, but the real rewards are for conformity to standard practice - oblivious to the wreckage it may cause." The message is not wasted.

RULE - In matters conflicting with status quo preservation, **no good deed goes unpunished.** (author unknown, but appreciated)

The critical element behind all these shenanigans is human nature, which is no more than a particular kind of animal nature. It is the nature of a primate, a biological creature dominated by biological rules - performing unconsciously, spontaneously and without self-analysis. **Replace.**

The answer to **WHY** is simply because people choose to follow their instincts rather than lead with their intellect. Looking at all the wreckage this option has generated, we still wonder why man blocks the corrective feedback mechanisms.

Organizational Weak Spots

FRONT VIEW

FLAWLESS SERVICE CORP

OMNIPOTENCE IS OUR TRADEMARK

TOP

SIDE

A basic function of an organization is to create and perpetuate the myth of total organizational potency. Whatever the issue, the corporation has the answers all tidy in the policy manuals. Supremely competent, the organization knows best and does best for all concerned. Once past the marble lobby, corpoworld is seen as competent only to inflict punishment on those who would try to repair deficiencies. When vulnerabilities are denied in general and undiscussable in particular, they provide unrestricted access for unrelenting failure.

HAVE FUN AT WORK

Chapter Eight

<u>Why Organizations Can't Cope</u>

These days, it is quite common to encounter behavior considered as irrational. When we define irrational as acting discrepant to **one's own** value system reference, however, we find irrational behavior to be extremely rare. What is normally called irrational is just a collision between internally consistent but mutually conflicting reference value systems.

Organizations, like their individual members, have reference value systems too. In contrast to the great diversity in individual values, organizational doctrines have little variation. The need for a communications network is an affliction possessed by the organization. It occupies prime real estate in corporate doctrine. Train yourself to note the reference value system, including myths and taboos, any time you observe irrational behavior. Remember, the purpose of a social system is what it does (POSIWID), not what it says it does. When you understand the priorities, which the references reveal, the capability to predict behavior is enhanced and irrational behavior fades back into plain stupidity.

RULE - See what the others see and then think differently about what is seen.

Vulnerabilities of the organization

Understanding the reasons for self-defeating organizational behavior during conditions that scream out for innovation, is absolutely necessary in order to **have fun at work.** One reason is the inherent limitations in the hierarchical form for any activity but routine operations. When innovation is used as the reference model, the hierarchical framework by which organizations arrange themselves automatically defines a communication system network with all its gaping voids, gross distortions, and major roadblocks.

From a technical perspective, there are inherent strengths and weaknesses in **any** particular communication system. The most suitable network for one set of circumstances can be pathological for another set. Like many issues in solving problems, it is a case of matching form to the application. However, few issues are more undiscussable than limitations in the instinctive organizational arrangement.

RULE - Exposing wickedness is a legitimate form of sadism.

When the structure chosen from genetic imperatives is a mismatch to the situation, the corporation contracts a case of cognitive dissonance. Aberrant behavior, to cover up the fact that the hierarchy is not working, becomes the norm. Good reference structures to gauge the world around you are fun, especially when no one around you has them. It is nice to understand what is going on with the herd and be able to predict its movement.

Voids

I. CROSS-DISCIPLINE, COMPLEX PROBLEM SOLVING AGENCIES

   A. The complex problem receiving and solving division
      1. The department junction subject matter department
   B. The total systems responsibilities department
   C. The life-cycle perspective department
   D. The systems think training department
   E. The look outside of our field for improvement group
   F. The decision-making process improvement department

II. COMMUNICATION IMPEDIMENT COMPENSATING AGENCIES

   A. The common semantic language communications division
      1. The specialization translation department
   B. The plant configuration and cross-reference department
   C. The common up-to-the-minute corporate data bank group
   D. The tower of Babel demolition department
   E. The camouflage unwrapping department
   F. The discussion of the undiscussables department

III. CORPORATE STRESS REDUCTION AGENCIES

   A. Policies and doctrine overhaul departments
      1. The new working assumptions department
      2. The POSIWID ombudsman department
      3. The disaster project feedback department
      4. The dogma and doctrine complaint resolution group

   B. Awards agencies
      1. The innovation encouragement department
         a. The maverick and innovator reward department
      2. The whistleblower honor and huge reward department
      3. The accurate mess forecaster huge reward group
      4. The fuzzball eater honor and huge reward department

   C. Management evaluation agencies
      1. The management requalification worker review board
      2. The incompetent manager ejection department

IV. THE DEMING METHODS FOR QUALITY DEPARTMENT

HAVE FUN AT WORK

RULE - The human social system is a global unity much larger than the sum of the cramped views of the individual social sciences.

Organizations are complicated network entities that appear to be different every time a different perspective is taken. By changing paradigms of reference, you can even get a new look from the same direction without changing your vantage point. The mismatches presented here flow from comparing the instinctive organizational structure in common use to the model of what is requisite to cope with complexity (threshold-crossing matters). Prepare for voids, omissions, oversights, vacuums and blank spaces on the one hand and distortions, barriers, biases, trap doors and mirrors on the other. That's why we call corporate quarters, once you understand them, The Fun House.

The archaic social structures and behavioral norms, behind which man hides to avoid the turbulence of change, only increase the fury of the storm. Organizational defense of the status quo makes matters worse and thereby highlights organizational dysfunctions. The causes of the discrepant behavior so commonly exhibited have been sorted into compartments. Three of these bins are labeled Voids, Roadblocks and Distortions. Diversions have already been covered in the discussion of "eliminations."

By "voids" we mean organizational parts and practices, essential for corporate health, that don't exist. "Roadblocks" refer to the hidden barriers that confound innovative initiatives all along the way. "Distortions" are the visible and available organizational resources that are allocated grossly out of proportion to need. The most dangerous category of pathological behavior of the institution, the Inversion, is presented as Livingston's Law in the next Chapter.

Voids

Organizations clearly display what they are and how they behave, even though the motivational web-work of rules, unspoken conventions and values is undocumented. When the corporation screams for the status quo in the face of encroaching obsolescence, its logic is sound ... nothing but sound. POSIWID gets you on the fun side of the event horizon. Using the language of success and looking back on the scene, all sorts of voids can be noticed.

The departments most essential to sustaining the modern-era corporation are missing. What are not missing are intentional controls and rules to maintain these voids. Every now and then something sneaks in to fill a vacuum and you can watch the organizational immune system respond to filter out the impurity. This happens, for instance, every time the champion of a systems department moves on. The vacuum is quickly filled by mediocrity and the entire systems department evaporates without even an obituary. The list of missing departments undoubtedly can be expanded to include functionalities that are not vital to solve complex problems, but would help in regular affairs. Some of these voids will be explored further.

The Junctional Node

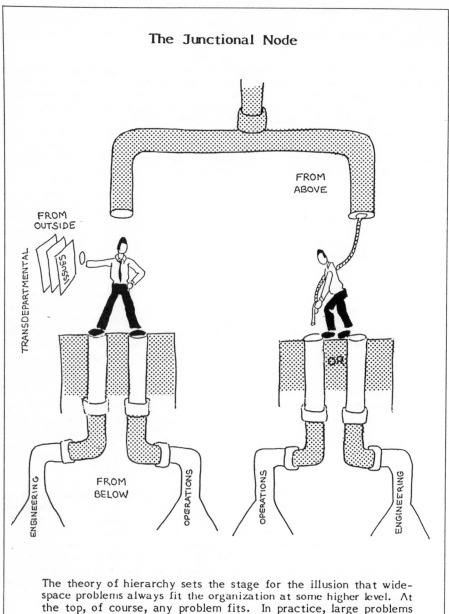

The theory of hierarchy sets the stage for the illusion that wide-space problems always fit the organization at some higher level. At the top, of course, any problem fits. In practice, large problems bubble up through the hierarchy encountering levels increasingly incompetent to deal with them. The facilities for the illusion include a set of valves installed in the communication channels. One valve type diverts information to one **OR** the other pipe. Block valves stop all information of the third kind from getting in. Check valves permit information to flow only in one direction. These expedients breed great disasters.

HAVE FUN AT WORK

Tyranny of the executive - the junctional node

View any organization chart and note the box where two departments come together, such as engineering and operations. What is missing is the staff support for that box which handles matters involving **both** functions (matters which relate to engineering **and** operations are many), such as computer integrated manufacturing. Without staff support, the box has three options. For orders that flow down from on high, the junctional node can act as a diverter valve and deflect the whole assignment into one department **or** the other. If the transverse problem comes up from below, the junction must act as a check valve and prevent the problem from rising out of its cage. But for the wide-band issue that comes from the outside, the junction deflects and disavows all knowledge of same.

Kirchhoff's law states that nothing can be stored at a junction point (it is not a storage tank). The law applies in full measure to the organization chart, real or imaginary. Many engineering laws, such as Kirchhoff's, apply very well to organizational affairs, especially when the institution is being studied as a communications network.

Some of the most crippling voids are those which would serve as an interstitial glue to paste separate, independent organizational fragments together for joint affairs. Without such super glue, people focus on parochial interests and not the goals of the total organization. Organizations are very quick to fragment and form additional subunits when complexity strikes. Specialization blocks an attempt to understand another's job and viewpoint. Missing is the compensating function to maintain a healthy level of integration. This is the singular reason why attempts to manage corporate information are so disastrous. Any innovation can only be implemented by simultaneous adjustments of a number of departments with disparate objectives. They are quite paralyzed to make the required decisions themselves.

RULE - The time to get required approvals is inversely related to the size of problem that can be solved.

An example of the common effects of disintegration without super glue integration (voids) can be found in the US Interstate Highway "system." Before work on the Interstates began, billboard advertising was prohibited on highway land. While this presumed the absence of billboards (and no further legislation necessary), legal ways were found by opportunists to circumvent the prohibition: they constructed billboards further back from the roadways, still in view of the motorists. And so in a subsequent highway beautification act, funds were provided to remove non-conforming billboards and make cash payments to the owners for the inconvenience. About 2,000 non-conforming billboards are so dismantled every year. Meanwhile, new billboards appear at a 15,000 per year rate. This mismatch is only one dimension to the lunacy as the billboard demolition crew is preceded by the separate forest management crew of the highway department - who are busy cutting down trees that block the motorists' view of the non-conforming billboards.

The USA celebrated the bicentennial of its Constitution in 1987. That doctrine survived the most tumultuous era of mankind principally because of a key provision for orderly change that can be exercised by the public. The Constitution prescribes an extended process for change by which two-thirds of the states can call a convention and then three-quarters can install an amendment. These amendments have typically been for the good of the people. The ruling class does not have to be assassinated. The Capitol does not have to be sacked

117

Feedback

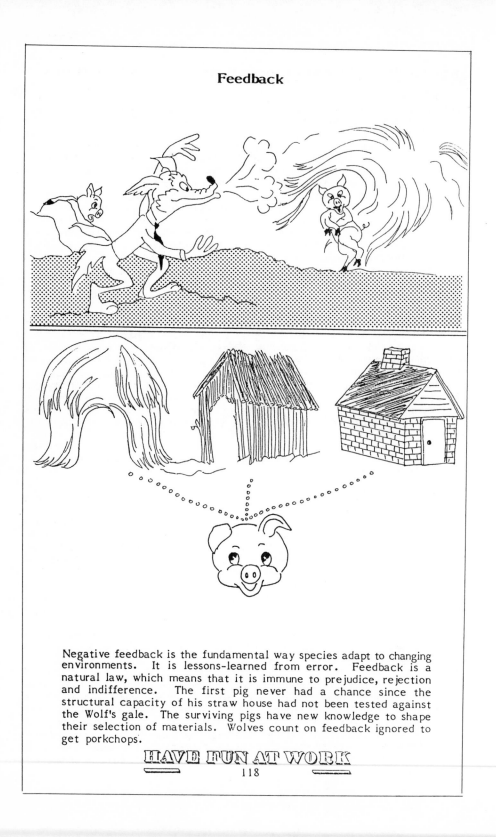

Negative feedback is the fundamental way species adapt to changing environments. It is lessons-learned from error. Feedback is a natural law, which means that it is immune to prejudice, rejection and indifference. The first pig never had a chance since the structural capacity of his straw house had not been tested against the Wolf's gale. The surviving pigs have new knowledge to shape their selection of materials. Wolves count on feedback ignored to get porkchops.

by foreign powers. The adaptive process is written down. It has a starting block and a finish line. The U.S. Constitution is recognized as one of the seven political wonders of the world.

Organizations have no equivalent arrangement for change. It would be considered peccant. Without the ability to alter doctrine, less than one in ten thousand corporations reach their centennial. Many of those described as the world's greatest in 1920 have already expired. Organizational "constitutions," chiseled without provisions for change by the governed, seldom fit the prevailing conditions for even five years.

There is a set of voids in providing compensating mechanisms for noise and error in communication channels. Quick to form another work specialty, corporations do not realize when the next specialty concession costs it the communications ball game. Compensating mechanisms like a common data base and cross-reference list have proven to be among the most difficult and unstable tasks existing in organized society and, once achieved, quickly decay.

Roadblocks

Unlike voids, organizational roadblocks are easy to find. Try solving a complex problem at high speed and you get married to them. Scientists have a standard roadblock expressed by "we don't know enough yet," followed by "we don't have the necessary support equipment yet."

Everyone is familiar with the roadblocks of "red tape." When companies require frequent reports and review meetings, they are placing barriers to progress. One terminally-sick company we worked for had a sign-off sheet which could not be completed in less time than it took to perform the task. Utilities are gripped by a budgeting process so inane, there is no time for anything else in the yearly cycle. The pursuit of "gas tight" specifications makes everyone forget the subject matter. The quest for "binding" contracts becomes a game unto itself that has no referee and no end.

A monster roadblock is the prohibition of non-standard problem-solving techniques. Social order depends upon the acceptance of rules by the led. The social rules of conduct prohibit actions induced by other causes (other than sorcery itself). Individual behavior is constantly monitored and appraised by this common framework of socially recognized and sanctioned standards, which are antithetical to innovation. Coupled with the edict to use only "approved" practices for all problems is an amendment forbidding the use of non-approved practices. That is precisely how the status quo is maintained.

RULE - "That which is not compulsory, is forbidden." Orwell.

The roadblock to feedback, by itself, is quite sufficient to destroy any system, animate or inanimate. When there is no consideration of the results of actions (connecting practices to the wreckage they cause), there is no means to differentiate the good from the bad. The obedience to standards without an avenue for learning from feedback, is the linear-think link to calamitous misjudgment. The block to bad news from linear think has been used by pathological organizations in this century to sanctify psychotic acts and normalize their criminality (e.g., the Third Reich). Feedback blocks have allowed institutions to engage in human sacrifice, war, slavery, forced labor and arbitrary distributions of wealth for the last 5,000 years. On the other hand, the great achievements of the Renaissance were obtained precisely because the opinions of

119

THIRTY-SEVEN COMMON DENIALS

DENIAL OF HISTORY

1. Problems in operating the process concealed (RBF)
2. Vital plant staff knowledge from on-the-job experience withheld (cover-ups)
3. Problems in previous projects hidden (even destruction of records)

DENIAL OF PROJECT RESTRAINTS

4. Support staff withheld
5. Adversarial relationships forced by the project environment (unions, intra-organizational competition, accounting, legal, etc.)
6. Critical nature of informal, undocumented, dynamic organizational communications (sneaker net) concealed
7. Little interest in training, even after the equipment is shipped
8. Little interest in testing, even before the equipment is shipped.
9. No plan for processing, handling, and maintaining new information available from the new system
10. Disregard for established human factors principles in man-machine facilities
11. No plan for functioning without familiar information in convenient locations
12. Operations refuses to participate during development to avoid any potential blame for project failure.
13. Even when willing to cooperate, Operations is made unavailable due to "production requirements."
14. Refusal to change previous control strategies

DENIAL OF STATUS

15. Claims that, this time, they are doing "right" when it is still being done the same as for all other failures
16. The problem statement for the project is wrong (usually and totally).
17. Incorrect and missing documentation of existing process configuration
18. Equipment areas are overlooked, ignored, incompatible and not operable as assumed for project scope
19. Inappropriate system support, such as in power supplies, grounding, shielding, cable routing, separation, isolation, surge protection, heating, cooling, cleaning, signal types, etc.

20. Ineffective in-house maintenance, preventative maintenance absent, difficult to obtain valid measures on existing process as benchmark
21. An undiscussable social value system dominates over the technical value system (objective cost/benefit project justification impossible)
22. Plant staff not familiar with "high-tech" elements

DENIAL OF OWNERSHIP

23. Serious attempts to understand system undertaken only after turnover activity starts ("We never knew the system did that.")
24. Avoidance of the fact that manpower requirements for new system may increase, not decrease
25. Late change requests for items known since project beginning
26. Project scoped without basis or realistic plant survey
27. Reluctance to learn new system or aspects in another "territory"
28. Lack of provisions for expansion and life-cycle needs
29. Fragmented and dispersed system responsibility
30. Poor or missing changeover transition plans

DENIAL OF STEWARDSHIP

31. Poor enforcement of primary project commitments
32. Identification and planning for contingency conditions avoided (e.g.new hazards from using electrical vs existing pneumatic devices)
33. No criteria for limiting incremental additions until the system saturates before project completed (uncontrolled scope-creep)
34. Lack of comprehensive, common-language data base and cross-reference lists
35. Lack of effort to obtain operator and key staff participation and acceptance
36. Adjustments based upon developing knowledge avoided (it would be recorded as a "mistake")
37. Little support in documentation and in preparing design information requirements

OMNIPOTENCE IS OUR TRADEMARK

the ancients were no longer accepted without question. A healthy skepticism led to a new outlook on natural phenomena, and things haven't been the same since.

The connection of practices to results is feedback of results compared to a "specification" as a basis to revise practices. This connection monitors the fit of the solution domain to the problem domain. Feedback is a success word. The language of success is a language formed from connecting practices to the results they produce, good **or** bad. Sounds simple, doesn't it? Yet, the roadblock to feedback is woven into the basic fabric of our society. Between closing our eyes to reality and looking the other way from the truth, no place is left for seeing. History shows that history itself has rarely been used to modify decision-making by gut reaction.

RULE - Never encourage another group to act rationally. It wastes your time and annoys the organization.

The periodical **Business Week** is filled with stories of business success. The articles of this typical establishment stooge illustrate two types of the feedback blindspot. The first type shows how the rich get richer, i.e., starting with a success and going on to greater everythings. The second type always begins with how Mr. X took over a "sick business situation" and via fiscal surgery made a success out of failure. Note that the direction is always up, always successful and already proven (never in process). The bumper crop of sick business situations which enables the fiscal surgeons to achieve fame, is conveniently omitted.

The fact that 65,000 business organizations expire every year in the USA, does not lead Establishment minions to wonder. Obviously, whatever is being preached as success models for the solution space is totally bankrupt for the vast domain of the problem space. Don't learn from 65,000 failures, Establishment, most of whom you trained. Don't connect Their practices to Their failures, managers. They are on the other side of the event horizon. Let them die.

Organizations save their best block party dance for preventing the adoption of successful, but non-standard, methods. The overwhelming success of quality came to our shores from Japan more than a decade ago. The demonstration of the quality virtues has been and continues to be blocked by the USA Establishment as necessary and sufficient reasons to change the anti-quality network of vested interests.

The common practice in blocking change is to promise requisite support for the change project and then renege on the promises. This ploy is in such common use that a large array of "acceptable" phrases has developed. The list of denials only gets bigger. The withholding of vital support does not suspend its necessity. Denial is the principal method used for crippling the modernization project. It never fails.

Distortions

Organizations, whether in or out of routine states, always allocate their attention and resources by an undiscussable, obscure set of priorities. The function of placing resources where they will do the most good (allocation) is distorted like the Fun House wiggly mirrors. For the complex situation, POSIWID shows us the allocation decisions are so far off the mark, and by such large margins, that it **cannot** be by accident. A recent example of the phenomenon of distortion is that, even though behavior causes 97% of the grief, the USA only

VULNERABILITIES OF THE IMPENETRABLE ESTABLISHMENT DEFENSE

I. VOIDS (Missing vital parts)

   A. Trans-territory agencies for cross-territory problems. i.e., the junctional node working staff
   B. Compensations for communication impediments, i.e., common knowledge base in a common language
   C. Correcting mechanisms
      1. Policies and doctrines
      2. Awards
      3. Management
   D. Deming's methods for quality performance

II. ROADBLOCKS (Some are avalanches)

   A. Forbid non-routine, require routine
   B. Mismatched working environment
   C. Specialization
   D. Denials
   E. Accounting and purchasing
   F. Administration red tape
   G. Forbid feedback learning
      1. Organizational performance history
      2. Project history
      3. Linear think and action

III. DISTORTIONS

   A. Allocating resources to significant issues
   B. Reward non-performance
   C. Punish competence
   D. Intolerant of error and experimentation

IV. LIVINGSTON'S LAW OF INVERSIONS

V. ELIMINATIONS, especially negative incentives

VI. INCREMENTALISM to unnoted lock-in switch of major issues

VII. PERCEPTUAL LIMITATIONS

VIII. BAD DECISION-MAKING

   A. Criteria for process and groundrules for application
   B. Objectively including soft factors with hard factors

HAVE FUN AT WORK

spends 3% of its research and development budget on behavioral science, and virtually zero per cent of that on organizational dysfunction (budget dollars for research are dispensed by organizations).

RULE - If more is being spent to get less, the purchase is being made by an organization.

Organizations are subject to Pareto's Law (90% of the work is done by 10% of the staff) and respond by a system of compensation that rewards the 90% who do only 10% of the work with at least 90% of the pay. If corporations were to compensate their employees on the basis of their contribution to the success of the firm, the "system" would go berserk. It has become commonplace for the corporation to reward only those who behave according to established mediocre norms - and remain indifferent to productivity.

The medical industry allocates research resources on a basis that obviously has little to do with human life. For cancer, which causes about two million years of lost life annually, the federal government spends one billion dollars. That is a ratio of $500 per year of lost life. For heart diseases, which exceed two million years of lost life every year, the ratio is only $300. For the largest cause, injury, losing over four million years of life annually, the ratio drops to $30. A nation-wide study of mortality shows that a majority of New York City hospitals are drastically worse than USA norms. The doctors in the spotlight counter the evidence with, "There is no connection between mortality and the competency of health care." Marvelous news for the ill.

The institutions entrusted to transmit culture to the keepers of the other zoos (schools) convey a value system with little resemblance to reality. The fetish for growth, glory and success shuns the lessons which can be taken from the study of failure. Equipped only to deal with success, priests of the faith shatter at the first waves of trouble. Academics attempting to get financial support for study of organizational failure are shown to the door. This self-sealing cycle prevents a legitimate look at the very dragons eating away on the corporations. Academia, a basic component of the Establishment, dutifully complies with the order, and failure remains a forbidden topic. **Erase.**

RULE - Fast cycle failure feedback has no equal for learning how to cope with complexity. Don't leave home without it.

One distortion growing by small increments has been enabled by advances in computer graphics. The decision-making process is now being warped through validation by viewing. The apparent credibility of data is enhanced by clever graphics and it is warmly embraced by the uninvolved. Graphics stand in the way of thinking. While the work behind the numbers behind the pictures has always been the hardest to sell to management, the underlying models of the system get worse as graphics get better. No good can come from this distortion.

Distortions, voids and roadblocks are everyday dishes on the menu in The Fun House cafeteria. Don't step outside of the small territory assigned to your group to solve a problem you can't solve otherwise. The passive defenses are already in place. The active defenses will spring to the parapets and drive off your threat to the status quo. For now, enjoy the show of dystopia, but stay in the stands. You haven't seen the entire beast yet.

Alice In Control

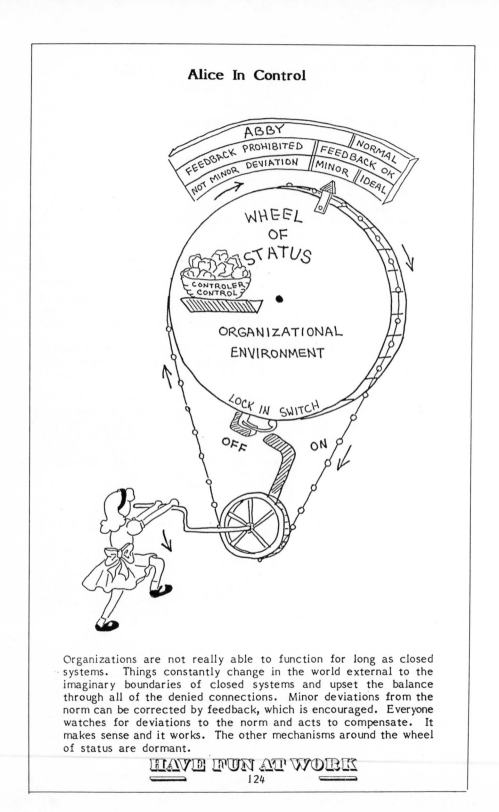

Organizations are not really able to function for long as closed systems. Things constantly change in the world external to the imaginary boundaries of closed systems and upset the balance through all of the denied connections. Minor deviations from the norm can be corrected by feedback, which is encouraged. Everyone watches for deviations to the norm and acts to compensate. It makes sense and it works. The other mechanisms around the wheel of status are dormant.

Chapter Nine

The Why Factory

Livingston's Law

Like the discovery of most statutes of nature, the identification of this most incredible, counter-intuitive pattern of animal behavior (Livingston's Law) came about by noticing that, in certain situations, the shape of our many wounds was the same. Naturally, we would have preferred a flash of genius to contusions of similar appearance. Now, equipped with 20/20 hindsight, the telltale blunt instrument of this "unnatural" law is obvious - everywhere.

There is a conditional switch, as when Alice fell down the rabbit hole into Wonderland, that suddenly snaps on Livingston's Law, and the world turns abruptly upside down. In the weird world of Livingston's Law, like that of Alice's Mad Hatter, the rational rules of behavior are the same, but they are inverted. For every rational act there is an equal and opposite irrationality. When Livingston's Law is in effect, the organizational balance beam between activities aimed at preservation and those directed towards adaptation, points to the ancient African savannah.

The switch that forsakes sanity is set at a high level of organizational stress (complexity confrontation). That is, if the times of interest are reasonably routine times, Livingston's Law lies dormant. Use your rational faculties and mental models with impunity for those situations. When the level of stress rises above the setpoint into cognitive dissonance, knowing Livingston's Law is the only thing that can save your hide. It is the logic of a madhouse.

RULE - Orgman is haunted by the grossest superstitions he dutifully transmits.

Like roadblocks, inversions are easy to see once you learn to change polarity on your intuitions at the snap of the switch. An inversion is a situation in which the organization compulsively acts in a direction exactly counter to the demands (control signals) placed on it. What is so monstrous about an inversion (positive feedback) is that the demander, which could be you, may fail to notice that his efforts are achieving results in direct opposition to his goals, and try to correct the situation by pushing harder in what he still mistakenly believes is a helpful direction. Through inversions, energy spent to remedy a problem ends up making matters worse.

In spite of great perversity, inversions are but one organizational strategy to maintain the status quo by matching active defenses in proportion to the perception of threat. Whatever their strength of logic, inversions automatically compensate for and nullify any and all efforts to reason with the organization. The harder the push to move right, the harder the instinctive reactions push to the left. The size of the regulating force is immaterial. No new orders have to be issued to deal with a large threat. The threshold switch is the social trumpet call that always mobilizes sufficient forces to preserve the status quo - which is **always** sustained. Inversions are more common than is generally appreciated.

RULE - An organization in process of self-destruction considers any interference as encouragement to accelerate the pace.

Alice in Invertland

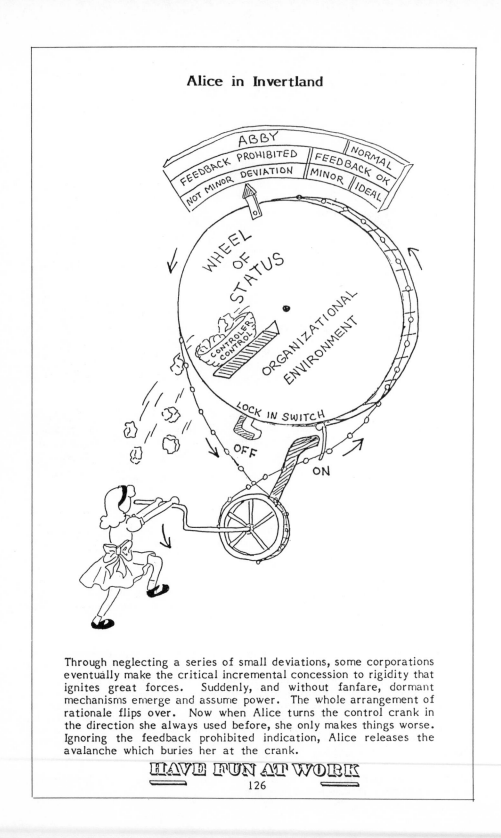

Through neglecting a series of small deviations, some corporations eventually make the critical incremental concession to rigidity that ignites great forces. Suddenly, and without fanfare, dormant mechanisms emerge and assume power. The whole arrangement of rationale flips over. Now when Alice turns the control crank in the direction she always used before, she only makes things worse. Ignoring the feedback prohibited indication, Alice releases the avalanche which buries her at the crank.

HAVE FUN AT WORK

The frequent encounter with inversions, once it was realized they existed, led to the formulation of the general law. While the rules, as offered in this book, are spears of insight which are prone to exceptions, a law is revelation from which corollaries can be drawn with impunity. The unnatural law is stated in two parts, the threshold situation and the rule.

Livingston's Law

When an organization has become significantly discordant with its supporting environment, any regulating action directed to reduce the discordance will precipitate an organizational response with opposite polarity to the intent of the regulator. The response evoked by the signal contains at least enough power to silence the regulator and to increase the discord beyond what it would have been if no control action had been initiated.

One observation which may help decipher some of the technical wording of the law is the dictum - "No good deed goes unpunished." The intuitive sense of an effort at regulating something to stay within desired limits (maintain stability), is to take an action that travels around the loop and arrives back with a size and sign which, when added algebraically to the initial discord, reduces it. When the threshold value of organizational discord is crossed, and Livingston's Law erupts out of La La land, your same well-meaning regulating action travels around the loop and arrives back with a sign additive to the discord, of appalling size, and delivered to you by a squad of trigger-happy corporate assassins. Your efforts to achieve stability only create more instability.

The organization is well aware of its condition when it is far out of alignment with its environment. The situation develops into the stupid gridlock of World War I trench warfare, where, as time goes on, all sides suffer casualties without advantage. Livingston's Law is always in force during project status camouflage time. It is still difficult, but we have learned restraint for shouting remarks about the emperor's clothes when the big parade of waste is marching by. There are just too many assassins.

The law does not apply when the corporation is in phase with the real and changing needs of its markets. In those happy situations, control actions to correct a small imbalance with the outside world will achieve their intended, harmonious result. This pattern matches our intuitions. It is in consonance with our mental reference model.

The law also does not apply when the corporation is drifting awry and the normal defenses are still doing their job. For these conditions, the control signal is effective with routine rationale. A great many organizational dysfunctions are protected by the array of standard subterfuge.

Livingston's Law of Inversion in Action

Discrepant situation	Action signal	Response
Poor quality	Automation	Poorer quality
Unanticipated failures	ID early and fix	More big failures
New problems surface	Add staff	Staff turnover
Changing requirements	More flexibility	Rigid rule enforce
Wrong reflex decisions	Supply more data	Less data used
Misunderstood messages	Coordination	More specialization
Specialties isolated	Team work	More specialization
Mgt power display	Earn control	More impotent
Central control lost	Decentralize	Manage by slogan
Products obsolete	New products	Repaint old products
Innovation discouraged	Reward innovators	Innovators punished
Information deficient	Computerize	Less information use
Poor program transport	Standardize SW	More SW languages
Inefficient operations	Cut red tape	More red tape
Heavy traffic tieups	Add police	Slower traffic flow
Too many rules to work	Reduce regulations	More rules enforced
Frequent errors	Locate error cause	More errors
Boring work	Humanize job	Smaller task scope
Knowing bad from good	Define job goals	Supply of bad grows
Confused directions	Clarify goals	Fewer directions
Vital issues uncovered	Discuss core items	Fewer topics allowed
Reduce labor content	Computerize	Labor costs increase
Relate to real world	Adjust practices	Focus on internals
Coordination tougher	Reduce agency #s	More disintegrations
Risk averse	Count and account	More risks taken
Narrow skills	Broaden competency	Social control hit
Big surprises	Ashby knowledge	More surprises
Complex	Systems methods	More complexity
Uncoordinated	Integrate	Demand for autonomy
Punish mavericks	Adopt innovation	Reward conformists
Costs uncompetitive	Increase quality	Costs go up
Problems unsolved	Different way	More problems grown
Forced outages high	Study causes	More breakdowns
Organization is wrong	Learn from history	All money to defense
Managers disconnected	Reduce # of levels	Levels added
Big, obvious trouble	Get help	Trouble denied
Better forecasts	Feedback	Good predictors hit

Masking Decisions

Deception and lies are common in the animal kingdom. Many species have to deceive other species in order to survive. Only man, among all other living things, it should be observed, lies to himself. That he should continue to believe his own lies is a wonder of the universe. A major self-deception occurs in believing that Livingston's Law is not in effect when it is.

The organization has an impressive storehouse of self-delusions and protective reactions which cover all of the situations it encounters, except the escalating messes which it makes for itself in the defensive process. In practice, the only thing these defenses protect against is survival. These myths have been invented to communicate illusions about the defensive response to control signals. Myths have a long life of their own. They will persist long after the fallacies of their corresponding illusions have been exposed. They already have. Livingston's Law does not have to be invoked when myths are doing their job.

Livingston's Law is the defense of last resort, brought out after all lesser defenses have been exhausted. The bear trap of the law slams onto the legs of unwary Samaritans who have failed to observe when organizational harmony has gone quite sour. Going down the garden path as before, the concerned detectors of disharmony dutifully create an error signal to warn the organization of its collision course with EOPMD. This time, the control direction provokes a response opposite to intent and instead of moving towards harmony, moves further away from it. This speeds up the process of degeneration. Livingston's Law explains why good intentions (and accurate predictions) are met with hostility and increasingly vicious counterproductive behavior.

Livingston's Law is easy to test. Start with a small control signal and note the sign of the response when it completes the loop. If it is counter to the control intent, the law is in force. If you value your hide, do not make large scale tests. Remember, eliminating the source of the control signal is part of the response.

Livingston's Law conditions are common around modernization projects, like office automation, where the new gizmos to be installed mean a big redistribution of social status and authority. The goal of the modernizing effort may be to keep the company in business. The goal matters little. The affected groups will do whatever it takes to sabotage the project so as to retain the status quo-even groups that may have requested the modernization project in the first place. Studies keep showing that the complaints about degraded health due to computer display screens (CRTs) are really masked complaints about the rotten organization they work for. You can watch Livingston's Law right in your own town government as it deals with the impending crisis in waste disposal. Using this reference model, you can note many examples at work.

The sampling of general exhibits of Livingston's Law has been provided to show you the range of issues that are covered when the law is in force. When you install the law into your diagnostic toolbox, it can be a powerful predictor of organizational behavior. The only precondition which has to be known is that the threshold settings have been exceeded. Like any law, Livingston's Law defines a constraint on the great variety of behavior the organization can exhibit. Once identified, constraints can be put to good use. This is the only hope for understanding the complex natures of the corporate organism and on which to base an increase in coping capabilities - the prime mover to **have fun at work.**

Over The Walls

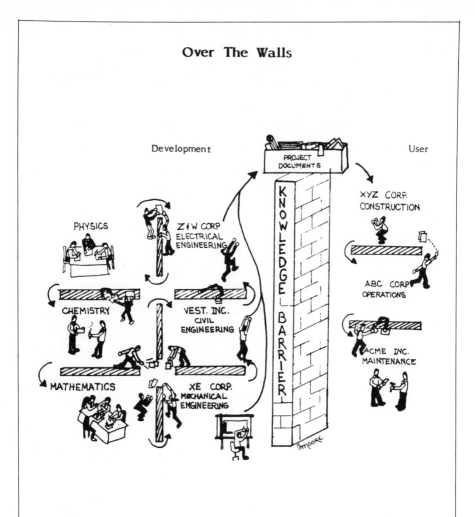

This cartoon has been a popular favorite throughout the ten years of its life. Tribal life survives today in walled cells, often called departments, where every effort is made to make all who are not insiders - strangers. Specialization has created so many cells and so many foreigners that translation activity takes up most of the time. Rather than install and enforce a common language, so that everyone can get on with doing the job, cells build cloisters where all communication with the outside world, as they have defined it, must pass over-the-wall like mental popcorn. Everyone does it. There is no cell assigned to oversee the integration of the other cells and remove the errors of translation, so popcorn gets all over the place where it eventually accumulates enough to suffocate the project. Once established, department members defend their walls to the death.

The switch for Livingston's Law is snap-action and latch-in. Once installed, there is no going back. The action of the law itself prevents a reversal until all the players are gone. We often wish that healthy tendencies would only reinforce each other just as well as pathological ones do.

Self-reinforcing behavior patterns which exclude the regulating influences of feedback, seem to be a trademark of mankind. For instance, the development of electric power was certainly one of the most significant innovations of all time to improve the quality of human life. When Edison's practical lighting schemes were starting to gain, the gas lighting industry responded, not by participating in the revolution at their doorstep, but with a complete updating of products for using gas. The big dollars spent in a frantic effort to extend their reign sealed their fate for an early demise. The pattern of behavior was repeated for mechanical calculators and watches.

The computer-driven engineering work station (CAD) is in the same script. The huge influence of the powerful computer on the desk-top has, technically, forever changed how engineering and engineered projects will best be done. This innovation is no mere electronic slide rule, which mechanizes tasks that would be done anyway. The computer has changed the entire approach to problem-solving itself. New tools, new tasks and new skills shout change in the ears of vested interests much louder than they announce an opportunity to grow.

Engineering associations, like the American Society of Mechanical Engineers, quake at the thought of such rapid and significant change. Representing a microcosm of the motley guild of all engineers, the ASME faces a major restructuring of the work of engineering it can not prevent. Like any paralyzed bureaucracy, the ASME went outside to hire a consultant to tell them what any member could, that the winds of change are howling.

The entire work-task distinction between Mechanical Engineer and Civil Engineer, for example, is fading away. It is too much too fast for the senile, arthritic institutions and, paranoid about discussing the undiscussables, they will resist the inevitable changes to the end. The same turbulence exists throughout the engineering communities and, everywhere the same reaction. The list of control signal generators, who have already bitten the dust, will grow. It's only a matter of time until some senior designer with thirty years on the drawing board, and skills developed over a lifetime now no longer valued, comes barging into the CAD computer room with gun blazing.

Livingston's Law teaches that the least harm you can do to an organization in trouble is to leave it alone. By itself, the situation will continue to deteriorate, but any efforts to reverse the direction, no matter how noble, will only trigger reactions that will accelerate the degeneration. Organization Man, under stress, has an imprisoned mind which has no capacity for appraising the results of his practices. His final demand, of course, is to make the world over in his own shrunken image.

Don't be tricked into confusing real innovation with "distress" innovation, and beware the good intentions of unconsciously biased minds. Organizations are very creative in maintaining their status quo. Remember, the organizational decision just before the choice to change itself is suicide - a crazed Kamikaze raid on one of its own airfields. It takes time to get used to that one.

<u>Abandon the pursuit of the impossible</u>

Our belief systems are those the mind, as a biological structure, is designed to construct, and people are especially programmed to be indoctrinated. The refusal of insight, the roadblock to feedback, betrays these pathological rules for

THIRTY-FOUR ORGANIZED DECEPTIONS

STANDARD SUPERVISOR TRAINING
FOR STATUS QUO DEFENSE

FOCUS ON TECHNOLOGY

1. Preach faith in technology and technologists. Problems encountered are only indications of imperfections in the technology - all of which can be eliminated by giving enough attention.
2. Reject all non-technical factors. Avoid issues which can not be quantified and expressed by equations and models. The non-technical context is the ultimate cause of all system failures.
3. Use profile comparisons between separate entities (technical and/or social) to create the illusion that an actual, intelligible correspondence exists.
4. Exclude any issue or factor which can not be expressed in scientific notation. There are no standard methods to reveal biases.
5. Promote the illusion that a build-up of competence within a particular technical specialty constitutes a guarantee that system problems will not be encountered.
6. Instill confidence that technology goes from certainty to certainty and that deviations from the expected never occur. Show the transfer of information between disciplines as like an electrical system with easy-to-identify connections.

FOCUS ON STANDARD PRACTICES

7. Attribute problems only to manageable deficiencies in "the" process and, therefore, correctable through time and resources.
8. Enforce the policy that quality, reliability and safety are fulfilled only if the standardized rules are followed.
9. Base an implementation of ends upon the grounds of means. That principle never provides a workable solution to the problem.
10. Extend the same practices proven for small systems to large systems. Large systems induce systems effects that permit failure processes to become critical before they can be prevented.

FOCUS ON GRANULATION AND SPECIALIZATION

11. Separate issues according to the disciplines represented by the specialists assigned. Differing perspectives will further polarize the parties involved. There is no common language to shape concepts distributed over several disciplines into a coherent solution.
12. Disassociate with the outside world when it intrudes. Disciplines do not want to interact with those outside of their own guild on conditions other than in their own scope.
13. Appoint specialists to the problem. They will represent their narrow discipline and shun the broad view. Integrating the results into conclusions that might correspond to the real problem will be left to Providence.
14. Support the notion that every discipline has an independent intrinsic value. This will lead to the fantasy that a complete and accurate solution to any problem can be obtained by pushing the submission of evidence hard enough with the aid of only one discipline.
15. Treat quality, reliability and safety as single-discipline issues. It makes certain these vital matters will remain unsatisfactory.
16. Permit safety considerations to be made only for the obvious. Failure modes that can not be unilaterally accommodated within the conceptual boundaries of one discipline are always badly handled.
17. Confine the scope to small individual factors. Never investigate the pattern they form.

HAVE FUN AT WORK

FOCUS ON INSTINCTS AND REFLEX ACTION

18. Make quick conclusions and follow with impulsive, far-reaching decisions. These acts flow from instincts rather than rational principles and they are invariably wrong.

19. Accept fundamental discrepancies between mathematical models and physical realities without examination. Same as school.

20. Communicate only by estimating the interests of those at whom the activities are aimed.

21. Take whatever is necessary to link expectations to the reality for granted.

22. Act first. Buy something. There will be plenty of time before the error surfaces and it removes the social heat.

DENY, IMPEDE, GIVE LIP SERVICE AND IGNORE

23. Encourage workers to associate the world of fiction with their daily lives.

24. Accept arguments in principle and then continue on as before. This conceals a lack of understanding and concern.

25. Ignore any questions about the incompatible parts of the system. Confuse the real with the model.

26. Block any ideas of the need for more knowledge and competence to improve abilities to handle the complex issues of a multi-disciplined problem. Personal and commercial interests will easily justify the obstruction.

27. Conceal truth, in order to appear positive and uncontroversial. Social pressure will automatically squeeze the truth from other expressions of opinion.

28. Manifestly exclude any other judgement on the quality of the information and knowledge drawn upon - but that possessed by the vested interest.

29. Rely upon self-searching by others. Maintain that the quality, reliability and safety criteria existing in the respective disciplines constitutes a guarantee for the system. This will deflect any consciousness of risk of failure.

30. Address only problems shown by disaster. Never explore the reasons for the vulnerability in the first place and never inquire about the lack of preparedness.

31. Acknowledge non-technical aspects merely by indicating them. Whether indicated in general or specific terms, they will remain invisible.

32. Ascribe any resistance to undue pessimism. Conditioned reflexes think the problem will be overcome sooner or later by the force of some natural law bringing everything into order. Quantity develops into quality. Therefore do the same effort as before and be patient.

33. Assure that the performance of the designer is independent of the setting. The natural arrangement is always a mismatch.

34. Stall for another increment of status quo time with the Facade of Futile Feigned Faith (F4) in the "system." Memorize the following list for quick response to threat (repeated from Chapter 4 for your convienence).

- Let's give the "new" organization time to work.
- The new policy should solve the problem.
- We are confident that these adjustments will work.
- Things should start to look better next month.
- We have added two more assistant project managers.
- We are going to install a more powerful computer.
- We are suing the vendors for non-compliance to the spec.
- The new software will be put online next week.
- We see some signs that things are turning around.
- There is plenty of safety factor built into the seals.
- It just needs more time to straighten itself out.
- If we all work together, we can make the schedule.
- Today we start mandatory overtime, seven days a week.
- We have hired a consultant with a great track record.
- The last meeting really cleared up the misunderstandings.

HAVE FUN AT WORK

behavior. Orgman is not taught to understand himself. As a consequence, Orgman is marked by a sense of helplessness, not by a sense of adequacy. Every new spurt of technology increases his dependence upon others and reduces the proportion of things that can be checked by referring to experience. It is hardly surprising that we have problems getting on well together when we know so little about the mechanisms by which we interact. These factors do not augur well for having fun at work as a natural condition.

The wreckage of our day is the cumulative product of refusals to understand. In 1988, more than half of the Third World deaths result from archaic community hygiene practices for which remedies are readily available and cheap. The renewed famines of East Africa bring forth many familiar control signals for action. Control signals fail in these areas for the same reason that preaching has never eliminated sin. Once again, the Establishments of those nations are seeing to it that the basic social mechanisms which created the catastrophe in the first place survive intact. The communal flight from understanding prevents the insights these concrete situations demand. Real people die in these unnecessary messes.

The language of failure will now be given a rest. We have pounded without mercy upon the Bad Seventies of the basic references you use for daily living. Those subconscious structures which have failed you with such dependability, should have been shaken and extracted. The new mental models need room to grow.

The language of success is rich with vocabulary because success needs to be understood in any discipline. It is not a language for the glory of the organization. It is a language of celebration for the individual. Learn to speak it and **have fun at work.**

THE LANGUAGE OF FAILURE

Eliminations, diversions and pursuits of the impossible

Universal Scenario & transitional behavior indicators
    Project assessment factors for go/no go
    The zone of indifference (ZOI)

Vulnerabilities
    Voids, roadblocks, distortions
    The decision-making process
    Livingston's Law of Inversion

Standard organizational practices impact for Tracks A&B
    Linear think and prohibited connections
    Conditional feedback block

Management's toolbox
    Management by objectives = managing by rules
    Performance reviews & Zero Defects slogans
    Mix and match entreaties

Status quo defenses
    Denials of requisite support
    F4
    Organized deceptions

Communications
    Specializations/Babel
    Steep hierarchical gradients
    Filters, compressors and modifiers

Social controls
    Punishment of mavericks & accurate prophets
    Reward non performance and conformity

Human perceptual limits and mismatches

The Language Of Success

A. SOCIAL SYSTEM
   1. Connections
      a. History & performance record
      b. Inherent limitations to communications
   2. Feedback
   3. POSIWID
   4. Vulnerabilities as darts
   5. Innovation
      a. Outside practitioner (path of max resistance)
      b. Skunkworks
         (1) Elimination of adversarial relationships
         (2) Value systems and definitions
         (3) Discussion of the undiscussables
   6. Territorial imperative
   7. Two level abstraction
   8. Cognitive dissonance
   9. Separating victims from enemies
   10. Erasure and replacement of the Bad Seventies
   11. Environmental assessment
      a. Viable options
   12. Structure pack

B. TECHNICAL SYSTEM
   1. Complexity indicators
   2. The critical mass of essential principles
      a. Scoping, boundaries and penetrations
      b. Scrutable connectivity
      c. Part number detail
      d. Model building, model testing, simulation
      e. Development of Ashby knowledge structures
         (1) Blowout sessions
            (a) The unintended count/account
            (b) Prohibition of solutions
      f. Allocation of common "currency"
      g. Black boxes and constraints to variety
         (1) Count and account for variety
      h. Fast cycle RBF
   3. Systems engineering analytical tools

C. SOCIAL - TECHNICAL SYSTEM INTEGRATION
   1. Task descriptions by cycle of control
      a. The cross reference list
   2. Law of equivalent significance (footprint)
   3. Job performance aids
   4. Combined TDBD + communications chart format

D. HFAW levels
   1. Defense: Stress surgery and disposal
   2. Offense
      a. Personal revenge: awareness + loyalty
      b. Building a PWG coalition: 2 track think
      c. Building a constituency of PWGs
         (1) Instant cognitive dissonance
         (2) Taking functional control

Chapter Ten

So then always that knowledge is worthiest ... which considereth the simple forms or differences of things, which are few in number, and the degrees and coordinations whereof make all this variety.

Francis Bacon

Fundamentals

The language of success is a contrived but exoteric language. The fashionable one, the one worshipped by the Establishment, is based upon a constant world - an hallucination. You can not **have fun at work** just by shifting emphasis around the corporate language you have been taught (more, more-harder, harder - faster, faster) recast here as the language of failure.

The language of success is a garden of known, validated issues that relate to the complexities of the real world. The language describes a solution domain that encompasses the domain of **any** problem. The terms are borrowed from a wide variety of sources and experience. Think of it as a foreign language that should be learned before you can become a citizen of Successville. We doubt this patchquilt language will ever have a legitimate home in society. Most successes are illegitimate anyway.

We often wish it were otherwise, but dealing with the elements of complexity and their relationships takes some effort and persistence. We would prefer passive ways to obtain knowledge - something we just happen to acquire. Learning the language of success, unfortunately, is an active process that will require your conscious participation. Don't blame us, we didn't invent complexity. Know that by understanding the few laws and rules which constitute success, the terrible complexity monster blocking the path to fun at work can be domesticated.

RULE - Because the herd is always wrong and always races away from complexity, YOU must march toward it.

To **have fun at work,** install the language of success as a major benchmark in your replacement mental reference set. The vernacular provides a new, insightful, healthy vantage point from which to view the world of work. It is the difference between success references and reality that matters most, not just distinctions between gradations in mediocrity and failure. There are many tools for mapping between the surfaces of your environment and the landscape of success. Understanding this "foreign" language, a symbolic model, allows you to develop a continuous weather report on the chances for error and the opportunities for error prevention or, failing that, error recovery. You cannot escape the necessity of increasing variety in your coping competencies, and you need skills in imaging complex matters to begin the training. Confidence in your ability to control a situation is exactly how you learn to **have fun at work.**

The Fat Ladies of Feedback Sing

To make success happen, there is no fooling around with practices known to fail and wasting energy trying to suspend natural laws. Engineer John Stevens inherited the disastrous Panama Canal project after it had been botched by the French and the USA government and had consumed 20,000 heroes. His first order was to stop all work on the canal itself. He knew the time had come to control Yellow Fever and build infrastructure.

The language of success involves a set (rules) and structure embedded in structure. These structures form islands of high, dry rational ground out of the muck in complexity swamp. When enough islands of sanity have been formed, they can be joined together. Eventually, the numbers of things to be mentally manipulated becomes manageable. That is, once you are familiar with the tools, you can learn to use them to take hold of a complex matter which **no one** can understand and make a valid translation that **is** understandable. This is a secret the Establishment does not want you to know.

RULE - When you have an increasing slew of complexities with large technical and social components managed by a bunch of lawyers and accountants, you get what we're getting.

Acquiring knowledge about complexity is hard on the neocortex, but it is now only a question of time and labor. You need no magic. Rules let you recognize situations without heavy diagnosis (as has been and **may** be). Joining knowledge with rules in a structure equips you to adapt the paradigm of success (as **can** be) to the particulars of your work scene. Assaulting complexity is a skill, like any other, that gets easier and more natural with practice. It all can be boiled down to context, process and content.

Some key pieces and parts of the language, like POSIWID, have already been introduced. While some items can work as stand-alone tools, many concepts use tools together. They are not listed in any particular order of importance. The language of success includes spotlighting natural (but troublesome) distortions in perception and intuition, the cycle of control, organizational communications, limits of the hierarchical design, the territorial imperative, feedback and POSIWID, and Ashby's Law of Requisite Variety. These related topics introduce some tools for understanding the organism, hazards to avoid, and tools for coping with complexity. The best way to see the interconnections and how it all fits together is in application. The next Chapter will illustrate how the language of success is deployed by practitioners in the vast field of complex-problem solving.

RULE - The Establishment has no vocabulary by which the language of success can be expressed. That takes care of that.

The cycle of control

Preparing to **have fun at work** is not a simple task. While the mental exertion aspects are most regrettable, at least there is a way. One pillar of the language of success is the cycle of control. This cycle starts with **awareness** and goes on with **cognition, diagnosis,** identification of **viable alternatives, selection** of the action plan, **implementation** and **closure.** Being out of control is stress, not fun.

Monitoring of your environment must be constantly upgraded with more and better references so that you can become **aware** that "something is not behaving as it 'ought to.'" The spectrum of things (preconditions) which should trigger awareness is large, and that's what the rules are for. There is no expedient to avoid the requisite of reliable surveillance. Without awareness that something isn't "right," mechanisms for error prevention and recovery are comatose. Remaining oblivious to alarm conditions (threshold crossings) can ruin your day. Not fun.

The subliminal instincts that detect the discrepancy must be trained to bump the issue up to higher authority - your consciousness. Knowing that "something

Twenty Perceptual Limitations and Perversions

INFORMATION PROCESSING CAPABILITIES

1. Equivalent of 60 pages of new material per day
2. Ingestion rate 14 bits/sec (ears) to 40 bits/sec (eyes)
3. Seven plus or minus two discriminators (Fitts' rule)

COMPREHENSION

4. Very small numbers
5. Very large numbers
6. Geometric progressions
7. Complexity
8. Risks and chance (gambling)
   Size of samples used to judge
9.   Avoid risk when seeking to gain
10.   Choose risk when avoiding loss

INSTINCTS

11. Faith in the unfamiliar
12. Obedience to social controls
13. Territorial imperative

CONSISTENT AND PREDICTABLE DEVIATIONS FROM RATIONALITY

14. Decisions flip depending upon how problem is posed
15. Regression
    Punished for giving rewards
16.   Rewarded for punishing others
17. Mental short cuts
    Representation by wrong model
18.   Cognition of situation by irrelevant experience
19.   Ignoring baseline background data for risk estimate
20.   Loss-avoidance overrules gain-seeking

is up" focuses rational cognitive faculties on the issue. It is your chance to demonstrate the only surviving difference between man and the other animals. Gathering of related facts leads to some sort of situation diagnosis. Diagnosis leads to the appropriate tool box of remedies.

Knowledge helps you to select among the viable alternatives. In deference to the Law of Least Effort, meaningful knowledge reduces the amount of detail that has to be weighed before choosing. The decision environment "noise" is a variable which, together with your variability, increases the value of rules for this task. One rule that always applies here is to discount your intuitive and socially-controlled perception of uncertainty. You have a magnificent opportunity to fail and it should not be delegated to your human nature or the herd-mentality influence. Implementing the choice for **action** is relatively normal and straight-forward. The trick is usually to **hold back** on action until the brain is put into thinking gear. Not popular.

RULE - When in doubt of a proper course of action, observe non-Brownian movement of the human herd and order yourself in the opposite direction.

The cycle of control is never over until the fat lady of feedback sings. Normally placed last or not at all, you place feedback first in line. Closure (feedback) is the most significant, if not the most elegant, word in the language of success. Fast cycle comparison of your practices to the results they produce (the effect of your actions compared to a good reference), is how you learn to **have fun at work.** Actually, error is how you learn everything.

Most large, old institutions are too far gone to sanction feedback. One large authority in our region makes a habit of trying massive, fad experiments and punishing anyone foolish enough to suggest the impact be assessed by impartial outside agencies. Let them have their policy. Yours is closure.

RULE - Without closure, the cycle of control becomes a one-way path to Hell.

The mathematics of organizational communications

There is an homologous aspect about laws which govern the technical side of the dilemma and those which apply to the social side. While the human factor is denied in practice, denial only increases its significance. For instance, most problems in the complexity business relate to information and its movement around a network. Extra heavy communication traffic causes breakdowns in human networks just as it does in physical devices. The "garbage in - garbage out" axiom is not confined solely to computer processing either. For success purposes, much of communications traffic is a matter of arithmetic and it belongs in the vocabulary.

Since the Stone Age, humans have been limited in the rate of incoming data they can absorb to 40 bits/sec. This upper limit shows up in various forms wherever the capacity is measured - "I can't take it any more." For example, a jet fighter pilot flying at 800 miles per hour at high G forces is not able to watch his cockpit displays at the same time he is trying to avoid enemy missiles and launch his own towards a respectable target. For less stressful situations, the information ingestion rate is equivalent to 60 pages of unfamiliar written material per working day. That feat must be reduced when the individual is engaging in another activity. Other reductions in the rate can come from the mental "system" need to transfer from short term to long term memory - "I need time to digest this material."

In order to process information, a person must first ingest it. This is accomplished through various sensors, such as eyes and ears. Limits for each sensor are set by the ratio of data capacity (the brain) to the communications flow through the bandwidth of these sensors to the outside world. Our eyes have a wider bandwidth than our ears and so we store more information obtained visually than we do aurally, because we get more bits of data that way. Communication is symbolic. Even miscommunication is symbolic.

Always consider human information processing capacity limits. As a biological limit, no human component in any organization is spared. It is a reference rule. The software of the brain has special programs for getting around those limitations for some situations. For example, we use an inherited ability, called the cocktail party effect, to selectively reject auditory inputs that threaten our ability to focus on a conversation of interest. Likewise, when we can not comfortably process the information at the rate we are ingesting it, we hit the stop button. So far, Napoleon seems to be the modern era champ, and even he met his Waterloo.

All expedients-of-instinct to get around the information handling limitations of the individual, such as committees and hierarchies, introduce new, massive difficulties in network communications. Most of these short-sighted devices merely exchange one constraint, which is only intuitively recognized, for a different set of constraints which are habitually disregarded. When restrictions to communication are ignored, they develop into errors.

With his memory bank of experience and aided by his computer, man can generate information at much higher rates that he can ingest. This can be either very good or a major problem, depending upon the form and destinations of his product. The ability to create more raw novel information than can be ingested is the most critical aspect of organizational communications. Like the nation's mountain of rubbish, these quantities do not go away because you slight them. Once created, they grow all by themselves.

RULE - Hear no evil, see no evil, and speak no evil. The world can fall apart without you.

Consider the match-up between the facilities installed by the organization to deal with information and the rate that information is developed. While corporate information processing rates usually change very little over the years, the supply of information is rising at incredible rates. In 1500 AD, humanity produced three books a day. There are some individuals who can read three books a day and many who can comprehend placing three books a day on a shelf. In 1950 AD, the world grew by three hundred books a day. That rate is far above what any individual can read but a few places, like the Library of Congress, had people who could still understand placing this production on a library shelf. In 1988 AD, three thousand books a day come off the presses. Now we don't even have many individuals who can read all of the book **titles**. The critical thing to appreciate here is that suddenly, buried among the gradually increasing rates, **something big has been lost**.

The organizational design itself is a product of human information handling limits. A species that can communicate telepathically among all its members all of the time with all of the information that is being sensed has no need for an organization in general and a hierarchical organization in particular. It is surprising how seldom these basic limits are consciously connected to organizational changes, although they dwell at the very heart of the matter.

While the espoused rationalities may be technical or political, there is a linear relationship between complexity (information content and quantity) and the number of levels in an organization.

RULE - Complexity only grows when you neglect it.

Demands for greater handling capacities, no matter how boisterous, will increase human limits not one bit. Human communication systems (organizations) transmit information incessantly. To be non-destructive, the variety in the receivers must not be less than that in the original senders. Each behavioral relationship between two or more members in an organization constitutes a unique communication channel, subject to the laws of any communication system. High channel capacities are a necessary resource to reduce error in communication systems, all of which are subject to noise. In communication, the noise comes over the channel just like the message.

To "live" with a situation they cannot change (large quantities of information to be transmitted), people code information they incessantly transmit. This compression increases the opportunities for error, as well as noise, and often makes the communication not fully reversible. By the time the executive order reaches the machine room gang, the CEO would never recognize himself as its author. Should the understanding of the order at the production floor be returned back through the system to the CEO, the recycled message would be incoherent. When the order-givers do not show up at the working level destination for their orders and remove errors in transmission and interpretation, they have abdicated control. All the rest is commentary.

Count and account

Complexity is typically "sensed" rather than measured with scales and micrometers. Things that are simple are easy to show as simple by a complete accounting of their parts and connections. Furthermore, the accounting process itself is comprehensible. The language of success applies the same strategy to complex matters. Through structure, recipes and tools, complexity becomes comprehensible by investing time and labor. Through a systematic approach especially developed for complex issues, we learn which factors are significant about an organization related to its stability.

Most things in daily life are far too complex for our primitive intuitions, so we "guess" at complexity by other unconscious mechanisms. Unfortunately, in assessing complexity by instinct, people habitually and grossly underestimate the innate complexity of most things, including many familiar things. It is strange stuff. To be so predictable in behavior driven by complexity, it is puzzling that man is so poor at estimating the very complexity that hits his behavioral tripwires. Whether or not he knows the true variety in information related to a demand, it is variety that flips his switch. It is when madhouse logic is poised to take over the scene, that complexity-busting methods reveal their power.

RULE - You can't change your limits to complexity, but with the right tools you can chop complexity down to your size.

Compression / Expansion

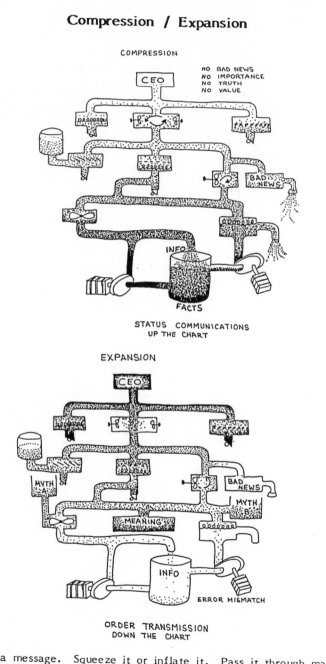

COMPRESSION

NO BAD NEWS
NO IMPORTANCE
NO TRUTH
NO VALUE

CEO

INFO

FACTS

STATUS COMMUNICATIONS
UP THE CHART

EXPANSION

CEO

MYTH A

BAD NEWS

MYTH B

MEANING

INFO

ERROR MISMATCH

ORDER TRANSMISSION
DOWN THE CHART

Take a message. Squeeze it or inflate it. Pass it through many converters. Assume error-free transmission. You just played Russian roulette with six bullets in the revolver. Bye.

Variety is measured by counting things related to the system and human limits constrain that process as well.   For instance, the spoken Onondaga language had unique words for individual integers up to about the number sixteen (many tribes provided words for no more than five).   All higher numbers were lumped into a single gesture for conversation which consisted of grabbing a handful of hair.   Whether there were twenty or two thousand Buffalo, the description was the same.   Counting hairs and discriminating among large numbers was considered a waste of time.   In our language, "a lot" often serves the same function.

The intrinsic complexity of communications builds exponentially with additions to the system (a fact we dependably fail to appreciate).   High complexity (variety) is managed by knowing applicable constraints.   The world is rich with constraints, some slight, some severe.   Intense constraints, like Livingston's Law, are your pals.   They reduce the possible variety in a system so you can count things and understand how it works.   Any object, animate or inanimate, is a constraint.   **Replace.**

Limitations of the hierarchy

The hierarchical organization structure is good at some kinds of information handling (vertical) for some kinds of situations (routine).   The hierarchy form is a good match for mass production in the same way as custom-built automation is best for the high volume assembly line.   The same structure, however, is a barrier to high fidelity **lateral** communications, which are necessary to handle non-routine situations that hit the hierarchy broadside.   For these situations, flexible programmable robots are the choice for the assembly line.

Since an individual can easily produce more information than he can absorb, even without computer assistance, there are major problems of screening, filtering, compressing (coding) and selecting information which is created. Policy rules for transmitting information are everywhere, but the rules for **choosing** information to be transmitted are at best sketchy and ambiguous, and at worst, nonexistent.   Added to an already chthonic situation is the common problem of information screening to remove items potentially threatening to the status of the communicator.   History shows, without variation, that bringing bad news to the King is an occupation which has little to recommend it.

RULE - It doesn't take many translations to lose the message.

In an organization with a steep hierarchical gradient, the translation problem exists also for downward communications.   When the big boss gives the order to increase sales, it is not at all obvious what that means at a departmental level. When the chief engineer then gives the order to create a new product line (to increase sales), it means a different thing to every member of his department. Lateral communication has the problem of traversing up and down the translations of a hierarchy to get from side to side and that route has obstacles of its own. Information costs and the lack of information to translate information costs even more.

The scope of activity and the amount of information that Orgman will process are quite constant, consistent and small.   At times you can even observe Orgman comparing the demand for more scope and information processing to his mental reference standards.   The more levels and rigidity in an organization, the smaller the span of responsibility that Orgman will assume.   The shrinkage process is accelerated when complexity strikes and the excess falls through the cracks until EOPMD.

Reorganization Triggers

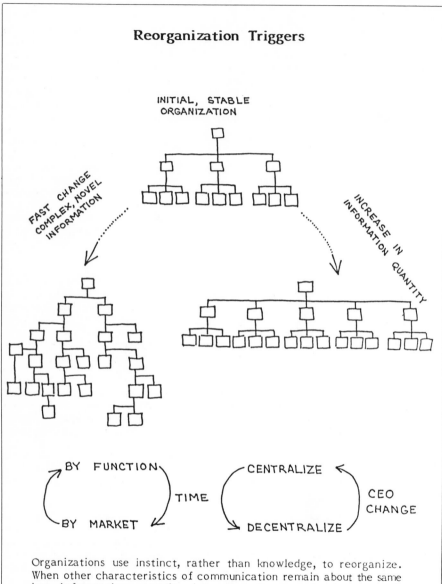

INITIAL, STABLE ORGANIZATION

FAST CHANGE COMPLEX, NOVEL INFORMATION

INCREASE IN INFORMATION QUANTITY

BY FUNCTION / BY MARKET) TIME

CENTRALIZE / DECENTRALIZE) CEO CHANGE

Organizations use instinct, rather than knowledge, to reorganize. When other characteristics of communication remain about the same but information quantity increases, the organization expands horizontally while its number of hierarchical levels stays the same. When messages to be communicated increase in novelty, change style often, or contain information not familiar to the recipients, the organization swells the number of hierarchical levels between the source of the novel information and its management. Time or a change in management, especially one brought in from the outside, switches from a corporate alignment by function to one by market category. Another switch is from centralized to decentralized administration and back again with a frequency directly proportional to organizational stress.

Once it is understood that the limiting factor in communications is the individual (the maximum self-integrated unit of human information processing capacity), understanding organizational communications is a matter of simple arithmetic. The serf and the squire alike can only intake 60 pages worth, or its equivalent, during a regular day. If the boss has six managers directly reporting to him, he can only deal with 10 pages, average, from each one. Even if the manager only generates as much as he absorbs, he still has the problem of compacting 60 pages down to 10 before transmission to the boss.

Routine matters compact very nicely. In those situations the boss can have many managers and still have time to spare. Novel, complicated matters, on the other hand, may not compact without grave damage to fidelity. When those conditions are sustained, another layer will be added, like clockwork, to the hierarchy. Now the boss has fewer managers to worry about and they are sending very compressed information - which is, invariably, less true and meaningful. The executive price to remain below 60 pages per day in input load and avoid the perception of stress (be within his span of control), is loss of control. However instinctive, it is a short-sighted expedient that fosters the very consequences it seeks to avoid.

RULE - The more information should be used in decision-making, the more decisions are based upon hearsay, prejudice and hunch.

Triggers that lead to reorganizations and other dysfunctions

When the situation is one of increasing information quantity rather than one of increasing novelty, the organization maintains the number of levels - but spreads out. In this case the compression ratios are good but there is just a lot of routine information. Compared to the seismic event of information novelty, quantity alone is a trivial problem. Organizations are unable to perceive or comprehend messages other than those referring to the machinery of their own activities. By knowing about the kinds and quantities of information flowing about the organization, flashes of madness (reorganizations) can be predicted with great accuracy. More importantly, when the complex problem enters the hierarchy it is easy to determine where the organization will go tilt. Knowing the innate schedule of organizational rearrangement, so that you can take advantage, or take cover, is one way to **have fun at work.**

There is an abundance of case histories about small companies that do great things. A young, dynamic concern is busy creating value to establish a niche, and information flows in all directions (non-hierarchical). People with tools and skills to solve problems are encouraged to do so directly, without a worry given to formality. The technical leadership in supercomputers, for example, was once lost to a company consisting of twenty-three people, including the janitor. Such loosely organized companies bring our innovations because they have not removed themselves very far from the great efficiency of hard-wired intracranial communications in the free individual. They form a Skunkworks.

There is a more abundant supply of case histories about the transformations that take place when the success of fledgling outfits leads to growth. It is well appreciated that, at a staff level of between 50 and 300 members, all hell breaks loose. Many companies and their founders do not survive the transition in organizational structure from amorphous to crystalline.

The trigger for shifts in organizational design is information variety in the form of communication traffic amounts and novelty content. If you have measures of the actual traffic in one hand and Shannon's theories of communication in the other, you can predict the whole affair. Changes to the organizational chart are always made by gut reaction. Instinct is the constraint that turns the variety possible into a pat formula.

The first element to examine is the intrinsic variety in communications as staff size increases. Viewing an individual communicator as a dot or node and each possible line of communication with others as a link or line, the number of links rises geometrically as the number of nodes rises linearly. Whereas the company founder can know enough about 200 individuals to make meaningful personal conversation as he chats along the production line, there is no way he can track all the communications chatter of the workers. Above 200 staff he can't even keep track of their names. To this must be added the variety of markets and the problems of a changing business environment.

"We tend to meet any new situation by reorganizing. And a wonderful method it can be of creating the illusion of progress while producing confusion, inefficiency and demoralization." Petronius Arbiter 50 BC.

There is nothing new about communities swelling to over 200 members, and through long experience, some taboos have evolved that take care of the problem rather nicely. For instance, the Mennonites practice the dogma of 400. When a local enclave of believers approaches 350, the congregation goes out and buys new land some distance away. When the ranks swell to 400, colonists designated among their numbers are sent away to the new territory to start another settlement. They have learned that people can not be well (comfortably) acquainted with more than 400 individuals and any time everyone doesn't know everyone else, clan life goes awry. This same lesson was first learned by the military over two thousand years ago.

As variety increases, the first triggered reaction of the organization is to impose a more disintegrated structure for itself, still in hierarchical form. In this arrangement only the CEO retains a link to every other node. A group on the tree that has unrestricted communication within the group (the primary working group) is called a leaf. This structure reduces variety in sanctioned communication channels to manageable proportions all right, but at a price. Except for leaves, information can legally flow only up or down. Not only does no one know all the problems, but only problems fitting within the tiny province of a leaf (as delineated by the organization) are allowed to be solved directly. Thus, only toy problems can be solved.

The tree expedient is, at best, extremely error-prone. Translations are notoriously imperfect. Each ecosystem of the organization has its own language and there are no perfect translators. Original meanings are lost and new meanings are injected, and the organizational chart contains many junctions of translation. For those few cases that make the effort, a fidelity assurance procedure to detect and correct errors is also error-prone. Unfortunately, the steps taken to reduce apparent variety, ostensibly to enable managerial control, create a structure that, by its very design, destroys control. No wonder we have great difficulties in understanding interdisciplinary relationships. The human DNA design software for organizing is still programmed for isolated tribes consisting of less than fifty individuals.

RULE - When in doubt, reorganize. The frequency of reorganizing is directly proportional to the domain of doubt.

Human limits in handling complexity by instinct

Complexity influences show up in various repositories. In the computer software zoo there is an established index of complexity (developed by McCabe) that measures the complication of a particular software program. Years of experience with the quantitative measure has identified the equivalent of a handful of hair. As the complexity index of a piece of software goes from one to about ten, the error rate in that software is low and constant. In other words, for comprehensible software, the chance of incorporating errors in the code is the same. Five pages of code will contain five times as many errors as one page.

At a complexity index of ten or more, the rate of error generation in software suddenly jumps much higher. Twenty pages of complex code will contain a hundred times as many errors as two pages. The software is no longer understandable or testable, and control by the designer is lost. The loss of control, seldom recognized as such, can cause considerable mischief downstream and usually does. Software that cannot be understood by its designer is not going to be understood at any other niche in the organization. Like Frankenstein, such designers become casualties of their own creation. Common stuff.

RULE - Faith in a solid base for predictions is a conspicuous feature of influential representatives of the technical trade, who always know it is a lie.

A manager of a primary working group has control limits that cannot be extended through increased managerial competence. If he devotes less than about 20% of his time to keeping up with the work of a subordinate, he will not have much influence on what the subordinate actually does. If all the manager did was to interact with subordinates, he could theoretically be in control of the work of five individuals. Above these nominal limits, whether he likes it or not, he cannot handle the communication variety, and autonomy is delegated by default.

When groups are messing with a complex problem, managers have very little technical knowledge about what is going on. Such loss of control, unrecognized, does not always lead to remedial action. Also, forming new branches of the hierarchy does not automatically lead to a recapture of control. Instincts provide extremely poor organizations and by denying feedback, there is no natural correcting mechanism. Bad.

The painful lesson is that conventional human expedients to cope with high variety communications do not reduce the variety. They do, rather, introduce new constraints, unnoted and temporarily obscure. Through awareness of the arithmetic of organizational communications, the reactions of the organization to upsets of the equilibrium can be predicted with great accuracy. There is a mechanical lawfulness to these seemingly random events.

RULE - If you think they are acting strangely, what you have detected is a difference between their reference mental model set and yours. Acting contrary to the reference is extremely rare.

Count & Account

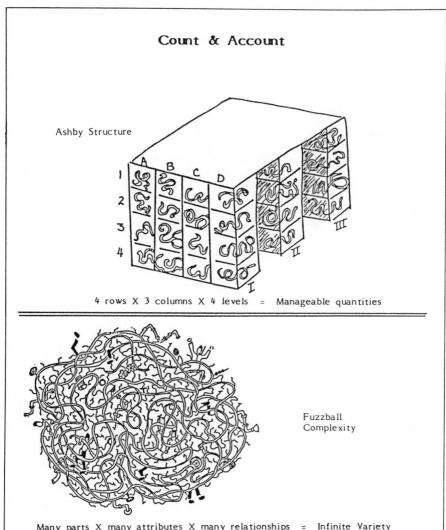

Ashby Structure

4 rows X 3 columns X 4 levels = Manageable quantities

Fuzzball
Complexity

Many parts X many attributes X many relationships = Infinite Variety

Ashby's Law is suspended for no one. There is no place to hide.
Since it can't be avoided, it is best to face the law head-on.
Cosmic variety is assaulted with structures which contain no more
compartments than can be understood by an individual. Structures
come with ground-rules and definitions for each compartment so that
chunks of variety can be assigned to their proper containers. The
first use of the structure is to count the variety and make sure it's
all there on the racks. Empty cubicles act as pointers to round up
any variety that got away. After counting, there are many ways to
account for the variety in each niche. Building knowledge about
variety is the foundation for success.

HAVE FUN AT WORK

Understanding human limits in the context of information handling and communications defines the limits of the organization to deal with a given situation. If you know the dimensions of the communication system related to a situation, you have begun to understand the situation as well as the organizational dysfunctions it will cause. This tool is a winner. **Replace.**

Count and account structures for coping with variety

Structure is essential for measuring complexity in quantitative terms. For instance, if there is going to be a battle, it is very helpful to know the strength of the adversary in detail and in advance. In warfare, providing a table of the enemy arsenal may be tough but it can be done and understood. The major parts, like rifles and tanks, can be counted and listed. Some parts, like bullets, have big numbers but not many varieties. In complex problem matters, the number of unique states is intimidating. Cosmic quantities of unique states are inherent in complex systems and they cause organizational D&D. That's why we call them complex.

Cosmic variety in complex systems is a fact of life. If the variety is not accounted for, it does not evaporate. It lies in ambush waiting for its time. The language of success warns us to **count** the variety, regardless of its enormity, as a requisite step to **account** for the variety.

Small or large, human faculties are notoriously unreliable with extreme numbers. At the tiny end, the usual reference is a strand of hair (one thousandth of an inch). Hair fails as a reference when physicists ask us to comprehend vast open spaces between the nucleus and the orbiting electrons in the atom of an element. Today, science can see into the small in the same magnitude relationship we have with our Milky Way galaxy. For most of us, the high end doesn't exceed a handful of thousands (ten thousand parts can be counted between coffee breaks). We hear "billions and billions of stars" from Carl Sagan, without the faintest grasp of what that means.

RULE - When they talk about the very small or the very big, they can't comprehend it either.

The example called "Caesar's Last Breath" better helps to convey the immensity of large numbers. While the Earth's atmosphere is vast, so is the number of molecules in your breath. With each one you take, you inhale a single molecule of the same air exhaled by Julius when he was assassinated.

Our given mental machinery is considerably worse at geometric progressions and the rapidity of exponential growth. We count physical items as one each and overlook the fact that every interconnection counts one each also. As legend has it, the Indian King Shirham used typical human intuition when he wished to reward the Grand Vizier Sissa Ben Dahir for inventing chess, a game played on a board with 8 rows by 8 columns of squares. When Sissa merely asked for a geometric progression of wheat on the chessboard starting with a single grain (to be placed on the first square, then two on the next, four on the next, etc.), Shirham called him a fool and granted the wish.

The Territorial Imperative

Instincts about territory run deep. There is only so much land and not everyone can have all he wants. When tribes remain on their own territory, order is the result. When tribal territory is violated, big troubles begin. For matters of practical living, and there is only so much of that, activity territory is deeded to guilds just as if it were physical land. There can be no overlaps in assigned activity any more than the same land can be deeded to two owners without a shootout. The only activity turf left for new guilds is air-rights. Specialties which claim to diddle with multi-guild matters build their edifices on abstraction. To avoid violating turf, they can only solve abstract problems. Meanwhile, Rome burns.

Things went on track for the king's intuition until about the thirtieth square when he noticed that the wagon trips bringing in grain from the royal stores were more frequent. Before the fortieth square was reached, the nation was out of wheat. Sufficient grain to fulfill the wish through 64 squares will cover the surface of the earth to the depth of an inch. So much for majestic intuition.

The variety in complexity often works the same way because of the interdependencies. Things go well up to, for instance, the equivalent of the twenty-fifth square (only a 5x5 array). Then the next element to include drives the variety, not from one grain to two (which we can easily appreciate), but clear out of comprehension. The behavior indicator of overload is borborygmus and D&D, signalling the end of reason and free fall to gut reaction. The language of success displaces gut reactions that are known to be grossly inaccurate and unreliable. Outside of tribal life on the bountiful savannah, not many instincts are good decision-makers. While man does well with linear relationships and their superposition, he is naturally incompetent with non-linear matters. Structure tells us what to do when we only know we are in a situation where our instincts betray us.

The software shop in one Wall Street brokerage house has established a popular quantitative index (memory size) for signalling a mismatch between the ability to cope and the demand. The measure is used to size up an issue as well as the brain space currently available to deal with it by an individual. There are simple problems, like working out vacation schedules, which get a rating of 1K. Tough problems, like keeping up with the Chicago Board of Trade, can be ranked above 20K. When approached with a problem, the recipient states his current available memory space.

At the end of a hard day, bringing a 20K problem to a person warning of only 3K available saves the situation. It is quick feedback at the best possible level. At that time, the choice is either to chop the topic down to 3K size or save it for tomorrow - no hard feelings. This practice is a working example of using the language of success and a great tool to **have fun at work**.

The Territorial Imperative

During those hundreds of thousands of years on the East African savannah, where the evolution process had enough time to do some serious remodeling, tribes were limited in size and turf by the top priority value they placed upon the meat of large animals. The cooperative male hunting band handled the problem of killing large game, including competing carnivores. They also had the job of carrying the meat back to the families. This set the hunting range from home to about eight miles. In abundant animal times, which was most of the time during that era, contact with adjoining tribes was infrequent.

Territory represented a food supply. Maintaining control of an area which could supply the tribe with meat was necessary for survival. The territorial imperative (TI), the strong, instinctive association of humans to their domain, has long roots. Few people adequately appreciate the intensity of the TI. It is so basic to human nature, it is taken for granted.

Law, being what law is, has always sided with the territorial imperative. When you are in your home, and that turf is under attack, real or perceived, you may consider yourself in a sanctuary from which you need not further retreat. It is the **one** issue lawyers do not debate. If you are in the park and a gang of thugs comes after you, you are expected to make every effort to flee. If these same dudes break into your home, you can empty your Uzi with impunity. Held territory, when deeded by society, is a sanctuary with considerable community benefits. As such, the instincts to defend and control territory are far more deeply rooted in the brain than the neocortex. The reptile brain is the custodian of that program. Give it great respect. It is one of the tools for having fun at work. If you can get anything in the reptile brain's program library going for you, you have it made.

The territorial imperative at work at work

The territorial imperative explains much in the workings of the organization. It is the territory of the primary working group, the tiny microcosm of the corporation, that is the sanctuary for the individual. Walls and moats are erected around groups, not individuals. We often call these elemental groups "cloisters" to remind us about turf sanctity.

RULE - When they say "get off my land," they mean it!

Turf that is a sanctuary for you, if you want to retain the deed, must be defended against intruders. The door swings both ways, however. When you are in someone else's territory, you must behave as a visitor. The only reward you can expect as an outsider, if you act out-of-line to house rules, is banishment. You set the rules in your home and they set the rules in theirs. The rules can be in direct conflict. It is not whether or not your intrusion is helpful, but it is the intrusion itself that is forbidden. In other words, no meaningful help can be accepted from outside the group - by instinct. It is why no good deed goes unpunished.

The territorial imperative has the unfortunate propensity to take poor situations and promptly make them ludicrous. The population can be on the docks dying of starvation and the customs department will not allow food to be unloaded from the ships until two weeks of routine paperwork has been processed. The TI ranks close to the top of the motivational ladder. In corporate life, we do not know its equal.

Modern society provides all kinds of examples of the TI at work. One favorite is the perennial discovery that academia and industry do not interact. They certainly don't. Some sort of convocation is then arranged by the discoverers of this terrible oversight and moguls from both sides are invited. After everyone is through extolling the virtues and benefits of mutual cooperation, they all go home and forget the whole thing.

Like corporations, universities don't even interact with themselves. This fact is on public display every time the university teaches a 'systems' course. Since there can be no recognized systems territory, the expedient is to hold the students in a fixed position while the twig-of-science representatives are rotated, merry-go-round fashion, across the lectern. To show the many dimensions of a "system," such as hydraulics and chemistry, the students are exposed, in sequence and with enough time interval so that one professor can get out of the building before the other arrives, to a civil engineer and then an alchemist. Of course, each recites only the narrow specialized set of knowledge in custodial protection of his guild.

The vital interactions among the dimensions of the system, the essence of systems thinking, are taught by no one. That critical issue is left as an assignment for the students. The only message that gets through to the pupils is that the territory of systems thinking is a social No Man's Land. It is. You can get hurt there. Meanwhile the **need** for systems thinking, and systems-based doing, rises.

RULE - Everyone knows about systems problems. They are the ones which are not recognized until it is too late.

With the determined coercion of an appropriate maverick, some universities condone a tiny (always tiny) systems department. This shows another side to the territorial imperative: where territory-intruding functionalities are allowed to exist without persecution, they are only given deeds in blue-sky land. Social territory has both area and elevation. The area on the earth's surfaces constitutes the practical world that makes things like parts for automobiles. Elevation, or blue-sky land, opens up unlimited territory that is not otherwise related to the real-world terrain, and will thereby be uncontested. Elevations rise above the reach of criticism. The systems man can ridicule the telephone repairman for inferior service, but the electrician doesn't even know what systems freaks do.

The systems department is socially licensed only in so far as it remains aloof from reality, develops a corpus of knowledge that does not intrude on any other abstract territory already occupied, and never attempts to apply its stuff to university operations. And so it is. The guild which espouses system can **appear** to intrude upon other established territory, but as a matter of course, the guild can dwell only in its private abstract. The systems department remains decoupled from the very real-world issues over which it claims a governing influence. The blue-sky land rule was given a trial.

THE BLUE SKY RULE - Things cloud up fast when you cross territorial borders.

A test of the Territorial Imperative in complex problem-solving

In 1987, the Quality Assurance Institute (Orlando, FL) produced a conference on "Quality Assurance in the Healthcare Industry." Quality assurance (QA) is a blood relation to systems engineering. The conference organizers and speakers were from the ranks of the systems community. Applications of systems technology to the horrible problems of health-care QA was the main theme. We obtained a spot on the program thanks to the foresight of Bill Perry, Director of the institute.

Long before the convention, we located a nurse with impeccable credentials and wide experience in clinical practice to participate in the experiment. The professional nurse was gradually exposed to the systems world, and in several months a practical application of systems practice (the Design for Complexity) was mapped onto the hospital QA fiasco. Several specifics were developed. The nurse, now familiar with both the language of systems and the world of medicine, prepared her presentation.

The people who attended the conference were from the middle ranks of the health-care industry. Most came from hospitals. When the systems gurus attempted to put the world of systems thinking into focus for the medical practitioners, mismatches of language and concept became readily apparent. For two long days the pattern was the same: the lecture material was met with silence, and speakers and audience alike wondered, "Why am I here?"

155

The Shuttle Craft

The territorial imperative is the prime directive for man and it stands directly in his own way to solve problems that spill over many borders. An effective expedient must respect the condition. The winning design is the skunkworks shuttle. Skunkworks claim no territory at all and do not call for a violation of territory. A temporary, mobile band without role distinctions and rank, the skunkworks shuttles between the theories of systems and reality, acting as guests wherever they dock. Practical application of relevant systems doctrines solves complex problems, nothing else.

The nurse ringer implant, meanwhile, was relating as a peer with the other attendees during coffee breaks and interacting with the systems freaks in their own language during the lectures. No other attendee could even figure out the topic. The conference-goers wanted to listen in their own language to the presentation of quick-fix solutions. But they complained of getting a bunch of "theoretical nonsense" about viable systems models. The nurse defused the situation by informally assuring the audience that she would fill the relevancy vacuum.

By the last day, the day for the ringer, the dissention towards the systems speakers had gotten so far out of hand that all parallel sessions of the conference were cancelled to allow everyone, systems and healthcare specialists alike, to hear the nurse. The presentation was superb. A workable process, in systems form, was presented in the language of the medical world by one of its own, in familiar details that could not be misunderstood. The experiment itself was executed on plan and it was time to record the results.

The reaction, as predicted, was immediate and clear. The systems freaks, astonished at what had just taken place, could not fathom the violation of territory. Imagine, actually doing what was preached! The nurses, also stunned by the experience, could not believe that a person could at the same time be a professional nurse, be conversant with so abstract a subject, and dare to make the abstract practical for nursing (intruding on turf). The result was, of course, that the nurse was, from the moment of joining the two domains and thereafter, socially excommunicated by both sides. The significance of the problem of quality health care didn't matter. In comparison to the implied violation of the territorial imperative (an unforgivable sin), all else is picayune. The visitors from Duke University even went through legal proceedings to recover the conference fee.

It is important to recognize that had the nurse dwelled within one regime or the other, she would have received applause oblivious to the value of the material, which only could have avoided the vital issue. The conference would have been merely considered a waste of time and quickly forgotten. The demonstration of territory violation, however, required the highest expressions of outrage - especially because it was **practical** and could have been executed by anyone there back at home base. The point is that complex problems, like hospital QA, **require** the coordination (read violation) of territory in order to accomplish the slightest good at all.

Orgman speaks: The genetic policy for Territorial Imperative issues in the organization is simple. For entities that **espouse** systems integration, check that they are sufficiently abstract (blue-sky) and take credit for advanced thinking in forming them. As long as they remain impractical, reward them with a modest place in the establishment - and religiously disregard their efforts. Trans-territorial entities that reside directly on the surface of reality, such as quality assurance and training, must be crippled and overpowered. See to it that they are understaffed and under-funded, intimidate them with promises of punishment for any interference with normal business, and sabotage any efforts that might do good.

POSIWID #2

When all the rhetoric of defense fades away, the purpose of any
social system is still what it does. The purpose of the World Bank
and the International Monetary Fund, for example, is to burden
their targets with money and explicit instructions on how to spend
it. The benefactors remain studiously ignorant of prevailing
complexities and Ashby, so the injection of capital brings starvation
and economic ruin to their clients. These agencies consume only
one billion dollars a year to generate more human suffering than
the Pentagon manages to deliver with a budget of 300 billion dollars
a year. Now that's cost effectiveness!

HAVE FUN AT WORK

RULE - Thou shalt not trespass on fenced domain.

Without such chains, any trans-departmental entity can usurp the power of management. We know one company where the dominant organizational force resides with the clerk of the warehouse, who knows more about the production process than anyone there. No one can get parts without his approval. At another site, no activity dares to proceed without the blessing of the efficiency engineer, including those with direct orders from the president. Arrange a prominent place in your have-fun toolbox for the territorial imperative. In a later Chapter, you are encouraged to develop your skills with it.

Feedback and POSIWID

Like the TI, feedback is a main girder for your replacement reference mental structures. The significance of feedback can not be over-emphasized. Through a DNA design glitch, organizations are able take advantage of a hidden control switch, provided without your consent, in your cranium. The switch allows the vital feedback function to operate in some situations, and shuts it off for others. The threshold setpoint rule is simple. If the issue is a slight excursion from routine practice, feedback is encouraged. The organization may even run a contest, for instance, to select the best candidate for the new safety slogan. The employee who suggests a better packing material for the product may even get a reward.

RULE - As long as all the practices and all vested interests in jobs remain the same, feedback is welcome.

Appropriately drugged with feedback trivial pursuit, we fail to notice that this prime directive of nature has been violated for the topics that really matter. Don't think that the barrier imposed to feedback is just another item on the long list of constraints to organizational life. It is a tyrant with enormous implications. Let "them" impede your task with other constraints, like paperwork, but never let them tinker with feedback. It is the essence of how we learn.

The Purpose Of a System Is What It Does - POSIWID

The protective shield for feedback is the 'law' expounded by Stafford Beer, and it is a sleeper. Give it time to grow on you. At first it will shock the old mental models you have not yet erased from the Bad Seventies. Like any law, denial will not make it go away. POSIWID is your friend.

Never look at an existing animate system from the front end. Never, ever. Hide your eyes when they show you the policy manual. Flee when they recite the great mission statement. Instead, go to the back end and work your way up towards the middle. The real purpose of the social system will have been illuminated before you get to the first line of supervision.

When wreckage relentlessly appears at the loading dock, the purpose may be to make wreckage or, more kindly, it may be an inherent effect from a higher-level purpose. When rework occupies half the factory, the purpose may be to make jobs. When 25% of **all** illness is caused by the industry ostensibly devoted to the restoration of wellness (iatrogenic diseases like nosocomial infections), the purpose may be to increase business. When regulations are not enforced, the purpose may be to protect the regulated from competition.

The purpose structure of an organization can make radical changes, but they are rarely for the better and usually for the worse. In one pathological scenario, illuminated by POSIWID, the sequence starts with the persistent violation of national laws by a particular institution in a heavily regulated industry. When the 'regulator can not excuse the extreme deviations from the norm any longer, the offending facility is ordered closed. Consultants are brought in. The next step involves radical surgery of the target organization. New levels in the hierarchy are added at the top and new managers are hired from the outside to occupy them. The new recruits immediately hire more consultants.

This move bifurcates the organization into two cultural groups. The new guard in the power positions, waving the reports of their consultants, invokes a new culture (always with the word excellence somewhere included) by fiat. Executive orders notwithstanding, the old guard at the controls of the facility retains the culture they had. From that point on, the purpose of the organization changes, from whatever productive function it was established to perform, to maximize effectiveness at civil war. What the old guard does, is to do everything in its power, which is considerable, to make the new hired guns look bad. The purpose of the new guard is to secure their beach head and disenfranchise the established groups - sparing no expense to the inherited institution.

RULE - No issue unifies independent corporate departments more than an external threat to the status quo.

We are eyewitnesses to three independent expositions of this behavioral trajectory, now in progress, all following identical paths but offset in launch time. The institutions at stake are huge and the amount being wasted in the civil wars is incredible. They are systematically and inexorably destroying their own organization's in full view. The commitment to corporate suicide is a most horrible affair. Human debris is everywhere.

The wreckage of this scenario includes a regulator organization that failed to achieve the results intended from its powers of enforcement, a regulated corporation that is dramatically and permanently worse than it was when the penalty was applied, and many billions of dollars wasted. The espoused purposes have achieved **only** the very consequences they sought to avoid. The only thing the regulator can do is to impose more penalties and escalate the wreckage. POSIWID keeps the shipping lanes of feedback open. Otherwise the sea is boiling and the moon has turned to blood. It is stress city.

When feedback has been disconnected by the temple priests, situations like this are much more likely to develop. Without feedback, there is no compensating mechanism for errors. Many tolerable errors have the unfortunate tendency to manufacture situations that reinforce and escalate the error. Escalated errors have the habit of locking-in and developing an immunity to remedies that normally have a beneficial effect. In these cases, the restoration of feedback comes too late. Feedback is preventive medicine, not a crisis cure. Feedback is your benevolent companion for fun at work.

It is important to note the Establishment disdain for history (as a primary form of feedback). As historians have ventured into areas other than praising Establishment heroes, they have found their numbers decreasing. When a balanced account of major events is presented, unsuspecting historians find their financial support withdrawn. Showing that the Establishment does not learn from their disasters is a ticket to some form of punishment. POSIWID teaches that a fundamental value system is on display here which goes "We have the system we want. There is no point to learning about reasons to change it. Don't rock the boat." This lesson is much more than a curiosity. It is marking a clear danger, as well as a waste of time, to pontificate change to the social power structure.

Ashby's Law of Necessary Variety

The long excavation to locate conceptual bedrock for the language of success ended at W. Ross Ashby's Law of Necessary Variety. With Lord Ashby, we no longer have to worry about going further down through the midden heaps of assumptions. Ashby's Law occupies the throne of the **have fun at work** palace.

Ashby's "Law of Necessary Variety" states that in order to achieve control of a system, animate of inanimate, the control means must be able to deal with whatever conditions the system can exhibit.

Embedded in this statement are ordinary words with extensive meanings. The key words include **control, conditions, can exhibit,** and **system.** Traversing the law in reverse order, "can exhibit" means literally "all possible." It doesn't mean to stop counting the conditions when the thermometer reaches "all intended" or at "all likely." It pertains to **all** possible conditions that are enabled by virtue of the design of the system. We subdivide "all" into two categories - intended, and contingency (unintended). Ashby himself explains this feature of his law with "Only variety can destroy variety."

People have great anxiety about the concept of contingencies (they are undiscussable until after they happen). For instance, most steam-driven electric generating power plants have great big pipes for conveying some river water to carry away waste heat. The pipes are so large that trucks can pass through them when they are empty. The water is pushed through these huge pipes into and through the basement of a large building by powerful pumps. When the warmed water emerges out of the building on its way back (through more big pipes) to the river as intended, the pumps are called, appropriately enough, circulating water pumps.

Inside of this building the pipes are fitted with rubber booties so that things can jiggle around without breakage (unfortunately they didn't start off with that idea). Every now and then, these flexible sections blow up (one of the "can exhibits"). When they do, the big pumps keep sending water down the big pipes to the building basement, where it collects. And collects. During this contingency period, since they aren't circulating water any more, the name of the big pumps is changed to the "building pool-filler pumps." Actually the pumps do a great job in their new function and, in short order, turn the building into the largest indoor swimming pool in the county. In the event of a flood, the pumps could be called the "river level reduction pumps."

RULE - "Intendeds" are what you wanted when you bought the system, "contingencies" are what happens when you use it. Results are what you expect, consequences are what you get.

Ashby Control

FOR THE VARIETY OF CONDITIONS
THE SYSTEM CAN EXHIBIT.......

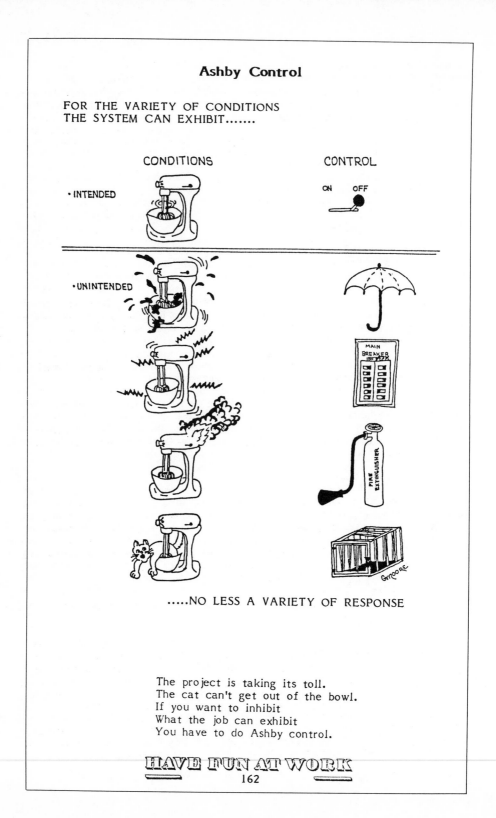

CONDITIONS   CONTROL

• INTENDED

• UNINTENDED

.....NO LESS A VARIETY OF RESPONSE

The project is taking its toll.
The cat can't get out of the bowl.
If you want to inhibit
What the job can exhibit
You have to do Ashby control.

More Ashby definitions

Condition means status. **Conditions** means unique states. Your car may cruise down the freeway at a constant speed for a long time and that would be only one state. Every change of speed entails passing through many conditions uniquely describable one from the other. Even at the same velocity, system states can vary depending upon which gear is being used to hold the speed. Complex systems have many, many possible states. Zillions.

The meaning of **control** has to do with keeping the productive system intact and functioning within defined, intended state boundaries. Control includes control means for contingencies, like the pool-filling pump episode, as well as control for making a product within specifications with all of the system parts intact. Stafford Beer explains this aspect of Ashby's law with "Only variety in the control system can deal with variety in the system controlled." To have control by Ashby's definition, is no mean feat.

RULE - Complicated problems sire complicated governments.

There are two kinds of control objectives, physiological and operational. Physiological goals of control (as a joined subsystem) are simply to endure and to persist. There are basic needs and consumables involved in just having the system around. Organizations need physiological support also (that means that somebody has to keep paying the wages). One way to stop an organization from spreading its havoc, suggested by Parkinson, is to curtail its income until it withers away.

Once the basic support needs are met, operational goals are to prevail over the environment and get the purposive job done over a range of conditions. In a manufacturing company, this means to create the product to specifications of quantity, quality and price. Organizationally this means, "Now that order is established, start the production line."

Variety measurement

Structure is the vehicle that enables us to make progress in waging peace with the unfathomable. In complex systems, the degree of unfathomability at the finish is little reduced from the unfathomability at the outset. Often the complexity of the solution system is more complex than the problem. The definition of stress as an individual mental state obtained from comparing your ability to cope (your control system variety) to the demands made on you (situation variety), is another expression of Ashby's law.

RULE - Embrace all natural laws. Honor those in particular which the Establishment tries to slight.

System variety is so high that coping structures are needed just to begin comprehension. Consider a 8x10 array of light bulbs. Each light can be in a state of on or off. To enumerate the variety inherent in this array would take a computer, performing one billion calculations per second, the entire age of the universe to complete the job of listing possible states. This sets a **boundary condition** because a system which exhibits unique states that cannot be enumerated in possible time cannot be completely understood. A new identification strategy for credit cards is based upon the same principle (there are so many connected states possible that only the "key" can bring order). In the real world, variety becomes unfathomable at much lower levels.

163

Variety

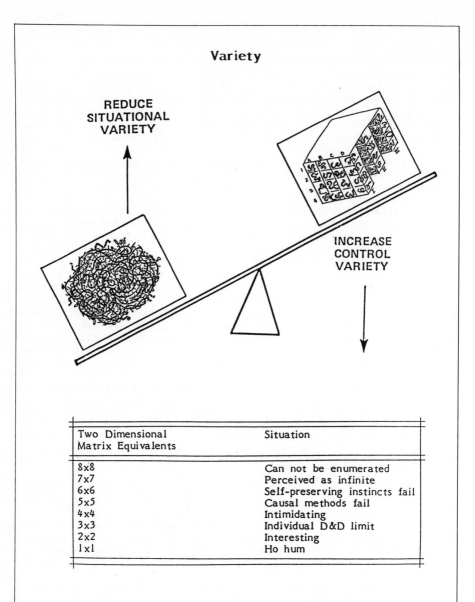

REDUCE SITUATIONAL VARIETY

INCREASE CONTROL VARIETY

Two Dimensional Matrix Equivalents	Situation
8x8	Can not be enumerated
7x7	Perceived as infinite
6x6	Self-preserving instincts fail
5x5	Causal methods fail
4x4	Intimidating
3x3	Individual D&D limit
2x2	Interesting
1x1	Ho hum

The issue of variety the system can exhibit compared to variety in the control system (to inhibit the variety of the purposive system) is what is at stake whenever two basketball teams take the floor. The purpose of each team is to show the other more variety (moves) in plays than the opposition has variety in control (defense). As the ball changes sides, the goal quickly shifts from exhibiting variety (offense) to inhibiting variety (defense). Should one team have a large advantage over the other, the game is boring. When everything is in balance, you have an infinite number of overtime periods. The variety that can be displayed by two teams of five players is so large that it can not be enumerated.

RULE - However complex you imagine daily life to be, it's much more complicated than that.

Consider the variety in the possible composition of a football team actually appearing in the stadium at game time. Since the number of players on a given day could vary from zero to the full squad, the variety exceeds the daily printing capacity of the world to list the unique rosters that could be fielded. In practice, the program lists the full squad and the announcer identifies the missing. The cosmic variety is hidden from our perceptions. Ordinary intuition fails, and fails by huge margins, to credit the real degree of complexity that surrounds us.

Importantly, this conceptual yardstick (variety measurement) also defines what technical tools have a chance to be effective. Above the limit where causal methods (what an action in one element does to the others) must fail by virtue of sheer quantities, methods which depend upon an examination of each state can be eliminated. The language of success includes keeping book on the variety in the technical system and its inseparable companion, the social system. You cannot ignore the natural law of necessary variety and expect to **have fun at work**.

Ashby's law, although several decades old, is mentioned sporadically in a few academic circles and avoided in all others. Taken by itself, Ashby's law is easy to understand. It is usually accepted as sensible and self-evident. Nevertheless, Ashby is routinely placed on the shelf and forgotten in a classic D&D maneuver. Ashby's law forces an extended confrontation with the true complexity of the system and runs roughshod over human instincts. As the foundation of the language of success, it is a pillar in the reference structures for having fun at work.

We have found the law to be so basic and palmy that it is applied as a matter of course. Whether physical systems or computer software systems, whether institutional systems or managers as systems, Ashby's law and its derivatives do the trick. It is most interesting that such a dominant, natural law would be ignored by the Establishment. Natural laws are inert to social deceit. Measures of complexity help to distinguish between simple and not-simple on an objective basis.

This Chapter was devoted to presenting and discussing basic tools to **have fun at work**. Just like the dilemma facing the curator of a museum, the tools can be exhibited together by category or they can be shown in application context in a diorama. We chose both forms. The diorama form is presented in the next Chapter.

Design For Complexity

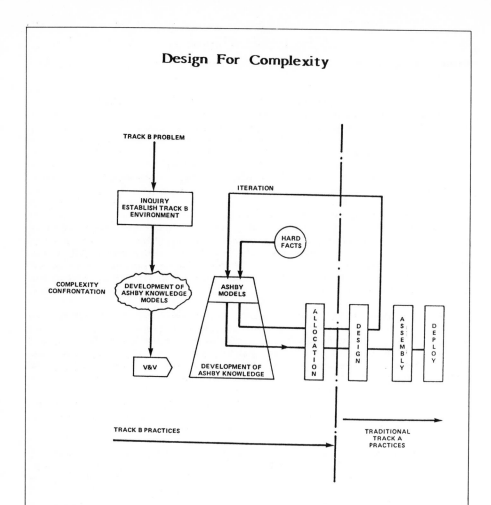

This roadmap covers the major sections of the DfC that deal with the technical system. The procedure features short cycle RBF with a good model of the system as the vehicle to exercise the system before it is materialized. System knowledge is developed through a rigorous structure applied to the models especially adapted for unintended conditions the system can exhibit. The DfC process has been around for years and is applied to software (FUBAR) as well as hardware (SIPOD) systems. The DfC explores system behavior as a support function to, not as a replacement of, the system design process. The DfC only performs functions that are omitted by the typical project, stopping at the border of knowledge building.

Chapter Eleven

All aboard for Track B

This is the most "technical" Chapter in the book. While we do not expect every reader to be comfortable with the material, it will be helpful for you to inspect part the process that **has** to go on to solve a complex problem. A successful methodology that intuitively appeals to anyone whose perspective does not extend beyond the range of desk calculators does not exist. Since becoming competent to **have fun at work** is a problem linked to gaining competency with complexity, there is no alternative. Knowledge must be translated into abilities to solve problems, which then develops into competence. An outline of the approach is provided for reference and a diorama is presented to show the first stage of the drawn-out process.

The Design for Complexity (DfC), also known as Track B, and its environment, more widely known as the Skunkworks, is a prescription for solving a complex problem - any complex problem. The fact that Track B works so well is assurance enough that Track B is suitable, potent magic to avoid the complexity hangover. Experience shows that propaedeutic nuances hardly matter to those stricken with the complex project affliction.

RULE - The integration of any large-problem project is an illusion created by the many independent activities which have agreed to cooperate on only one temporary expedient: to fly in close formation.

The DfC provides a framework on which complex matters may be ordered, related and understood. Whether the complexity is an inanimate system of pipes and pumps or an organization in crisis, the principles remain valid. The concepts of designing, building, testing, constructing, and maintaining a system share a common property. The act of creating a system is an act of **communication** from the designer to the system designed. The designer functions as a regulator, an error-controlled regulator, selecting and arranging particular solutions out of the many available. Note that designers (regulators) are chosen by a selection process involving another regulator. Communication theory applies across the board.

For the solution of a complex problem, there is only one success model. It's not in any management book, to be sure, because management is dedicated to the preservation of the familiar model for mediocrity and failure. The special Skunkworks environment is occasionally touted in "excellence" books, but in them you won't find any tools and structures for systems. Solutions to technical systems problems abound in engineering manuals, but the only twig of science that supports its own weight in social systems problems is, of all things, cultural anthropology.

RULE - Natural human instincts are unable to interpret the dynamic, non-linear, complex multi-loop systems of which humans have now become components as well as major contributors.

The DfC is a methodology based upon governing principles, natural laws, and standard innovation that is shaped to suit a specific complex problem. It is a prescription for innovation of a special kind which leaves the organization essentially as it was found - minus one complex problem. We have no magic bullet for higher order institutional dysfunctions per se, and no suggestions will be found here to bring sensible, rational behavior to the organization on a permanent basis. History has been pretty clear on the hazards of that ambition.

The normal, expected approach at this point would be to show off "the solution." We could go the usual technical-fix route with case studies, graphs, charts, calculations, savings and encomiastic testimonials. The academic fiction for rational review teaches that if substantial proofs were presented, cool heads would prevail and remedy would follow. Through experience, we have learned that such strategy is a front-door trap. The natural intelligence of man got him into this mess in the first place. Do not think that reflex reasoning will get him out of it. Impartial logic is precisely the ingredient that is missing.

RULE - If the road to Hell is paved with good intentions, then its furnaces are fueled by the cool heads of reflex action.

It is fun for others, like yourself, to work in the DfC environment. The atmosphere is filled with happy chatter and productivity, and opportunities for personal growth are abundant. There is a welcome sense of pride in work. But it is not often fun to lead the DfC, to be a practitioner. The point man must be an outsider possessed of a set of thick psychological armor.

We tune in on the DfC spectacle in order to show you that the practitioner works with the same tools you will use to **have fun at work.** The practitioner requires more structural tools than are found in your toolbox, but everything you will use, he uses. He wants to prevail too.

It is the outside practitioner (popularly known as the damn fool) who is responsible for making the prescription work. Heading up the job of solving a complex problem is not for Orgman. To the xenophobic salariat, the DfC is absolute gibberish. Corporate insiders (mavericks) can certainly provide the necessary practitioner functions as well as any outsiders, but they can't survive the escalating punishment of censorious social control. No member of an organization can be considered a good employee while he is advocating disorder in place of entrenched practices. Those deviants must be promptly punished. Like the Hollywood stunt man, the practitioner has tools and tricks to reduce the risk in the job down to reasonable levels. The key to his tool crib is to be an outsider.

The biggest hurdle of all is to get organizational entry. For problems of imprimatur and access, systems engineering technology is a barren desert. The unbroken string of failure is a tribute to the effectiveness of the corporate defenses from front door assaults. Inaccessible to the logic of its own needs, the organization is militant towards any motion which comes close to the mark. There are some enclaves in the USA that solicit clients laden with complex problems for treatment. They have credentials on top of credentials and feature a procedural gimmick, like Warfield's concensus methodology for allocation (which is excellent), for complex matters. The record shows little corporate interest in systems help for their disastrous projects. POSIWID comes to the rescue once again. The front door approach doesn't work.

There are no known side-doors either. Livingston's Law explains that the organization in dire need, when exposed to a control signal ("Let's get professional help"), will make matters worse while quenching the control signal generator. The lengthy, laborious process described in Chapter 14 is the only way devised which can arrange for practitioner entry. Unfortunately, it must be done by insiders. That is, we know of no procedure by which an outsider can get access to an organization through logic and credentials. One necessary ingredient seems to be a large ration of luck.

Overview of the Design for Complexity

The technical paradigm of the Design for Complexity is based upon Ashby, system practices such as model-building, structured knowledge building, and the process of innovation. Ashby knowledge is developed from bedrock in increasingly comprehensive stages with each layer connected to, and dependent upon, the layers that precede it. The ground rule for control of cohesiveness and validity, as one stage is attached to the work of another, is called scrutable connectivity. Everything is scrutable back to the Ashby foundation - no gaps.

1 - Establish the Skunkworks environment
    A - Scope the technical system problem
    B - Ashby the social system as a communications system
    C - Confrontation

2 - Solve the technical problem
    A - Devise model for building Ashby knowledge
    B - Team-build Ashby knowledge
    C - Allocation

3 - Develop the solution
    A - Establish validation environment
    B - Initial solution designs
    C - Surcease and iterate
    D - Release to the all-natural process

The project never starts on level, dry ground. Practitioners always inherit a multidimensional, Track A, alligator-filled swamp (the Big Muddy). The matter of linkage escalation is painfully real. It is not fun at work. Track B must face a gauntlet of awesome organizational constraints that are established and waiting. In the Design for Complexity, the practitioner leaps out of the box and pounces directly for Orgman's throat. He follows the Law of Maximum Organizational Resistance and starting the DfC is his precondition.

RULE - Only the practitioner gets to see just how big a mess has been made out of the project by the organization.

The Path of Maximum Organizational Resistance

There are several ways to arrange for the necessary Track B Skunkworks environment, but all involve conflict. Organizations have hidden "special handling" mechanisms to accommodate track B that don't require a formal change in doctrine. For example, a prominent men's club in London has an ancient policy to exclude dogs from the premises. When one of the cherished members went blind and needed a seeing-eye dog to continue service, the organization quickly produced a simple expedient that preserved their ancient policy intact. A notice was posted on the club bulletin board, for those who might be concerned, informing the members that "The particular animal accompanying Mr. Caruthers shall be deemed a cat."

169

The Path Of
Maximum Organizational Resistance

Environmental protection is the top priority for the practitioner. He must perform the necessary norm-breaking before the temple clergy have time to organize a defense. The practitioner's life is not for the timid, the socially sensitive, or the mediocre. Solving complex problems that the organization cannot solve with its arrangements is not a popularity contest. Usually there are many departments which are part of the established roadblocks. Fortunately, they typically hate each other and it takes time for them to coordinate against the common menace. The practitioner must have the environmental issue in control long before the roadblockers wake up.

The organization will have a long history of in-house war stories about its past and present, on-going, complex projects. The standard practices which produce the wreckage are assembled into the approved corporate POSIWID model for disaster. Mindful of the territorial imperative, the practitioner visits each organizational compartment, such as accounting and contracts, with a bill of particulars. The confrontation is held very early before any project details have had time to develop into defensive ammunition. To help identify the built-in **roadblocks,** issues are handled in generic form.

RULE - Managers in power do not permit questioning the incompetence of the institutions from which their power is drawn.

Through persistence, the target roadblock department will suggest an acceptable procedure for the subject project (Track B has been deemed a "cat"). In practice, its only way to avoid further embarrassment from the systemic impact of the POSIWID tool. For hard cases, the practitioner threatens to stop the project and blame The End on the failure of the target department to cooperate. That always works. Orgman doesn't like his performance spotlighted by an outsider who is immune from social controls and who has nothing to lose. Orgman needs the comfort of the herd. It takes time for the herd to organize a defense to the POSIWID threat. The practitioner races down the Path of Maximum Organizational Resistance before the window of opportunity afforded by the communication lag closes off. It is a chase scene worthy of a Hitchcock story ending.

RULE - Feeding a complex problem on a diet of standards and regulations makes it grow bigger.

Of course, rules that conflict with the Law of Least Mental Effort are rarely followed. The government is flooded with edicts, orders, laws and advisories calling for elements of Track B practices to be used in its own work. In fact the more on-target, the less likely it will be given even lip service. The government has a labyrinth of regulations that require contingency plans for its computer systems (a basic Track B task derived from Ashby). In practice, not one government computer system in a hundred has such a plan. One application, which had complied in substance, placed the sole copy of the contingency plan in the same room that went up in flames with the computer.

Picking a fight with the bully

Since the Skunkworks requires a flat organization (no role distinctions), the practitioner searches for the elements of linkage escalation and any doctrine or practice that inherently forces an adversarial relationship between main project participants. The principal offense is the tying of a contract to a specification. In the Skunkworks, all team members are functionally equal. As applied for Track B problems, the "me buyer, you vendor" distinction forced by a contract linked to a specification is the most counterproductive invention ever made by industrial society. The practitioner eliminates specifications on both sides of the fence. Pussies need not apply.

The organizational response follows a predictable course. The purchasing department thinks management has been eating out of the wrong mushroom patch. However, it is easy to demonstrate, using the records of the organization itself, that an inverse relationship exists between the "tightness" of a specification and the success of the complex project. Project disaster is often blamed upon loose

Adversarial Relationship

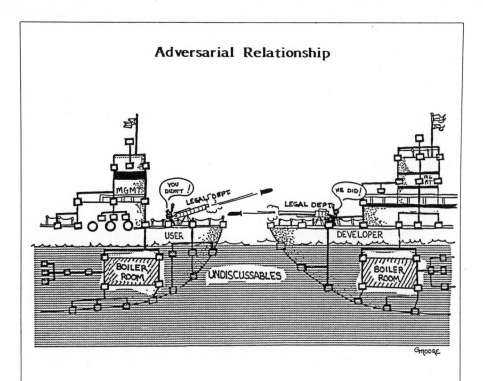

No one claims that adversarial relationships lead to good productivity. POSIWID shows, however, that forming hostile arrangements must be a high priority since so much effort is directed towards that end. One set of uncoordinated groups in the user organization scribes a specification that has little relationship to the real problem and is unintelligible even to its authors. Another set of disjointed groups in the developer institution, in response to the specification, assembles a functional description of a solution to a different problem, but which could not be delivered anyway. This tangle of disinformation, a crime which is committed at the start of the project, is as good as things get. Downhill from there, everyone treats everyone else as an adversary. The POSIWID goal must be to keep law schools filled, because that's what the arrangement does.

specifications, even while the evidence demonstrates the opposite. The same inverted thinking is witnessed regarding the cost of quality.

The penalties for the practitioner differ in important ways from those of an insider. An observant employee who points out the relationship between "tight" specifications and failure to management (gives a control signal) will be punished for his trouble (Livingston's Law). Since the practitioner knows that Orgman will shy away from what he intuits is another's "land," he creates the idea in Orgman that what the practitioner does is standard practice "back at home." The territorial imperative can work **for** you too.

RULE - Any time the organization thinks it possesses the gas-tight specification to solve its large-space problem, the cause is lost.

In one suite of cases, where the identical complex problem was confronted by many separate conglomerations, the specifications were progressively expanded as an epidemic of EOPMD horror-shows struck project after project (that law again). One group we monitored spent over a year, and well over two million dollars, to prepare a "gas tight" specification in a futile attempt to avoid a repeat performance (we had it bronzed as the perfect Track A specification). Buried in endless circumlocution, the vendor is held accountable for every item. Payments are withheld for the slightest infraction. The "ultimate" specification, of course, ran into trouble from the outset. In reality, the only thing perfect about the specification was the guarantee of failure. It soon became obvious.

RULE - All expedients to eliminate the risk of failure form adversarial relationships which guarantee disaster.

The claustral workers, who knew nothing about the suffocating specification before the contract was signed, quickly found themselves caught between a client who demanded compliance and a specification that couldn't be met (leading to withheld payments). Turnover on the project, including project management, reached fifty per cent in nine months. Management costs exceeded performance costs by a factor of three. The result was equivalent disaster at a higher price (about fifty million dollars at last count) and trauma to the people in both organizations. The buyer had wreckage instead of a system and the vendor his dire financial straits. The EOPMD announcement was appended with a new schedule which had its next milestone further out than the **entire** original project schedule. There are no winners in games like these. The RECYCLE disaster is a hopeless undiscussable, mired deeply in Livingston's Law. The perpetrators have been sentenced to life imprisonment in Track A. No parole.

RULE - The project operated on any other basis than mutual trust and open communication is headed only towards courts of law.

The practitioner explains, using **connections** of practices to results, that while it is helpful to develop a specification of intent, and it is necessary to have a contract (so that the vendors can get paid by the Track A system), it is instant death to connect the two together in Track B. Ashby shows that a perfect specification is impossible. The closest approximation to a specification allowed is that of Ashby knowledge as it develops during the project.

The Toolbox is an arsenal of coping mechanisms with sufficient variety to deal with whatever variety the organization may exhibit. Such preparedness also demonstrates our respect for the considerable power and variety of the enemy forces. We hope the enemy doesn't wake up and increase his variety.

Connections

Track A Standard Practice	Track A Results	Track B Results
Assume problem definition	Routine	Wrong problem
Issue specifications	Covers item	Deficient, bad estimates
Award on low price	Reduces cost	Maximizes cost
Contracts and lawyers	Protection	Adversarial relationships
Decomposition	Work proceeds	D&D isolation
Preach Zero Defects	Errors concealed	Progress stops
Use standard procedures	Accomplishment	Errors
Work independently	Parts fit	Mismatch grows
Professional management	Valid status	Camouflage
Administration	Supports work	Prevents work
Assign blame for errors	Errors reduced	Errors increase
M-B-O reporting	Corrections	Camouflage x 2
Report problems upstairs	Problems solved	Problems grow
Punish Deviants	Efficiency grows	Errors hidden
Reward conformance	Productivity grows	Headway stops
Audit programs	Identify errors	Camouflage x 4

RULE - The practitioner has many tools and the handle that fits them all is to be an outsider.

Securing the Skunkworks

The first phase of practitioner endeavors is devoted to bringing the organization to its knees so that a Skunkworks can be formed. The Skunkworks (whose motto is: "I Stink Therefore I Am") has to last for the duration of the project. The practitioner knows that all promises made by the organization are lies. To avoid the disruption of false starts, the practitioner follows a procedure that gets the job done for real. It is in this phase of the DfC where most of the **have fun at work** tools are used. Since the practitioner can predict the outcome in advance, it **is** fun at work.

Imposing proven structure is a basic means of making the complex much more manageable. It greatly reduces the number of items that have to be considered at the same time. Since the complex problem, like any project, facility or institution, is an inseparable union of a technical system and a social system, an organizing structure was developed which accounts for these two joined systems. It is the Law of Equivalent Significance. It accounts for the taboo of overt operation on anything but technical matters. Although we function within the social system atmosphere, organizations only give licenses to work on the technical content. Complex problem-solving is not, and will never be, organizationally neutral.

RULE - Whenever a technical system is coupled to a social system, the grand overall problem is a social system problem.

The structure obeys the Law of Equivalent Significance by including the essential social system **in its context,** by the practitioner, as one of many communications and information processors. There is an intentional parallel procedural treatment of the technical system and the social system. What the practitioner does for one he does for the other. The necessities of good communications are not altered because part of the total system is human-driven.

RULE - Large-space problems shrink only through innovation. Innovation requires an innovator. Innovators require a constituency. Together they comprise a Skunkworks.

The practitioner starts by defining the **boundaries** of the two systems. The technical system includes the problem to be solved and the connections to the larger world (the problems that are **not** going to be solved by the project). The social system includes the organizations involved in developing, processing and communicating information relevant to the problem and lists the satellite organizations, such as regulatory agencies and vendors, which will be excluded. Every penetration through the boundaries drawn to the larger outside world is marked.

Technical and social system models

The algorithm used by the practitioner to develop the model begins by a building a top down functional breakdown chart (TDBD) which describes the technical scope in functional terms (standard systems practice). Functions are systematically described to a level of detail which defines pieces of information (part numbers) related to the task. The goal of the TDBD chart is to define and

175

Have Fun At Work TOOLBOX

I. TOOLS WHICH FIT BOTH THE TECHNICAL SYSTEM and THE SOCIAL SYSTEM

    A. Eliminations
    B. Ashby's Law of Necessary Variety
        1. Variety count and account (complexity indicators)
        2. Black box design criteria
    C. Communication assessment
        1. Shannon's theorems
        2. The cross-reference list
    D. The Language of failure
    E. The Language of Success
    F. The critical mass of Essential Principles
    G. Boundaries and Penetrations
    H. The Law of Equivalent Significance
    I. The Cycle of Control (technical-to-social system linkaging by task)
    J. Part number detail
    K. Fast cycle RBF
    L. References

II. SOCIAL SYSTEM TOOLS

    A. Two level plus abstraction
    B. Territorial Imperative and the ZOI
    C. Performance history
    D. Innovation and the Skunkworks
        1. Error tolerance
        2. Test then design (validation-driven projects)
        3. Fast cycle feedback
        4. Common semantic language
        5. Prohibition of solutions
        6. Emphasis on unintended functions
    E. The Universal Scenario
    F. Cognitive dissonance
    G. Impaired intuitions and perilous perceptions
    H. Limitations without outside practitioner
    I. Voids, roadblocks, distortions and inversions
    J. Structure pack for social interactions
    K. Job performance aids (JPAs)

Practitioner's Toolbox Supplement

III. TECHNICAL SYSTEM

    A. Systems engineering analytical techniques
    B. Procedural manuals and structural templates (e.g., SIPOD)
        1. Ashby knowledge development (Blowouts)
        2. Value systems development
        3. Scrutable connectivity
        4. Operational requirement assessment criteria
        5. Allocation with operational requirements
    C. Fuzzball eater personnel resource

IV. SOCIAL SYSTEM

    A. An outsider respecting company orders
    B. Path of maximum organizational resistance order-of-battle
    C. Skunkworks environmental protection requirements
    D. War story reference library
    E. Standard practices connections for Track A and Track B
    F. Flee vs flight criteria
    G. Disguises for social system matters as technology
    H. Bullet-proof vest and silver cross

HAVE FUN AT WORK

classify the array of functional requirements (abstract) in a hierarchical structure that guarantees the problem won't get lost, and get down to physical details in small, related bunches that are specific, unambiguous, and understandable. "Part Number Power" is being developed.

RULE - The more complex the technical system, the less it will be tested. This is done to avoid leaving a user catastrophe to chance.

Each box on the TDBD chart contains the fixed equipment used to provide the function and a list of associated input/output information particulars (such as sensors and actuators). The TDBD chart covers all items **not** involved with the social system. The principal goal of the TDBD diagram is to identify the definitive list of physical tasks which, in the aggregate, join to provide the topmost function (abstract). At each node of the TDBD chart is listed any related (custodial) fixed equipment for process and control as well as the tasks associated with operating and maintaining that fixed equipment, both automatic and manually assisted. This is hard work for the practitioner but it is relatively calm. The structure of TDBD is driving for a classification of all possible behavior that the system **can exhibit**, not just what is intended.

RULE - Think in structure, think in sets, think in boundaries.

The next step works with the formal organization chart of each institution having an important role in the project. The formal lines of communication expressed in the organization chart are presumed sanctioned to provide information to and receive information from the technical system. In full parallel to the TDBD chart strategy, the communication system is driven down to the primary working group level and associated with details of information, such as part numbers (as contrasted to a progress report), that are unambiguous, measurable and understandable. Each box on the chart is labeled with the tools and the information library classified by that set for which it is custodian and that set it uses in the conduct of its affairs for which it is not responsible to develop or maintain. Unlike the TDBD chart, however, there is no structure for fashioning what the complete list of information is. Pieces of information originate in media (humans, documents, lists, data bases) somewhere in the organization and transformed information has an organizational destination.

RULE - Working on technical solutions oblivious to social system factors is an extinct luxury.

The Cycle of Control connecting technical and social systems

It is the technical task (or performance element or functional unit) which connects the technical system to the social system. In the TDBD chart, tasks are only identified; a separate step is then taken to structure each task to organize definition and detail for **connection** to the social system. The task structure is the familiar Cycle of Control and consists of the functional elements of input, processing, output and closure. An example of a task description is a recipe for preparing a dish of food.

Task input is structured to contain task triggers, workers, information, tools, materials and specifications. The input information is identified in categories of live and recorded, in part numbers, listed with their immediate sources in the technical and social systems. In recipe form, input means to identify (so they can be obtained) all the ingredients for the dish and its preparation.

Law of Equivalent Significance

ANY   • INSTITUTION
        • PROJECT
        • FACILITY

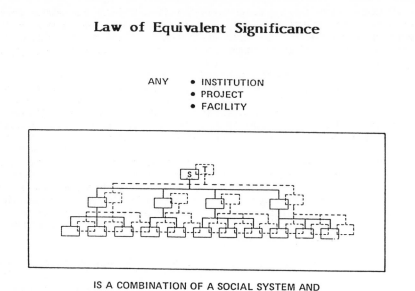

**IS A COMBINATION OF A SOCIAL SYSTEM AND
A TECHNICAL SYSTEM**

Treating any system as a collection of independent elements flying in close formation is the kiss of death. When the greatest piece in the system, the social system component, is left out of the cauldron, Pandora's Box is opened for the duration of the project. It is traditional and customary to treat all problems as technical problems, functioning as if the social system aspects didn't exist. The territorial imperative demands, for instance, that Mechanical Engineers tend to their gearboxes and leave human communication matters to the sociologists. This arrangement produces unworkable systems. It is the social system itself which blocks open treatment of the social system, creating a self-destructive and counterproductive situation. The practitioner, as an outsider, avoids such morbid folly. The ceremony of marriage of the social system to the technical system (the two have been living together for eons anyway), is performed at the beginning to legitimize the relationship and prevent another slew of idiot progeny. What is done for the gears is done for the guys. In organizations, differences in their behavior are hard to distinguish.

Task processing is structured to contain the knowledge and tacit experience requisites for executing the procedure, a list of fixed equipment, and the procedure instructions. This is the action part of the recipe (e.g. mix two ingredients for five minutes) and it always assumes some identifiable threshold of competence.

Task output is structured to contain products, byproducts, information and triggers for other tasks. Information outputs can be live and/or recorded. They are listed with their immediate destinations in the technical and social systems. In the DfC recipe form, output means the dish goal, the mess to be cleaned up from creating it, and the trigger for ringing the supper bell.

Task closure is feedback, a comparison of task product to the specifications for which the task was triggered. It is tasting the dish to check that it met the specification for which the recipe was created. Closure locates discrepancies which can be detected to trigger corrective tasks. In the task description structure here, so far, it is assumed that everything works perfectly. The purpose of the task description is to identify the task components and all the communication links of **potential** error.

The task description is the treachery that ties the people to the technology. It sets the stage for putting the mess on the table for view. It is clearly legitimate at the same time it is intimidating. Exposure to lots of technical "part numbers" acts like a narcotic on Orgman. The quantity of work and the lack of ambiguity anesthetizes him (there is nothing to argue about, so he goes back to sleep). The list of unknowns will be larger than the list of knowns by an order of magnitude. Tasks are described one at a time and accumulated. It gets to be a lot of documentation and a big data base.

The communications system for information

The task, which originated from operational requirements of the technical system, is connected to the social system through workers, tools and information involved in the task. In the structure for the social system, information homes have been identified. The pathway that gets the information from its home to a task input is defined by a cross-reference table, developed as a separate activity, and this defines the communication network involved (directly and indirectly) in the task.

RULE - The failure to develop a language which spans discipline boundaries defeats any command for the disciplines to cooperate.

Tasks are defined one at a time in terms which include the communications network for handling task information. The communications network, except for automatic information processing by machines (live technical data to live control actions), is the heartland province of the social system. The information data base now contains the relationship of organizational elements to tasks in terms of who and what information. When all the tasks have been described by the structure based on the Law of Equivalent Significance, the aggregate task loading and communications load for each group on the chart is obtained.

The task description, via the cycle of control format, provides a mechanism for assembling one of the most incriminating data bases ever devised - the cross reference list of part number information. The cross reference list shows the information contained in tasks and organizational documents (classified by many characteristics). This list is then used to show the propagation network of a

The Cycle of Control

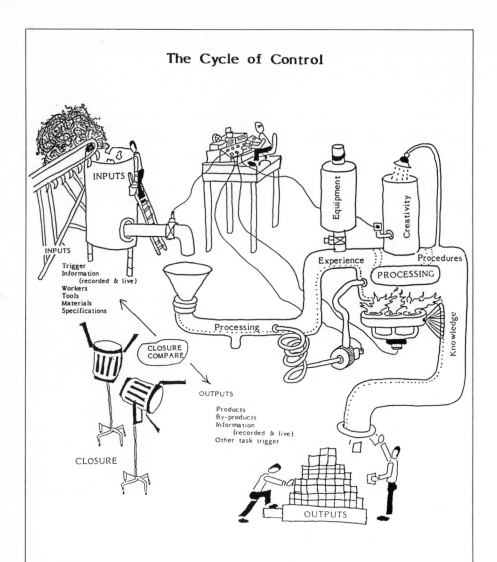

The cycle of control represents how things are in the real world. All tasks, whether by inanimate matter or cellular congress, have the basic elements of initialization, processing, output and closure. While any element can be ignored, none is suspended by indifference, or deference to social hierarchies. When we displace the cycle of control by intuition, and depend upon the magic of the millennia, DNA, to order our lives, what we discard is the element of closure -- the primary engine for growth, adaptation and improvement.

HAVE FUN AT WORK

piece of information. That is, the impact of a "part number" change (or error) to documents and tasks (part of Ashby knowledge development).

While one might be inclined to think that a corporate information cross reference list would be a basic operating document, such lists do not exist. Cross reference lists are forbidden documents because they tell too much about the organization itself. Departments have little idea what information they use in performing their asssignments. They do not know where the information they generate ends up in use. Both the significance of information and the damage bad information can create are deliberately unknown. The hostility of the organization to the preparation of a cross reference list is so acute, it takes the outside practitioner and knowing deception to pull it off. The mismatches, voids, replications and gross misunderstandings about company information is there for anyone to see in glorious part number form. It is an indictment of the "system" that no one can dispute.

The communications pathway descriptions show the nodes where information is handled (translated) and thereby subject to error. A review of the opportunities for error and the capacity of the control system to recover from such errors, forms the basis for estimating the probability of encountering errors which will not be controlled. The numbers or error points involved are always enormous. The Cycle of Control tool shines bright searchlights on the risks peppered throughout the system.

RULE - The path of **least organizational resistance** is paved with unknown risks.

Unfortunately, the human perception of risk is another genetic distortion in the real world of complexity. It stinks. Orgman, obsessively worried about vague and distant dangers, blithely ignores clear and present ones. Human perceptions of risk often have little to do with reality. They are classified as either preference risks, which are voluntary, familiar and piecemeal; or shunned risks which are involuntary, dramatic and bunched. The long evolutionary balancing act (between safety and excitement) has produced a most imperfect reference model. Corporations are adept at cloaking their risks in taboo and ritual.

Structure guides developing knowledge as an objective basis for identifying and selecting which risks to take. Gut feelings about risk are so consistently and so significantly wrong that strong measures are necessary to bring about objectivity.

RULE - The stigma of error is the engine of self-destruction.

Each organization has a unique culture which determines automatic preferences. Some institutions even have phobias, extreme fears that trigger the autonomic nervous system, about issues like doing work for the government. Note well that phobias have roots back to the ancient savannah, not the nuclear age. People often freak out because of thunderstorms, heights, water, snakes and spiders. On the other hand, phobias are rarely invoked by guns, automobiles, explosives and electricity. The trick of the contingency knowledge bank buries these cultural and emotionally-controlled distortions in part-number detail.

Footprint

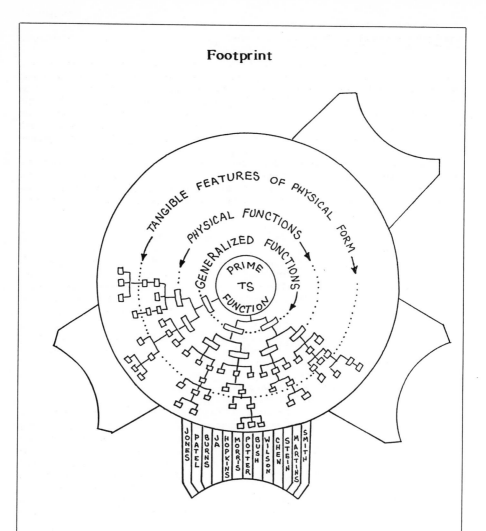

This diagram is only an outline of a footprint chart, to show the basic elements of the tool. The technical system TDBD is arranged in concentric circular form in the center. The social system is arranged in working group bunches around the circumference of the largest circle. Every individual in the group has his slot and the concave end allows placing lines representing active channels of intragroup communication participating in a task. The other end of the slot can be connected to the technical system, as appropriate, and to other groups to indicate intergroup communication channels. Used in conjunction with the data shown on page 184, most tasks related to a system make the footprint look like a birdsnest. Reality.

Task environmental assessment

Tasks performed by people using information, also handled by people, are greatly influenced (to put it mildly) by the environment within which those activities are performed. You cannot assess the environment without an idea of what the task load is. Just like their machine counterparts, environments appropriate to the tasks will increase the probability and reliability of the tasks to be carried out (e.g., clean rooms for making silicon wafers). Task environments for people are designed by and dominated by the social system.

Measuring the corporate **structure** as an environment includes counting the number of hierarchical levels, nodes and specializations (distinctive language). Also thrown into the cauldron are organization age, size and how finely it has granulated functionalities (e.g., the number of separately delineated departments reporting to marketing).

RULE - Work flows toward competence.

Measuring the corporate **doctrine** includes counting how widely scattered (the number of separate groups involved in a task) responsibility has been cast. This measure is obtained by enumerating how many social system elements are involved in a task. Also evaluated is how closely the doctrines (policies) and the bases for those doctrines match up with the tasks and the facts of the environment surrounding the organization. Organizations clutching to ancient doctrines in a turbulent external setting establish an entirely different environment for executing tasks (Livingston's Law) than that prevailing in the organization which is in harmony with its external environment.

Aggregate measures

The task setting is then used as a frame of reference to evaluate the **communications** network. This is done by counting impediments to the development and transfer of information and noting compensating mechanisms for those impediments, if any. The reliable, timely communication of information is jeopardized by high densities and novelty, by frequent change, by translations and over-the-walls, by secrecies and filters, by data compression and expansion, by rivalries and adversarial relationships, by policy conflicts and higher emphasis on group status than reaching corporate goals. These factors generate error and noise on the communication channels, and error propagates directly to the technical system.

RULE - The instinctive formation of a hierarchy, with the number of levels proportional to the degree of complexity confronted, is proof of the finite intelligence of man.

The Law of Requisite Variety says that the ability of the compensating control to regulate such things as noise and error, cannot exceed the controller's capacity as a channel of communication. Shannon's Theorem 10 reiterates the law when it says that if noise (error) appears in a "message," the amount that can be removed by a correction channel is limited to the amount of information that can be carried by that channel.

The Communications Balance

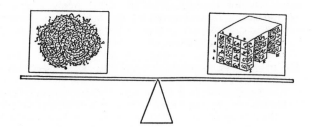

CHANNEL FIDELITY IMPEDIMENTS

Regards for status filters
Specialization
High transmission densities
Rivalries
Many translation junctions
Secrecies
Over-the-wall style
Adversarial relationships
Data compression/expansion
Stigma of bad news
High novelty of content
Conflicting internalized values
High change rates
Time mismatches
Propagation incomplete

INFIDELITY COMPENSATORS

Minimize role distinctions
Common semantic language
Error detection mechanisms
Skunkworks environment
Feedback and closure
Team format
Flat organization
Remove role distinctions
Clear rules for translation
Failure tolerance
Systems engineering structures
Undiscussables discussed
Common cross reference list
Coordination function
Cross reference matrix

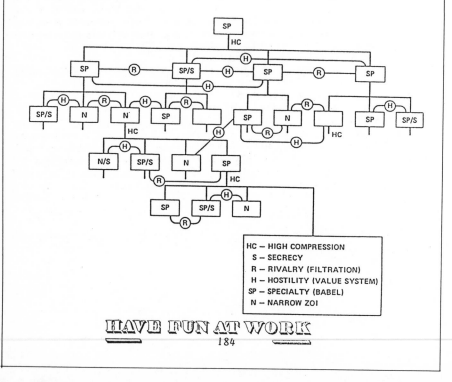

HC — HIGH COMPRESSION
 S — SECRECY
 R — RIVALRY (FILTRATION)
 H — HOSTILITY (VALUE SYSTEM)
SP — SPECIALTY (BABEL)
 N — NARROW ZOI

HAVE FUN AT WORK

RULE - Accurate communications up the hierarchy are inversely related to promotions.

At this juncture, the practitioner has found many errors, many more opportunities for error, and has measures on the maximum ability of the social system and technical system to correct those errors. All this in glorious part number, technical detail. There's more.

Compensating factors to communication blockages include such social system functions as feedback, integration, validation, common language, quality, open discussion of the undiscussables, and clear rules for compressing and expanding information. In this way impediments are balanced with compensators. When the balance tilts hard towards impediments, the communication network reliability is accordingly degraded (by high variety) and more work load is added (bad information costs).

The data base of task descriptions contains the specifics of interaction between the technical system and the social system. The balance of communication handicaps and compensators can be mapped on the defined information pathways to derive a set of overall measures.

- The number of involved organizational entities
- The number of translators and filters
- The number and duration of time delays
- The degree of granulation and specialization

These measures provide direction for selecting where error is most likely to occur. At this point, the practitioner reviews the capability of the systems to respond to contingencies (the error conditions which the system **can exhibit**). This step is RBF on the cheap (fast **feedback**). The system is exercised in model form to check how it might respond to the error situations which it may encounter or create itself. Typically, the volume of error potential is so high that it becomes clear that the formal communication system is inoperative, even for normal business.

RULE - Without a reference of success, constraints to success remain invisible.

Human limits set the standard

As discussed previously, humans, like machines, have capacity limits for handling information. Much is known about these human limits from empirical evidence and hard science. For example, the moon astronauts insisted upon manual control of the lunar lander engines until simulation clearly established that they were unable to juggle all the parameters at once and prevent running out of fuel. Air traffic controllers routinely demonstrate their human limits in keeping up with the traffic. On-line reserve capacities, in the context of life on the East African savannah, have long been occupied by the problems of civilization.

RULE - The human machine for thinking has not been programmed to deal with the world of today.

The Skunkworks

The skunkworks is not just the most productive show in town, it is the only way complex problems get solved. Every alternative to the skunkworks is known to fail. Millions of attempts to bypass the skunkworks, because feedback is prohibited, are going on now. Fools! The vital issues must be discussed. Errors must be made. Learning must take place. Feedback must flourish. These requisites come as a surprise?

Comparing status to human limit standards

The status of the situation has been defined in terms of the task load on the communications systems. The loadings can be directly compared to human limits in these same categories. An example of one human limit is the information processing rate of one symbol every 25 milliseconds. If the social system has more capacity than the tasks require (to meet specifications), then the situation is in control or capable of being in control with the prevailing arrangement.

RULE - Trained managers, over time, reach their goal of stability in organizational performance only at conditions featuring the least productive relationships.

If the requirements exceed the "technical" limits of the social system, much can be determined. Particular problem areas can be identified and specifics of the cause of the problem can be enumerated. Measured mismatches also point to problem-solving methods that can work in the existing social system and those that can not. Mismatches between reality and reference models act like signal buoys to locate the areas where control has been lost, where the formal communication network can't do the job, and where error rates will be the highest. For planning purposes, this kind of information is priceless.

RULE - The solution of a complex problem is only possible when the belief system of the workers designing the solution has been expanded to include the whole problem.

At this juncture, the situation described by following the Technical-Social system structure is little different than what was common knowledge at the outset. The organization is a critical mess. Of major significance, however, is the difference in how the conclusions were obtained. The cumulative data base developed by the practitioner is the repository of specifics showing the "technical" elements that generate the situation. The informal sources, which are much faster, contain only generalizations and they are undiscussable.

What the practitioner has done is to stimulate and simulate the project for solving the complex problem. He may have proved that it can't work as it is. On the one hand, the complexity has been illuminated by the spotlight of the Cycle of Control data, and on the other, the mismatch in communications is painfully exposed.

Using the mismatches for planning

With the situation defined in detail and the performance requirements defined in detail, a solid technical basis is available to select methods which can meet the requirements. In order for methods to work, they must be provided a suitable environment. If the methods required do not match with the methods sanctioned by the social system, then the environment will not match either. Thereby the mismatches of the existing arrangement invariably mean that different methods are necessary and a different environment will have to be installed to allow them to work - period.

RULE - Bad estimates are natural products of the organization.

Boundaries & Interfaces Structure Checklist

I.   LIST EXTERNAL ENTITIES/SYSTEMS IN ENVIRONMENTAL SUPPORT

    A. Regulators
    B. Codes and standards
    C. Financing and taxes
    D. Legal and patent
    E. Purchasing
    F. Human resources
    G. Training and schooling
    H. Corporate procedures
    I. Accounting and payroll

II. LIST EXTERNAL ENTITIES/SYSTEMS IN DIRECT SUPPORT

    A. Vendors
    B. Clients and customers
    C. Other departments and disciplines
    D. Consultants
    E. Management
    F. Other organizations

III. PENETRATION FACTORS TO DESCRIBE FOR EACH EXTERNAL ENTITY

    A. Information, in part numbers, required from system
    B. Information, in part numbers, required to system
    C. Language translations, number and type
    D. Variability with time

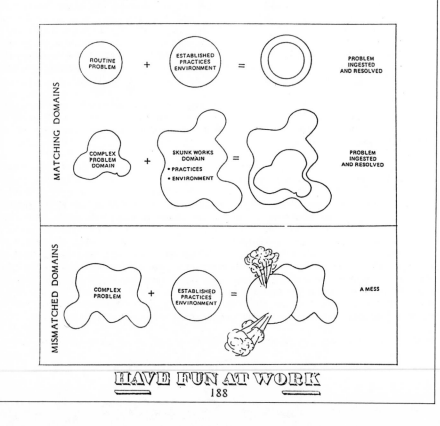

The organizational path of least resistance insures quiet in the early going but it sets the stage for great commotion at EOPMD. Over time, the difference between published estimates and actual results is a prime measure of organizational dysfunction. The Track B strategy, through early, cheap RBF with the Ashby model, reverses the procedure. As long as it's the practitioner who is taking the heat, no one seems to mind. Voila! Fun at work.

RULE - The workable solution to a complex problem will introduce only problems which already have a workable solution.

The wealth of particulars that illuminated the mismatches permits planning to be done with confidence and in considerable detail. A correlation exists between the number of nodes where error could occur, and the probability of error occurring in a set of tasks. A cursory look at the contingency control means available was done by the practitioner in the course of developing the project. This phase we call Ashby 1. Knowing the probability of error and the probability of error recovery provides estimates of the magnitude of the problem, and the levels of effort it will take to provide control. POSIWID with this quantity of dirt is like shooting fish in a barrel. Fun at work!

Having the requisite plan does not automatically lead to its acceptance, but it does provide a frame of reference for assessing alternatives. It is a simple matter to show that alternative plans, which do not address the vital issues identified, are doomed to fail. At that point the decision to continue the project, or not, can be made. Unless the requisite conditions are established, there is no point to proceeding further.

RULE - Role distinctions between communicators destroy any opportunity for a productive exchange of information.

If the decision is made to proceed with Track B, the practitioner can then get down to technical business without worry about corporate termites destroying the Skunkworks. The organization will shift into the position that the Skunkworks isn't really there. That is the highest possible score. After the Skunkworks has been in business for about three months, a welcome event takes place.

The transformation

As the mess is deeply rooted in a labyrinth of psychological astringents (thanks to the organization), there is a major leap in productivity that occurs when those restrictions are lifted. The awareness that the Skunkworks is going to make the project go comes all at once, during the blowout era (a knowledge-building phase of the DfC described in the first book).

The participants, now free to grow to their potential, are able to see the course of Track B. They gradually realize that something special is going on. They're having fun at work. The productivity is so abnormally high, the feeling soon develops that any problem which emerges is going to be solved. There is positive reinforcement for the project in the Track B environment that knows where it is going and has the tools to get there. The capability, of course, was there all along.

RULE - No one buys in on owning a project that is intolerant of mistakes.

Fuzzball Eater School

Making every effort to avoid learning about the complex problem itself, a popular expedient is to turn the problem, which is not understood, into a problem of personnel, which is. The idea is to find the hero (always the technology side) who can solve (eat) the problem (fuzzball) and arrange an introduction. Managers think fuzzball eaters can be grown like wheat. Candidates are rotated in assignment around specialty enclaves to, it is hoped, by adsorption, become systems-oriented (there is no systems department by intent). Graduates of the merry-go-round are injected into the grotto of issues which can not be dispensed to perform the necessary miracles. Most fail. Fuzzball eaters are born, not raised. Humanity has no more valuable resource, nor one it punishes with more regularity.

The practitioner works to achieve the transformation as soon as possible. Once it has happened, the entire focus can be set upon the technical matters of the problem. It is a major milestone of the project and it comes as a surprise to Track A onlookers (who are hoping instinctively for Track B to fail). The potential embarrassment of the host organization to the great productivity of Track B is avoided by carrying on as if the project didn't exist. Track B is stable and resilient to adversity from that point on. Work becomes, as it should always be, fun. Regrettably, such vital factors are not discussable outside of the Skunkworks. Somehow, psychological well-being is supposed to take care of itself.

What the practitioner does is to use the **have fun at work** tools to hoodwink the corporation into doing something in its own best interests for a change. Note that it was structured, socially safe, definitely not front-door, and it got the job done. The corporation is left with its reptilian tendency to view the world as a particular medley of sounds, sights and smells.

This is just the front-end phase of the DfC. The prescription continues with knowledge development using various structures for completeness. Value systems are constructed and the operational requirements data base is created. A phase called "allocation" precedes the validation-directed system development process. Documents that delve into the nitty-gritty of these innovations are reviewed in Chapter 15.

Establishment Profile

WHAT THE ESTABLISHMENT:

KNOWS

* The system provides health, wealth and privilege
* The workery is not organized

DOES

* Defends the status quo of its system
* Provides increasing affluence for its members
* Inbreeds
* Attacks any threat to any acquired privilege

REWARDS

* Conformance to Establishment rules
* Protectors of the status quo

PUNISHES

* High performers, innovators, mavericks and inventors
* Accurate forecasters of doom and whistleblowers

IGNORES

* Espoused incentives and supplications for change
* Failure of its principles and practices
* History

KNOWS THAT YOU THINK IT DOESN'T

* Quality is a winner
* Sanctioned practices don't work on big or new problems
* Its institutions are out of control and ineffective
* A small portion of the organization does most of the work
* There are more humane and effective methods

DOESN'T WANT YOU TO KNOW

* The exchange of loyalty for job security has vanished
* Innovators are the source of civilization and its advances
* You have the power to bring change

HAVE FUN AT WORK

Chapter Twelve

Insight to the Establishment and its professional management

> "The century of progress - Science explores:
> technology executes: **mankind conforms**." Theme
> of the 1933 Chicago World's Fair.

Fasten your seat-of-learning belts. POSIWID (the purpose of a system is what it does) is going to take you for a rough ride. If you haven't jettisoned a lot of the Bad Seventies (your wrong, self-harming mental models of reality) by now, do not read this Chapter. Your mind has grown in the genetic legacy of an extinct social environment. It has been conditioned based upon a particular history embedded in the archives of those who perform the indoctrination service. It's enough that the notions of the world you create in your mind are genetically constrained. You do not need to let the Establishment add to the handicaps. Where do you think the Bad Seventies came from?

POSIWID is a great tool for quick validation of espoused top-down models of animate systems. Models promoted by the same Establishment that gave you Viet Nam need particular scrutiny. If the view of a social system observed through POSIWID produces the same picture as the air-brushed version from Madison Avenue, you have verified the situation through diverse independent means - a very powerful tool for establishing reliability and confidence in the vision.

If the view through POSIWID does not jibe with the official scripture, however, raise a hurricane-force flag as a warning to investigate further. Mismatches between POSIWID and stated policy are always accompanied with blocks to feedback. For taking X-ray pictures of human society, POSIWID has no equal. With the penetrating power of POSIWID rays, which pass right through snow, smoke, fog and camouflage, you can see the facades, counterfeits, hidden agendas, mirrors and trap doors of the social enterprise. When management is burning that incense again to narcotize their workery (chemical warfare on their own troops no less), POSIWID pictures show the deadly plume in bright colors.

RULE - Management loves the briar patch of short term results.

The prime reason for jarring your perceptions of these artifacts of human society is that you have been trained to rely on the same places to obtain justice which committed the atrocities. Alfred Hitchcock created some of his most frightening scenes when the intended victim, escaping from an attack on his life, would unwittingly seek aid from what he thought were his allies - who were actually the attackers. The real horror of that scene is the absence of a correcting mechanism. That is, there is no hope for the criminal's target. With feedback going to exactly the wrong place, it is only a matter of time until the adversaries win. Just like playing the slot machines.

Visionaries, illusionists and mythologists

When you go to the lawyer or the doctor, e.g., the chances that your problem will be amplified and extended by the very agents you trust for remedy are excellent. One hundred years ago, most of the people living in the USA were more than fifty miles away from the nearest lawyer. Incrementally, as dueling was replaced with laws written by lawyers, other lawyers were able to mesmerize

Motivation

Failure in the "system" to solve a problem, like illegal drug traffic, must be blamed upon everything but the system itself. POSIWID shows that the ability of the "system" to reward its executives (the true goal) has never been higher. One excuse in vogue for failure is to accuse the workery of insufficient morale. Accordingly, in place of substance, motivation firms are hired to promote morale. No matter how hard the drums are beaten, the oars do not grow to reach the water. The oarsmen, chained to their specialties, can neither make longer oars nor change their position.

their clients into thinking their new problems were being generated by their adversary when actually they were dispensed by their own lawyers using stock programs (laws).

RULE - The first record in the history of any Establishment profession is a client complaint.

When you call City Hall to complain about slow garbage collection, you are passing on your complaint to the same dysfunctional social machinery which created the annoyance in the first place. What happens is that you are now listed as a trouble maker and the next time your garbage is scattered over your yard. If you persist in feeding back results only to the offending system, you end up with a lawn full of garbage decorated with a citation from the board of health. It's not that you don't have a legitimate grievance, it's that you are feeding back only to its source - a source known to relish its quirks and biases of cognition and behavior.

For this cycle there is only failure - yours. The enemy is being told information helpful to direct resources to cause you the most harm, and you have no compensating mechanism going for you. You lose. Russian roulette with no empty cylinders. For the Establishment, it is a automatic machine for winning. They own the slot machines and the natural programs of human nature do the rest. Neat.

The model of human behavior today calls for total reliance upon managers and blind obedience to authority. Take all your problems and all your ideas (deviations from the routine) to your manager. The organization and its priesthood know best. In other words, your genetic inheritance and social conditioning implant mental models that social institutions are your primary (and only) resource for achieving your goals. That their self-perpetuating desires, however counterproductive, take precedent over your basic needs, is not mentioned.

RULE - Executives manage to an oversimplified model of the world that exists only in the shrunken mind of their own consensus.

The Establishment and its management minions rely upon instinct-driven behavior of their victims to retain their control and their privileges. The Establishment was born (in existence less than 1% of human existence) through POSIWID on your kind. You can be free of its power by using it back on them. The more you feel compelled to follow the garden path (all prepared in roses for you by your antagonist) without thinking and self-analysis, the more you are certain to be a victim. The Establishment maintains control simply by limiting the options you will (properly conditioned by elements of the Establishment itself) perceive as viable coping mechanisms. In Ashby speak, they have more variety in control means than the variety you exhibit as a constrained system. The more limited your capacity for variety (regulating tools and skills) as a "solid citizen," the more likely you can be controlled by built-in mechanisms of the Establishment. Not always fun.

RULE - Organizations in trouble transfer all command to blind instincts and reflexes.

The whole plan to **have fun at work** is based upon increasing your variety of coping mechanisms and decreasing the variety in the demands you cognitively accept. It is pure Ashby. While much of this book is about increasing your

Healthy, Wealthy & Wise

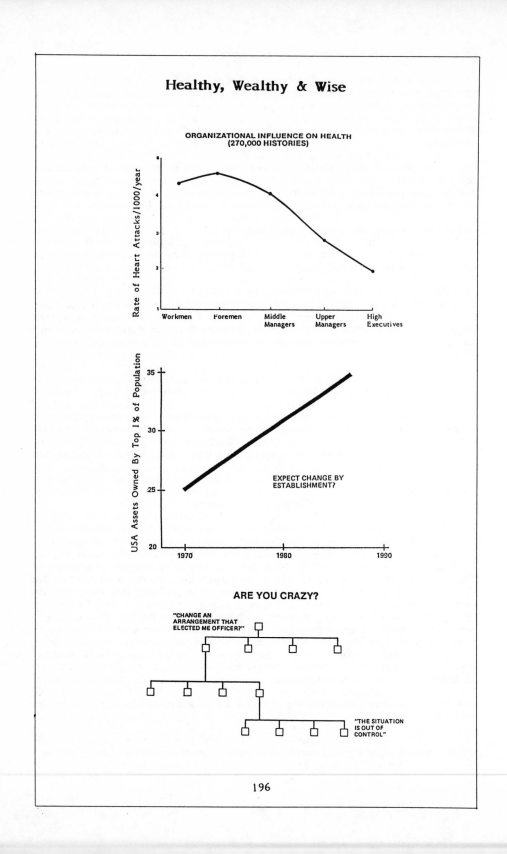

**ORGANIZATIONAL INFLUENCE ON HEALTH
(270,000 HISTORIES)**

Rate of Heart Attacks/1000/year

Workmen — Foremen — Middle Managers — Upper Managers — High Executives

USA Assets Owned By Top 1% of Population

EXPECT CHANGE BY ESTABLISHMENT?

1970 — 1980 — 1990

ARE YOU CRAZY?

"CHANGE AN ARRANGEMENT THAT ELECTED ME OFFICER?"

"THE SITUATION IS OUT OF CONTROL"

control system variety, this Chapter will dwell on reducing some variety in the situations you have to face - **especially the ones you create for yourself**. The Establishment is not your friend. It is your enemy. Management is not your friend. At best, management is an artificial reef acting as an obstacle to information and support services. Otherwise, management is your enemy. If you can refrain from aiding your antagonists, you will have much more opportunity to **have fun at work**. The POSIWID case on the Establishment and management is so clear and extensive that to put all the examples here would interrupt the flow of thought. The history of four sections of the Establishment as contained in the Bibliography, including the undiscussables inherent in health care, education, finance and industry, is a trail of tears.

POSIWID's report card on the Establishment

Because success is assured with the machinery it has, and it has been doing very well for itself, the Establishment is dedicated with fanatic intensity to preserving the status quo. Since feedback has no value to the inbred, the Establishment has never bothered to take an objective view of itself. The Establishment only listens to its own recordings, while the press, as a compliant servant of the privileged fraternity, builds up the wrong legends. Innovators don't write (the Establishment controls the publication industry anyway) and reading about innovation is discouraged. People who really make a **difference** to society have always been relentlessly persecuted by the Establishment.

RULE - Organizations only support innovators in desperate times, knowing all along that the Skunkworks works.

When the government fiddles with a tax simplification act, for example, it is deluged with influence from vested interests from the rest of the Establishment. The remainder (that's you) don't write letters to their representatives even though they directly provide 75% of the tax money to support the arrangement which taxes them. The salariat have no lobbyists and exercise no influence. It is helpful to review how well the power structure deserves the authority that has been entrusted to it.

The Establishment has grown very large, very complicated and has done so very quickly in terms of the evolutionary clock. Today, the Establishment is a bird's nest of specialization and departmentalization of decision making, lacking any kind of glue to integrate itself and focus diverse interests on joint affairs. Without a coherent plan, as the complexity of the Establishment increases, it loses the ability to make any changes at all, even ones that it says it wants to. The basic assumptions of the Establishment are so out of date that most are now known to be ludicrously false.

The Army communicates on equipment that cannot understand, by design, what the Navy equipment is transmitting. Foreign policy wants a strong dollar but unfathomably large deficits make it weaker. Forbidding feedback, the Establishment can not even meet its own needs. Today it runs on autopilot, set for conditions no longer existing, and completely out of its own conscious control. Any system that subsumes control to a range of conditions that are self-harming will, sooner or later, expire. They **all** did. By seeing the outputs that known inputs elicit (POSIWID), the strategic purpose of the Establishment must be to self-destruct.

RULE - Small short-sighted decisions create large, forever unworkable systems.

Out of Control

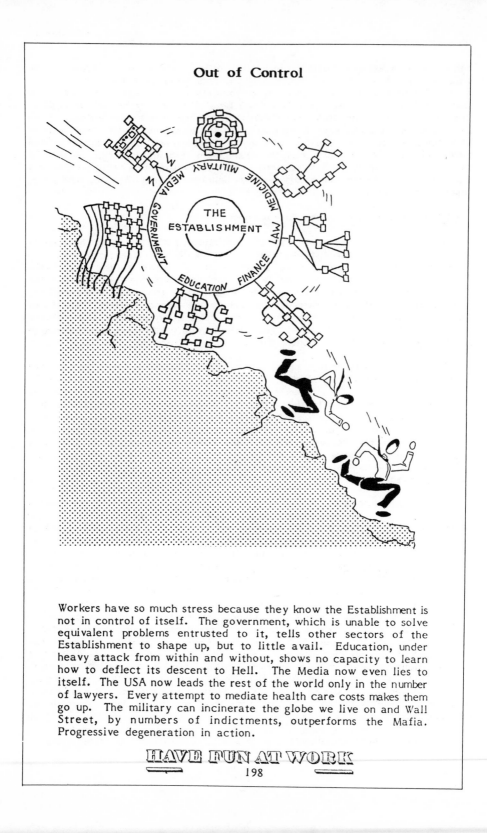

Workers have so much stress because they know the Establishment is
not in control of itself. The government, which is unable to solve
equivalent problems entrusted to it, tells other sectors of the
Establishment to shape up, but to little avail. Education, under
heavy attack from within and without, shows no capacity to learn
how to deflect its descent to Hell. The Media now even lies to
itself. The USA now leads the rest of the world only in the number
of lawyers. Every attempt to mediate health care costs makes them
go up. The military can incinerate the globe we live on and Wall
Street, by numbers of indictments, outperforms the Mafia.
Progressive degeneration in action.

HAVE FUN AT WORK

The nature of the governing class

The Establishment is an archaic human artifact, an organism with a heavy crust of habit, custom and tribal wisdom supplemented by a natural mental sluggishness and maladaptive attitudes. The Establishment evolved less from intentional design than from a genetic self-organizing mechanism spontaneously producing social orders. Unfortunately, there is no test (feedback and connections) for the Establishment to provide evidence of its special fitness for controlling the future of the community. The Establishment has grown to be a superstructure of huge organizations that accentuates, in turbulent times, their most harmful features. As if you didn't know, overstructured organizations generate dysfunctional motivations of their components.

RULE - Establishment spokesmen filter information in a manner to balance present and previous representations of a situation. Reality is hidden to prevent challenge to strongly-held doctrines.

All organizations have a tendency to increase rigidity when changing times upset established procedures which, at some point, constituted the organization's success. Institutions create a Berlin Wall, where all conflict is designated as disloyalty and all dissent (feedback from loyal members) as enemy action to be suppressed (Livingston's Law). Critical issues, such as complexity, uncertainty, mutualities and interactions, are denied. Privileged classes have always resisted change as a threat, usually correct, to their privileges. When the big tenured guns from Harvard have a convocation to develop a cross-science entity, the outcome from the barnyard of vested interests, as it must be, is to pronounce the project impossible. Large corporations hand over work to small, adaptive companies with the same rationalizations. The logic of the Establishment in these instances, of course, is to keep the status quo at any cost.

RULE - Any significant real-world problem that can no longer be ignored by society has already been abandoned by science.

The belief that the deepest problems of society are being solved along with the deepest technical matters is a delusion propagated by the possessing classes. The total amount of material destruction brought about by the Establishment in the last fifty years far exceeds, in raw brutality and purposeless destruction, the most sustained efforts of the Assyrians, the Aztecs and the Mongols. Mindless violence of the Establishment is sanctified by debased customs and blinded minds conditioned by its own power system.

In 6,000 years of history, only 300 were without war. Since the UN was founded some forty years ago, over 100 wars have taken place. Many governments have seen fit to spend, in terms of their GNP, far more on their military than on their schools. While Japan spends eight times more for education than war, the Arab countries happily spend twenty-eight times more on their guns than their textbooks. The military budget is not for the defense of the free world against communism. It is for the destruction of ancient enemies.

The allocation of scarce resources to warfare shows the relative importance of national rivalries, compared to citizen well-being, in national value structures. Latin America doesn't even know where its $365 billion in foreign loans went. It also seems to have incessant trouble remembering what it does to those who monitor human rights.

The concept of basic human rights has taken hold in recent years and various coalitions have formed to monitor the progress or lack thereof of human rights as practiced by the world's Establishments. Several hundred monitors are out there observing the bottom line of rights delivery all over the planet in reference to the Stockholm accord. Do you know what an enlightened Establishment calls a professional whistleblower using POSIWID for human rights? That's right: target practice.

More than half of the world's monitors of human rights are rewarded for their POSIWID reporting with torture, imprisonment and removal of their rights of employment. Threats and harassment aren't even counted. About 10 monitors a year are simply murdered outright. In some countries, like Saudi Arabia and North Korea, the chances of being exterminated exceed 100%. That record pretty well sums up the basic character of the Establishment. **Replace.**

RULE - Suppressing innovation is the ultimate act of self-destruction.

As Establishments go, the USA has no claim to special distinctions one way or the other. Like its European models, the USA Establishment has encouraged slavery, genocidal treatment of its natives, and war for profit. The USA Establishment has increased its national debt by two million-million dollars in the last ten years. Even two world wars couldn't accomplish that defeat. A perceptive POSIWID audit was provided in 1850 by Chief Luther Standing Bull.

"The great chief in Washington says he wishes to buy our land. One portion of the land is the same to him as the next, for he is a stranger who comes in the night and takes whatever he needs. The earth is not his brother but his enemy, and when he conquers he moves on.

"The Whites too shall pass - perhaps sooner than other tribes. Continue to contaminate your own bed and one night you will suffer in your own waste. When the buffalo are all slaughtered, the wild horses all tamed, the secret corners of the forest heavy with the scent of many men, and the view of the ripe hills blotted out by the talking wires, where is the thicket? Gone. Where is the eagle? Gone. And what is it to say goodbye to the swift and the hunt? The end of living and the beginning of survival."

The American Aztecs did not provide a very civilized precedent either. Having consumed all the game, commoners were able to get meat only on occasion through cannibalizing the victims of human sacrifice. When Cortez entered the Valley of Mexico, the local consumption was 15,000 humans per year. The conquistadors found 100,000 skulls stacked in neat rows in the plaza at Xocotlan and another 136,000 at Tenochitl'an. To prevent the same scenario in India, the public forced the priests to reclassify the cow as a sacred animal just before they were all gone.

RULE - Complex problems are never solved by legislation or regulation. Laws send lettuce by rabbit, while regulations send rabbits by coyotes.

Our omniscient government today claims there was no harm done to its own taxpayers by radium, Agent Orange, open atomic testing, etc. It supports 200,000 law firms to handle such matters, whose sheer existence and operating rules increase the number of cases in a kind of morbid geometric progression. The same negligent attitude observed by the Great Indian Chiefs has been on public display without interruption. The endless preening of Establishment members, with their reflected glow in the media, supports the prevailing impression that history progresses through elections, summit meetings and militant movements. **Erase.**

Snatching defeat out of the jaws of victory

While politics in the USA has always been a form of mass entertainment, the Establishments of Europe have provided a model for themselves that is nothing short of a guarantee of disaster. Science did not leave its mark until **after** the greatest age of industrial advance had passed. Guild organizations, founded upon social solidarity, were quick to denounce the ingenious as unfair competition. During the Industrial Revolution, innovation was carried on by anybody, but only at a safe distance from the guild hall.

Although they were the clear leaders of engineering innovation at the Great Industrial Exhibition of 1851, the British easily managed to lose their lead to rivals by the time of the Paris Exhibition, sixteen years later. The highly-esteemed equipment and techniques of the British had, by then, already grown obsolete. Saddled with an Establishment that makes any change painful and erratic, Britain retains a fierce resistance to innovation that is oblivious to consequences.

RULE - Policies based upon linear thinking always fail. Unable to adapt processes to reality, prisons become schools for crime, new freeways increase congestion, and housing for the poor adds to their misery.

The rigid educational system of the Germans also discourages entrepreneurs as well as innovators. Placing their chips on highly efficient smokestack industries, an area of traditional supremacy, now has Germany vulnerable to change. Simultaneous French efforts at centralization and decentralization have Frenchmen preoccupied with their civil tug of war. Meanwhile, the USA is being hustled to adopt Japanese practices which the Japanese are about to jettison.

The Russians have an Establishment that strangles them at every turn. Scandal is conducted on a huge scale and one recent case involved no fewer than 100,000 officials falsifying records in collaboration. It would be hard to change the system and make it worse. The Establishment is so counterproductive that Gorbachev has been given an opportunity to deploy a devastatingly powerful weapon for which the USA has no defense. In fact the USA couldn't create one with all the might of the military-industrial complex and unlimited resources. Gorbachev has given the order to cut military red tape to USA levels or less.

As incredible as it seems that any nation could aspire to the hexing of Pentagon paper mills, the Russians have promoted the arthritis of red tape to record lengths. Estimates by the CIA indicate that should the red-taped Red Army reach the Pentagonal paper model of Nirvana, their effectiveness in war would increase four-fold. Facing a prospect perceived to be more horrible than germ warfare, the USA military (Livingston's Law again) has planned to respond by increasing its paperwork. This time the Communists have gone too far. The Establishments of the world are united in common cause. The Geneva Convention will have to be amended to ban such atrocities. It's OK to kill millions in warfare, but to change an Establishment by any other means is unthinkable.

RULE - Old ways provide flawless directions for new sins.

No Good Deed Goes Unpunished

Helping social systems to avoid self-destruction is perilous work. The natural reaction to the innovators is to thank them for their troubles with the gallows. POSIWID on the system indicates mediocrity as the rewarded goal. Mediocre performance makes heroic messes.

HAVE FUN AT WORK

Anyone can make a bad guess about the future, but the Establishment has no mechanism for learning from its past tragic failures. Great energies are spent in covering up this inherent flaw. Establishments grow by a process of internal elaboration to maintain the status quo, despite a wide range of external changes which should be feedback to shape the future. Everything depends upon everything else and the system quickly breaks down. Refusing to accept its fate in order to influence its destiny, the Establishment has a very low survival value (coping system variety) in modern times, low enough in some Latin countries to eliminate the need for elections.

Designed for times of zero change, the Establishment design has outlived its usefulness. Right for thousands of years, the complex has run into environmental conditions created by "civilized" progress for which its essence is a total mismatch. The Establishment has met its Ice Age wearing only a pith helmet.

Innovators are the sworn enemy of Establishments. Innovators threaten the order and power structure rather than support equilibrium at mediocrity. Even though the future of the Establishment in turbulent times depends entirely upon how it advances or retards the creative work of the innovators, the innovative process must be furtive and alert to sabotage actions by the very organizations it labors to support.

RULE - Order is established by intuition. Disorder, the soul of innovation, is established by intellect.

The **now**, hip, chic, "in" method of dealing with the Establishment, spontaneously ratified, is through individual people. The instinctive starting place is someone from management. The folly of that expedient is discussed next.

A POSIWID report card on professional management

A relatively new class of professionals, called management, has been created by the Establishment to deal with some complications of control and provide productive working conditions for the salariat. Professional management is a guild occupation, begun in earnest about a century ago, based upon specialized intellectual study and training involving the practice of certain techniques.

Management operates according to a body of theory, supported by a collection of knowledge organized in an **internally** consistent library. Like any guild, management is a closed, self-serving system involved with the maintenance of behavior and aimed at controlling norm-breakers. The history of treatment provided to whistleblowers, a lasting disgrace of human civilization, shows how well management minions have served their masters.

RULE - Managers do not leave project failures to chance.

Workers have an atavistic relationship with professional management that is a combination of respect and expectations. This relationship has developed into a dogma that, like any hidden agenda, is an undiscussable. POSIWID can be used in the general area of quality to take an X-ray of management to reveal the obscured underlying value system.

The spotlight on quality

Few issues have provided more vivid insight into the basic driving forces of professional management in the USA than the matter of quality. In being forced

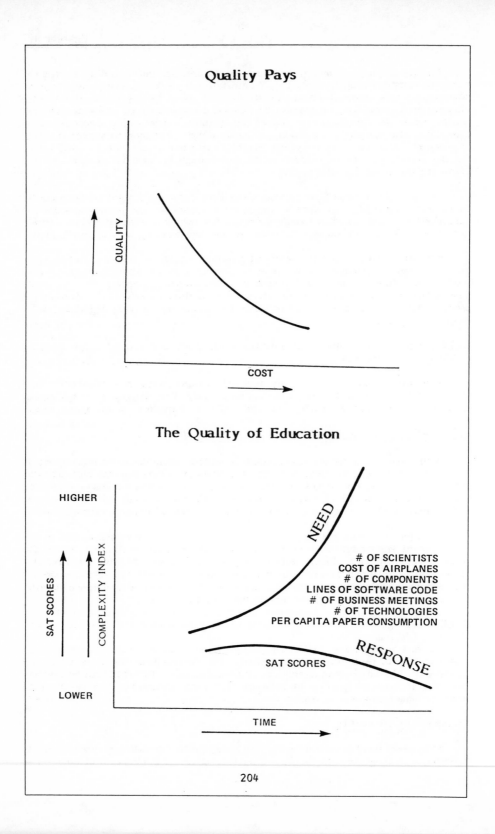

Quality Pays

QUALITY

COST

The Quality of Education

HIGHER

COMPLEXITY INDEX

SAT SCORES

NEED

OF SCIENTISTS
COST OF AIRPLANES
OF COMPONENTS
LINES OF SOFTWARE CODE
OF BUSINESS MEETINGS
OF TECHNOLOGIES
PER CAPITA PAPER CONSUMPTION

RESPONSE

SAT SCORES

LOWER

TIME

by external circumstances, which threaten the life of the corporation, to deal with the quality dimension as an internal matter, management has publicly exposed many aspects of their cult normally kept well hidden. While the temple priests have always promoted a common value system, their treatment of the quality issue has surfaced a clear pattern of reaction that speaks volumes about the far side of their common culture, a side taking various dark forms which are shared by all cultures.

The technical matter of quality (quality assurance, quality control, reliability, safety, etc.) contains little of an objective nature for rational men to debate. Aspects which may have been in some doubt a decade ago have all been answered through case histories, the passage of time, and the superabundance of demonstrated, documented successes. The contemporary manager has to contend with a surfiet rather than a dearth of published information. Quality theory or practice does not now have to be accepted as a matter of faith. Any questions about quality can be settled with site visits and balance sheet reviews. Starting from a base situation where quality gains are necessary to survive, there is nothing material about quality improvement that is negative.

High quality products and services are better for everyone than those of low quality. They are superior all around for the buyer/user and, as such, enhance the standing of the supplier in the world marketplace. Customer satisfaction leads to increased customer acceptance and market share. In other words, quality helps to secure and perpetuate the business. Nothing bad about that.

Increasing quality cuts costs, just like Juran and Deming say. Savings in the 20% to 25% range are typically achieved. Even assuming the same market share, any cost reduction of that magnitude has to generate much more income. Nothing bad about that.

Increasing quality increases worker happiness. They take more pride in their work, stay on the job longer, and are much more healthy. Medical records have long attested that in quality-supporting corporations, employee mental/physical health is significantly better than it is in quality-negligent agencies. Good health reduces medical and insurance costs to everybody's benefit. Nothing bad about that.

There are many, many examples where quality has been increased and the benefits, summarized above, realized. Most of these models are open for inspection. A competitor of Smuckers, for example, merely has to attend one of their public tours through the factory to learn in detail how they do it. The technology of quality improvement is well established, proven and the basic elements are the same independent of industry. Accordingly, getting into the quality business today involves little risk, if any, no matter what the application. Nothing bad about that.

The cost to begin quality improvement can be quite modest. Using the existing staff, many simple, small corrections can pile up to provide huge benefits. Few industries need the big-ticket automation investment so often reported in the glossy publications. Quality improvement can often be a pay-as-you-go proposition, virtually eliminating economic risk altogether. Nothing bad about that.

Quality improvement is an established, proven technology that increases markets, reduces costs and enhances worker health. All this can be obtained at low investment cost and negligible risk. Not a bad proposition at all. Yet, everyone knows about the widening gap between quality delivered by the USA and foreign competition. Poor quality is ranked today as the number one drag on USA productivity and competitiveness. Many companies have to choose between improving quality or facing extinction. Yet, over 65,000 USA corporations per year elect to go out of business. In spite of billions of dollars thrown at attempts to improve quality with quick-fix fads, the USA is far behind the world's best. Rather than closing the gap, reactions have only made the gap wider. Livingston's Law rides again.

Why this growing gulf? The list of popular excuses espoused by management, providing an element of social comfort, is long and includes such issues as labor unions, government regulation, high labor costs, and trade barriers. Regrettably for the public image of American management, the Japanese have taken over such plagued facilities right in the USA homeland and turned them into quality winners - with all of the claimed 'handicaps' intact. Knowing the excuse list is a diversion, the search for the answer must rummage around in what's left, and, as usual, it's undiscussable.

Quality is still shinning bright lights on the true priority structure of the temple clergy. For the corporate elite, making profits and perpetuating the business don't rank near the top of their value structure at all. Taking care of the very employees that enable their privileged status doesn't place very high either. Demonstrated success, sometimes inhouse, has thrown out the comfortable excuses of risk and investment along with all the other fabricated objections.

RULE - The Establishment has never hesitated to choke off the rich array of problem-solving talents of its governed - exactly what it needs to survive.

The Deming Atrocity

The saga of W. Edwards Deming tells all one needs to know about management priorities. The father of quality control, a national hero in Japan, has been abused by American management to a degree that leaves no uncertainty about the management value system. The success of the Deming "way" has been demonstrated for four decades. Few households in the USA do not have at least one product from the Deming "system" by way of the Far East. The important relationship to appreciate is that increasing quality reduces costs.

The Deming approach is not taught in any management school in America because what is taught there has always been in direct conflict. It was only natural, then, that the 1987 President's blue-ribbon panel to advise on productivity problems did not mention Deming's name. The blame was placed upon the American worker, taxes, regulations and social decay - as usual. Meanwhile, the dilemma with world competition deepens and you ultimately pay the price to many accounts. Managers still demand an allegiance, which they do not reciprocate, because of a pathological grip on acquired privilege. Follow the Deming story with POSIWID vision and any residual mysteries about management will be answered.

Status quo again

Management exhibits so much aggressive reluctance to embrace quality simply because it is guided by a hidden array of social system values which supersede the technical system list published for public consumption. **Quality is not organizationally neutral.**

Management fights quality improvement with such vigor because it means a reduction in authority and a redistribution of power. Inbred with a strong case of misoneism, regard for status among peers in the organization takes clear precedent over what else may be espoused. What management **does** in the name of quality is to reinforce the party line with new jingles and slogans (e.g., zero defects). Since there is no way to improve quality with the existing arrangement, a new arrangement is required which carries along with it a rearrangement of the vested interests in jobs. People who are competent in the quality scene will increase in status while those skilled only in the old scheme of things (the scheme now being called BAD) must lose status. Managers are not particularly bad people. They are just conditioned to be extremely bad leaders.

The sheer quantity of wreckage, animate and inanimate, caused by these hidden priorities of management to thwart quality improvement, is colossal. That such wholesale destruction is routinely condoned is a testament to worker resignation, however misplaced, on the manager cult. In times past, workers believed that in blind obedience to the dictates of the organization, their future was assured. In this age of merger and acquisition, where worker security is never considered, that grand fallacy is exposed. Throughout history, management has been very consistent and loyal to its doctrines. POSIWID shows us what they are.

RULE - Job security has vanished. The commodity exchange of loyalty for protection from change has closed operations.

Despite an increasing volume of complaints, management largely ignores the quality issue until competition, usually foreign, eats into the markets. In the instance of color TV, managers did not begin to concentrate on improving product reliability until the Japanese had won a lead large enough to be fatal to many American firms, including the pioneers of the technology itself, like Dumont.

Note well that there are virtually no reliability data on products and services in use. Management's refusal to carry out studies of user experience is caused by a studied lack of concern. Shoddiness is encouraged as a means of enhancing short-run profitability. The neglect of quality data should be treated as a criminal offense. Instead, it has become the norm.

RULE - Six hundred business schools now produce 63,000 MBAs per year in order to keep pace with the annual number of businesses which perish (63,000).

The quality of incompetence knows no limits

There have been other insights to the executive value system besides quality, such as pollution/waste control. It is the same story. In most cases, reducing waste products by recovery and recycle has, rather than adding to operating expenses, provided a significant source of new revenue. Some plants make more money from recovered "waste" products than they did from primary material. Rather than being embraced by management, pollution control is fought at every turn. Government intervention to provide sufficient incentive has produced mostly investment in coverups, lawyers and public relations. The records, such as with asbestos, are too many, too consistent and too clear to mislead POSIWID. The waste disposal issue will yield yet another flood of management horror shows. Social control shennanigans do not work on garbage.

Triple Analysis

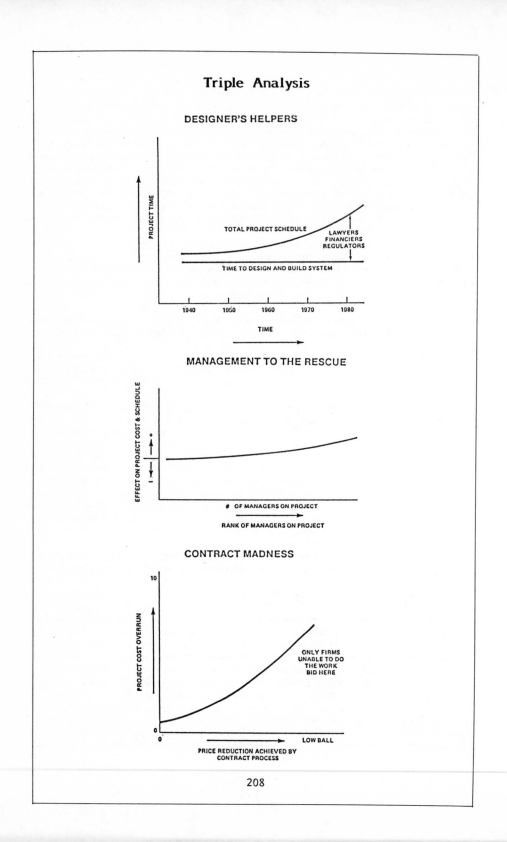

DESIGNER'S HELPERS

TOTAL PROJECT SCHEDULE

LAWYERS
FINANCIERS
REGULATORS

TIME TO DESIGN AND BUILD SYSTEM

PROJECT TIME

1940   1950   1960   1970   1980

TIME

MANAGEMENT TO THE RESCUE

EFFECT ON PROJECT COST & SCHEDULE

+

–

OF MANAGERS ON PROJECT

RANK OF MANAGERS ON PROJECT

CONTRACT MADNESS

10

PROJECT COST OVERRUN

ONLY FIRMS
UNABLE TO DO
THE WORK
BID HERE

0

0

LOW BALL

PRICE REDUCTION ACHIEVED BY
CONTRACT PROCESS

RULE - Institutional activities have made the world more complicated and less stable. Instability from complexity defeats human instincts. The October 19, 1987 stock market crash mechanism consisted only of standard, routine transactions.

While the real value system of professional management has not changed since the occupational specialty was invented, it has never held open house for inspection. History shows that professional management, routinely taking care to arrange for suitably-colored parachutes, can only be entrusted to perpetuate the status quo of the culture. This propensity is so strong that cases have occurred where a factory which had already gone through the quality leap (and still in process of reaping great benefits) reverted back when infiltrated by traditional management inherited in a takeover. Such examples serve as a constant reminder of the great power of primitive herd instincts, including those of the bell-cows, over reason and logic.

RULE - With the disconnection of feedback, the amount and kind of issues in jeopardy are irrelevant to decision-making. The overriding priority is preserving process.

When managers tell each other the facts of life about world commerce, no one is listening. The preaching, cajoling and threatening, even when originating from within the Establishment, fall on ears especially adapted to reject any distraction from financial reports. All the energy spent to persuade management to embrace new truths, by any measure an impressive amount, is a diversion and a waste. As one must be impressed by management's defenses, one must also be in awe of the foolhardy persistence of the barnyard ruckus for management to change. POSIWID shows their solution space is not related to the problem space.

RULE - Commercial-grade managers thrive in decaying organizations.

While professional management is entirely suitable for running undisturbed routine operations in a stable environment, history has shown that its basic value system and skills must be jettisoned when change is necessary. It is a common wartime practice to bypass the established system when there is a clear need to solve a novel problem quickly. The special military forces available to the President to handle sticky situations operate with a budget that is secret, unlimited and discretionary. There is no other way short wars are won.

This discussion of management, as seen from the perspective of the mess, is not polemic. If management was the main malefactor of the mess, we believe, the issue would have long been settled. As mentioned before, the **a priori** acceptance of managerial culpability is not only wrong, it is diversionary. The literature of this century is filled with all sorts of advice and admonitions for management and their ukase - as if management were somehow at fault and had withheld their power to remedy the situation. Managers do what is expected of them as members of the professional management guild as it has evolved, not necessarily what is needed to save the organization.

RULE - Every one of the solutions which institutions believe in are known not to work.

If the situation calls for action which fits management "rules of behavior," so much for the good. On the other hand, if the situation requires duty which falls outside of its culture, the choice is simple. The failure to understand

Petitions to Management

Mix and match

Imperative	Instruction
Management must	Be aware of changing conditions
Management should	Recognize the _____ problem
Management has to	Adapt to changing markets
Management can not fail to	Modernize the operation
Management can only	See the damage being done
Management will	Stop the waste
Management will act to	Produce a quality product
Management is obliged to	Remove the deadwood
Management has a duty to	Lead us out of this mess
Management is responsible to	Come up with new products
Management is expected to	Increase our market share
Management is entrusted to	Be in control
Management is compelled to	Take action necessary to solve
Management is supposed to	Safeguard the institution
Management is presumed to	Care about worker health
It is imperative that Management	Act in a moral, responsible way
It is vital that Management	Respond to new competition
It is crucial that Management	Think more long term
It is essential that Management	Improve working conditions
It is necessary that Management	Read the reports

management as just another discipline doing its thing by the same basic rules of misoneism that drive other guilds, is a failure to reckon with the mess. The important issue is to understand what professional management does and what it does not.

RULE - Management stops at the first solution that looks workable, selecting disaster on the installment plan.

In earlier times, the owners of the enterprise (feudal lords) did the managing and set the conditions for work. The seigneurial manner of management kept life for the serfs simple, if routinely uncomfortable. For instance, the high frequency of war placed a premium on the production of reliable gunpowder to preserve the Establishment. Large supplies of dependable gunpowder were the result of good ingredients, quality control and factory organization. The only problem was that gunpowder manufacturing was a notoriously dangerous trade with the loss of life so high that recruiting enough staff was difficult and insurance impossible.

Europeans came up with a simple expedient that solved the safety problem. The owner-operators of a gunpowder factory placed their homes in the middle of the works. With the lives of their own family at risk and the factory self-insured, management convinced the workers, without palaver, that safety would be first. Examples of such arrangements in this strategy are open for public visit at Hagley on the Brandywine river in Pennsylvania.

RULE - Managers are only trained to hold together organizations which have already failed.

The Industrial Revolution precipitated a change in management class activities, as fewer managers were owners. The change accelerates to this day. This change is not trivial. The culture of management has evolved along smart lines to meet the new challenges of modern times while maximizing its own self-interest. With the dominance of management by professionals rather than by owners, the radical idea of the golden parachute and no-lose employment contracts was quickly adopted. It is considered smart of a manager to obtain a golden parachute as a demonstration of his dedication to the culture. Placed into a position where he has no real control and exposed to complex messes he can not solve, no-lose employment contracts **make sense.**

Workers seldom appreciate that such adjustments made by management are powerful indicators of the absence of control. Workers are also slow to recognize that clever management has made the necessary arrangements, in advance, to win personally no matter what wreckage is caused in the organization they temporarily lead. Not only does the manager have his office and home far away from the gunpowder factory site, he has secured a cheap insurance policy by which he will gain if there is an explosive event.

Any organization in a mess features a management clique that is out of control. The situation soon triggers a disconnect and distance (D&D) response. Management abandons the uncontrollable scene for one more suitable to its capacities and training, such as divesting or acquiring another corporation. The acquisition process, which can be learned in any MBA university, is simple and fun. Those who play in this sandbox are called conglomerate executives and they gain prestige, win or lose, through the publicity that surrounds the game. Their perfunctory handling of organizational chaos at home, which should be hailed as opprobrious, is overlooked. Smart.

Handicapped Management

Like any specialty, professional management must stay within the narrow pathways deeded to its guild. Accordingly, information which would lead to the violation of territory has no useful value and can cause big troubles. Managers are issued blinders and ear plugs at graduation from management school to certify that they have achieved the appropriate level of illiteracy. Decisions are made by reflex and gut feelings. There is no use for information and feedback. Managers do very well without all the turmoil and thinking associated with change. Organizations self destruct while managers take the money and run.

HAVE FUN AT WORK

RULE - Be wary of any management decision untainted by relevant experience.

The relationship of manager to worker is a product of organizational structure and doctrine. There is nothing unique about the role of gentry, nobility, masters or executives that separates its relevance from the prevailing environment. As organizations are buffeted by the turbulence of a fast-changing world, so is the traditional linkage between manager and worker. As today's organizations still posses a design more suited to the conditions of the 17th century, management is encumbered with a cultural heritage more suited to the Model T assembly line. Organizations and managements alike are limited in their ability to adapt to change in environment. Their evolutionary clock runs too slow to keep pace with the realities of today and there is no built-in provision for a suitable correcting mechanism.

The manager animal, courtesy of POSIWID

There are many segments of society that constantly attempt to communicate with management. Since people cling to the illusion that management is in control of the Establishment, rather than the other way around, managers are mistaken to be the vehicle for remedy to perceived ills, real or imaginary. Managers are flooded with advice and instructions for action.

The imperatives for management (control inputs) are visible in so many places and have been for so long a time, we are driven to the conclusion, because they have so perfectly failed (system outputs), that the manager animal is blind.

Management is bombarded with verbal imperatives to take action from so many places and has been for so long a time, we are forced to the inference that the manager animal is deaf.

Studies of management information practices show that managers do not use the flood of data books relentlessly extruded by their management information systems department in making decisions. Basically, managers do not read. The literature of the management profession is not prepared by managers but is produced by university professors who, by practical necessity, owe their allegiance to the cult of education. Since they neither read nor write, the evidence carries us to the deduction that the manager animal is illiterate.

It seems quite unrealistic to expect a professional management guild member to cope with complex matters, a challenge difficult enough with a full set of faculties, when he is handicapped with a psychological contract that renders him illiterate, deaf and blind. History certainly bears this view out. Management failures and its inputs to avoid them are everywhere to be seen. The monotonous stream of duties for management end up in the organizational black hole and constitute a colossal diversion and waste of effort.

RULE - The more complicated the situation, the fewer and more selective the information channels managers use to direct actions.

Most efforts in the management assistance field are devoted to solving the basic dilemma of misguided human behavior and organizational dysfunction. Afraid to suggest an alternative, systems scientists focus on management as the means to bring about needed change. The hidden agenda of professional management has been shown by POSIWID. As with any organized guild, its scope is relatively narrow and rigid. The idea that management is in control and responsible for anything that can not be handled locally is as fallacious as the doctrine of corporate infallibility. People who believe such myths richly deserve to be officials in this life - and the next. **Erase.**

RULE - No instrument is fast enough to clock the speed attained by mangers detaching themselves from the complex problem.

While management is fully aware of its limitations, it is caught between the prescribed role of omniscience and the lack of effective options sanctioned by its guild. Managers, as interpreters of the organizational imperatives, are expected to reinforce doctrine, not to challenge it. The organizational process has selected managers for the material displays of social success. It is difficult to expect a manager to propose change to a social system which has elected him to high office.

It is more ridiculous to expect colleges to train managers to step out of line with the established dogma and to get in line with the truth, when they can't do it themselves. University factories destroy creativity and innovative thinking while emphasizing analysis over synthesis. Learning is reduced to discrete and unconnected bits of obsolete information. Students are taught to ignore situational dependencies on truth. "If it worked in the past, it will work in the future. If action produces the results you are looking for, a lot of action will produce a lot of results. Disregard complexifiers, you will be making decisions from your reflexes anyway."

RULE - Management by committee is, and always has been, a disaster. Some one should tell the business schools.

Obedience based upon a faith that management has magic powers is misplaced. It's not that workers really believe the party line, it's that, by plan, the organization provides no socially-acceptable alternative. There is, fortunately, an alternative and it begins with you.

Complex-problem solving requires a general framework for showing the interconnectedness of data in many different disciplines, an attribute notably absent from the coterie. The management guild, like all guilds, has provided no practical self-correcting machinery, particularly in the captive training institutions which dutifully transmit the same diseases. Guilds develop proficiency in enforcing standard practice, not in encouraging innovation. If top down is inoperative, the only viable alternative is bottom up. This expedient has made sense to the herd several times before.

Back to POSIWID on the Establishment

The ancient Greeks, with the normal inherited aversion to a change of cultures, set the early record for quick bottom-up enlightenment of their officials. One of the many invading countries convinced the Greek populace that, if it would only cooperate and let the well-meaning invaders in, the Greek way would be spared. When resisted by the prevailing Greek bureaucracy, the people assassinated the lot and installed a new set already known to possess the desired inclinations. The persuasive invader soon proved to be unbearable. When the population realized their first error, it was corrected by mass murder of the replacement Establishment and installation of another with like minds to what they possessed at the outset. The whole cycle was completed within 9 months.

The modern speed record was set by the French two centuries ago during the Reign Of Terror. When the revolution got into high gear slaughtering the prevailing government, the job was finished in four months. It only took the Parisians 30 days thereafter to execute the entire organization behind the revolution. While we may think the process was savage and excessive, other methods have taken a far higher toll in carnage. The unlearned lesson is that society has sanctified no civilized methods of change. War is the usual means by which Establishments (of the losers, that is) are normally "shaped."

In this century, the military process employed by Germany to shape its Establishment, for example, was slow and not at all cost-effective. Once modernized, however, the German Establishment outdid the victorious Allies. In spite of $80 billion invested in the effort, General Motors has hardly made a dent in modernizing its culture in the last ten years. By itself, $800 billion won't do the job either.

Spanish conquistadors found a native population so highly regimented and so completely deprived of initiative that when Montezuma fell, the communities offered no resistance. The Spanish forces were so small in comparison to the natives, they could have been overwhelmed, in spite of their weaponry, by sheer numbers. Instead of losing a few hundred in a battle with the conquistadors, which they could have easily won, within six years after Columbus discovered the new world, the natives suffered more than one million casualties. Today, the price for blind obedience to the Establishment can be much higher. Billions of people will die in a nuclear war.

While the large array of successful alterations to the Establishment have all been written with red tooth and claw, it does show the kinds of extreme physical action that it takes to achieve tangible results. In most cases, every intermediate step was taken before escalation reached guillotine logic. Note that Establishment changes, in spite of the need obvious to all, have been achieved by a process of displacement, not one of conversion of the tenants. Imagine what large driving forces must exist to invoke such drastic moves. To resort to such uncivilized measures is just one clue to the tremendous power of societies to control the behavior of "civilized" man.

RULE - No one knows the ultimate motivator.

Human nature of the species is slower to change than the living can imagine. While that feature of evolution has shown its strength in getting us here, it is a weakness in rapidly changing times. The same social inertia applies in full measure to our governing institutions.

The Orgman Era

Having no reason to plan for contingencies, Thomas Jefferson designed a political system based upon agriculture. Even in 1900, four out of every five USA citizens lived on a farm. The agricultural industry then was a loose confederacy of fiercely independent families. The influence of the humongous organizational form on everyday life in the country was minimal. Aside from the social role of the Grange and the Masons, each farmer was in control of his resources and his opportunities for risk. Beginning with a reverence for independence, the culture of agriculture was built upon trust and informal mutual support. Responsibility for one's own actions has always been fertile ground for thinking and innovation.

215

By 1980 the situation had become completely reversed. Only one out of every five USA citizens lived on a farm. The alliance of independent individuals having infrequent, optional relations with organizations has been displaced by a society highly dependent upon, and servant to, the organizational format. In exchanging a society characterized by independent self-determination for one that is organizationally dependent and controlled, much has been lost. The notion that an organization is superior to an individual in every way is a dangerous, unhealthy myth.

Insane leaders have never had difficulty in recruiting people to carry out any officially-sanctioned fantasy, however debased and dehumanizing. Their labor pool for inhumane activity is Organization Man, not the farmer. In now times it leads to technological exhibitionism and an annual untaxed eighty billion dollar drug business.

Mutual dependence upon a inherently flawed organizational structure does not lead to the design of more appropriate or adaptive structures. Any organization that forbids feedback is a menace to itself in particular and to society in general. The lack of a correcting mechanism has brought the downfall to every organization of man except the tribe.

RULE - Modernization exacerbates long-standing problems.

Man has designed organizations and granted these artifacts great powers of social control over himself in order to obtain the predictable behavior that delivers stability. Through no fault of man, it just happens to be that his marvelous organizational design is acutely counterproductive when environmental conditions have crossed the thresholds of turbulence set for an ancient age. Since the organization is his chosen idea, man becomes trapped by the awesome power of cognitive dissonance (part of his human nature) in a dynamic organizational cobweb. That is, he will do anything to defend his organization choice as correct - even when institutional walls are crumbling about him.

Fooled you!

Forces for change, rather than leading to organizational adaptation, lead to a stronger defense of the status quo (Livingston's Law again). Take a POSIWID look at the employment ads to see what is valued by the organization. While the self-description of the company will espouse grand plans and wide visions, you will not find a solicitation for the integrator, systems thinker and the innovator. What you will find, in spite of proclamations about new developments, are job descriptions for narrow slots already defined in detail.

Two superstars we know have amassed an array of credentials and cachets which answer all the pleas made by the organization featured in business section articles of the newspaper. In an experiment, we asked these gentlemen to respond to a wide variety of advertisements for superstar help - which they did. When organizations found the living answer to their written prayers, they ran. Our gifted collaborators were astonished at the hostile reactions. After a lifetime of preparation to qualify at everything our society proclaims as desirable, they found out that society doesn't want them. They haven't been the same since.

RULE - Nothing illustrates the capacity of management to lie better than the employment ads of the company.

The painful ongoing lesson from history in this matter is that to make a change, another route, which avoids the Establishment defenses (until things stabilize again), must be found. The only non-violent process known to succeed begins with the victims, through conscious recognition of the basic problem, and open discussion of the situation. The multitudes of isolated outposts of reason need to communicate with each other. Don't expect the government to grant a FCC license for that purpose.

Final preparations for having fun at work

Unfortunately, the natural process that created the Unfun problem in the first place has it retrograde. We don't have an eon of time to solve the **have fun at work** challenge via the evolutionary clock. Strategically it may be a "force majeure" race between deriving a solution and launching a nuke. Hope for the future of man in this man-made situation most certainly depends entirely upon the victims. We have concluded, most reluctantly and only after exhausting every other avenue, that Unfun at work will only be brought under control by your instigation, sapience and sweat. This is a monition, not a plea out of desperation. **Fun at work** has a much more durable foundation when Unfun has been eliminated. Don't feel glum about demolishing the familiar, but bad part of your mental models. They had to go.

In spite of continual media efforts to portray otherwise, the great bulk of our population is comprised of workers. It is the workers who produce the wealth and it is the workers who pay the taxes. Regarding the latter, it is noteworthy to witness the pomp and circumstance surrounding the tax reform circus that comes to Washington every few years. The song and dance is conducted by a snake-charming elite to hypnotize the workery into a comatose state. During the trance-of-the-salariat the cards are stacked so that the deal, as it must be to support the whole social structure, remains the same.

RULE - The manager that can stop system and environment from co-evolving hasn't been born.

Workers don't get issued golden parachutes when they sign up. It is the workery which suffers the most with the complexity mess. It is the workers who fell for the pitch to dutifully follow the dictates of the organization in exchange for security. When the mill closes, it is the worker who is set adrift in a poorly-run welfare state to find another occupation. Managers know better. Not surprisingly, the principles and ethics of management do not coincide with those of their employees.

It is becoming increasingly apparent that, without a change initiated by the workers, there will be no change in the Unfun stress situation. Ignorance is not bliss for the workery, and some mighty significant issues are still waiting to be understood. For instance, two years after Hiroshima, only one in a hundred understood that an extraordinary event had occurred. The journey from irresponsible to responsible in this matter is admittedly full of hazards. But, if we must have an enemy, let it be the silence of our unchallenged mental models.

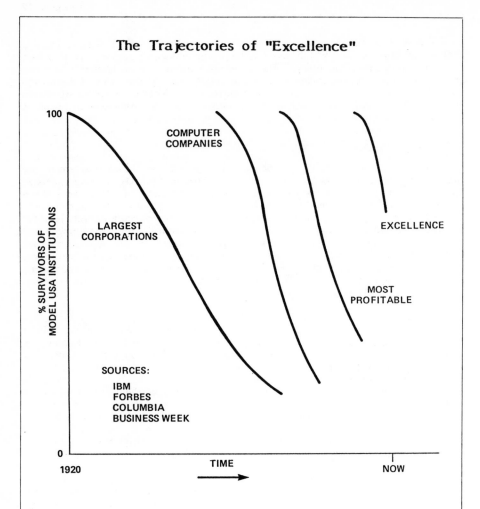

The Trajectories of "Excellence"

% SURVIVORS OF MODEL USA INSTITUTIONS

100

COMPUTER
COMPANIES

LARGEST
CORPORATIONS

EXCELLENCE

MOST
PROFITABLE

SOURCES:

IBM
FORBES
COLUMBIA
BUSINESS WEEK

0

1920

TIME

NOW

The fact that performance history is ignored does not mean it is missing. The Establishment is so sure of itself and so confident that feedback will be automatically neglected, that bottom-line evidence is everywhere. The record speaks for itself. Not only must we use the wrong measures of merit, what we think are its sources must also be in error. The best, the biggest and the richest are attributes which quickly perish through natural organizational processes. Anyone who thinks he knows what makes for "excellence" is headed for a banquet of crow. It is embarrassing to have your assessments proven so wrong so soon after the ink dries. There ought to be a law. Ooops!

While you have been confined in a prehistoric psychic eggshell of your own construction, there is much that you can do to **have fun at work** when you break out to the outer world. The problem is really so big and so bad that even starting to move in a positive direction (getting your cognitive models to match with reality) is dramatically happy. Like the man who placed stones in his shoes in the morning to increase his pleasure in taking them off at night, you have been running around with irritating adornment and there is nowhere to go but up. Unlike a weight-loss diet regimen, payoff results here are quick and obvious. Undoing Unfun is just regaining some basic inalienable rights that you have unwittingly, in a series of little concessions to passive regimentation of your actions, given away. Leaving the paradigm of failure frees up your values and makes room for growth. You grow just to know.

We paid big dues to get this far and POSIWID has cleared the way for progress. The wicked witch of the Establishment blocks our mission no more and the gleaming gates of Emerald City are just ahead. The Wizard of Oz is waiting to grant our wishes for fun at work. Just please don't ask the Wizard for a quick fix. Only losers clamor for simple cures to this mess and they are thrown out empty-handed. The Wizard doesn't want to blemish his record.

HAVE FUN AT WORK

HFAW Checklists CHECKLIST

I. The common semantic language

    A. The language of failure

        1. Eliminations
            a. Entreaties to management
        2. Vulnerabilities
            a. Voids
            b. Livingston's Law of Inversion
        3. Organizational communications
        4. Organized deceptions
            a. F4
            b. Denials
        5. Track connections to standard practice
        6. Perceptual limitations and perversions
        7. Establishment profile

    B. The language of success

        1. Boundaries and interfaces
        2. The HFAW toolbox
        3. The practitioners toolbox supplement
        4. Elements of complexity
            a. Signs of complexity perceived and the ZOI
        5. Project factors for go/no go assessment

II. The HFAW order of battle
    A. Structure for situation assessment
        1. Viable options
            a. Darts
            b. Structure pack

III. The erase and replace summary

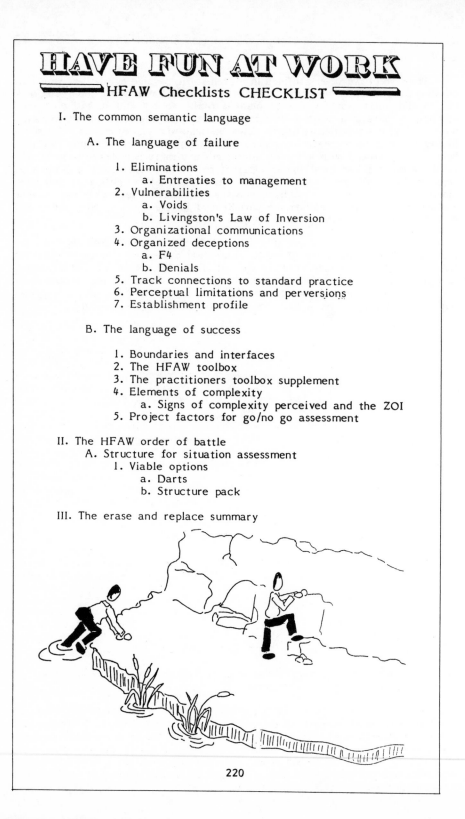

Chapter Thirteen

Have Fun at Work Level One

"If a man does not keep pace with his companions, perhaps it is because he hears a different drummer. Let him step to the music which he hears, however measured or far away."

Henry David Thoreau

Well, it's about time for the different drumming. The demolition derby for subconscious subterfuge, the hardest part by far, is over. While the tessellation of thought trails on mental model madness are counter-intuitive, tedious and tiresome, destruction was the only way to start building fun at work from level ground. If you paid your dues, most of your Bad Seventies and academic fictions will be gone. It was crucial to stop momentum towards self-defeating ends so, as a basic requisite to **have fun at work,** we have mercilessly hammered away at the inherited injunctions to fail. An expedient solution to Unfun at work simply doesn't exist. Now, like Mohammed, it is time for your hegira to rationality.

This Chapter is not a prescription for your management to fill. It is a step-by-step procedure for **you** to implement. You already have the experience, the knowledge, the creative potential and the necessary talents to pull it off. You have witnessed these same qualities in your peers at off-site company functions like retirement parties and picnics (ever wonder where all that imagination and coordination was concealed at work?). What you have been lacking are appropriate references, tools, ingredients and a recipe, nothing more. Now, it is only an investment of time and labor.

GITLIN'S DICTUM - Let's not do anything stupid.

The initial objective, level one, is to eliminate stress, your stress. Saving yourself from stress at work is a goal towards fun you can achieve without asking anyone for permission to try. Start anytime. You have full control. No one and no organization can give you stress without your consent and, if you have given it, call it back into court. While a major goal is to greatly increase the variety of your coping capabilities, the key to stress reduction begins with a stringent analysis of the demands being placed upon you by the situation. The first phase of having fun is completely self-contained. It is within you.

RULE - Control starts from knowing what is significant and what is needed. All else is the technology of foolishness.

The structure of the recipe is the cycle of control. It starts with assessing the situation, which consists of the environment and the project. You have been given the ubiquitous reference model for failure and the priceless reference model for success. The situation is measured by comparison to the two bracketing reference models. The measurements are used to prevent premature conclusions and minimize prejudice. No drug gives quicker stress relief than working on a rational process for gaining useful, relevant knowledge. And work it is.

Jamming Corpo Radar

Social control activators have exquisitely sensitive pick-ups on instincts and reflexes. The trick to prevent social punishment from being inflicted is to prevent the detectors of behavioral deviations from firing. One way of going in under, and effectively jamming sensor systems is to provide a stream of loyalty displays. Our man from Posiwid wears the corpo hat and tie, waves its flags and owns its stock. But note, in addition to the policy manuals and retirement plans, that in his hands at all times is a case full of corporate vulnerabilities. Displaying an abundant and continuing stream of loyalty-and-awareness acts to cause the Deviant Detector mechanism to fail.

Pursuit of the attainable

Next comes synthesis of the measurements. The many indicators mean something in terms of influencing actual environmental status. The study will lead to conclusions about the situation. In this organizational behavior business, situations are never grey. Corporate situations are painted on a white canvas from a palette loaded with only one color - black. The conclusions drawn can then be connected to viable courses of action. The execution of the plan will connect to results. The feedback loop can be short - it can't be too short. This structure does not confine, it sets you free. You know you can't trust your instincts.

The two categories of situational variety are the possible and the impossible. The tables provided are job performance aids (JPAs) to help you distinguish between the two. If the situation **is** hopeless, there is little reason for stress. The demand to pursue the impossible is no demand at all - what you have exposed is a fraud. If the situation **is not** hopeless, there is little reason for stress. If you have made an authentic situation assessment, you have already determined (sensed) that you can cope. We know you are not mentally lazy or you would never have gotten this far in the book - even if you started in the back.

RULE - Stress is punishment, inflicted by the Almighty, for attending school.

The basis of the recipe for stress elimination is safety. None of the steps in the recipe for Level One involves the slightest risk of social controls. In fact, you will remain far from the bleeding edge. You do all the cooking by yourself, telling no one. You need to experiment and experiments mean that errors will be made. You need to be able to fail and be the only one who knows. While failure along the way is normal, it needs to be "managed" and that is what the recipe is for.

Any paradigm shift is a painful learning process because, in nature's plan, we learn from error and error alone. We encourage you to experiment with the methodological magic because unless you make mistakes you will not own the recipe. The beginner experiments are designed to learn something. In organizations, the safe space you need to experiment comes from not breaking the rules. The recipe is the most direct route to **have fun at work.**

Psychological armor

From the reference-languages perspective, ultimately pragmatic, you will become increasingly aware and knowledgeable about dimensions of the situation that you didn't know existed. This new-found awareness will probably be noticed by others and, since it is a deviation from their norm, it will arouse suspicion of malicious intent. The antidote for all triggers of social control is institutional loyalty. Bake awareness and loyalty together into an inseparable combination. Never display awareness without displaying loyalty in equal or greater amounts. When you must err, overdo loyalty. It jams their radar.

RULE - Finding a place to fix blame for stress does nothing to diminish it.

The triggers of social control are instinct-driven and subconscious and so, fortunately, is the perception of loyalty to the enterprise. Break no rules, display fealty and the safe zone for awareness is your property. Experiment with your neutralizer until the pattern is accepted as the new norm. You might as well brush up on your acting skills anyway, there's more scripts to come.

Loyalty display is an active process. Wear the company tie, become a stock holder, praise the heroes, recite the folklore, profess appreciation for sound policy, work extra, join the bowling team and don't break any rules. Come to work on time, return early from lunch, wave the company flag on cue, speak only praise for management decisions, and keep a straight face. You are sending mixed signals to the attitude detectors in your environment and it confuses their social control computer. Don't get caught laughing when the computer goes tilt.

Now add abstraction to the cauldron of safety. Abstraction means safety. When your awareness grows close to the cataract, and it will, fill your balloon with the superheated air of abstraction. You can sail over any social control precipice by elevating your discussion to at least two levels of abstraction removed from the local particulars. If your department fiddles with software, e.g., you can talk about similar problems in the industry. Stay away from the software mess in your department and the mess that is your institution. Cultivate two-level-minimum abstraction as a habit. The science fiction industry, as an example, is involved with neither science nor fiction. Science fiction stories are abstract assaults on dysfunctional organizations (evil empires). Abstraction works anywhere.

RULE - Software does not respond to enthusiasm.

Who's the boss?

The right of popular resistance to the Establishment is traditional. In feudal society, vassal homage was a firm contract and a bilateral one. The workers, or vassals, were obliged to pay part of what they produced to the king and the king, in turn, was obliged to protect the land and maintain order. The right to resist unjust authority was never bartered away by the workers. In 1090, an Alsatian monk described the king's obligation to the vassals as "like the swineherd to the master that employs him."

Workers, being the number and substance of the organization, are still the primary source of power. Workers outnumber, by far, all other categories lumped together. If they don't shovel coal into the boiler, the ship doesn't go. It is the privileged sect of the organization that is vulnerable, not you. Do you think they make so much fuss because they are in control? You have been given the references to expose elitist, Establishment vulnerabilities whenever and wherever you wish. It is a most potent weapon in the arsenal for Level Two (next Chapter).

In this Chapter, Level One, the tools and the knowledge are used by you to extract yourself from stress. Stress is basically caused by feeling out of control. You can soon put an end to that. The recipe is a defensive strategy and it is safe. After your mental fortress is in good working order, we will show you how to take the fun offensive. The same weaponry can take you all the way to functional control of the organization - and you don't even have to change your job title.

RULE - Officials only display rational faculties when they have retired from any position in the organization where they might be expected to act on rational directives.

To **have fun at work,** allow that the situation **can** be impossible. It can be truly hopeless. The recipes for corrective action to the situation assume a threshold of possibility. For hopeless situations you can adapt, knowing that the organization will not change for the better, and have all the fun there is to have. Adapting to a sick organization does not make you well. The same process shown here can be used to evaluate the prospects in **any** situation. You already know that most organizations are sick.

Assessing the situation

Start with the social system environment. It always dominates situations and the recipe calls for assessing environment in two levels. Before looking at your local weather, take measures of the institutional climate in general (remember the first DfC step is always **context**). Determine its age and its size. See if the business it thinks it's in is dynamic or stable. Count the number of vertical levels in the hierarchy between the top and the bottom. Figure the ratio of good departments to bad departments. Observe how often top management mixes it up with the troops. Note the frequency and severity of control signals and reorganizations.

Scrutinize management. Learn the ratio of good leaders to deadwood. Check the time lag to kick out the managerial misfits and the speed of rewarding the stars. List the discrepancies between what the company espouses (and advertises) and reality in the trenches as you know it. Measure the number of departmental rivalries and the number of twig-of-science dialects. Determine the general attitude about experimentation, risk and failure. See if the history of corporate growth is one of sporadic incrementalism or radical innovation. Learn what their clients and competitors think about them.

Study the organization as a communication system. Notice how information is compressed and expanded on its way up and down the hierarchy. Estimate where the disconnect occurs which separates the knowledge of the actual situation from that fantasized by management. After you have identified the channels in the network over which information travels, check the quantity of information flow and its novelty. Search for any mechanisms which compensate for the installed impediments to good communications. Note how management uses the data flood from MIS to make decisions.

The purpose of this audit is to gauge structural rigidity and communication effectiveness. If the superstructure is in rigor mortis, a common state of affairs, it places a limit in your span of influence. It also means that Livingston's Law is generally invoked. Our own experience with corporations show only too clearly that bad habit patterns have much greater social inertia than good ones. Good cultures and bad cultures both can exhibit lock-in. The bad situations naturally get worse. The good cultures need constant cultivation. The basic plan of the Bad Seventies, we have learned from POSIWID, is self-destruction. The fact of a hopeless organization does not mean that the local environment is necessarily impossible. Every "stiff" organization species has its marvelous, supple exceptions.

Structure For Situation Assessment

I. Environment (Chance for success with **any** non-routine issue?)

    A. External to the organization
        1. Turbulence and rate of change
    B. Organizational climate
        1. History and mythology
        2. Age, size, rates of change
        3. Management, number of layers
        4. Communication effectiveness
    C. PWG weather
        1. Punish and reward system
            a. Skills encouraged and used
            b. Desired performance punished
            c. Non-performance rewarded
            d. Performance matters
            e. Performance restricted

II. Particular project (Chance for success with issue at hand?)

    A. Technical system check list
        1. Elements of complexity check list
    B. Social system check list
    C. Place in the Universal Scenario (Window for alteration?)

VIABLE OPTIONS

I. Impossible situation
    A. Timely exit
    B. Accelerate to EOPMD
        1. Use structure to identify more problems and errors
    C. Join as an EOPMD firefighter

II. Possible situation
    A. Refer to HFAW levels attained

HAVE FUN AT WORK

If the official, documented communications system is unworthy of the name, the informal, undocumented one will be flourishing as much as the constraints will allow. First examine the physical arrangements. Functionally-related groups can be scattered around in separate buildings. (It doesn't take much in the way of physical obstacles to thwart communications. A common cafeteria or gathering place, however, can compensate.)

Context established, time for target matters

The first measures taken of the institution reveal the nature of the general environmental climate. After the institutional framework issues are recorded (context), assemble the local weather report. Note that the mental ghettos of the organization can be counted upon to act in a manner opposite to needs and espoused goals. If flexibility is essential, management will demand loyalty to traditional practices. If coordination is vital, parochial interests will stiffen (Livingston's Law).

Having fun at work is mostly concerned with the local environment - the one that counts. The organizational context for the local scene is not trivial, although its influence on shaping behavior falls off dramatically the further away you get from the far side of the Primary Working Group (PWG) moat. Different variables relate to the local scene. Your goal here is to determine if the home base setup is the norm or the exception compared to the corporation as a whole. If exceptional in the plus direction, all to the good. If not, a different tack must be set. You want to learn the degree to which your associates are intimidated by the system. This can be done, fortunately, without making any direct inquiries at all.

Construction of the local cognitive weather report is guided by another structure. The first checkpoint is to assess how much of the talent actually possessed by the local band, the PWG, is used at work. Of the skills they have, check the match with job demands. Large mismatches always raise warning flags. If there is no problem with an insufficient cushion of know-how and experience, ignore the talent-to-demand matchup issue. There is not one corporate job in a thousand beyond what can be learned by any high school kid in a month.

RULE - Dealing with stress is just like working with complex numbers. There is a real part inseparably linked to an irrational part.

The remaining steps call for comparing the reward and punishment system-in-use to proclaimed performance criteria. Once again the search is for gross mismatches rather than imperfect alignments. Look for punishment for "desired" performance. One common example of that mismatch is in production quotas. If the spread around the bogey is large, see how the stars are treated in practice. If the local social control weather is cold on performance labeled by supervision as "hot," then hot performance will be avoided.

RULE - No corporation has ever invented a punishment terrible enough to outweigh the ridicule of peers.

The other side of that coin is to check the reward and punishment practice regarding non-performance. For example, the espoused goal of schooling is to infuse the mentally malleable with knowledge, skill and understanding. The attainment of such goals are measured via artifacts called examinations. Academic management, possessed with the full cycle of control, rewards on a basis that has little direct relationship to effective teaching. Instead, raises and promotions are

Stress Disposal Program

Work Context

Problem Content

Problem Solving Process

Track A Methods
or
Track B Methods

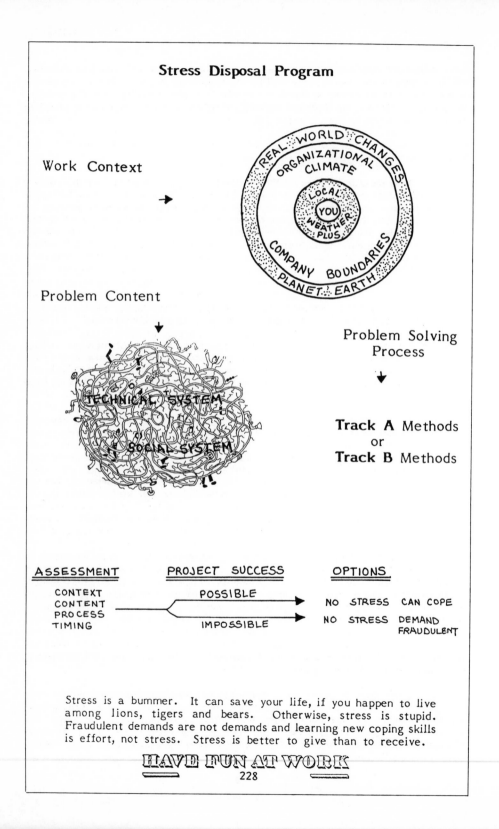

ASSESSMENT	PROJECT SUCCESS	OPTIONS
CONTEXT CONTENT PROCESS TIMING	POSSIBLE →	NO STRESS CAN COPE
	IMPOSSIBLE →	NO STRESS DEMAND FRAUDULENT

Stress is a bummer. It can save your life, if you happen to live among lions, tigers and bears.   Otherwise, stress is stupid. Fraudulent demands are not demands and learning new coping skills is effort, not stress. Stress is better to give than to receive.

HAVE FUN AT WORK

based **only** upon time served and academic credit hours earned. At the university the distortion is carried to more grotesque proportions as rewards are connected **only** to quantity of money granted by outside contracts obtained and the number of published pages. Exhorted to achieve one set of objectives, the institution rewards another.

RULE - Nothing provides more excuses to avoid work than an elaborate job specification.

The pressure placed on education to correct itself, always directed to its officials, is amplified and transmitted to the teachers in the front lines with your children - where the delivery of education transpires. In another display of Livingston's Law, the control action achieves an end opposite to its well-stated intentions. As officials become progressively insecure, because they are out of control and in the spotlight, they abuse teachers with scorn and indifference. The real vulnerabilities of the Establishment, in yet another display of convoluted logic, are always expressed through distraught trickery to make the workery feel vulnerable.

RULE - The more headquarters is out of control of the situation, the more they punish the troops. Instinctive management, in stress, demotivates.

It is common to find that "misbehaving" is rewarded. Supervisors who keep their subordinates uninformed so as achieve status, for instance, become petty tyrants with acquired power. If not punished, their behavior is rewarded. In the organizations which operate processes, like production lines, it is common to have such tyrants. Their subjects serve silently in humiliation and abuse - waiting for their turn to become "licensed" for tyranny. When they finally inherit the dictator's throne, they know exactly how to behave. The contrasts in behavior we have witnessed in this situation are too dramatic to escape notice.

More local weather indicators

The most critical factor to measure is the perceived significance of the work itself. If the work doesn't really matter to the rest of the organization, it will tend not to get done. In our conglomeration, nothing good happens to those who perform and nothing bad happens to those who don't. For our life of experimentation in La La land, where failure is the norm, indifference is great. For less-crazed citizens, it takes away dignity and self-worth. Not fun.

In operating organizations, the prime measure is the balance between the penalty (or reward) for mistakes and the rewards for "failure-free" performance. If the balance favors minimizing bad marks much more than getting gold stars for good marks, the distortions can get bizarre. In most operating scenes, there are no rewards for keeping the rickety bucket of bolts going, but if the production line stops because of an error previously committed and deemed bad, it's cause for great negative fury. At one plant we know, this policy has reduced efficiency to the tune of several tens of millions of dollars annually. The bill constantly escalates, and it is paid without a whimper.

In the military, this prevalent value-system mismatch causes great anxiety for operators of sonar screens. His cost of missing an approaching torpedo still leaves a chance that the contraption for destruction will miss. If he sounds the alarm when the torpedo is really a shark, the price to be paid is in no doubt whatsoever. Punishment for disturbing the peace will be swift and certain.

Safety systems are disabled by the punishment and reward system for employees, not by terrorists.

Last of all, look at the routine impediments to doing the job. Things like paperwork and the obligation to comply with rules imposed for the internal sake of external agencies, can sap the enthusiasm out of a rabid zealot. When an operating organization is dominated by the purchasing department, for example, the obstacles to getting parts and materials can be so great that all hope for preventative maintenance activity is turned into neglect. When a machine fails and big damage is suffered, parts get ordered fast. Unfortunately, there is no correcting feedback path that connects the wreckage to purchasing practices. Accountants see to that.

RULE - Any reprimand for error deletes all possibility for solution.

A new accountant at a western railroad noticed a large annual bill for replacing broken doors in passenger stations. Going further, he found that washroom doors were kept locked and needy passengers had to get the key from the ticket agent. His predecessor saved the railroad $200 by only authorizing one key per station. When customers walked off with the key, there was no way to get the door open. To obtain a new key, forms had to be supplied for a "capital expense" - which took the approval of the superintendent of passenger service and six months. For 'emergency repairs' however, the agent was given a cash account to use at his own discretion. A busted lavatory door is clearly the greatest emergency possible in a passenger station - and every station had an ax. The tale of the observant accountant who exposed the mismatch is another story.

Your home base will either "feel" intimidated by the system, as they define it, or not - no grey areas. Either side of the threshold switch is self-reinforcing. Groups that feel secure to act on their own will not easily give that feeling up. Cloisters that quake when the boss yells are brain dead. It's easy to tell one class from the other. You can almost trust your instincts.

Through structure and supporting JPAs, you have been able to assault the nebulous complexities of organizational climate and local weather, and determine status with a high degree of reliability. Furthermore, you have acquired some Ashby knowledge which will be helpful in day-to-day activities. You grow just to know.

At this point, gather together all of the factors and judge whether or not **any** complex project would have a chance to succeed in the current environment. Using the language for success and its requisites, look at the facts and draw your conclusions. There is a simple check on your decision. Take a look at the historical record of your company with complex projects. If you have determined that **any** complex project must fail, the record will show the trail of tears on particulars. Once again, the frequency and severity of its failures are helpful measures. You can also estimate the inverse relationship of specification sophistication to damage caused. While tiny specs are unrelated to project outcome, comprehensive specs and elaborate contracts always cause disasters.

RULE - The more resources spent on specifications and contracts, the sooner the project will turn into a larger mess.

Evaluating your project

Knowing the nature of the underlying structures, you know that projects either follow the yellow brick road to the junk yard or they proceed through the Skunkworks to triumph. Telling one from another is simple. If you have ascertained that **any** complex project must fail, don't be surprised if yours is giving you fits. Chain yourself to these sturdy structures so you don't fall into the cosmic abyss of associating your problems with particular people. As people, always remember that it is the Bad Seventies that see them through the day. That is quite a handicap. Think of them as impaired rather than pernicious - a feat easier said than done. If you can't resist retribution, in **have fun at work** level two you will be given the invisible weapons of torment. Sometimes the devil wins out and we sin a bit ourselves.

Use the Universal Scenario as a template and road-map to locate your project's position. The Universal Scenario is in regular performance at thousands of locations and hasn't missed a curtain call yet. (If you are fortunate enough to work in a Skunkworks, you are having fun anyway. The DfC scenario will locate your position in the Skunkworks factory.) The location on the map fully describes the situation and connects directly to the list of options. If you are between D&D and EOPMD, the threshold has been crossed and Livingston's Law is in effect. You now know the herd is inaccessible to reason. When reason can only bring punishment, scratch reason. When you have done your homework, determining project status is a snap.

Alternatives

Stress relief is your moral duty, not an option. A "demand" to perform that is wildly hopeless is a Kamikaze run. If you were asked to melt the polar ice caps, it would only bring a smile. One college professor submitted a proposal to the Pentagon to neutralize the Russian submarine fleet by boiling the oceans. The complex project in the Track A environment (between D&D and EOPMD) is no less ridiculous. You have accepted stress only because you have not been supplied suitable measurements of demand. The head shed counts on those Bad Seventies to keep you in line. Always start off by evaluating the demands of the job.

RULE - The more you detect faults in the working environment, the less the environment will allow you to accomplish.

If you are neck-deep in the Big Muddy, leave your physical self mired - but get your mental self the hell out of there. You only have to appear to be "stressed" with the others, as before, to duck social controls. When you shed the demand side, **you** have removed stress and gained command of your senses. To avoid punishment, just don't tell anybody. When you have ejected stress, **you** are in control, not the "system." Your awareness has set you free. Loyalty display will keep you there. It is a great relief to be out of the swamp and standing on dry, level ground. You deserve it.

You can now choose to stay put and accept the unalterable situation without the frustration of thinking it should or could be otherwise. Your alternatives then lie in how to display loyalty. You can go through the motions of conformity with fanfare and without complaint. Echo whatever the mindless herd recites. Do whatever is rewarded and avoid whatever is punished, while saving your knowing smirk for private times. You go with the flow by conscious choice, not under the social whip.

Go/No Go Assessment

TECHNICAL SYSTEM FACTORS

- Are there more than two technologies or disciplines involved?
- Can the technologies change much during the project?
- Will the solution system require a lot of maintenance?
- Is the **real** problem poorly understood by the project officials?
- Will standard, conventional practices be used?
- Any new or unfamiliar technologies involved?
- Are there more than two adequate solutions?
- Is the project time frame more than two years?

If more than one "yes" answer to the questions on the technical system checklist, proceed to its inseparable companion, the social system.

SOCIAL SYSTEM FACTORS

- Is the organization large (>250 persons)
- Is the organization over five years old?
- Is the project controversial?
- Are there more than three departments involved?
- Will standard corporate practices be used?
- Is prime project responsibility distributed?
- Is project control assumed by professional officials?
- Any built-in adversarial relationships?
- Are there more than two organizations involved?
- Many lawyers, bankers, regulators, insurers, consultants?

If more than three "yes" answers to the questions on the social system list, failure of the project has not been abandoned to speculation. The communication needs are out of control.

COMPLEXITY FACTORS

- Many unfamiliar, new elements
- Many parts, many dissimilar parts
- Many relationships between parts, many kinds of relationships
- Many technologies, crafts, skills, disciplines, arts
- Many departments, many organizations, many regulators
- Long time exposures, changing conditions, shaky assumptions
- Large risks, large consequences, large staffs
- Political controversy, conflicting objectives
- Big dollars, long time to recover investments
- Many solutions, many constraints, many requirements
- Many lawyers, bankers, brokers, consultants
- Many managers unfamiliar with the problem or the technology

HAVE FUN AT WORK

You can now knowingly chose to abandon the pursuit of the impossible for other domains. The only time when that strategy is frowned upon is at the EOPMD marker. Smart money leaves the doomed ship with a cushion of time before EOPMD. The reverse is also true. Join a scene that is in or soon will be in EOPMD (advertising that **the** mess is not **your** mess) and you will receive the firefighter's reward. People think, to the end, that the disaster is caused by particular people failing to use the sanctioned tools with sufficient skill. You can use that ridiculous instinct to advantage.

Fire-fighting for profit

It is the **act** of firefighting that is rewarded, not the number of flames extinguished. As long as you are perceived to be engaged in firefighting, e.g. by long hours, you can do anything you want. Rewards are dispensed in direct relation to the height of the flames. Spend most of your time ferreting out hidden problems to make the flames higher. There are **always** tons of problems that are unknown and overlooked. The systems structures work like magic to identify issues which fell through the cracks. It is fun to find them and pass them up to management. Always keep a reserve of unidentified problems ready to transmit and always have an elaborate **technical** description ready to explain the complexity of the mess. Show how one thing affects another until the absorption limit of your audience is reached. The more they see what you know about the extent of the wreckage, the more you will be left alone. The quick-fix artists get a lot of publicity before their remedies prove worthless, but they don't last. The skills you acquire in using Ashby develop into a competence you can use anywhere.

Knowing the behavioral imperatives that drive the scene gives you many options to capitalize on your knowledge. You can make silent predictions and reap the joy in watching them unfold on cue. Getting rewards by understanding how the machinery works is both profit and fun. That's double fun. You can laugh at the human folly surrounding you and cheer your escape from the mental ghetto. That's fun too. So is confirming that your investment in learning is paying off. No one can have too much variety in coping mechanisms. The world hasn't stopped growing more complex. You can predict a bright future for complexity.

The other dimension of the stress equation is the variety in your abilities to cope. The more and varied skills you have to "regulate" situations, the wider the variety of demands you can handle without stress. As you have learned, any complex matter can be converted with appropriate structures and tools into just a difficult matter that can then be licked with time and labor. The work situation may be hostile to such heresy, but at least **you** know the true score. It has been precisely the exercise of complexity-resolving tools, and the increase in coping variety they bring, that relieved your stress.

RULE - Structures filled with facts, in a fair fight, will always win over emotion, generalizations and intellectual indolence.

Level One of **have fun at work** will take time to implement. It is safe and sure, as long as you keep it to yourself. Gain a cushion of experience with this new language system. Like most things, the amount of fun is related to the risks you are willing to take. The next phase will mark the switch from defensive fun to offensive fun. You were issued your bullet-proof vest here. The thrill of the hunt starts in the next Chapter, and we're not chasing after bunny rabbits.

The HFAW Order Of Battle

LEVEL 1 - Basic defense

    1 - Stress removal, extraction from the Big Muddy

        A - Situation assessment
        B - Comparing demands to possibilities
        C - Increasing coping competency

LEVELS 2, 3 & 4 - Offense

    2 - Individual offense

        A - Awareness + loyalty display
           1 - Discrepancy detection and reporting
           2 - Darts for defense
           3 - Balancing distortions
           4 - Structure pack
           5 - Cognitive dissonance implantation

    3 - PWG offense

        A - Recruiting a PWG coalition
           1 - Escalated discrepancy detection
           2 - Common language (failure/success)
           3 - Structure pack
           4 - Discussion of some undiscussables
           5 - Group darting for defense
           6 - Group cog dis implantation

    4 - Multiple PWG offense

        A - Recruiting PWG constituency
           1 - Escalate undiscussables discussion
           2 - History identification
           3 - Connections of practices to wreckage
           4 - Promotion of two-track think
        B - Magna Carta time
           1 - Instant cog dis implantation
           2 - Track B decision

Chapter Fourteen

Have Fun At Work Level 2 and Beyond

Achieving Escape Velocity

When you have reached the comfort level promised by the do-yourself-a-favor strategy, a sanctuary-building operation, you are ready for more fun. Once security is achieved, it quicky slips in priority. In this Chapter, we leave the sanctuary and take the arsenal on the offensive, level by level. Like many adventures in life, the higher the level of excitement, the more efforts you have to make and the more chances you have to take. Since the opportunities to experiment are unlimited, we favor incrementalism (pioneering by gradual steps) rather than living at the edge. Big trials and their attendant big risks are only necessary when opportunities are sparse. The social situations you need for experimentation, involving people under oppressive corporate control, are everywhere.

The annual amount of organizationally-caused waste in 1988 (USA) is about one trillion dollars, including institution-caused worker health problems (mental and physical). A wreckage-prevention challenge of this magnitude is certainly no pushover for anyone. The Unfun and waste persist, not because of greedlock, but simply because the value system encoded in our genes ranks survival matters on the African savannah in higher importance.

RULE - Half of the organizations formed fail within two years. The other half avoided the methods taught in business school.

The most important fact to keep in mind, and the primary purpose for writing this book, is that **you are not alone.** You do not have to accept the social system dystopia as an obedient, isolated drudge who is unable to challenge the huge institutional machinery (as in the old saying "You can't fight city hall"). There are many kindred souls (they are just scattered and unconnected) and lots of accessible, friendly help. There is a growing list of tested tools specifically designed to help achieve advanced levels of having fun at work. There is a growing catalog of tangible, ready-made job performance aids (JPAs) that you can obtain to use right at home base. There is first-rate art, by Rob Schouten, based directly upon the principles disclosed in this book, which you can proudly display on the wall. You are not alone, and you do not have to experience all of the mistakes made by others who are engaged in the same struggle. Anything we use, you can use.

This Chapter uses the diorama perspective, showing the procedures and tools in general context. The next Chapter employs the display-case format for the arsenal. Each aid is discussed in some of the various ways it can be used. Thereby you can get a handle on this funny business from two directions. Mix the tools to situations by random chance and surprises are guaranteed. Note that we only certify the surprise part. For some of these surprises you should be prepared to duck.

When you leave the sanctuary of your own intellectual domain, there is risk of error and social punishment. It is inherent. The farther away from the cranial fortress you venture, the more fireworks you can create by hitting an unmarked tripwire in peopleland. As there is a direct relationship between fun intensity and the deviation from the norm (if the norm was fun you wouldn't need this book), be aware there is also a direct tie between social resistance and deviation from the norm. You will be adventuring into the heartland of social controls to **have fun at work** Level Two.

RULE - Failure is bad. The absence of failure is really bad.

To create new norms in social situations, incrementalism is always more reliable than sudden force. Erosion wins over dynamite. Forget the flawless rationale of your case when dealing with others. If you present a struggle between emotion and reason to (and even **within**) rational people, emotion always wins.

This axiom holds invariant whether the subject matter is rules for football or weaponry for strategic defense (SDI). In our land of randy pentagonal fantasies, rational men in high office have determined that SDI success is letting only 3,000 USA military targets get destroyed by enemy missiles. No defense has been considered, by this elite, for our cities at all. So with POSIWID vision it is clear that rational leaders of society place more value on protecting their machinery for exterminating other societies than preserving their own neighbors from a nuclear miscalculation made in a foreign country. It figures.

Some preliminaries

Never make a permanent association of rational thought with rational man. In this Chapter you will find how to elicit an irrational response out of any Orgman. When you see how easy it is, you will be shocked. Before you leave sanctuary for the world of instinctive error, make sure your supply of self-confidence will last through several encounters of the absurd kind. Never let them see you flinch. The application probability of social controls is inversely related to the vulnerability perceived by the monitors of behavior. If they think you don't much care what they do, they won't bother going to the trouble to do anything. Instinctive.

RULE - The more susceptible you are to social controls, the more you will be punished.

The productivity record on changing corporate cultures is not good. The searchers for "excellence" have found less than a handful of happily-revised cultures (towards a healthy direction) in a haystack of attempts numbering in the thousands. You can get better odds at the million-dollar slots. When change is achieved across the organizational chart, it is **always** done with fanatic determination of top leadership displayed without letup over a long period of time. These leadership qualities, by themselves automatic cause for expulsion from management school, are quite rare.

What is at work behind the culture reframing task are basic survival instincts of the human herd. These instincts have long roots and involve social cooperation to improve social competition. Those groups that cooperate better compete better against other human groups and become ancestors. Instincts for survival on the savannah, applied without question to global affairs in this atomic-bomb age, must eventually provoke the very consequences they were designed to avoid.

RULE - The organizational mind is incapable of grading entrenched practices by order of significance. All change is forbidden.

In spite of the obliquity and unnecessary grief that an organization brings to its members, there are no prospects offered for massive, fundamental changes from the turpitude that would solve all the social system problems at once. Such grand visions for expedient solutions must be abandoned. It is more healthy to acknowledge and accept that the basic stupidity of organizations, and it is the rankest form of stupidity, will prevail for a long time. Let the abundant history of perfect failures with culture-remodeling put a cap on end goals and aspirations. You do not have to be obnubilent in your dealings with the claque. Succor is at hand.

Think of organized society as a herd milling about on a giant playing field enclosed in a stadium. Herd life is dominated by two permanent conditions. The herd never leaves the stadium and the game being played is never changed. Next, think of yourself as a deviant member of the herd able to go back and forth between the stands and the field.

The built-in strategy of the herd is to confine all activity to the game and be impervious to all else. If you wish to communicate with the herd at all, you must play their game by their rules in their stadium on their playing field. By this tactic, deviants are easily spotted and neutralized. Note that HFAW level 1 operated completely within these conditions so that no deviation occurred.

The strategy of higher HFAW levels also lives by these unchangeable conditions. The herd rules are followed in exposing herd vulnerabilities but the exposures are coupled with tactics which prevent deviation detectors from sounding the alarm. Just like in cracking the bank vault, the security system must be disarmed first. It turns out that there are plenty of ways to communicate heresy with the herd through their own rules, after their defensive radar is jammed.

Social influence can be extended with a practical prescription in well-defined steps out to areas of coalition that are achievable. While the zone of fun will be some segment of the organization smaller than the whole, each level up increases the variety and magnitude of opportunities for having fun at work. As mentioned earlier, "Pockets of Excellence" are common in large icky institutions. New pockets can be developed, in time and with the plan of persistent incrementalism provided in this Chapter, from almost any raw material. Since the human species is so clever at lying to itself, it makes the crusade to help humans refrain from harming themselves, exciting.

RULE - Organizations concentrate on **process** as a defense against the **content** of an innovation.

Avoid aiding the enemy

Management is the enemy of fun at work. It has been trained to be ultimately clever at social manipulation to maintain order. Part of the fun will be for you to be able (by control variety increase) to turn the tables. Don't worry, they really can't stop you and there is no need for management support for constructing your Fat City. Actually, compared to the task of awakening your own associates out of their stupor, handling management is a snap. Managers are especially coached to be limited in capabilities and to be predictable in response, a kind of robot programmed only with the company doctrines.

Management's Toolbox

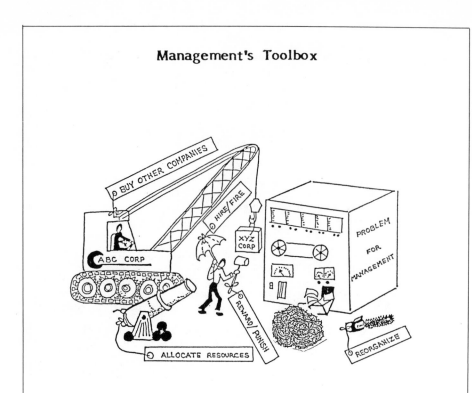

The model T automobile often broke down, but anything which went wrong could be fixed with the half-inch wrench provided in the glove compartment. Today, the toolbox which could cope with any problem on the new computer-laden car costs far more than the car itself, and could barely fit into a tractor trailer. Today, the era of increasing specialization is coupled with disintegration of whole issues. The war on drugs is waged by no fewer than ninety major and independent agencies, which consume ninety percent of their available energy fighting for and defending turf among each other. Meanwhile, drug shipments have tripled in six years. The problems for management today demand tools of integration, coordination, systems-think and a life-cycle perspective. The one-half inch wrench won't hack it anymore.

Managers have but few tools, and with them, managers create more problems than they can solve. Managers can hire and fire, but they can only hire to narrowly-defined slots and they habitually drive away the very talent they need to solve the problems which plague them. This is definitely not the kind of help you need. Managers can allocate resources, but having no objective criteria to guide them, gross distortions are inevitable. Managers dispense rewards and punishments, but since they do not know what is going on, their instincts only reward the mediocre who aggravate the worst features of the situation. Managers can reorganize, but their gut-reaction basis, which is to reduce their own information processing load, comes at the expense of losing their last remnants of control. Many CEOs today were trained as accountants, whose tool box contains but two implements - a calculator and an ax.

RULE - Managers never repeat the mistakes of their immediate predecessors. They repeat the mistakes of their forebears once-removed.

Every sanctioned management tool has been custom-designed for routine problems in a stable environment. Because they were created during an era when changes were the exception, management tools are impotent for complex matters. They always were. The cardinal sign of management stress is exhibited when it functionally abandons the problems which its own inappropriate tools have created, and takes up the business acquisition game. It copes with the stress of being out of control by abandoning its most basic in-house responsibilities altogether. The popularity of the conglomerate-forming game is directly proportional to the widespread management stress from having to cope with today's problems using last century's toolbox. You do not have these constraints. You can expand your coping toolbox without limit. You **have fun at work.**

Navigating through Dystopia

Since few even try, few appreciate how spontaneously the forces of social control can escalate in destructive power to counterbalance the severity of an attack on encysted customs. When the only reaction is ridicule, it is easy to escalate the pressure - erroneously thinking that this is the extent of the defense. Any overt attempt at dealing with the core issues, however, and social control erupts with whatever force that it takes, psychological or physical, to prevail.

RULE - A constant concern of the Establishment is to keep workers ignorant of their own heroes.

We caution against any plan for a frontal attack on the organizational defenses with an assault of logic. Once again, the military provides a benchmark. The British Special Air Service, formed from the Long Range Desert Group, trains only for innovative entries. In action continuously since 1945 (Kenya, Malaya, etc.) except for three years, and **never engaging in a frontal attack,** the service has lost but half their force in 100 tours of duty. Whenever the regular army goes into action, each tour of duty only spares one out of three. So much for front doors. If the policy manual worked as espoused, there would be no need for a lot of things.

Few instances bring the ability of Orgmen to cooperate into sharper focus than the savage attack they spontaneously inflict on the whistleblower. Otherwise sane executives who, in their zeal to dispense the prescribed social controls and demonstrate that they were proper members of the Establishment, assassinated the "Challenger" disaster forecasters under the glare of national TV.

Climbing Out Of The Big Muddy

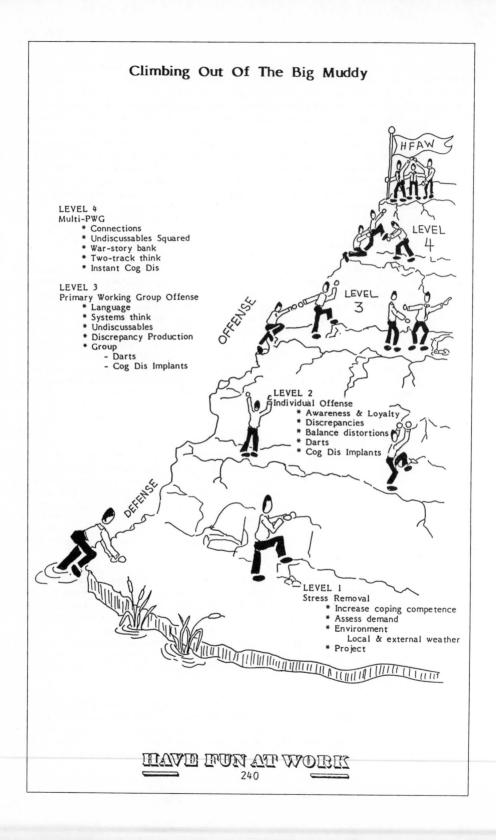

LEVEL 4
Multi-PWG
* Connections
* Undiscussables Squared
* War-story bank
* Two-track think
* Instant Cog Dis

LEVEL 3
Primary Working Group Offense
* Language
* Systems think
* Undiscussables
* Discrepancy Production
* Group
    - Darts
    - Cog Dis Implants

LEVEL 2
Individual Offense
* Awareness & Loyalty
* Discrepancies
* Balance distortions
* Darts
* Cog Dis Implants

LEVEL 1
Stress Removal
* Increase coping competence
* Assess demand
* Environment
    Local & external weather
* Project

OFFENSE

DEFENSE

HFAW

LEVEL 4

LEVEL 3

The executives easily survived the publicity of the Senate hearing room (Establishment behavior review board) while the forecasters lost their jobs.

RULE - The last thing the Establishment wants published is a scorecard on their achievements, especially if the scores of the innovators are on the same card.

By now, you should recognize these erratic manifestations of madness in the eristic scene around you and be unafraid of their progeny of menacing irrationalities. Organizations don't force men to act, they restrain them from acting and so keep them in a constant state of childhood. When you can distinguish the objective from the instinctive, you can make more conscious decisions for your own actions. Progress, however tiny, begins with a discerning percipient awareness. When you don't differentiate, you get what you have been getting.

Level Two: Getting even, not mad

When you have escaped the stress quicksand, you can **have fun at work** on your own steam by going with the flowing. Now you comply by **your** choice and the differences are not trivial. You can fit into the reward system-in-use and get the material benefits without taking the game seriously (avoiding the attendant stress). You only have to **appear** to be under full social control to disarm the security system. The issues brought out in this book can provide some humor while provoking some thought on the unthinkables. You gain in status with your peers by flashing your awareness. It keeps them loose when you jar lazy minds without evoking social punishments. They think you are even smarter than you are.

RULE - Always work backwards from the wreckage towards the causes until the organization makes the connection. Never admit recognizing the connection yourself.

The trick for solo work is to bring up the issues normally overlooked in the form of naive questions, as a stockholder, and then get out of the room. Time delay bombshells. Make them think and never let them see you smirk. Always use broad questions based upon a sincere desire to help the company. Never use statements of local fact. Orgman has no capacity to see problems as a whole. Having fun at work is getting revenge on and getting rewarded by your targets at the same time. By specializing in areas where Orgman is weak, you can bake his brain.

Almost any sort of revenge can be obtained by avoiding the front door (think of it as sealed), taking your time, adopting incrementalism, and by never using a weapon without connecting it to a display of organizational loyalty. Avoiding the front door means to shun all sanctioned methods by which employees are supposed to communicate with upper levels of the organization. Taking your time means to try out one increment of "fun" before you try another. Loyalty is your radar-jamming camouflage for inciting riots.

Develop skill and sincerity with your repertoires. When you bring up non-routine subject matter, there are only two safe forms - both extreme. Have a case so simple that obviously there are no deficiencies **OR** make it so complex and detailed that there are no obvious deficiencies. There is more in your arsenal.

RULE - Always keep someone between you and the doomed project.

Achieving Invisibility

The power of cognitive dissonance can intercept the sensor data of the actual scene and translate it into one of consonance with a preconceived model already in cranial residence. With corpo radar jammed, a dart of vulnerability awareness hits the victim right where his sensor data is processed - and you vanish from the scene. Pooof! You can even see the paralysis process happen.

The invisible blow gun

The ability to expose a vulnerability of any Orgman at any occasion is one of your omnipresent weapons. You can keep it to yourself or teach it to others in Level Three. We have assembled a set of phrases which we call darts (curare-tipped, of course). Send any of these darts off to your target by speaking them (the blow gun). The darts achieve paralysis of your victim within seconds. Make sure you really want to immobilize the creature. Once hit, he is no longer able to perceive that you exist. There is, however, no known antidote. You can make yourself vanish but we don't know how you can make yourself rematerialize in the mind of your quarry.

Your quiver is packed with a starter set of darts. They are based upon organizational voids and other mismatches to the success model. The victim is asked a question which makes him conscious that you are aware of organizational imperfections. You can make up your own darts from the local list of vulnerabilities. The question, or dart, forces a brief cognitive encounter with the unprotected weakness. Orgmen and managers alike have great problems with matching the promise of invulnerability taught at business college with the reality at work. The darts easily find their mark in the large land of misallocation. To reduce the dose, make the questions more abstract. To increase the potency, make the questions more specific to the local scene.

The starter set hits upon some of the prevalent defense mechanisms, passive and active, against change to the status quo. We have seen darted supervisors physically freeze in their tracks. After becoming speechless, the next reflex action is to D&D. The most confident manager will fall like a rock when he realizes you are aware of his misoneism and the impotency of professional management. Merely maintain an air of innocent inquiry as a loyal team member and stockholder trying to do a better job (remember: harder, harder - faster, faster - better, better). Let the victim escape with his excuses, thinking he handled the situation to your complete satisfaction. A darted manager will continue his defense of the guild, of course, but you don't exist in his cognitive world any more. It is better security than an electrified fence.

Implanting cognitive dissonance

Your basic offensive weapon against Orgman is cognitive dissonance - you dispense it. The most skillful implant of cognitive dissonance (cog dis) will render your victim a helpless blob of anxiety - while preventing a connection of his affliction with your handiwork. It is your only safe offense as a single.

There is a narrow window of opportunity for implanting cognitive dissonance and you must be alert to the impending occasions. Situations that qualify are ones where fresh activity is about to be mobilized. Given that setting, you must make a **connection** between the standard approach and the wreckage it leads to. There are always lots of case histories. Point out the structural similarities between what is starting off and what has taken off so many times before - and crashed. Point out how, at other companies which use these popular practices, the same results are obtained too. Our library of case histories is maintained just to aid this maneuver. (Homework, homework, homework)

RULE - The "least-noise" solution in development always produces the loudest fireworks in production.

Starter Dart Set

DARTS ABOUT STANDARD COMPANY PRACTICES AND FEEDBACK CONNECTIONS

1. How do we keep our practices current to these changing times?
2. Where is the policy manual to cover procedures for situations not covered in the manual?
3. How do we change practices when we prove they don't work?
4. Where is the procedure describing the decision process in use?
5. Why do we have so much grief when we try to modernize?
6. What's being done to reduce red tape? It only grows.
7. How does the organization distinguish simple problems from complex ones? How does the organization handle complex problems differently than it does for standard business?
8. Is the business situation which prevailed when the company got its practices going, the same as today?
9. How does the company commensurately reward the outstanding performance of its high producers, accurate prophets of disaster, mavericks and innovators?
10. How does the company handle issues that cover more than one of our separate departments?

DARTS ABOUT COMPANY DESIGN FOR MISCOMMUNICATIONS

11. What happens to correct the problem when the party receiving your message doesn't understand it?
12. How do we know we are making correct message interpretations?
13. Where are the groundrules for compressing information to be sent upstairs? How do we know what to leave out?
14. Why does everybody have different computers and software?
15. Where are the official written ground rules for correctly expanding the orders from above into action items where we work?
16. Where are the proper communication channels for important bad news where you don't get punished?
17. Where is the cross-reference list showing information propagation and use?
18. Where is the official, common data base? Where is the company configuration control data base available?

DARTS ABOUT MISSING KNOWLEDGE

19. Where is the corporate dictionary of common language terms and abbreviations?
20. In what ways are our fundamental practices different & similar to the competition's?
21. What data is used by the company to allocate resources?
22. How does the company allocate resources between short term goals and long term health?
23. Where is the list of methods that are prohibited?
24. Where is the common corporate language for exchanging information? How does the company learn about morale? Where is the list of topics which can not be discussed?
25. How do we know when all the hard spots have been identified?
26. How many work specialties are there in the company (make sure you already know the approximate answer) and how many translators are there to check on fidelity?

DARTS ABOUT MISSING ORGANIZATIONAL FUNCTIONS

27. What is the governing rule for handling lateral matters (ie computerization)?
28. Where is the staff related to the junction node of ____ and ___ to handle matters that relate to both ____ and ___.
29. Where does the company match methods appropriate to the complexity of the issue?
30. Which department handles life cycle matters and system-thinks?
31. Where are errors detected?
32. Why is it that the only thing we can deal with out in the open is technology?
33. Where are they using Deming's methods in the company?

Explain that the stuff which **does** work on projects (like the one being undertaken) is always the same too, and, of course, quite different (and therefore non-standard). You can use any book in the "excellence" series as a reference for that point. While Orgman may act dumb, everyone knows what you are talking about (heresy). Stay with facts and only make conclusions which those facts support with lots of margin. Showing detailed, structured knowledge about the subject will always temporarily win over vague defenses. (The odds are on the side of the quantifier with a systematic analysis.) Your goal is not to convince for the DfC, but to create a situation that would otherwise never develop.

While pledging your devotion to the established practice manual (after all, did the company score any victories any other way?), force management to make a conscious decision about project methodology. Make it clear (it can't be overdone) that you will support **either** path chosen. The odds are, the first time, that management (Orgman) chooses the routine process. Advertise that decision with due credit, another show of loyalty itself, and then devoutly work the routine like a good soldier, not as a loser but as a winner. Usually you are forced to support the mismatched scene with no hope of a correction. No fun. This time they have taken the bait.

RULE - The management strategy to suppress innovation relies upon Orgman's entanglement with a car, kids and a mortgage.

Now as the project unfolds along the Universal Scenario as predicted, as it must, just make sure the connection previously made is kept alive by regular low-key feedback. Just another name on the dishonor roll of fallen projects, but this time through a deliberate choice by management to stay with the normal routine. The consonance of management's mental model of **their choice** with a happy project outcome is turned into dissonance. Since management can not reconcile the facts with the mental models fabricated in management school, they must deny the plain truth to ease the pain of cog dis. The project members, buried in truth up to their ears, can not avoid noticing the irrational display. Now **that's fun**. The managers impaled on cog dis are further afflicted with a loss of credibility and status. This time, in a reversal of roles, it is you that achieved control of the situation and management that was punished for making a bad decision. And, **you** arranged it!

RULE - Obvious risks are easily averted. Therefore, the search for unknown risks is forbidden.

There is no guarantee that the next time management will make a different decision, but at least you have learned how to preserve your sanity while dispensing certain paranoia to the well-deserving. Should the lesson eventually be learned and they choose skunkworks, you can have fun with a productive situation too. It's the greatest.

Attack weapons

One offensive weapon is counteracting distortions. For example, computerworld only speaks in technical solutions. Make a few missiles out of generic problems and errors endemic to computerworld and computer wizards will freak out right in front of your eyes. Display your rationale first, always at least two levels abstract. Announce that you are going to discuss the undiscussables (the ultimate distortion) before you do. Make like you are doing it as a last resort because the vital issues are there and you want to see the problem get solved. They become paralyzed and unable to function until your question session has been set on "event disavowal." Any time you go where the herd avoids, carry a large load of logic. Orgman quickly gets very confused in taboo subject matter.

Livingston's Law is the doomsday machine. If you can dupe your victim into making a loud control signal when the Law is in effect, the organization will automatically do the rest. This deception is rarely achieved. Accomplish it and you score extra points. No weapon is more damaging than to set up a target as a whistleblower. His calls for organizational reform will soon fade as he is carried away in the padded van.

Keep in mind that the world of solo flying in Orgspace, up to this point, is confined to the status quo. That is, nothing you can accomplish by yourself can make any difference to the situation at large. Orgman instinctively knows when his sacred doctrines are being threatened and he blindly rallies to their defense. Whatever the question, the answer is always status quo. While you can **have fun at work,** you can't increase the airspace. The next increment is directed towards the acquisition of new maneuvering room for the Fun House.

RULE - Managers arrange their affairs for bad news. Their indifference to good news soon justifies their precautions. POSIWID.

Level Three - growing into fun at work

Give yourself plenty of time to get used to your new mental models of organizational behavior. Like the revelations obtained by astronomers when they first viewed the heavens with instruments that could detect x-rays, radio waves, and infra-red radiation, the new library of behavioral patterns at your disposal will provide many "discoveries" in the world you live in. Nothing will appear the same. Brace yourself for some surprises at every level.

RULE - Any system created by the Establishment to efficiently and peacefully settle controversy will quickly become the greatest source of conflict.

We doubt that you will be able to resist trying out the weapons, even if you aren't in a particular snit. Prudence suggests that you get some experience with the big guns on the practice range before the need is real and urgent. The firepower is proportional to risk and we again suggest incrementalism. Humanity is so uniform in social contexts that you can experiment anywhere. Don't start the testing at work but move your experience from "safe" testing elsewhere into the work place. What you observe is what you get.

The basic strategy of having fun at work, Level Three, is to share your fun knowledge with others in your immediate work group with a view towards building a PWG coalition. Unless you are content inflicting revenge to selected targets, your associates will have to be let in on the game - and that's where the risk comes in. Start them as you started, with the eradication of stress. Help them to get up to level ground first. You can sympathize with their anguish in revising the Bad Seventies mental models. It hurts!

RULE - Bad tendencies automatically reinforce each other. Each good tendency needs continuous support to remain viable.

Having fun at work beyond Level Two is a strange combination of social subterfuge and worthwhile achievements. If the ultimate fun scene is one of happy honest cooperation of people reaching out to their potentials and having success solving significant problems, realize that the only way to get there is by trickery and treachery. It feels good to work hard and achieve something you know is worthwhile in an atmosphere of openness, learning and truth. In order to arrive at the goal, however, you will have to be skilled at acting out most of the deceptions which, in other circumstances, honorable men despise. It is recommended that you keep these disparate models in separate mental compartments and consciously know which is on the front burner. Never give Orgman an even break.

Job Performance Aids (JPAs)

In this mental-frame remodeling business, it takes a good plan of small steps, acting worthy of an Oscar, the persistence of gravity, and lots of calendar time. As mentioned earlier, the first subterfuge is your apparent innocence. You must appear as purity supreme at the birthing. If your pals suspect for a minute that you are trying to put something over on them, it is you that is over.

There are issues which they already know that are buried deep in the subconscious (undiscussables) and there are issues about which they are ignorant. Since you can't differentiate without being found out, don't try. The only way to launch intramural enlightenment in safety is to start with abstraction. This is where the JPAs come in. To aid abstraction, an ever expanding set of JPAs is being created to provide relevant, abstruse material for the whole affair. You begin simply, by casually supplying JPA information in document form to your target(s). Additional JPA tips are provided in the next Chapter.

Act like the JPA is some information you ran across which you thought might be of interest, and don't be in any hurry to obtain a reaction. Step one is to raise awareness that there is a problem up to the talking level. As we now know where Earth is spotted within our Milky-Way galaxy, you can show where the organization is located in the ubiquitous mess. Dwell on ubiquity. Once they can discuss how common the mess is, your pals can be exposed to the process of elimination which the knowledge supports. Use appropriate JPAs as needed. You can start connecting results to practices. While you stay in abstraction, let your recruits discuss local specifics. Note that, so far, you have taken no risks of social reprisals and, if you get just this far (discussing the vital undiscussables within your own group), you can already expect a happy outcome.

Once the subject matter has been accepted as discussable (give it several weeks), hang the Universal Scenario poster. This JPA helps introduce the language of failure in code words and sorts your local audience. Place the poster where the local traffic can get up close to it and you can discreetly observe their reactions. This JPA is well tested and the subject matter is recognized within five seconds or less. Instinctive reactions to the topic fall into one of two categories and tell more about the viewer than the qualities of the poster.

One US Marine Corp facility, for example, displays the poster on corridor walls in their office complex. Those individuals who are interested in the Universal Scenario and resonate with the scripts, will spend minutes and make sounds like "Ah Ha!" while looking at the poster. These people are high-potential recruits. Those who avoid contact after the five-second identification period are already into knowledge disavowal and are low-potential recruits. Help the persons with enough self-confidence to dare cognition of the truth. Ignore the others.

The Marines have learned that the first beachhead to secure is the common, neutral language. The poster helps others to start using the language of failure code words, such as EOPMD and D&D, to describe events at work. This step is crucial. The code words provide a vocabulary for discussing the undiscussables that is safe and compact. When you have said that the project is in the Camouflage Squared phase, you have really transmitted a lot of information in compact form.

RULE - Complexity is a tool to increase autonomy.

Ordinarily, organizational dysfunction is a more taboo topic than illicit sex. Ministers can give sermons on any sexual topic they choose as long as they use neutral language like "reproduction" and "copulation." The same thing can be done for aberrant organizational behavior. The ability to make safe conversation on these socially-controlled topics is a fundamental milestone that must be reached first. There is no rush.

One-on-one, one at a time

You should start Level Three by concentrating on one recruit. Ideally, he will be one of your current PWG pals and mentally tough. Assuming he passed poster, supply more JPA material related to the new terms. While there is nothing sacred about our starting vocabulary, it is vital to use code words with your ally. The JPAs provide an abstract medium for discussion that allows dealing with the undiscussables in safety. People from other PWGs that are around when the code words are used will not know what is going on and thereby have no deviation alarm for activating social control. Safety first. When you have jointly agreed to use the code words around the shop, it will be a quantum gas. So much of what goes on in an organization is a farce and downright funny. People who would howl at the antics in the monkey cage are solemn when the same scripts are being enacted at work. It is great to be able to discuss the undiscussables in safety to get confirmation and support of your assessments. It is fun to laugh at the accuracy of your predictions. With just one peer you can **have fun at work** Level Three.

RULE - All intelligence reports to management are unreliable, filled with wrong topics, and devoid of bad news. That is how intelligence reports make stupid managers.

The language provides an important new information source. The code words that describe complex scripts save time. In short order you will find the organizational language system to be your most important source of critical information. For example, if your associate reports that Project X is in the Camouflage stage, you automatically know both project status and how to relate to the victims.

Build your constituency by one-on-one communications. This affair is too much for larger meetings. Stress removal is a very private affair. After your first disciple is comfortable, he can help you convert others in your PWG. Abide with the language system for a while before escalating into new territory. If you think this recipe resembles the formation process of the male hunting band, good. You are going after the brainiest of beasts and you need to have group communications working smoothly. You may decide to continue organizational life as usual until the urge for adventure overwhelms the faded need for security. Be sure you have your act together every time you cross the sanctuary drawbridge.

Cooperative action for fun

The same defensive weapons for your solo work are available to the enlightened group. The awareness phase can be accelerated considerably when there are multiple players, because of crossfire opportunities. The quiver of darts is ready to go and the more darter experience, the better the darts can become. Loyalty displays can also become more elaborate without drawing suspicion. Group darting can make your entire group disappear in the minds of other entire groups - even if some members are absent. Group power greatly multiplies the power and the fun of the individual.

Other groups will quickly notice a change in fun level, but they will be confused about a need for countermeasures. No infractions of dogma have occurred. They do not have enough time to get Their communications network functioning. It's a pain. The mere fact that your group is having fun and showing much fewer signs of stress is enough to rivet Their attention and increase Their stress. If misery loves company, fun groups provoke curiosity. The success of your group safely upsets the equilibrium in the organization. That's good, because you are gaining on Them. It, actually.

RULE - Control is the power of deliberate actions to secure rewards.

The jump in offensive firepower is more dramatic than the improvement in defenses for having fun. The discussed connection of practices to results can take as many specific forms as there are participants. The larger pool of experience will have more and varied cases to reinforce the connections. Once the tide is turned on the discussability of feedback, the battle is over. There are many pent up feelings here that are anxious to escape. The essential nature of feedback always sounds more vital with a group chant that a single cry in the wilderness. Once the barrier is broken, it can become a flood.

RULE - The refuge of the non-conformist mind is abstraction.

The various structures provided in this book can be used in regular work to identify and quantify discrepancies. Having a large shopping list of items that are wrong and have been overlooked is a great way to increase power and influence. Everybody loves to have problems to solve and when you control the problems list, you are controlling activities. People would much rather work on solving problems, which is rewarded, than finding them, which is discouraged. So, hit them where they ain't.

Discrepancies are for the workery, not for management. Provide valid discrepancies to the workers directly and they will be your silent allies. Supply discrepancies to the management and they will be your enemies. For sheer **quantities** of errors, nothing beats the cross reference list. Study your own work first and get your own act together. Then, pick out suitable targets and keep a pile in reserve as a cushion. What they think they don't know (that you might) is a form of blackmail to prevent entertaining any thoughts of social controls.

Cognitive dissonance gifts also increase in frequency and severity. Managers can hardly escape cog dis stress when the group is of like mind to what management should decide. For example, the cross reference list can show that any attempts at automation are doomed to only automate error. Other groups who witness the injection ceremony will be in awe. The method to apply cog dis by the group is basically the same as it was for the solo effort, but with more impact at decision time and more reminders as the project runs amuck.

Sorter Grader

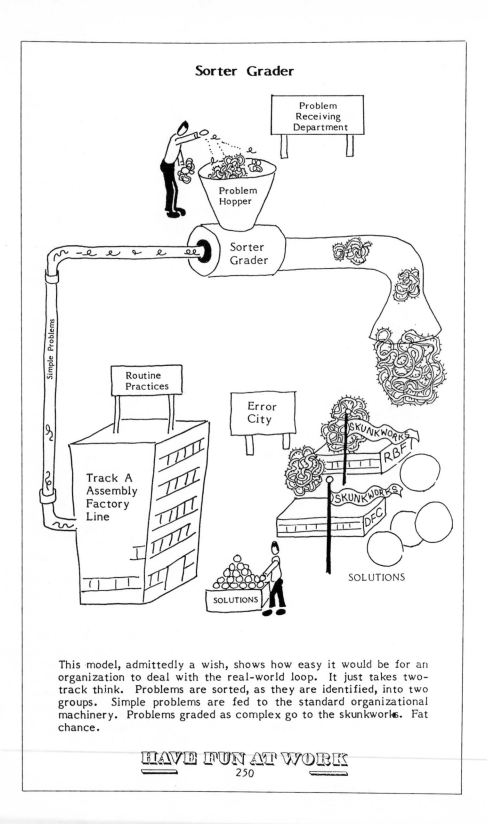

This model, admittedly a wish, shows how easy it would be for an organization to deal with the real-world loop. It just takes two-track think. Problems are sorted, as they are identified, into two groups. Simple problems are fed to the standard organizational machinery. Problems graded as complex go to the skunkworks. Fat chance.

History break

The few cases where the Establishment has been successfully modified to perform a needed function (which it should have been able to do for itself) echo the same methods. The only way victims of organizational dysfunction ever achieve relief is when they get themselves together and work out their own solutions, in a framework which fits the prevailing arrangement of the "system." An organized assault by victims is the only way.

When the needs of the handicapped in California were addressed by a maze of uncoordinated government agencies, the services never matched the requirements. Unable to adapt, the social agencies escalated the very miseries they were created to alleviate. As was painfully evident to the handicapped, the resources that could very well help their condition were never directed to them. Finally fed up with state of affairs, the handicapped formed their own groups. They learned about the "system," they worked out detailed plans which both fit their needs and the structure of the social service zoo. When they finally assaulted the walls at Sacramento, there was little resistance. It was a win-win situation for all sides.

The same course was taken by the AIDS victims in San Francisco. Abused by the terrible, inhuman treatment of the prevailing "system," the local community took direct charge of the situation. Patients are quartered in rooms furnished in the best that decorating arts can deliver. Meals are prepared by gourmet chefs. Friendly, caring conversation is available around the clock. The atmosphere is most unhospital-like and AIDS victims from all over the country have come there to die in dignity and pleasant surroundings. Bottom up is the only way that works. **Replace.**

Two track think

It is the group, rather than the individual, that can start advertising the two track think culture. It's potent and it's fun. Only one voice and two track speak never gets out of the group. Rather than Track A being all bad and Track B being all good, it is time to make the bad vs good scene situationally-dependent. Preach glowing stuff about Track A for Track A problems, the critical need to have Track B for Track B problems, and how easy it is to tell the difference. The acceptance and differentiation of both tracks does not seem to put any one "culture" on the spot. When two track think can be openly discussed, the Establishment is in for a hard time. The group can move forward or stop at any place in this level without needing or stirring management interaction. That is, in Level Three the group can achieve everything in Level Two with more defensive influence around the organization and with much more fun. Man is, after all, a social animal.

RULE - Rigid institutions can only be saved by fanatics. Flexible organizations can be sustained by everyone.

Two track think tests the peripheral groups in preparation for Level Four. The logic is unassailable and politically neutral. If other groups resonate with the concept, they really are consciously recognizing that Track A has given them fits. If the reception to another track is cool, they are really up tight about the work scene.

Level Four is Magna Charta time

If you have saved yourself and your group and are into the languages and weaponry for fun at work, you have done very well. While the organization is still a Track A mess and management is still wreaking havoc with the minds of your peers, your group has achieved escape velocity. Once you are able to discuss the undiscussables and exhibit an awareness about what is going on, performance can only increase. Management is afraid to tangle with your crowd so you have more autonomy. Let the born-again group adjust to the new norm. It's a slow process at best. Besides, others are watching with great interest. Groups aren't supposed to be able to change cultures and if they are having fun at work they must be up to something improper. Some managers believe that if workers are happy on the job, they're not working.

RULE - Preventing feedback prevents everything.

When the group has become bored with the security and achievements of level three, they are ready for high adventure. There is no reason, following the plan provided, why the group cannot, if it chooses, take over functional control of the institution. No new skills have to be learned. They have already demonstrated having what it takes. For Level Four fun at work, other groups have to be recruited. It is still a one-on-one process and you start where people in your group already have pals in other groups. One advantage is the reputation of your group, the exploits of which will be featured in coffee-break discussions as regular fare.

Don't bother with individuals in other groups tied up in a mess that is in the camouflage stages. While they are the most in need, they will be the most resistant to aid. Catch the same men between messes and they will be highly receptive. There is no need for dolor. Livingston's Law is frequently in force. Knowing when to run is just as helpful as knowing tricks that work. The experience gained in getting this far will have identified likely groups from the hopeless ones. You do not need many recruited groups. You can do well with two, three is plenty.

There are joint affairs to establish. It is time to build a common experience and evidence bank. Corporate history should be revisited and feedback energized. You are going to attack management and you want to be well prepared. Just using the same organizational language system of failure and success will be a wow.

Management does not have many tools (coping variety) and the ones they have don't fix much. So, the basic management strategy is to reduce variety in the situations, which dispenses stress to others. The level four goal is to present management with a situation variety which does not fit their toolbox, is impervious to their breast-beating, and transfers some heavy duty stress to them.

RULE - Bad information sources do not improve with age.

Multiple group cooperation escalates the fun in all directions. Somewhere between one group and two groups, the organizational Gestapo loses its bite. Social controls seem to get confused when more than one group culturally metamorphoses. Perhaps others sense that norms are changing and that, God forbid, it may be **them** that is deviating. The scope of discussables explodes to include vital issues and everyone not in - is out. The first meeting when two groups display their weaponry, the other groups in attendance will freak out, totally disoriented.

Likewise, the firm connections (practices to wreckage) and feedback can be openly discussed to set the stage. When two groups are using the same organizational language system, the other groups do not know whether it's them or you. The issue of who is the deviant becomes blurred. Whatever the balance of people in the meeting room, the situation is perceived by Orgman as pure risk. His goal is to stay within the norm and he is not as sure as he was what the norm is. If he takes your groups on, he may be advertizing his own deviation more than yours. These kind of uncertainties give Orgman cardiac arrest.

Joint operations can include connections and two track thinking as featured items. The homework on local history pays off here. In joint operations, the scene can be taken from the abstract levels and brought closer to home where it stings. The attack of connections is offset by two track thinking but a great display of loyalty should accompany the whole show. Lots of company devotion is mixed with lots of feedback on practices and wreckage and on that matter, you can dig in your heels. No more sidestepping and no more retreats to avoid social controls. With joint operations you don't have to.

Time to take on management

By this time, management will be aware that strange things are going on but will have no evidence of non-conformance. In some cases they have openly praised the cooperation between groups. So far, lots of fuss has been made but no social control alarm has gone off. Work goes on as stupidly as it always did. The trap is sprung when a window of opportunity for "cog dis" arrives. This time, when the choice is presented by the joint groups for management decision, cog dis is instant. Make it clear that the choice should go to Track B. Explain what will happen to managers who choose Track A (guaranteed failure with lots of publicity). It's time for the Magna Charta to be rolled out.

RULE - The entrenched order is the enemy.

You have presented a variety of situation (entirely achievable with the human systems we have) which greatly exceeds the variety which management is trained to handle. For relief from the responsibility for failure, it is time for management to get the outside practitioner and get out of the Track B way. With joint operations, you don't have to be nice - just loyal. You have transferred the power.

The ultimate fun at work is Track B. There is an endless supply of complex problems waiting to be solved and no two are alike. The Design for Complexity is a learning experience that has no equal. Everyone grows (coping variety increase). People can find and expand to their potential which, in the final analysis, is what being human is all about.

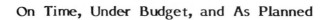

On Time, Under Budget, and As Planned

Chapter Fifteen

The Toolbox of Fun at Work

Many tools for having fun at work have been presented throughout this book. These devices can augment your coping competence and provide ready-made structures of reference. The requisite handle that fits them all is your intellect. While a summary of tools and aids is provided here, you are the judge of when and where to apply them at work. They **never** fail to uncover aspects that are being overlooked.

You are not alone. More and more workers are becoming aware of the common thread of unnecessary bondage to the "system" and that something can safely be done about it. There are many kindred souls. They use and contribute war-story material. The wealth of ideas for tools and tool usage is directly related to the diversity of respondents and we encourage you to participate as you think best. The exchange benefits all, and all have volunteered to assist others. No one has found a quick fix. If you have an overnight cure, you will be the greatest hero of the modern era.

In order to participate in the informal association, send a note via the publisher and particulars will be provided. The pile of fun aids grows, and improvements are being made via constant experimentation and feedback. Participants are from many countries and working in every industry and profession, and they have proven to be quite clever at finding novel uses for the fun aids. In diversity there is strength. Experiments lead to more tools. No one knows it all.

Posters

Summary charts of the material in this book include the Common Semantic Language, the Erase and Replace list of the Bad Seventies, Vulnerabilities, Organized Deceptions, Denials, Livingston's Law, the Rules, Eliminations, Diversions, the Tool Box, Project Assessment checklist, Communications checklist and Connections, the impact of Standard Practices (and environment) on Track A and Track B problems. All of these charts are available in an upgraded poster format, supplemented with cartoons and cartoon characters. There are few situations encountered in corporate life that are not represented on one or more of these posters. The whole point is that having fun at work is a very practical competency. Rather than a thought experiment or an esoteric flight of philosophic fancy, the ability to solve a wider range of problems adds to self-confidence in positive reinforcement. The structures can be put to work at work. They work.

"ORGANIZATIONS," a poster depicting the Universal Scenario, includes, in color, some of the cartoons found in this book. It's large (two feet by three feet) and very few people can walk by it on exhibition without registering an image and a smile. We tried it out with some business friends, and found that the traffic to any exhibition booth is increased threefold over normal amounts. Naturally, Mega-corpo-company Unwritten Policy waxes paranoic about getting near the truth, in writing, even while its employees flock over to get copies.

Eliminations

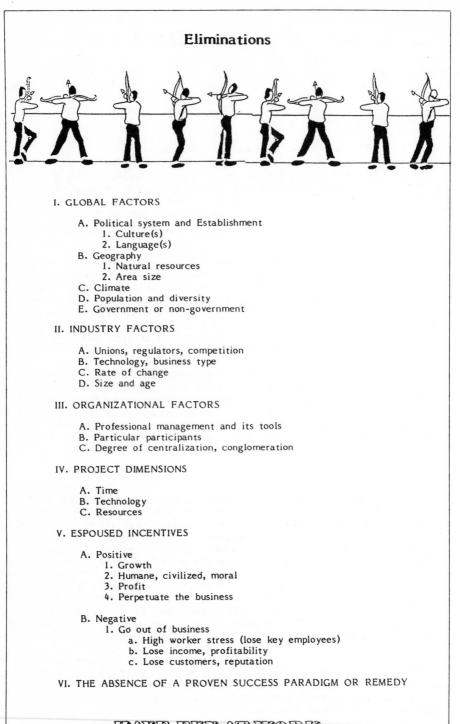

I. GLOBAL FACTORS

    A. Political system and Establishment
        1. Culture(s)
        2. Language(s)
    B. Geography
        1. Natural resources
        2. Area size
    C. Climate
    D. Population and diversity
    E. Government or non-government

II. INDUSTRY FACTORS

    A. Unions, regulators, competition
    B. Technology, business type
    C. Rate of change
    D. Size and age

III. ORGANIZATIONAL FACTORS

    A. Professional management and its tools
    B. Particular participants
    C. Degree of centralization, conglomeration

IV. PROJECT DIMENSIONS

    A. Time
    B. Technology
    C. Resources

V. ESPOUSED INCENTIVES

    A. Positive
        1. Growth
        2. Humane, civilized, moral
        3. Profit
        4. Perpetuate the business

    B. Negative
        1. Go out of business
            a. High worker stress (lose key employees)
            b. Lose income, profitability
            c. Lose customers, reputation

VI. THE ABSENCE OF A PROVEN SUCCESS PARADIGM OR REMEDY

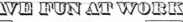

"DIPTYCH," the poster which expresses the opposite of the Universal Scenario, is in the works at Fuzzball Press. It includes many parts of the common semantic language of success. Unlike the language of failure, which everyone knows, the language of success hangs on the wall like abstract art. It is primarily for levels 3 and 4 of the HFAW recipe where it is very effective in letting other departments intimidate themselves by comparison.

"ORGANIZOOLOGY" is a supplement to the Universal Scenario poster which describes a newly-recognized snap-action, knee-jerk behavior pattern that organizations display. The first phase is performed by a cast of Establishment players, sans workers, who create a project that is a pre-fabricated disaster for the workers before ground is first broken. In this Scenario, there is no escape, because before the spade bites the sod, the project money is already in the pockets of the lawyers and bankers.

"RULES" Rules are shaftways of insight that help to make sense of the mess. It is impossible to have too many rules. This poster is a compendium from the books and other documents. Your contribution to the rule list is encouraged, and when used, you get the FES publication of your choice, postpaid. They do not have to be simple to be useful. Rules are constraints to variety and they are pals.

Essays

By now you have learned that trans-discipline areas are a neglected, avoided no-man's land. As you might expect, many "complex" problems which are quite impossible to solve in the narrow corridors of specialty prison are quite straightforward to solve in the wide spaces of Ashby-land. One family of impossible tasks includes simulation, system design, Artificial Intelligence (AI), configuration management, automation, quality and operations system design. These issues are governed by natural laws which, when ignored, natural laws being what they are, are not suspended. Unimpressed by the legions trying to solve large-space problems by heaping on thin-space solutions, natural laws expose the gross stupidity.

The family of "insurmountable opportunities" for socio-technical systems is addressed in an ingenious, proceduralized application of the DfC, entitled **SIPOD**. This cookbook agenda enables you to fashion a knowledge-based expert AI system, for instance, out of **any** tangible arrangement of parts. SIPOD provides a practical reference standard for success of heroic usefulness. Since it is a socio-technical system "fix," it is involved and not quickly understood. It is important to recognize that practical remedies exist for many common, complex problems which routinely give organizations fits. A variation of SIPOD for software systems is a book called **FUBAR: Test, Then Code.** These are technical books which deal with practical, proven Ashby cybernetics technology for solving **any** complex problem. It is not the kind of material one would consider fun reading for the general public, but note that it **is** available in concrete form. Both **SIPOD** and **FUBAR** are easier to perform than they are to explain.

THE DESIGN FOR COMPLEXITY: Only the front end of the Design for Complexity (DfC) was presented in this book. A full introduction to the DfC is given in **The New PLAGUE.** A full technical treatment of the DfC is available separately.

The PRACTITIONERS MANUAL is available, free, to owners of **The New PLAGUE.** The bag of dirty tricks of utility for practitioners in social system machinations, a mixture of jargon and filth, is updated twice a year.

Other essays available which show the application of the **have fun at work** mindset to particular real-world issues. Topical areas include: quality assurance in hospitals, testing software, and the modernization of industrial processes.

Art for the workery

Full-size color reproductions of Rob Schouten's paintings, especially commissioned for the series, are available for the workery. Each comes with its decoder key. Displayed at work, they are more a weapon than a conversation piece. Rob 's art will be featured in a book to be published in late 1989. He has fun at work, too.

On Time, Under Budget and As Planned: The triangle from the back cover of this book, reproduced in full color. Image size +/- 20 x 20 in. Artist: Rob Schouten Float lucite frame included, so you can hang it three ways.

Meeting Of The Members Of The Board: Full color reproduction of the cover of **The New PLAGUE.** Artist: Rob Schouten.

Savannah Man: Cover illustration for **Have Fun At Work** by W. L. Livingston. Artist: Rob Schouten.

St. Quo Plays Marionette In The Corporate Cathedral: The frontispiece illustration from **Have Fun At Work,** reproduced in color. Artist: Rob Schouten.

Hands-on exposure

We offer a lively one-day seminar which shows direct, practical application of the latest tools to the real-world situations of the participants. The hands-on, candid experience demonstrates how easy it is to apply the structures to gain a quantum leap in understanding complex situations and how to cope with them. Speaking engagements, which include a humorous slide show of material not interjected in this book, can also be arranged. The show has proven to be very unpopular with the Establishment, which is how the material is tested.

Books

The first book on the subject, **The New PLAGUE,** (1986) began the emphasis on the workery. This book provides background and an introduction to the Design for Complexity. A full Chapter is devoted to the stormy computer industry marriage to Wall Street. It is the first of a series of books of the workery, for the workery and (increasingly) by the workery.

Our next book, **HAVE (More) FUN AT WORK,** (1989) will report the results of the experiments with new material for day-to-day use at work. It is a structure upon which you may hang the daily data from the social system. The design of the rack itself is the basis for making higher-level sense out of the array of data. Basically, pieces and parts of communications are compared to reference sets to locate a "fit." As matchups are made, they are given pre-assigned weighting factors and the pattern they form points to higher-level matters. The purpose of this "system" is to shorten the time it normally takes to get to HFAW levels three and four. So far it is a lot of fun.

Bibliography

Several hundred books are reviewed every year to augment the bibliography and to identify key contributors. Most are recommended via feedback from readers. Relevant technical material is found in the sciences of control systems, human factors, cybernetics, automation, simulation, law, operations research, general systems theory, management information systems, military science, fuzzy sets and systems, stocastic processes, and statistics. Relevant social system material is found in the soft sciences of psychology, anthropology, sociology, history, philosophy, religion, politics, stress, and economics. Once you know what to look for, the daily newspaper serves quite well. Few realize the common connection among the great variety of fiascoes that society provides in a steady stream. The media mentality is the antithesis of systems think.

Ways of using the tools

The growing list of Perceptual Perversions is your personal checklist to intercept topical content, in those areas, and cognitively force them into your consciousness for audit and review before you let them out into the world. If the subject is risk awareness, for example, make sure you are dealing with good numbers rather than your viscerals and question everything in sight. Make everyone read Gustav Ostberg on risk and you will have a chance to restore sanity.

Several structures were presented in this book to enhance your assessment competency, including: Structure for Situation Assessment in Chapter 13, Perceptual Limitations and Perversions in Chapter 10, Communications Balance from Chapter 11, the complexity checklists in the text of Chapter 4, and the Go/No Go Assessment Table from Chapter 13. This suite of structures for situation and project assessment, as well as the Boundaries and Interfaces Checklist, applies to nearly everything. With part number power, the breakdown forces an objective view which can be shared with many. As the number of unfavorable aspects rises, it automatically sends the "We are in trouble" message without saying a word. This is the approach used in the seminar. The process doesn't deny the unwarranted optimism, but it handles the disease on a different, negotiable level. It is positive stuff to know that the situation is hopeless; knowing **why** is a bonus.

Connections in Chapter 11 describes pathological standard Track A practices for Track B. It is a handy reference early on in an activity. Evidence that the list is correct is available in your own shop. First, call attention to the problem by citing sources, such as this book. Wait until another person makes the first remarks about an in-house similarity until you unload your findings. Don't bring up the particulars first.

The lists of phrases that denote F4 or the ZOI are very useful in meetings. Keep them with you and when you hear a fit, note that the position of who said it is being located for you. The list of management entreaties can be used in the same way. Humor is the best way to handle such matters. Heaven help anyone who takes this silly stuff seriously.

The Organized Deceptions and the Thirty-seven Denials lists contain more social dynamite because they hit home and deep. The majority of projects are encumbered with every issue on the lists. In most cases it is better to distribute copies as a FYI item before discussion begins. Just act innocent and claim you provided the lists out of good intentions to help the effort as a concerned stockholder. In practice the lists can be used as another project road map to locate the position. Once again, it is important to refer to an outside source.

The key to the lists provided is the reference structure "rack" they form. It is the comparison of what **is** to a structured reference of what **could be** or should be which conveys the impression that you possess "powers" that others don't have. Let them retain the illusion. When you show Orgman a marked-up list of comments expressed at a meeting, in the checklists provided, it is the context that does the damage. Orgman knows well what happened at the meeting and he is quite prepared with his own home-grown library of cover-up responses. What he is **not** prepared for is structure. What rips off the top of Orgman's head (and his camouflage) is the framework of items on the lists that were **not** marked. Orgman knows that structure will eventually win out over gut reactions. This shock is why we take extra care to make the lists appear to be professional and, hence, abstract.

Keep the Establishment Profile and the charts of Vulnerabilities and Darts as private stock. Also, there may be an unnecessary risk in displaying the Communications checklist until you feel secure. Once the communications issue can be placed on the table for discussion, however, you've made a big step forward. In contrast, the Toolbox and the Erase and Replace summaries can be displayed with impunity because no one will know the language.

The Language of Failure and The Language of Success are your basic project status determiners. Plot a running total of the things that fit the failure list which **are** being done and a list of the requisites for success which are **not** being done at all. It makes a great monthly report. The idea is to keep the connections between practices and results continuously visible. It is the new context of success that does the damage to Orgman. When small enough increments are taken in forecasting you can deflect social controls. Refrain from saying, "I told you so."

The chart of Eliminations in this Chapter is your checklist of how not to spend your time. Once you are familiar with the supporting evidence and war stories, you can question the activities of others in hot pursuit of the impossible. Most people don't even think of the things they should be thinking of. It is helpful to convey the impression that the source of the Eliminations list is from the outside world. This lends it an air of credibility that, at the very least, raises some flags of thought. When you can show that similar efforts (usually very similar) always fail elsewhere, you can ask for distinguishable differences between what is being proposed and your history-book of disasters. The answers you will receive can be found on the F4 list. If you have a specific occasion, the odds are very good that at least one of the volunteers can provide an outside, precedent war story that fits like a glove and will send you supporting documentation. We have a pile of disaster specifications over three feet tall, some costing more than a million dollars to prepare. Typically, you will find more cases than you can remember.

Closing comments

The process of having fun at work is an active one. You have fun at work with your intellect as the navigator. Instinct captures you as a passenger, whose fate is up to the whim of a mindless mob noted primarily by a propensity to spin around in small circles. Accept the incongruity of the trick, to be objective in some areas and turn self-destructive in others, played by the human mind upon itself. You can see the trick on display everywhere you find pragmatic technologists, fully knowledgeable that the biggest constraints are in the social system, in linear-think pursuit of the technical fix for everything. Intelligence and stupidity can often be seen flowing out of the same animated spigot.

Always remember that you are dealing with the biggest problem on earth and that it got large and grows larger for lots of good, mutually supporting reasons. Remove one reason and there are plenty left to make the mess just as big. It is an honor to be conscious of the ubiquitous mess and a privilege to be working towards a remedy. If the civilized mind is not used towards that end, we wonder whose end it is used for.

When attempting to slay a dragon nearly the size of our planet, it is most advisable to respect its power and avoid a frontal assault - one in which you will surely lose. The plan is one of treachery and erosion and for that your best friend is calendar time. Nothing can make up for the gestation period. Just think how long it will take you to erase and replace and you will better appreciate the time factor.

You are not alone and there is no need for you to feel helpless against the juggernaughts of "City Hall." Many vulnerabilities exist there and they can be exploited. You will have to invest effort and time and take risks. Big deal. That's the price of excitement and there is no higher adventure than to **have fun at work.**

Erase and Replace Summary

Erase
- Purpose of organization is what it espouses
- Technology solves all problems
- Relevance of time, technology, money, people or management (the Eliminations)
- Loyalty exchanges for job security

- What you have been taught is true

- Failure and error are bad

- Complex organizations solve complex problems
- Standard procedures will solve all problems

- Orgman is guided by reason

- Management is in control
- Elaborate specifications reduce odds of failure
- The mess can't be helped
- The process is normal
- Problem complexity is no reason to change practices
- Resources are allocated by significance

- Organizational practices will solve all problems
- Preservation is prime directive of organization
- Organizations learn from their mistakes

- Skillful application of normal practices will solve all problems
- Things will work out by themselves
- The Establishment knows best
- The Establishment provides civilization
- Perceptions are equal to reality
- There are limits in what can be done

- Decomposition leads to control
- Organizations are designed and operated by neocortex intellect
- Stress should be accepted as part of the job
- Management responds to espoused incentives
- Specialization of labor adds control

- High performance is rewarded
- The organizational design is omnipotent

Replace
- Purpose of organization is what it does
- Technology brings problems

- Personal development is your responsibility
- What you have been taught is harmful to your health
- Error and failure are primary learning processes
- Innovation solves complex problems

- Standard methods make all complex problems impossible to solve
- Orgman is directed by social controls and instinct
- PWG is in control
- Specifications and contracts do not leave failure to chance
- The mess is unnecessary
- The Universal Scenario
- Complexity flips the switch from success to failure
- Allocation is by hidden agenda, always wrong
- Organizational practices are known to fail
- Defense of the status quo is the basic motivator
- Good or bad extremes of experience are ignored
- The solution space of popular practices is not related to the complex problem space
- Only errors grow by themselves
- The Establishment is your enemy
- Individual innovators provide civilization
- Instinct and intuition are usually wrong
- Systems methods can solve any complex problem
- Disintegration causes failure
- Institutions are products of the primitive limbic system
- Stress is always unwarranted, invalid or correctable
- Status quo is prime directive

- Uncompensated specialization destroys control
- No good deed goes unpunished
- The organizational design has big voids, roadblocks and distortions

Erase and Replace Summary

Erase

- Sanctioned practices lead to company success
- Exclude non-technical issues
- Controversy is to be avoided

- Gut reaction can substitute for knowledge in decision-making
- Technology goes from certainty to certainty
- Practices that work on small systems will work on large ones
- The corporate environment can support any activity
- The past is not relevant to today's problems
- The formal organization chart defines communications
- Productivity is the goal

- The Establishment is omnipotent

- Undiscussed issues are unimportant

- Compare your operation to others

- Consider only intended goals and obvious dangers
- Plunge in with solutions

- Received information is error-free
- Avoid trespassing on the territory of others
- Variety in the conditions the system can exhibit is to be ignored
- Everything has a technical fix
- The organization can adjust to complexity from within
- Because the organization wants the solution it will cooperate
- The technical system can be treated in an independent manner
- Quality is expensive
- Take complex problems to management
- "Excellence" companies know how to do it

- Projects fail because of the particulars of the effort
- The company is unaware of problems with its practices
- You can't buck the system

- Logic will prevail over emotion

Replace

- Traditional practices lead to organizational failure
- Social issues dominate all
- The path of least organizational resistance always fails
- Structure and content is all

- Technology is a mess of biased value judgments
- Extrapolated systems always bring new big problems
- The environment for routine destroys innovation
- The track record is the only adjustment to today's problems
- The informal communication system is the only one operative
- The organizational environment strangles productivity, its correction is key to complex problem solving
- The Establishment has a large array of vulnerabilities
- Discussing the undiscussable is the only way complex problems are solved
- Compare status to the language of failure and the requisite for success
- Count and account for contingencies

- Work only on problem definitions via failures
- All information received is wrong
- A common semantic language is essential

- Ashby's Law is a natural law

- Social system issues dominate
- Outside practitioners are essential for complexity
- The involved departments deny support and sabotage
- The technical system is inseparable from the social system
- Quality reduces cost
- Management is the enemy of quality
- Without constant support, all companies fail
- Projects fail because they never had a chance to succeed
- Corporation records are loaded with evidence of failure
- Combining loyalty display with action confuses radar
- Emotion wins every time

263

HFAW Reference Structure Pack

I. Social Interaction

    A. What **is** said and reported but not true
       1. Deceptions, Camouflage, and F4
       2. The Thirty-seven Denials
       3. Eliminations and Entreaties to Management
       4. The Bad Seventies and Connections
       5. The Territorial Imperative and the ZOI
       6. Misperceptions

    B. What is true but **not** said and reported (II must be done)
       1. Issues that are unidentified
          a. Through the cracks because of SOE shrinkage
          b. Unknown contingencies without Ashby knowledge
       2. Issues that are known, but avoided
          a. Conscious
             (1) Project dimensions
             (2) Cross reference
             (3) System configuration control
             (4) Life cycle perspective
          b. Subconscious
             (1) Boundaries and interfaces
             (2) Footprints

II. Technical - Social Systems Interactions

    A. Situation assessment
    B. Social system status
       1. Communication system
       2. Vulnerabilities
    C. Technical system status
       1. Complexity factors
       2. Go/no go factors
       3. The Universal Scenario
       4. The DfC reference

III. Personal reference

    A. The HFAW Checklist List
    B. The Common Semantic Language
    C. The HFAW Toolbox
    D. Establishment Profile
    E. The HFAW Order of Battle
    F. Starter Dart set

HAVE FUN AT WORK

BIBLIOGRAPHY

HUMAN BEHAVIOR

A Dynamic Theory of Personality, Lewin, K., New York: McGraw-Hill, 1935

A God Within, Dubos, Rene, New York: Charles Scribner's Sons, 1972

A Short History of Psychotherapy, Walker, N.,London: Routledge and Kegan Paul, 1957

A Study of Thinking, Bruner, J., Goodnow, J., and Austin, G., New York: Wiley, 1956

A Theory of Cognitive Dissonance, Festinger, Leon, Stanford: Stanford University Press, 1957

About Behaviorism, Skinner, B.F., New York: Vintage, 1976

Acceptable risk, Fischoff, B. et al, Cambridge: Cambridge Univ. Press, 1984

Adaptation to Life, Vaillant, George E., Boston: Little, Brown & Co., 1977

Anatomy of Reality: Merging Intuition and Reason, Salk, J., New York: Columbia University Press, 1983

Anthropology, Kroeber, A.L., New York: Harcourt, Brace, 1948

Before Philosophy, Frankfort, H., Frankfort, H.A., Wilson, J.A., and Jacobsen, T., New York: Penguin Books, 1949

Behaviour and Evolution, Roe, Ann, and Simpson, George Gaylord (eds), New Haven: Yale University Press, 1958

Being and Doing, Raskin, Marcus G., New York: Random House, 1971

Beyond Culture, Hall, E. T., New York: Anchor, 1977

Breakdown of the Bicameral Mind, Jaynes, Julian, RML

Centuries of Childhood, Aries, Phillipe, London: Jonathan Cape, 1962

Chance and Necessity, Monod, Jacques, New York: Knopf, 1971

Changing Images of Man, Markey, O. and Harman, W., Oxford: Pergamon Press, 1982

Contingencies of Reinforcement, Skinner, B.F., New York: Appleton-Century-Crofts, 1969

Coping with Stress, Meichenbaum, D.R., London: Century Publishing, 1983

Culture and the Evolution of Man, Montagu, Ashley (ed), Oxford: Oxford University Press, 1962

Decision and Stress, Broadbent, D.E., London: Academic Press, 1971

Decision Making, Janis, I.L. and Mann, L, New York: Free Press, 1977

Decision Theory and Human Behavior, Lee, W., New York: Wiley, 1971

Encounters with the Self, Hamachek, D., New York,: Holt, Rinehart & Winston, 1970

Evolution and Human Behavior, Alland, Alexander, Jr., Garden City, NY: American Museum of Natural History, 1967

Experimental Psychology, Woodworth, R.S., and Schlosberg, H., New York: Henry Holt & Co., 1955

Explorations in Personality, Murray, H.A., Oxford: Oxford University Press, 1938

Frustration and Aggression, Barker, H.; Dembo, T.; and Lewin, K., Iowa City: University of Iowa Press, 1942

Frustration: The Study of Behavior Without a Goal, Maier, N.R.F., New York: McGraw-Hill Book Co., 1949

Half the Human Experience: The Pyschology of Women, Hyde, J.S., Lexington: D.C. Heath, 1985

Handbook of Motivation and Cognition, Sorrentino, R.M. et al, New York: Guilford, 1987

Horizons of Anthropology, Tax, Sol (ed), Chicago: Aldine Books, 1964

Human Aggression, Storr, Anthony, London: Allen Lane, The Penguin Press, 1968

Human Behavior: An Inventory of Scientific Findings, Berelson, B., and Steiner, Gary A., New York: Harcourt, Brace & World, Inc., 1964

Human Growth, Tanner, J.M. (ed), Oxford: Pergamon Press, 1960

Influencing Attitudes and Changing Behavior, Zimbardo, P.G., and Ebbesen, E.G., Reading, MA: Addison-Wesley, 1969

Information Processing and Human-Machine Interaction, Rasmussen, Jens, New York: North-Holland, 1986

Insight: A Study of Human Understanding, Lonergan, D.J.F., New York: Philosophical Library, 1956

Instinctive Behaviour: The Development of a Modern Concept, Schiller, C. H. (ed & transl), London: Methuen, 1957

Introductory Lectures on Psychoanalysis, Freud, Sigmund, London: Allen & Unwin, 1923

Learning and Individual Differences, Gagne, R.M. (ed), Indianapolis, IN: Bobbs-Merrill, 1967

Learning From Experience: Toward Consciousness, Torbert, William, New York: Columbia University Press, 1972

Mind at the End of Its Tether, Wells, H.G., New York: Didire, 1946

Mind, Self and Society, Mead, G.H., Chicago, IL: University of Chicago Press, 1924

Models of Man, Simon, Herbert A., New York: John Wiley & Sons, 1957

New Technology and Human Error, Rasmussen, Jens, Dunkan, K & Leplat, J., Chichester: John Wiley & Sons, 1987

On Becoming A Person, Rogers, C.R., New York: Houghton-Mifflin, 1961

On Human Nature, Wilson, E.O., Cambridge, MA: Harvard University, 1978

Our Inner Conflicts, Horney, K., New York: W.W.Norton & Co., 1945

Personal Space, Sommer, R., Englewood Cliffs, NJ: Prentice-Hall, 1969

Personality Theories: A Comparative Analysis, Maddi, Salvatore R., Homewood, IL: Dorsey Press, 1976

Personality: A Psychological Interpretation, Allport, G.W., New York: Holt Reinhart & Winston, 1937

Physical Control of the Mind, Delgado, J.M.R., New York: Harper & Row, 1969

Powers of the Mind, Smith, Adam, New York: Ballantine Books, 1975

Primary Mental Abilities, Thurstone, L.L., Chicago: Univ. of Chicago Press, 1938

Principles of Psychology, James, Williams, New York: Henry Holt & Co., 1890

Programs of the Brain, Zachary, John, Oxford: Oxford University Press, 1978

Psychoanalysis and Anthropology: Culture and the Unconscious, Roheim, G., New York: International Universities Press, 1950

Psychological Stress, Appley, M.H. and Trumbull, R., New York: Appleton-Century-Crofts, 1976

Psychological Stress and the Coping Process, Lazarus, R.S., New York: McGraw-Hill, 1966

Psychology and the Human Dilemma, May, Rollo, Princeton, NJ: D. Van Nostrand Co., 1967

Quest for Identity, Wheelis, Allen, New York: W.W. Norton & Co., 1966

Rationality: An Essay Towards an Analysis, Bennett, Jonathan, London: Routledge & Kegan Paul,1964
Roots of Behavior, Bliss, Eugene L. (ed), New York: Harper & Bros., 1962
Schools of Psychoanalytic Thought, Munroe, R. L., New York: Holt, Rinehart & Winston, 1955
Scientists of the Mind, Karier, Clarence J., Champaign: University of Illinois, 1986
Sex and Behavior, Beach, Frank (ed), New York: John Wiley, 1965
Social and Psychological Factors in Stress, McGrath, J.E. (ed), New York: Holt, Rinehart & Winston, 1970
Social Causes of Illness, Totman, Richard, New York: Random House, 1979
Stress, Cox, T, London: Macmillan, 1978
Stress and Disease, Wolff, Harold, Springfield, IL: C.C.Thomas Press, 1968
Stress and Coping, Field, T.M. et al, Hillside: Erlbaum, 1985
Structure of Human Abilities, Vernon, P.E., London: Methuen & Co., Ltd., 1950
The Abilities of Man, Spearman, C., New York: Macmillan, 1927
The Biosocial Nature of Man, Montagu, Ashley, New York: Grove Press, 1956
The Center of the Cyclone: An Autobiography of Inner Space, Lilly, John C., New York: Julian Press, 1972
The Cognitive Revolution in Psychology, Baars, Bernard J., New York: Guilford, 1987
The Concept of Self, Gergen, K. J., New York: Holt, Rinehart & Winston, 1970
The Cultural Background of Personality, Linton, R., New York: Appleton-Century-Crofts, 1945
The Divided Self, Laing, R.D., London: Tavistock Publications, 1965
The Ecology of Human Intelligence, Hudson, Liam (ed), Middlesex, England: Penguin, 1970
The Effect of Air Traffic Control Experience Levels on Quality, Rhoades, J.R., and Samuel, C.E., Dayton, OH: WPAFB AFIT-LSSR 26-79B, 1979
The Evolution Man, Lewis, Roy, Harmondsworth: Penguin Books, 1963
The Factors of Mind, Burt, C., London: University of London Press, 1940
The Feminine Mystique, Friedan, Betty, New York: W.W.Norton, 1963
The Human Condition, Arendt, H., Chicago: University of Chicago Press, 1958
The Hunters, Service, Elman R., Englewood Cliffs, NJ: Prentice-Hall, 1966
The Language and Thought of the Child, Piaget, Jean, New York: Harcourt, Brace & World, 1926
The Making of Man, Calverton, V.F. (ed), New York: Modern Library, 1931
The Mature Mind, Overstreet, H.A., New York: Norton, 1947
The Meaning of Anxiety, May, Rollo, New York: Ronald Press Co., 1950
The Mind at Work and Play, Bartlett, F.C., London: Allen & Unwin, 1951
The Motivation to Work, Herzberg, Frederick, Mausner, Bernard, and Snyderman, Barbara, New York: John Wiley & Sons, 1959
The Naked Ape, Morris, Desmond, London: Jonathan Cape, 1967
The Natural Mind, Weil, Andrew, Boston: Houghton-Mifflin, 1972
The Nature and Destiny of Man, Niebuhr, R., New York: Scribner's Sons, 1949

The Origin of Species, Darwin, C., Middlesex, England: Penguin Books, 1968
The Origin of Man, Read, Carveth, Cambridge: Cambridge University Press, 1925
The Origin of Man, DeVore, Paul (ed), Chicago: Aldine Books, 1968
The Potential of Women, Farber, S. M., and Wilson, R.H. (eds), New York: McGraw-Hill, 1963
The Primal Scream, Janov, Arthur, New York: Putnam, 1970
The Problem Solving Approach to Adjustment, Spivak, G. et al, San Francisco, Jossey-Bass, 1976
The Psychology of Consciousness, Ornstein, Robert, San Francisco: W. H. Freeman, 1973
The Psychology of Decision, Hogarth, R.M., New York: Wiley, 1980
The Savage Mind, Levi-Strauss, Claude, London: Weidenfeld and Nicolson, 1966
The Scientific Analysis of Personality, Cattel, R. B., Chicago, Aldine Publishing Co., 1965
The Seasons of a Man's Life, Levinson, D. J., New York: Knopf, 1978
The Social Life of Early Man, Washburn, S.L. (ed), Chicago: Aldine Books, 1961
The Storming of the Mind: Inside the Consciousness Revolution, Hunter, Robert, Gaarden City, NY: Anchor Books, 1972
The Stress of Life, Selye, Hans, New York: McGraw-Hill Book Co., 1956
The Structure of Human Personality, Eysenck, H. J., London: Methuen & Co., Ltd., 1953
The Structure of Human Decisions, Miller D.W. and Star, M.K., Englewood Cliffs: Prentice-Hall, 1967
The Study of Behavior, Stephenson, W., Chicago: University of Chicago Press, 1953
The Study of Man, Linton, R., New York: Appleton-Century-Crofts, 1936
The Territorial Imperitive, Ardrey, Robert, New York: Atheneum Press, 1966
The True Believer, Hoffer, E., New York: Harper & Row, 1951
The Varieties of Temperament, Sheldon, W. H., New York: Harper & Bros., 1942
The Wisdom of the Body, Cannon, W. B., New York: W.W. Norton & Co., 1932
Theories of Personality, Hall, Calvin S., and Lindzey, Gardner, New York: John Wlley & SOns, 1970
Theories of Personality, Arndt, W.B., Jr., New York: Macmillan, 1974
Theories of the Mind, Sher, Jordon N. (ed), Glencoe, IL: Free Press of Glencoe, 1962
Walden Two, Skinner, B.F., New York: Macmillan Co., 1948
Who Shall Survive?, Moreno, J.L., Washington, DC: Nervous & Mental Diseases Publishing Co.,1934
Women and Madness, Chesler, Phyllis, New York: Doubleday, 1972
Work and Human Behavior, Neff, Walter S., New York: Atherton Press, 1968

GROUP BEHAVIOR

A Dictionary of the Social Sciences, Gould, J., and Kolb, W. L. (eds), New York: Free Press, 1964
African Genesis, Ardrey, Robert, London: Collins, 1961
Alienation and Freedom, Blauner, Robert, Chicago: University of Chicago Press, 1964
Autonomous Group Functioning, Herbst, P.G., London: Tavistock, 1962

Beyond Freedom and Dignity, Skinner, B.F., New York: Alfred A. Knopf, 1971

Clan, Caste and Club, Hsu, Francis L.K., Princeton, NJ: D. Van Nostrand, 1963

Cognitive-Behavior Modification, Meichenbaum, D., New York: Plenum, 1977

Communication and Culture: Codes of Human Interaction, Smith, A.G. (ed), New York: Holt, Reinhart & Winston, 1966

Conflict Among Humans, Nye, R.D., New York: Springer, 1973

Contemporary Sociological Theories, Sorokin, Pitirim, New York: Harper & Bros., 1927

Continuities in Cultural Evolution, Mead, Margaret, New Haven: Yale University Press, 1964

Current Perspectives in Social Psychology, Hollander, E. P., and Hunt, R.G. (eds), New York: Oxford University Press, 1967

Dynamics of Groups at Work, Thelen, H.A., Chicago: University of Chicago Press, 1954

Evolution and Culture, Sahlins, Marshall D.; and Service, Elman R. (eds), Ann Arbor: University of Michigan Press, 1960

Experiences in Groups, Bion, W.R., New York: Basic Books, 1959

Exploration in Group Relations, Trist, E.L., and Sofer, C., Leicester: Leicester University Press, 1959

Field Theory in Social Science, Lewin, Kurt, New York: Harper & Bros, 1951

Fights, Games, and Debates, Rappoport, Anatol, Ann Arbor: University of Michigan Press, 1974

For a Science of Social Man, Gillen, John (ed), New York: Macmillan, 1954

Foundations of Behavioral Research, Kerlinger, F.N., New York: Holt, Rinehart & Winston, 1964

Foundations of Sociology, Lundberg, G.A., New York: Macmillan, 1939

Frustration and Aggression, Dollard, John, et al, New Haven, CT: Yale University Press, 1939

Games People Play, Berne, Eric, New York: Grove Press, 1964

Group Decision Making and Effectiveness, Van De Ven, A. H., Kent, OH: University of Kent Press, 1974

Group Dynamics, Cartwright, Dorwin, and Zander, A., New York: Harper & Row, 1960

Group Dynamics: The Psychology of Small Groups, Shaw, M.E., New York: McGraw-Hill, 1981

Group Planning and Problem Solving Methods in Engineering, Olsen, S.A. (ed), New York: Wiley, 1982

Group Techniques for Program Planning, Delbecq, Andre; Van de Ven, Andrew H.; and Gustafson, David H., Glenview, IL: Scott, Foresman, 1975

Groups in Harmony and Tension, Sherif, M., and Sherif, C.W., New York: Harper & Row, 1953

Handbook of Social Psychology, Lindzey, G. (ed), Reading, MA: Addison-Wesley Publishing Co., 1954

Handbook of Social Psychology, Young, K., London: Routledge and Kegan Paul, 1946

Handbook of Small Group Research, Hare, A. P., New York: Free Press, 1962

How to Win Friends and Influence People, Carneige, Dale, New York: Pocket Books, 1958

Human Nature and the Social Order, Thorndike, E. L., New York: Macmillan, 1940

I'm OK - You're OK, Harris, T. A., New York: Harper & Row, 1969

Individual in Society, Krech, D.;Crutchfield, R.S.; and Ballachey, E. L., New York: McGraw-Hill Book Co., 1962

Initiation Ceremonies, Young, Frank, New York: Bobbs-Merrill, 1965

Instincts of the Herd in Peace and War, Trotter, Wilfred, London: Ernest Benn, 1916

Interpersonal Accomodation, Abrahamson, M., Princeton: D.Van Nostrand, 1966

Interpersonal Messages of Emotion, Dittman, A.T., New York: Springer, 1972

Introductory Sociology, Cooley, C. H., and Angell, R.C., and Carr, L. J., New York: Charles Scribner's Sons, 1933

Lord of the Flies, Golding, William, London: Faber & Faber, 1954

Men In Groups, Tiger, Lionel, New York: Random House, 1969

On Aggression, Lorenz, Konrad, London: Methuen & Co., 1966

Personal and Organizational Change Through Group Methods, Schein, Edgar H., and Bennis. W.G., New York: Wiley, 1967

Personality Dynamics and Effective Behavior, Coleman, J.C., Chicago: Scott, Forseman & Co., 1960

Primitive Secret Societies, Webster, Hutton, New York: Macmillan, 1932

Primitive Society, Lowie, Robert, London: George Routledge, 1921

Principles of Sociology, Giddings, F.H., New York: Macmillan, 1896

Psychology: The Fundamental of Human Adjustment, Munn, N.L., London: George G. Harrap Co., 1961

Schedules of Reinforcement, Ferster, C. B., and Skinner, B.F., New York: Appleton-Century-Crofts, 1957

Sensitivity to People, Smith, H.C., New York: McGraw-Hill Book Co.,1966

Small Groups, Hare, A. P.; Borgatta, E. F.; and Bales, R.F., New York: Alfred A. Knopf, 1966

Social Behavior: Its Elementary Forms, Homans, G.C., New York: Harcourt, Brace & World, 1961

Social Deviance, Wilkins, Leslie T., Englewood Cliffs, NJ: Prentice-Hall, 1965

Social Learning Theory, Bandura, A., Englewood Cliffs, NJ: Prentice-Hall, 1977

Social Norms and Roles, Rommetveit, R., Minneapolis: University of Minnesota Press, 1954

Social Organization, Cooley, C. H., New York: Charles Scribner's Sons, 1909

Social Pressures in Informal Groups, Festinger, Leon; Schachter, S.; and Back, K., New York: Harper & Row, 1950

Social Psychology, Brown, R., New York: Free Press, 1965

Social Psychology, Bird, Caroline, New York: Appleton-Century, 1940

Social Psychology of Modern Life, Britt, S. H., New York: Farrar, Strauss & Giroux, 1941

Social Psychology: An Experimental Approach, Zajonc, R.R., Monterey, CA: Brooks/Cole, 1966

Social Sciences as Sorcery, Ardreski S,, London: Andre Deutsch, 1972

Social Technology, Helmer, Olaf, New York: Basic Books, 1966

Sociobiology and Behavior, Barash, D.P., New York: Elsevier, 1977

Sociobiology: The New Synthesis, Wilson, Edward O., Cambridge, MA: Belknap Press of Harvard University Press, 1975

Strategy of Conflict, Schelling, Thomas C., Cambridge, MA: Harvard University Press, 1966

Swords of Silence: Chinese Secret Societies - Past and Present, Glick, Carl, Hwa, Hong Shenk, New York: McGraw-Hill, 1947

Systematic Sociology, von Wiese, L., and Becker, H., New York: Wiley, 1938

Talk, Work and Action, Richardson, F.L.W., New York: The Society for Applied Anthropology, Monograph #3, 1961

Team Building, Dyer, W. G., Reading, MA: Addison-Wesley, 1977

The Dawn of Civilization, Piggot, S. (ed), New York: McGraw-Hill, 1961

The Dynamics of Interpersonal Behavior, Zalesnik, A., and Moment, D., New York: Wiley, 1964

The Evolution of a Community, Willmott, P., London: Routledge and Kegan Paul, 1963

The Explanation of Social Behavior, Harre, R., and Secord, P.F., Totowa, NJ: Rowman & Littlefield, 1972

The Human Use of Human Beings, Weiner, Norbert, New York: Avon Books, 1971

The Human Group, Homans, G.C., New York: Harcourt, Brace & World, 1950

The Human Imperative, Alland, Alexander, New York: Columbia University Press, 1972

The Joiners: A Sociological Description, Hausnecht, E. G. Murray, New York: Bedminster Press, 1962

The Lonely Crowd, Riesman, David, New Haven, CT: Yale University Press, 1950

The New Group Therapy, Mowrer, O.H., New York: Van Nostrand, 1964

The Principles of Social Psychology, McDougall, W., Washington, DC: Robert B.Luce, 1918

The Psychology of Interpersonal Relations, Heider, F., New York: John Wiley & Sons, 1958

The Psychology of Affiliation, Schachter, S., Stanford: Stanford University Press, 1959

The Psychology of Communication, Miller, A., Baltimore, MD: Penguin, 1967

The Resolution of Conflict, Deutsch, Morton, New Haven: Yale University Press, 1973

The Social Psychology of Groups, Thibaut, John w., and Kelly, H.H., New York, John Wiley & Sons, 1959

The Social Life of Monkeys and Apes, Zuckerman, S., London: Routledge and Kegan Paul, 1932

Theory and Problems of Social Psychology, Krech, D., and Crutchfield, R.S., New York: McGraw-Hill Book Co., 1948

Toward a General Theory of Action, Parsons, Talcott, New York: Harper & Row, 1962

Transactional Analysis in Psychotherapy, Berne, Eric, New York: Grove Press, 1961

Two-Person Game Theory: The Essential Ideas, Rapoport, A., Ann Arbor: University of Michigan, 1966

Victims of Groupthink, Janis, Irving, Boston: Houghton Mifflin Co., 1972

ORGANIZATIONAL BEHAVIOR

A Behavioral Theory of the Firm, Cyert, R.M., and March, J.G., Englewood Cliffs, NJ: Prentice-Hall, 1963

A Comparative Analysis of Complex Organizations, Etzioni, Amital, New York: Free Press, 1961

A Great Place to Work, Levering, New York: Random House, 1988

A Theory of Social Control, LaPiere, R.T., New York: McGraw-Hill, 1954

Administrative Organization, Pfieffner, J.M. and Sherwood, F. P., Englewood Cliffs, NJ: Prentice-Hall, 1960

Analyzing Performance Problems, Mager, R.F. and Pipe, P., Belmont: Fearon, 1970

Assessing Organizational Effectiveness, Zammuto, R.F., Albany, NY: State University of New York Press, 1982

Attitude, Organizations and Change, Hovland, C.I., and Rosenberg, M.J., New Haven: Yale University Press, 1960

Augustine's Laws, Augustine, Norman R., New York: Viking Penguin Inc., 1986

Behavior and Organization, Golembiewski, R.T., Chicago, IL: Rand McNally, 1962

Behavior in Organization, Huse, E., and Bowditch, J., Reading, MA: Addison-Wesley, 1973

Behavior in Organizations, Porter, L.W.; Lawler, E.E. iii; and Hackman, R. J., New York: McGraw-Hill, 1975

Behavior in Organizations, Reitz, H., Homewood, IL: Irwin, 1977

Behavior in Organizations: A Multidimensional View, Athos, Anthony G., and Coffey, R.E., Englewood Cliffs, NJ: Prentice-Hall, 1968

Behavior of Industrial Work Groups, Sayles, L.R., New York: John Wiley & Sons, 1958

Bonds of Organization, Bakke, E.W., New York: Harper, 1950

Both Ends of the Candle, Ross, Denniston, London: Faber & Faber, 1943

Catch-22, Heller, Joseph, New York: Simon & Schuster, 1961

Changing Organizations, Bennis, Warren G., New York: McGraw-Hill, 1966

Complex Organizations, Hrebiniak, L.G., St Paul, MN: West, 1978

Complex Organizations, Etzioni, A. (ed), New York: Holt, Rinehart & Winston, 1965

Complex Organizations: A Critical Essay, Perrow, C., Glenview, IL: Scott, Foresman, 1972

Conflict Management and Organizational Development, Mastenbrook, W.F.G., New York: John Wiley & Sons, 1987

Control in Organizations, Tannenbaum, A.S., New York: McGraw-Hill, 1968

Crisis in the Workplace: Occupational Disease and Injury, Ashford, A.A., Cambridge, MA; MIT Press, 1976

Death on the Job: Occupational Health Struggles in the U.S., Berman, D.M., New York: Monthly Review Press, 1978

Designing Collateral Organizations, Kilmann, R.H., Pittsburgh, PA: University of Pittsburgh, 1982

Designing Complex Organizations, Galbraith, Jay, Reading, MA: Addison-Wesley Publishing Co., 1973

Dimensions of Organizations: Environment, Context & Structure, Zey-Ferrell, M., Santa Monica, CA: Goodyear, 1979

Dispatches, Herr, Michael, New York: Alfred A. Knopf, 1977

Dynamics of Bureaucracy, Blau, Peter M., Chicago: University of Chicago Press, 1955

Environments and Organizations, Meyer, M.W., San Francisco: Jossey-Bass, 1978

Escape From Freedom, Fromm, E., New York: Farrar & Reinhart, 1941

Existence and Growth: Human Needs in Organizational Settings, Alderfer, C. P., NY: The Free Press, 1972

Formal Organizations, Blau, Peter M. and Scott, W. R., London: Routledge & Kegan Paul, 1963

Group Cohesiveness in the Industrial Work Group, Seashore, S.E., Ann Arbor, MI: University of Michigan, 1954

Organizational Behavior: Theory and Application, Whyte, W.F., Homewood, IL: Richard D. Irwin, 1969

Organizational Communication, Spiker, Barry K. and Daniels, Tom D., Dubuque: Wm. C. Brown, 1987

Organizational Design, Pfeffer, J., Arlington Heghts, IL: AHM Publishing, 1978

Organizational Design, Galbraith, J., Reading, MA; Addison-Wesley, 1977

Organizational Development, Huse, E.F., St. Paul, MN: West, 1976

Organizational Intelligence, Knowledge and Policy in Industry, Wilensky, Harold L., New York: Basic Books, 1967

Organizational Learning: A Theory of Action Perspective, Argyris, C., and Schon, D., Reading, MA: Addison-Wesley, 1977

Organizational Planning: Cases and Concepts, Lorsch, J.W.; and Lawrence, Paul R., Homewood, IL: Richard D. Irwin, 1972

Organizational Psychology, Kolb, D.A.;Rubin, I.M.; and McIntyre, J.M., Englewood Cliffs, NJ: Prentice-Hall, 1974

Organizational Psychology, Schein, Edgar H., Englewood Cliffs, NJ: Prentice-Hall, 1970

Organizational Psychology, Bass, B., Boston: Allyn & Bacon, 1965

Organizational Renewal, Lippett, Gordon, New York: Appleton-Century-Crofts, 1969

Organizational Role as a Risk Factor in Coronary Disease, Sales, S.M., Administrative Science Quarterly:Vol 14 (1969)

Organizational Strategy, Structure and Process, Miles, R. and Snow, C., New York: McGraw-Hill, 1978

Organizational Stress, Kahn, R. L.; Wolfe, D.M.;Quinn, R. P. and Snoek, J.D., New York: Wiley, 1964

Organizational Systems, Azumi, K., and Hage, J. (eds), Lexington, MA; D.C. Heath, 1972

Organizational Transitions: Managing Complex Change, Beckhard, R., and Harris, R., Reading, MA: Addison-Wesley, 1977

Organizations, March, James G., and Simon, Herbert A., New York: John Wiley & Sons, 1958

Organizations and Their Managing, Gross, Bertram, New York: Free Press, 1968

Organizations and Environments, Aldrich, H.E., Englewood Cliffs, NJ: Prentice-Hall, 1979

Organizations in Action, Thompson, James D., New York: McGraw-Hill Book Co., 1967

Organizations: A Quantum View, Miller, Danny, Englewood Cliffs, NJ: Prentice-Hall, 1984

Organizations: Rational, Natural, and Open Systems, Scott, W. R., Englewood Cliffs, NJ: Prentice-Hall, 1981

Organizations: Structure and Process, Hall, R.H., Englewood Cliffs, NJ: Prentice-Hall, 1972

Organizations: Theory and Design, Connor, P.E., Chicago, IL: Science Research Associates, 1980

Organized Social Complexity, LaPorte, T.R. (ed), Princeton, NJ: Princeton University Press, 1981

Pay and Organizational Effectiveness: A Psychological View, Lawler, Edward E., New York: McGraw-Hill Book Co., 1971

People and Productivity, Sutermeister, Robert A., New York: McGraw-Hill, 1963

Performance in Organizations: Determinants and Appraisal, Cummings, L.L., Schwab, D.P., Glenview, IL: Scott, Foresman, 1973

Planning and Developing the Company Organization Structure, Dale, E., New York: American Management Association, 1952

Power in Organizations, Zald, M.N. (ed), Nashville, TN: Vanderbilt University Press, 1970

Principles of Organization, Caplow, T., New York: Harcourt, Brace & World, 1964

Process of Organization, Weiss, R.S., Ann Arbor: Survey Research Center, University of Michigan, 1956

Productivity and Social Organization, Rice, A. K., London: Tavistock Publications, Ltd., 1958

Readings in Organizational Behavior and Human Performance, Cummings, L.L., and Scott, W.E., Homewood, IL: Irwin, 1969

Readings on Modern Organizations, Etzioni, A., (ed), Englewood Cliffs, NJ: Prentice-Hall, 1969

Social Disorganization, Elliot, M.A., and Merrill, F.E., New York: Harpers, 1941

Social Science Approaches to Business Behavior, Strother, G.B., Homewood, IL: Richard D. Irwin, 1962

Stages of Corporate Development, Scott, B.R., Boston: Harvard Business School, 1971

Strategy, Change, and Defensive Routines, Argyris, Chris, Cambridge, MA: Ballinger, 1985

Stress and Satisfaction on the Job, Benner, P.E., New York: Praeger, 1984

Stress, Appraisal and Coping, Lazarus, R.A. and Folkman, S., New York: Springer, 1984

Studies in Organizational Design, Lorsch, J.W.; and Lawrence, Paul R., Homewood, IL: Richard D. Irwin, 1970

Systems of Organization, Miller, E. J. and Rice, A. K., London: Tavistock Publications, 1967

Technology and Organization, Woodward, Joan, London: HMSO, 1958

Technostructures and Interorganizational Relations, Gillespie, D.F., and Mileti, D.S., Lexington, MA: D.C. Heath, 1979

Ten Thousand Working Days, Schrank, Robert, Cambridge, MA: MIT Press, 1978

The Adversarial Economy: Management of Government Requirements, Marcus, A.A., Westport, CT: Greenwood Press, 1983

The Analysis of Organizations, Litterer, J.A., New York: John Wiley & Sons, 1973

The Art of War, Tzu, Sun, Oxford: Oxford Univ., 1963

The Characteristics of Total Institutions, Goffman, E., Symposium on Preventive and Social Psychiatry, 1957

The Design of Organizations, Khandwalla, P.N., New York: Harcourt, Brace, Jovanovich, 1977

The Enterprise and Its Environment, Rice, A.K., London: Tavistock Publications, Ltd., 1963

The Godfather, Puzo, Mario, New York: G. P. Putnam's Sons, 1969

The Hidden Dimension, Hall, E.T., New York: Doubleday & Co., 1966

The Human Organization, Likert, Rensis, New York: McGraw-Hill Book Co., 1967

The Lens of Perception, Bennett, H.Z., Norwood: Celestial Arts, 1987

The Limits of Organizational Change, Kaufman, H., Alabama: University of Alabama Press, 1972

The Logic of Collective Action, Olson, Mancur, Cambridge, MA: Harvard University Press, 1965

The Long March, Salisbury, Harrison, New York, McGraw-Hill, 1985

The Management of Organizational Design, Kilmann, Ralph H., Pondy, Louis R., and Selvin, Dennis P. (eds), New York: Elsevier North-Holland, 1976

The March of Folly, Tuchman, Barbara, New York: Alfred Knopf, 1984

The Organization Man, White, W. H. Jr., New York: Simon & Schuster, 1956

The Organizational Revolution, Boulding, Kenneth, New York: Harper & Bros., 1953

The Organizational Life Cycle, Kimberly, J. and Miles, R.H., San Francisco: Jossey-Bass, 1980

The Politics of Organizational Decision Making, Pettigrew, A., London:Tavistock, 1973

The Principles of Organization, Mooney, J.D. and Reiley, A.M., New York: Harper & Bros., 1947

The Psychology of Language & Communication, Ellis, Andrew and Beattie, Geoffrey, New York: Guilford, 1987

The Quality of Working Life, Davis, L.E., and Cherns, A. B. (eds), New York: The Free Press, 1975

The Social Psychology of Organizing, Weick, K., Reading, MA: Addison-Wesley, 1969

The Social Psychology of Organizations, Katz, Daniel; and Kahn, R. L., New York: John Wiley & Sons, 1966

The Structure of Organizations, Blau, P., and Schoenherr, P.A., New York: Basic Books, 1971

The Structuring of Organizations, Mintzberg, H., Englewood Cliffs, NJ: Prentice-Hall 1979

The Theory of the Growth of the Firm, Penrose, Edith, London: Basil Blackwell, 1963

The Working Class Majority, Levinson, Andrew, New York: Coward, McCann & Geohegan, 1974

Theories of Organizations: Form, Process, and Transformation, Hage, J., New York: Wiley, 1980

Understanding Organizational Behavior, Argyris, Chris, Homewood, IL: Dorsey, 1960

Vertical Mosaic, Porter, J., Toronto: University of Toronto Press, 1965

Vocational Psychology and Character Analysis, Hollingsorth, H.L., New York: Appleton-Century, 1929

What The Employee Thinks, Houser, J.D., Cambridge, MA: Harvard University Press, 1927

Where The Law Ends: The Social Control of Corporate Behavior, Stone, C.D., New York: Harper & Row, 1975

White Collar, Mills, C.W., New York: Oxford University Press, 1951

Work and the Nature of Man, Herzberg, Frederick, Cleveland, OH: World Publishing Co., 1966

Working, Terkel, Studs, New York: Random House, Pantheon Books, 1974

THE ESTABLISHMENT

A Scientific Theory of Culture and Other Essays, Malinowski, B., Chapel Hill: University of North Carolina Press, 1944

American Business Leaders: A Study in Social Stratification, Taussing, F.W., and Joslyn, C.S., New York: The Macmillan Co., 1932

Animal Farm, Orwell, George, New York: Harcourt, Brace & World,, 1946

Between Two Ages: America's Role in the Technetronic Era, Brzezinsky, Zbigniew, New York: The Viking Press, 1970

Beyond Boom and Crash, Heilbroner, Robert L., New York: W.W.Norton, 1978

Beyond The Wasteland, Bowles, Gordon & Weisskopf, Garden City: Doubleday, 1983

Beyond The Stable State, Schon, D., New York: Norton, 1971

Big Enterprises in a Competitive System, Kaplan,
A.D.H., Washington DC: Brookings Institution, 1964

Boards of Directors: Structure and Performance, Vance, S.C., Eugene, OR: University of Oregon Press, 1964

Brave New World, Huxley, Aldous L., Garden City, NY: Doubleday & Co., 1932

Civilization and its Discontents, Freud, S., London: Hogarth Press, 1930

Class and Class Conflict in Industrial Society, Dahrendorf, Ralf, Stanford, Cal.:Stanford University Press, 1959

Community Control, Altschuler, A.A., New York: Pegasus, 1970

Confessions of an Advertising Man, Ogilvy, D., New York, Atheneum Publishers, 1966

Conflict and Defense: A General Theory, Boulding, Kenneth E., New York: Harper, 1963

Corporate Control and Business Behavior, Williamson, O.E., Englewood Cliffs, NJ: Prentice-Hall, 1970

Design for Policy Sciences, Dror, Yehezkel, New York: Elsevier, 1971

Dollars and Dreams, Levy, Frank, New York: Basic books, 1988

Dollars and Sense, Bensman, J., New York: Macmillan, 1967

Ecological Psychology, Barker, R.G., Stanford, CA: Stanford University Press, 1968

Economic and Philosophical Manuscripts of 1844, Marx, Karl, London: Lawrence & Wishert, 1959

Economic Concentration, Blair, John M., New York: Harcourt Brace & World, 1973

Elites in the Policy Process, Presthus, Robert, London: Cambridge University, 1974

Elites in Western Democracy, Crew, Ivor (ed), New York: Wiley, 1974

Environment for Man: The Next Fifty Years, Ewald, William R., Jr. (ed), Bloomington: Indiana University Press, 1967

Essays on the Ritual of Social Relations, Gluckman, Max (ed), Manchester: Manchester University Press, 1962

Exchange and Power in Social Life, Blau, P., New York: Wiley, 1964

Expendable America, Brodeur, Paul, New York: Viking, 1973

Experimental Social Psychology, Murphy, G.; Murphy, L.B.; and Newcomb, T.M., New York: Harper & Bros., 1937

Friends of Friends: Networks, Manipulators, and Coalitions, Boissevain, Jeremy, Oxford: Basil Blackwell, 1974

From Generation to Generation, Eisenstadt, S.M., Glencoe IL: Free Press of Glencoe, 1955

Future Facts, Rosen, Stephen, New York: Simon & Schuster, 1976

Future Shock, Toffler, Alvin, New York: Bantam Books, 1970

Gifts of Poison: The Politics of Reputation, Bailey, F.G., Oxford: Basil Blackwell,1971

Hot Strip Tease and Other Notes on American Culture, Gorer, Geoffrey, London: Cresset Press, 1937

Human Betterment, Boulding, K, Beverly Hills: Sage, 1985

Ideas in Conflict, Gordon, T. J., New York: St Martin's Press, 1966

Images of Organizations, Morgan, Gareth, Beverly Hills: Sage, 1986

In Defense of Industrial Concentration, McGee, John S., New York: Praeger Publishers, 1971

Indicators of Social Change, Sheldon, Eleanor B.,

and Moore, Wilbert E., New York: Russell Sage Foundation, 1968

Karl Marx: Selected Writings, Bottomore, T. B. & Rubel, M., London: Penguin, 1963

Kinds of Order in Society, Hayek, F.A., Menlo Park: Inst. for Humane Studies, 1975

Leaders, Groups and Influence, Hollander, E. P., Oxford: Oxford University Press, 1964

Leadership in a Free Society, Whitehead, T.N., London: Oxford University Press, 1936

Life and Death on the Corporate Battlefield, Solman, Paul, New York: Simon & Schuster, 1982

Major Social Institutions, Panunzio, C., New York: Macmillan, 1939

Megatrends, Naisbitt, John, New York: Warner Books, 1982

Men, Machines and Modern Times, Morison, E.E., Cambridge, MA: MIT Press, 1966

Models of Doom, Cole, H.S.D., et al, New York: Universe Books, 1973

Modern Capitalism, Shonfield, Andrew, London: Oxford University Press, 1965

Monopoly, Goulden, Joseph G., New York: Pocket Books, 1970

Nader's Raiders, Cox, E.F., et al, New York: Grove Press, 1969

New Dimensions of Political Economy, Heller, W.W., New York: Norton, 1967

New Ideals of Peace, Addams, Jane, New York: Macmillan, 1907

On the Psychology of Military Incompetence, Dixon, N.F., New York: Basic Books, 1976

Patterns of Discovery in the Social Sciences, Diesing, W., Chicago, IL: Aldine, 1971

Political Elites, Parry, Geraint, London: George Allen & Unwin, 1969

Politics and Markets: The World's Political-Economic Systems, Lindblom, Charles E., New York: Basic Books, 1977

Politics as Symbolic Action, Edelman, Murray, Chicago: Markham, 1971

Politics, Power & the Church, Lader, Lawrence, New York: Macmillan, 1987

Power and Innocence, May, Rollo, New York: Norton, 1972

Power and Culture, Gutman, Herbert G., New York: Pantheon, 1987

Power: A New Social Analysis, Russell, B., New York: Norton, 1938

Problems of Economics and Sociology, Menger, C., Urbana: University of Illinois Press, 1963

Professional Employees, Prandy, K., London: Faber & Faber, Ltd., 1965

Reason in Society, Diesing, Paul, Urbana: University of Illinois, 1962

"Rich Countries and Poor", Brown, Lester, Daedalus, Fall, 1973

Roman Life in Pliny's Time, Wilkenson, Maud, Philadelphia: George W. Jacobs, 1897

Rural Poverty and the Urban Crisis, Hansen, N., Bloomington, IN: University of Indiana Press, 1970

Scanning the Business Environment, Aguilar, F., New York: Macmillan, 1967

Scientific Study of Human Society, Giddings, F.H., Chapel Hill, NC: University of North Carolina Press, 1924

Shooting Ourselves In The Foot, O'Keefe, P.J., Boston: Houghton Mifflin, 1985

Small is Beautiful: Economics as if People Mattered, Schumacher, Ernst F., New York: Harper & Row, 1973

Social Class In America, Warner, W. L., New York: Harper & Row, 1960

Social Control, Landis, P.H., Philadelphia: Lippincott, 1939

Social Indicators, Bauer, Raymond (ed), Cambridge, MA: The MIT Press, 1966

Social Institutions, Hertzler, J.O., New York: McGraw-Hill, 1929

Social Interaction, Argyle, M., New York: Atherton Press, 1969

Social Standing In America: New Dimensions of Class, Coleman, Richard P., and Rainwater, Lee, New York: Basic Books, 1978

Social Structure, Murdock, George P., New York: Macmillan, 1949

Social Theory and Social Structure, Merton, R. K., Glencoe, IL: Free Press, 1957

Society and Nature, Kelsen, Hans, Chicago: University of Chicago Press, 1943

St.Clair: Boom and Ruin In PA Anthracite, Wallace, Anthony F.C.,, New York: Knopf, 1987

Stranger in a Strange Land, Heinlein, Robert, New York: Berlkey, 1968

Strategic Behavior in Business and Government, Summer, Charles E., Boston: Little, Brown, 1980

Strategy and Structure in British Enterprise, Channon, D., Boston: Harvard University Press, 1973

Strategy, Structure, and Economic Performance, Rumelt, R. P., Cambridge, MA: GSBA Harvard University 1974

Structure and Process in Modern Societies, Parsons, Talcott, New York: Free Press, 1960

Studies in Social Power, Cartwright, D. (ed), Ann Arbor, Mich.: Institute for Social Research, 1959

Studies in Philosophy, Politics, and Economics, Hayek, F.A., New York: Simon & Schuster, 1967

Technological Change and Occupational Responses, Presthus, Robert, Washington, DC: US Dept of Health, Education & Welfare, 1970

The Achieving Society, McClelland, D.C., Princeton, NJ: D.Van Nostrand Co., 1961

The Adaptive Organization, De Greene, K.B., New York: Wiley, 1982

The Affluent Society, Galbraith, John Kenneth, Boston: Houghton Mifflin Co., 1976

The American Occupational Structure, Blau, Peter M. and Duncan, O.D., New York: John Wiley & Sons, 1965

The American Challenge, Servan-Schreiber, Jean-Jaques, New York: Antheneum, 1968

The American Future, Hayden, Tom, Boston: South End Press, 1980

The Anatomy of Human Destructiveness, Fromm, E., New York: Holt, Rinehart & Winston, 1973

The Big Boys: Power and Position in American Business, Nader, Ralph and Taylor, William, New York: Pantheon, 1987

The Civil Culture, Almond, G. and Verba, S., Princeton, NJ: The Princeton University Press, 1963

The Closing Circle, Commoner, Barry, New York: Knopf, 1971

The Comedy of Survival, Meeker, Joseph W., New York: Scribner's, 1974

The Coming of Post-Industrial Society, Bell, Daniel, New York: Basic Books, 1973

The Crisis of Industrial Society, Birnbaum, Norman, New York: Random House, 1956

The Economic Theory of 'Managerial' Capitalism, Marris, Robin, London: Macmillan, 1964

The European Administrative Elite, Armstrong, John A., Princeton, NJ: Princeton University Press, 1973

The Failure of Success, Marrow, Alfred J., New York: American Management Association, 1972

The Functions of Social Conflict, Coser, L.A., New York: Free Press of Glencoe, 1955

The Glacier Project Papers, Brown, Wilfred and Jaques, E., London: Heinemann Educational Books, Ltd., 1965

The Global Mind: Beyond the Limits to Growth, Perelman, Lewis J., New York: Basic Books, 1987

The Great Society: A Psychological Analysis, Wallas, Graham, London: Macmillan, 1914

The Greening of America, Reich, Charles, New York: Random House, 1970

The Harried Leisure Class, Linder, S., Irvington NY: Columbia University Press, 1970

The Health of Nations, Sagan, Leonard A., New York: BAsic Books, 1987

The Human Problems of an Industrial Civilization, Mayo, Elton, New York: McMillan Co., 1933

The Limits to Growth, Meadows, Dennis H.; Meadows, D.L.; Ronders, J.; and Behrens,L., New York: Universe Books, 1972

The Making of a Counter Culture, Roszak, Theodore, Garden City, NY: Doubleday & Co., 1969

The Manufacture of Evil, Tiger, Lionel, New York: Harper & Row, 1987

The Meaning of the Twentieth Century, Boulding, Kenneth, New York: Harper & Row, 1964

The Medium is the Message, McLuhan, Marshall; and Fiore, Q., New York: Bantam Books, 1967

The Myth of the Birth of the Hero, Rank, Otto, New York: Johnson reprint, 1914

The Nature of Human Conflict, McNeil, E.B. (ed), Englewood Cliffs, NJ: Prentice-Hall, 1965

The New Industrial State, Galbraith, John Kenneth, Boston: Houghton Mifflin Co., 1967

The Next American Frontier, Reich, R.B., New York: Times Book, 1983

The Next 200 Years, Kahn, Herman; Brown, William; and Martel, Leon, New York: William Morrow & Co., 1976

The No-Risk Society, Aharoni, Yair, Tel Aviv: Tel Aviv University, 1981

The Organization Makers, Collins, O., and Moore, D.G., New York: Appleton-Century-Crofts, 1970

The Palace Guard, Rather, Dan, and Gates, Gary Paul, New York: Harper & Row, 1974

The Police and the Public, Reiss, Albert J. Jr, New Haven, CT: Yale University Press, 1971

The Politics of Pollution in a Comparative Perspective, Enlow, C.H., New York: McKay, 1975

The Politics of Corruption: Organized Crime in an American City, Gardner, J.A., New York: Russell Sage, 1970

The Polity, Long, N.E., Chicago, IL: Rand McNally, 1962

The Post-Industrial Society, Touraine, Alain, New York: Random, 1971

The Power Elite, Mills, C. Wright, Oxford: Oxford University Press, 1956

The Protestant Ethic and the Spirit of Capitalism, Weber, Max, New York: Charles Scribner's Sons, 1958

The Psychology of Social Institutions, Judd, C.H., New York: Macmillan, 1926

The Rise and Fall of the Great Powers, Kennedy, Paul, New York: Random House, 1988

The Roots of Capitalism, Chamberlain, John, Indianapolis: Liberty Press, 1976

The Sane Society, Fromm, E., London: Routledge & Kegan Paul, 1956

The Science of Man in the World Crisis, Linton, R. (ed), New York: Columbia University Press, 1945

The Science of Society, Sumner, W.G., and Keller, A.G., New Haven: Yale University Press, 1927

The Secret Societies of All Ages and Countries, Heckethorn, Charles W., London: George Redway, 1897

The Self-Production of Society, Touraine, A., Chicago: University of Chicago Press, 1977

The Servants of Power, Baritz, L., New York: John Wiley & Sons, 1965

The Social System, Parsons, Talcott, London: Tavistock Publications, 1952

The Social Life of a Modern Community, Warner, W.L., and Lunt, P.S., New Haven, CT: Yale University PRess, 1941

The Social Problems of an Industrial Civilization, Mayo, Elton, Cambridge, MA: Harvard University Press, 1947

The State and the Poor, Beer, Stafford H., and Barringer, R.E. (eds), Winthrop, MA, 1959

The Strategy of Social Protest, Gamson, William A., Homewood, IL: Dorsey, 1975

The Strategy of Social Regulation, Lave, Lester B., Washington, DC: The Brookings Institute, 1981

The Structure of Society, Levy, Marion J., Jr., Princeton, NJ: Princeton University Press, 1951

The Symbolic Uses of Politics, Edelman, Murray, Urbana: University of Illinois, 1964

The Technological Society, Ellul, J., New York: Knopf, 1964

The Theory of Social and Economic Organization, Weber, M., New York: Free Press, 1947

The Third Wave, Toffler, Alvin, New York: Morrow, 1980

The Turning Point, Capra, Fritjof, New York: Simon & Schuster, 1982

The Uses of Enchantment, Bettelheim, Bruno, New York: Alfred A. Knopf, 1977

The Wealth of Nations, Smith, Adam, New York: The Bobbs-Merrill Co., 1961

The Will To Power, Nietsche, F., New York: Macmillan, 1929

The World In 1984, Calder, Nigel (ed), Baltimore: Penguin Books, Inc., 1965

The World of Work, Dubin, R., Englewood Cliffs, NJ: Prentice-Hall, 1958

The World's Police, Cramer, James, New York: McGraw Hill, 1985

This Endangered Planet, Falk, Richard, New York: Random House, 1971

Two Cheers for Capitalism, Kristol, Irving, New York: Basic Books, 1978

Waging Business Warfare, Rogers, David J., New York: Scribners, 1987

Warrant for Genocide, Cohn, Norman, London: Eyre & Spottiswoode, 1967

Ways of Worldmaking, Nelson, Goodman, Indianapolis, IN: Hackett PPublishing Co., 1978

Why Nothing Works, Harris, Marvin, New York: Simon & Schuster, 1987

FINANCE

A General Theory of Economic Process, Chamberlain, N., New York: Harper & Row, 1955

Accounting Conventions: A Cause of Economic Instability, Robb, Fenton F., Edinburgh: University of Edinburgh, 1986

Accounting Information Systems, Robinson, A.; Davis, J.; and Alderman, C., New York: Harper & Row, 1982

Greed and Glory on Wall Street, Auletta, Ken, New York: Random House, 1986

In Banks We Trust, Lernoux, Penny, New York: Doubleday, 1984

Takeover, Johnston, Moira, New York: Penguin, 1986

The Great Depression of 1990, Batra, Ravi, New York, Simon & Schuster, 1987

The World Economy: History and Prospect, Rostow, W.W., New York: Wiley, 1984

GOVERNMENT

A Primer for Policy Analysis, Stokey, E., and Zeckhauser, R, New York: W.W. Norton, 1978

American Bureaucracy, Woll, P., New York: Norton, 1963

American Espionage, Jeffreys-Jones, Rhodri, New York: Macmillan, 1977

American Politics, Dolbeare, Kenneth M., and Edelman, Murray J., Lexington, MA: Heath, 1971

Analysis for Public Decisions, Quade, E.S., New York: Elsevier, 1975

Big Democracy, Appleby, P.H., New York: Knopf, 1945

Bomber, Deighton, Len, London: Pan Books, Ltd., 1970

Bureaucracy in a Democracy, Hyneman, C.S., New York: Harper, 1950

Bureaucracy in Modern Society, Blau, Peter M., New York: Random House, 1956

Bureaucracy on Trial: Policy Making by Government Agencies, Boyer, W.W., Indianapolis, IN: Bobbs-Merrill, 1964

Capitalism, Socialism and Democracy, Schumpeter, Joseph, New York: Harper, 1950

Decision-Making for Defense, Hitch, C.J., Berkeley, CA: University of California Press, 1965

Deep Black, Burrows, William E., New York: Random House, 1986

Double Cross System, Masterman, John, New Haven: Yale Univ., 1972

Economics and the Public Purpose, Galbraith, John Kenneth, Boston: Houghton Mifflin Co., 1973

FBI-KGB War, Lamphere, Robert J., New York: Random House, 1986

Governmental Reorganizations: Cases and Commentary, Mosher, F.C. (ed), Indianapolis, IN: Bobbs-Merrill, 1967

Herman The German, Neumann, Gerhard, New York: Morrow, 1984

High on Foggy Bottom, Frankel, C., New York: Harper & Row, 1969

High Technologies and Reducing the Risk of War, Pagels, Heinz R., New York: NYAS v489, 1986

Human Nature in Politics, Wallas, Graham, London: Constable, 1908

Inside Bureaucracy, Downs, A., Boston: Little, Brown, 1966

Inside the Third Reich, Speer, A., New York: Macmillan, 1970

Intergovernmental Relations in Review, Anderson, W., Minneapolis, MN: University of Minnesota Press, 1960

KAL 007: The Cover-up, Pearson, David E., Boston: Summit, 1987

Neighborhood Government, Kotler, M., Indianapolis, IN: Bobbs-Merrill, 1969

On War, Clausewitz, Carl von, New York: Barnes & Noble, 1966

Policy Analysts in the Bureaucracy, Meltsner, A., Berkeley, CA; University of California Press, 1976

Policy and Administration, Appleby, P.H., Alabama: University of Alabama Press, 1949

Policy-Making, Anderson, J.E., New York: Praeger, 1975

Political Man, Lipset, Seymour M., New York: Doubleday, 1963

Political Parties, Michels, Robert, Glencoe, IL: Free Press, 1958

Political Psychology, Hermann, M.G., San Francisco: Josey-Bass, 1986

Politics and the Regulatory Agencies, Cary, William L., New York: McGraw-Hill Book Co., 1967

Power in Washington, Cater, D., New York: Vintage, 1964

Power in Britain, Urry, John; and Wakeford, John (eds), London: Heinemann, 1973

Psychopathology and Politics, Lasswell, Harold, New York: Viking Press, 1960

Public Administration in Modern Society, Corson, J.J., and Harris, J.P., New York: McGraw-Hill, 1963

Puzzle Palace, Bamford, James, New York: Penguin, 1977

Roosevelt and Churchill, Lash, J., New York: Norton, 1976

Running Critical: Rickover and General Dynamics, Tyler, Patrick, New York: Harper & Row, 1986

Sociology and the Military Establishment, Janowitz, M., New York: Russell Sage Foundation, 1959

Squandering Eden, Rosenblum, Mort and Williamson, Doug, San Diego: Harcourt Brace Jovanovich, 1987

Stalin and the Shaping of the Soviet Union, Jonge, Alex de, New York: William Morrow, 1984

State Department, Press, and Pressure Groups, Chittick, W. O., New York: Wiley, 1970

T.V.A. and Grass Roots, Selznick, Peter, Berkeley: University of California Press, 1949

The Budget's New Clothes, Merewitz, L., and Sosnick, S.H., Chicago, IL: Markham, 1971

The Bureaucratic Phenomenon, Crozier, M., Chicago: University of Chicago Press, 1964

The Deadlock of Democracy: Four-Party Politics in America, Burns, J.M., Englewood Cliffs, NJ: Prentice-Hall, 1963

The Death of a President, Manchester, William R., New York: Harper & Row, 1967

The English Constitution, Bagehot, W., London: Fontana, 1963

The Federal Bulldozer, Anderson, M., New York: McGraw-Hill, 1964

The General and the Bomb, Lawren, W., New York: Dodd Mead, 1988

The Guns of August, Tuchman, Barbara W., New York: Macmillan, 1962

The Interstate Commerce Omission, Fellmeth, R., New York: Grossman, 1970

The Military Condition, DeVigny, Alfred, Oxford University Press, 1964

The Nuclear Delusion, Kennan, George F., New York: Pantheon, 1983

The Paperclip Conspiracy, Bower, T., New York: Little, Brown, 1988

The Pentagon of Power, Mumford, Lewis, New York: Harcourt, Brace, Jovanovich, 1970

The Pentagon and the Art of War, Luttwak, Edward, New York: Simon & Schuster, 1985

The Perfect Failure, Higgins, Trumbull, New York: Bantam Books, 1986

The Policy Predicament: Making and Implementing Public Policy, Edward, G.C. III, and Sharkansky, I., San Francisco, CA: W.H. Freeman, 1978

The Political Process in Columbia, Corr, Edwin G., Denver, CO: University of Denver, 1972

The Political Process, Freeman, J.L., New York: Random House, 1965

The Political Economy of International Relations, Gilpin, Robert, Princeton: Princeton University Press, 1987

The Politics of Policy Making in Defense and Foreign Affairs, Hilsman, Roger, New York: Harper & Row, 1971

The Power of the Purse: Appropriations Politics in Congress, Fenno, R.F., Jr., Boston: Little, Brown, 1966

The Presidential Advisory System, Cronin, T.E., and Greenbergs, S.D., New York: Harper & Row, 1969

The Rivals, Ulam, Adam B., New York: Viking, 1971

The Secrets of the Service, Glees, Anthony, New York: Carroll & Graf, 1987

The States and the Urban Crisis, Campbell, A. (ed), Englewood Cliffs, NJ: Prentice-Hall, 1970

The Study of Public Administration, Waldo, D., New York: Random House, 1955

The Target is Destroyed, Hersh, Seymour, New York: Random House, 1986

Two Cheers for Democracy, Forster, E. M., London: Harcourt, 1951

Urban Outcomes, Levy, F.S. et al, Berkeley, CA: University of California Press, 1974

War on the Mind: The Military Uses and Abuses of Power, Watson, Peter, New York: Basic Books, 1978

Ways of Worldmaking, Goodman, Nelson, Indianapolis: Hackett Publishing Co., 1978

Weapons and Tactics of the Soviet Army, Isby, David C., London: Janes Publishing, 1981

Wild Blue Yonder: Money, Politics and the B-1 Bomber, Kotz, Nick, New York: Pantheon, 1988

HEALTH CARE

Accreditation Manual for Hospitals, Joint Commission for the Accreditation of Hospitals (JCAH), Chicago: JCAH, 1986

American Medical Avarice, Harmer, Ruth Mulvey, New York: Abelhard-Schuman, 1975

And the Band Played On, Shilts, Chicago: St. Martins, 1987

Cases in Nursing Management, Ganong, J.M., and Ganong, W. L., Germantown, MD: Aspen Systems Corporation, 1979

Changing Hospitals, Wieland, G.F.; and Leigh, H. (eds), London: Tavistock, 1971

Doctors in Hospitals, Roemer, Milton, and Friedman, Jay, Baltimore, MD: The Johns Hopkins Press, 1941

Financial Management of Health Institutions, Silvers, J.B., and Prahalad, C.K., New York: Spectrum Publications, 1973

Handbook of Health Professions Education, McGuire, C.H.; Foley, R. P.; Gorr, A.; Richards, R.W. et al, San Francisco: Jossey-Bass, 1983

Heartbeat: The Politics of Health Research, Springarn, N.D., New York: Robert B. Luce, Inc., 1976

Hospital Bureaucracy, Heydebrand, Wolf, New York:: Dunellen, 1973

Hospital Management Systems, Brown, M., and Lewis, H.L., Germantown, MD: Aspen Systems Corporation, 1976

Hospital Organization and Management, MacEachern, M.T., Berwyn, IL: Physicians Record Co., 1969

Hospitals, Paternalism and the Role of the Nurse, Ashley, J., New York: Teachers College Press, 1975

Medical Nemesis: The Expropriation of Health, Illich, Ivan, New York: Pantheon Books, 1976

Medicine, Science and Life, Yanofsky, V.S., New York: Paulist Press, 1978

Men, Money and Medicine, Ginzberg, E., with Ostow, M., New York: Columbia University Press, 1969

Nurses: A Political Force, Archer, S.E., and Goehner, P.A., Monterey, CA: Wadsworth, 1972

Nursing Perspectives and Issues, Grippando, Gloria M., Albany, NY: Delmar Publishers, Inc., 1983

Nursing Theory, Stevens, Barbara J., Boston: Little/Brown, 1979

Organizational Issues in Health Care Management, Sheldon, Alan, New York: Spectrum Publications, 1975

Society and Medical Progress, Stern, Bernard J., Princeton, NJ: Princeton Unviersity Press, 1941

The Care of Strangers, Rosenberg, Charles E., New York: Basic Books, 1987

The Community General Hospital, Georgopoulos, B.S., and Mann, F.C., New York: Macmillan, 1962

The Learning Mystique, Coles, G., New York: Pantheon, 1988

The Presence of the Past, Sheldrake, Rupert, New York: Times Books, 1987

The Quality of Mercy, Greenberg, Selig, New York: Atheneum, 1971

INDUSTRY

A Killing Wind, Kurzman, Dan, New York: McGraw-Hill, 1987

Collective Bargaining: Prescription for Change, Flanders, A., London: Faber & Faber, Ltd., 1967

Corporations on Trial: The Electrical Cases, Walton, C. C. and Cleveland, F. W., Jr., Belmont, CA: Wadsworth, 1967

Factors Affecting the Growth of Manufacturing Firms, McGuire, J., Seattle: University of Washington Bureau of Business Research, 1963

Industrial Behavior, Rose, M., Harmondsworth: Penguin, 1975

Industrial Dynamics, Forrester, Jay W., Cambridge, MA: MIT Press, 1961

Industrial Jobs and the Worker, Turner, A.N., and Lawrence, P.R., Boston: Harvard University Press, 1965

Industrial Man, Warner, W.L., and Martin, N. H.(eds), New York: Harper & Row, 1959

Industrial Organization: Behavior and Control, Woodward, Joan (ed), New York: Oxford University Press, 1970

Industrial Organization: Theory and Practice, Woodward, Joan (ed), New York: Oxford University Press, 1965

Industry and Technical Progress, Carter, C., and Williams, B., London: Oxford University Press, 1957

Institutionalizing Innovation, Jelineck, M., New York: Praeger, 1979

Leadership and Supervision in Industry, Fleishman E. A., Harris, E.F., and Burtt, H.E., Columbus: Ohio State University Press, 1955

Management in the Industrial World, Harbison, F., and Myers, C.A., New York: McGraw-Hill, 1959
Motivation and Morale in Industry, Viteles, M.S., New York: W.W.Norton & Co., Inc., 1953
My Years With General Motors, Sloan, Alfred P., Garden City, NY: Doubleday & Co., 1964
On The Shop Floor, Lupton, T., New York: Pergamon Press, 1963
Onward Industry, Mooney, J.D. and Reiley, A.M., New York: Harper & Bros., 1931
Patterns of Industrial Bureaucracy, Gouldner, Alvin W., Glencoe, IL: Free Press, 1954
Psychology in Industry, Maier, Norman R.F., Boston: Houghton Mifflin Co., 1955
Pulbic Utility Economics, Garfield, Paul J., and Lovejoy, Wallace F., Englewood Cliffs, NJ: Prentice-Hall, Inc., 1964
Renewing American Industry, Lawrence, P., and Dyer, D., New York: The Free Press, 1983
Surviving Failures: Patterns of Project Mismanagement, Persson, Bo, Atlantic Highlands: Humanities Press, 1980
The Automobile Worker and the American Dream, Chinoy, E., Garden City: Doubleday, 1955
The Bhopal Syndrome, Weir, David, San Francisco, Sierra Book Clubs, 1987
The Car Makers, Turner, G., London: Eyre & Spottiswoode, 1963
The Changing Culture of a Factory, Jaques, Elliot, London: Tavistock Publications, Ltd.,1951
The Choices of Power: Utilities Face the Challenge, Roberts, M.J., and Bluhm, J.S., Cambridge, MA: Harvard University Press, 1981
The Fall of the House of Labor, Montgomery, David, New York: Cambridge University, 1987
The Human Side of Advanced Manufacturing Technology, Wall, T.B., New York: John Wiley & Sons, 1987
The Japanese Factory, Abegglen, J.C., New York: The Free Press, 1958
The Man on the Assembly Line, Walker, C. R., and Guest, R.H., Cambridge, MA: Harvard University Press, 1952
The Organization of Industry, Stigler, George J., Illinois: Richard D. Irwin, Inc., 1968
The Social Psychology of Industry, Brown, J.A.C., London: Penguin Books, 1954
The Structure of Competitive Industry, Robinson, E.A. G., Chicago: University of Chicago Press, 1957
Three Mile Island, Ford, D. F., London, England: Penguin Books, 1981
Where Have All The Robots Gone?, Sheppard, Harold L. and Herrick, Neal, New York: Free Press, 1972

ACADEMIA

Academic Procession, Wriston, Henry, New York: Columbia University Press, 1959
An Examination of Examinations, Hartog, P., and Rhodes, E.C., London: Macmillan Co., Ltc., 1935
Beyond The Ivory Tower: Social Responsibilities, Bok, Derek, Cambridge, MA: Harvard University Press, 1982
Cult Of The Fact, Hudson, Liam, London: Cape, 1972
Democracy and Education, Dewey, John, New York: Macmillan Co., 1916
Deschooling Society, Illich, Ivan, New York: Harper & Row, 1971

Education and Jobs: The Great Training Robbery, Berg, Ivar, New York: Frederick A. Praeger, 1972
Education, Its Data and First Principles, Nunn, Sir T. P., London:Longmans, 1946
Insult to Intelligence, Smith, Frank, Ann Arbor: Arbor House, 1986
Organizational Behavior in Schools, Owens, Robert G., Englewood Cliffs, NJ: Prentice-Hall, 1970
Power and Conflict in the University, Baldridge, J.V., New York: Wiley, 1971
Science and Human Behavior, Skinner, B.F., New York: Macmillan Co., 1953
Science in Industry, Carter, C.F., and Williams, B.R., London: Oxford University Press, 1959
Scientists in Organization, Pelz, D.C., and Andrews, F.M., New York: Wiley, 1966
Studies in Management Education, Miner, J.B., New York: Springer Publishing Co., 1965
The Behavioral Sciences: An Interpretation, Thomopson, J.D., and Van, D.R., Reading, MA: Addison-Wesley, 1970
The Closing of the American Mind, Bloom, Allan, New York: Simon & Schuster, 1987
The Divided Academy, Ladd, E.C., and Lipsett, S.M., New York: McGraw-Hill, 1975
The Educational Significance of the Future, Shane, Harold G., Washington: World Future Society, 1972
The Influence of Federal Grants, Derthick, M., Cambridge, MA: Harvard University Press, 1970
The Politics of Personnel Research, Berry, D. F., Ann Arbor: University of Michigan Press, 1967
The Relevance of Education, Bruner, J. S., New York: Norton & Co., 1971
The Undergrowth of Literature, Freeman, Gillian, London: Thomas Nelson, 1967

MANAGEMENT

A Behavioral Theory of Labor Negotiations, Walton, Richard E., and McKerzie, R.B., New York: McGraw-Hill Book Co., 1965
A Concept of Corporate Planning, Ackoff, R. L., New York: Wiley Interscience, 1970
A Passion For Excellence, Peters, Tom, and Austin, Nancy, New York: Random House, 1985
A Strategy of Decision, Braybrooke, D., and Lindblom, C., New York: Free Press, 1963
A Theory of Leadership Effectiveness, Fiedler, F.E., New York: McGraw-Hill Book Co., 1967
Administrative Behavior, Simon, Herbert A., New York:Macmillan Co., 1945
Administrative Decision-Making: The Bounds of Rationality, Sutherland, J.W., New York: Van Nostrand Reinhold, 1977
Administrative Reform, Caiden, G., Chicago, IL: Aldine, 1969
An End to Hierarchy! An End to Competition!, Thayer, F.C., New York: New Viewpoints, 1973
Authoritarianism and Leadership, Sanford, Fillmore H., Philadelphia: Inst. for Research in Human Relations, 1950
Authority, Sennett, R., New York: Knopf, 1980
Authority, Paterson, T.T., Glasgow: Univ. of Strathclyde, 1963
Bitter Wages, Page, J.A., and O'Brien, M., New York: Grossman, 1973
British Business Schools, Franks, Lord, London: British Institute of Management, November, 1963

Comparative Management, Davis, S.M., Englewood Cliffs, NJ: Prentice-Hall, 1971

Complex Organizations: A Sociological Perspective, Haas, J., and Drabek, T., New York: Macmillan, 1973

Concepts and Issues in Administrative Behavior, Malick, S., and Van Ness, E.H. (eds), Englewood Cliffs, NJ: Prentice-Hall, 1962

Contemporary Management, Hampton, D., New York: McGraw-Hill, 1981

Contemporary Problems in Personnel, Pearlman, K.; Schmidt, F. L.; and Hamner, W.C., New York: Wiley, 1983

Contingency Views of Organization and Management, Kast, F.E., and Rosenzweig, J.E., Chicago: Science Research Associates, 1973

Corporate Strategy, Ansoff, H.I., New York: McGraw-Hill, 1965

Corporate Views of the Public Interest, Sonnenfeld, J.A., Boston, MA: Auburn House, 1981

Culture and Management, Webber, Ross A., Homewood, IL: Richard D. Irwin, 1969

Essentials of Management, Duncan, W. J., Hinsdale, IL: Dryden, 1978

Executive Behavior, Carlson, S., Stockholm: Strombergs, 1951

Executive Success: Stresses, Problems and Adjustments, Jennings, E. E., New York: Appleton-Century-Crofts, 1967

Explorations in Managerial Talent, Ghiselli, E. E., Pacific Palisades, CA: Goodyear, 1971

From Strategic Planning to Strategic Management, Ansoff, H.I., and Hayes, R.L. (eds), New York: Wiley, 1976

Fundamentals of Top Management, Davis, R.C., New York: Harper, 1951

Games and Decisions, Luce, R.D., and Raiffa, H., New York: John Wiley & Sons, 1957

General and Industrial Management, Fayol, Henry, London: Sir Isaac Pitman, 1949

Handbook of Leadership, Stogdill, R.M., New York: Macmillan, 1974

In Search of Excellence, Peters, Tom and Waterman, R. H., New York: Harper & Row, 1982

Introduction to Management: A Contingency Approach, Luthans, F., New York: McGraw-Hill, 1976

Is Scientific Management Possible?, Kelly, Joe, London: Faber & Faber, Ltd., 1968

Japan's Managerial System, Yoshino, M., Cambridge, MA: The MIT Press, 1968

Job Redesign and Management Control, Blacker, F.H.M., and Brown, C.A., New York: Praeger, 1978

Leadership, Burns, James MacGregor, New York: Harper & Row, 1978

Leadership and Decision-Making, Vroom, V. H., and Yetton, P.W., Pittsburgh: University of Pittsburgh Press, 1973

Leadership and Effective Management, Fiedler, Fred E., and Chemers, Martin, New York: Scott, Foresman & Co., 1974

Leadership in Administration, Selznick, Peter, London: Row Peterson, 1957

Leadership or Domination, Pigors, P.J.W., New York: Houghton Mifflin Co., 1935

Management and the Worker, Roethlisberger, F. J., and Dickson, W. J., Cambridge, MA: Harvard University Press, 1959

Management Behavior, Lamb, W., and Turner, D., New York: International Universities Press, 1969

Management By Participation, Marrow, Alfred J.,

and Bowers, David G; and Seashore, Stanley E., New York: Harper & Row, 1967

Management Games, Kibbee, J.M.; Craft, C. J.; and Nanus, B., New York: Reinhold Book Corp., 1961

Management Training and Corporate Strategy, Hussey, D.E., Oxford: Pergamon Press, 1987

Management: A Contingency Analysis of Managerial Functions, Koontz, H., and O'Donnell, C., New York: McGraw-Hill, 1976

Management: Basic Elements of Managing Organizations, Webber, Ross A., Homewood, IL: Richard D. Irwin, 1975

Management: Tasks, Responsibilities, Practices, Drucker, Peter F, New York: Harper & Row, 1974

Managerial Attitudes and Performance, Porter, L.W., and Lawler, E.E., Homewood, IL: Richard D. Irwin, 1968

Managerial Behavior, Performance, and Effectiveness, Campbell, John P., Dunnette, M.D., Lawler, E.E, and Weick, K.E., New York: McGraw-Hill Book Co., 1970

Managerial Behavior, Sayles, L.R., New York: McGraw-Hill Book Co.,1964

Managerial Breakthrough, Juran, J.M., New York: McGraw-Hill, 1964

Managerial Effectiveness, Reddin, W. J., New York: McGraw-Hill Book Co., 1970

Managerial Psychology, Leavitt, Harold J., Chicago: University of Chicago Press, 1964

Managerial Thinking, Haire, M., Ghiselli, E., and Porter, L., New York: John Wiley & Sons, 1966

Managing By Objectives, Mali, P., New York: Wiley, 1972

Managing For Results, Drucker, Peter F., New York: Harper & Row, 1964

Managing in Turbulent Times, Drucker, Peter F., New York: Harper & Row, 1980

Managing Organizational Conflict: A Non-Traditional Approach, Robbins, Stephen P., Englewood Cliffs, NJ: Prentice-Hall, 1974

Managing the Flow of Technology, Allen, T. J., Cambridge, MA: The MIT Press, 1977

Markets and Hierarchies, Williamson, O.E., New York: Free Press, 1975

Measurement of Responsibility, Jaques, Eliot, London: Tavistock, 1956

Men, Management and Morality: Toward a New Organizational Ethic, Golembiewski, R.T., New York: McGraw-Hill, 1965

Men Who Manage, Dalton, Melville, New York: John Wiley & Sons, 1959

New Patterns of Management, Likert, Rensis, New York, McGraw-Hill Book Co., 1961

Occupational Mobility in American Business and Industry, Warner, W. L., and Abegglen, J.C., Minneapolis: Minnesota University, 1955

Of Acceptable Risk, Lowrance, W.W., Los Altos, CA: Kaufmann, 1976

Organization - The Framework of Management, Brech, E.F.L., London: Longmans, 1965

Organization and Management, Bass, Bernard M., Cambridge: Harvard University Press, 1948

Organization and Mangement, Kast, F.E.; and Rosenzweig, James E., New York: McGraw-Hill Book Co., 1970

Organizational Relations and Management Action, Bergen, Garret L., and Haney, W.V., New York: McGraw Hill Book Co., 1966

Organized Executive Action, Albers, H.H., New York: John Wiley & Sons, 1961

Out of the Crisis, Deming, W.E., Cambridge: MIT Press, 1986

Parkinson's Law, Parkinson, C. Northcote, Boston: Houghton Mifflin Co., 1957

Participative Management: The Indian Experience, Alexander, K.C., New Delhi, India: Shri Ram Centre, 1972

Personality and Productivity in Management, Mullen, J.H., New York: Columbia University Press, 1966

Personnel Selection and Placement, Dunnette, Marvin D., Belmont, CA: Wadsworth Publishing Co., 1966

Personnel: The Mangement of People at Work, Beach, D.S., New York: Macmillan, 1970

Planning Under Pressure, Friend, J.K., Oxford: Pergamon Press, 1987

Power and Discontent, Gamson, William A., Homewood, IL: Dorsey, 1968

Power! How to Get It, How to Use It, Korda, Michael, New York: Random House, 1975

Principles of Scientific Management, Taylor, Frederick W., New York: Harper & Row, 1911

Principles of Management, Koontz, Harold, and O'Donnell, C., New York: McGraw-Hill, 1972

Psychology in Management, Haire, M., New York: McGraw-Hill Book Co., 1964

Reference Guide to Management Techniques and Activities, Bloor, Ian G., Oxford: Pergamon Press, 1987

"Skilled Incompetence", Argyris, Chris, Harvard Business Review, Sept-Oct 1986

Sovereignty at Bay, Vernon, Raymond, New York: Basic Books, 1971

Soviet Management, Richman, B.M., Englewood Cliffs, NJ: Prentice-Hall, 1965

Speaking Truth to Power, Wildavsky, A., Boston: Little, Brown, 1979

Staff in Management, Dale, Ernest, and Urwick, L.F., New York,: McGraw-Hill Book Co., 1960

Strategy and Structure, Chandler, A. D. Jr., Cambridge, Mass, MIT Press, 1962

Studies in Leadership, Gouldner, Alvin W., New York: Harper & Bros., 1950

Survival on the Fast Track, Kovach, B.E., New York: Dodd Mead, 1988

The Adaptive Corporation, Toffler, Alvin, New York: Macmillan, 1985

The Art of Japanese Management, Pascale, R., and Athos, A., New York: Warner Books, 1982

The Authoritarian Personality: Studies in Prejudice, Adorno, T.W.; E.; Levinson, DE.J.; and Sanford, R.N., New York: Harper & Row, 1950

The Basics of Supervisory Management, Black, J.M., New York: McGraw-Hill, 1975

The Big Business Executive, Newcomer, M., New York: Columbia University Press, 1955

The Changing World of the Executive, Drucker, Peter, New York: Times Books, 1982

The Concept of Corporate Strategy, Andrews, K., Homewood, IL: Irwin, 1980

The Elements of Administration, Urwick, Lyndall, New York: Harper & Row, 1943

The Essence of Decision, Allison, G.T., Boston: Little-Brown, 1978

The Executive and His Control of Men, Gowin, E.B., New York: MacMillan Co., 1915

The Functions of the Executive, Barnard, C. I., Cambridge, MA: Harvard University Press, 1938

The Gamesman, Maccoby, Michael, New York: Simon & Schuster, 1976

The Gerber Report, Gerber, Alex, New York: McKay, 1971

The Great Organizers, Dale, Ernest, New York: McGraw-Hill Book Co., 1960

The Healing Artisans, Konner, Melvin, New York: Viking, 1987

The History of Management Thought, George, C.S., Englewood Cliffs, NJ: 1968

The Implementation Game, Bardach, E., Cambridge, MA; MIT Press, 1977

The Key to Failure, Hannah, Norman B., New York: Madison Books, 1987

The Making of Decisions, Gore, W. J., and Dyson, J.W., New York: The Free Press, 1964

The Making of a Moron, Breman, N., New York: Sheed & Ward, 1953

The Management of Conflict, Scott, W.C., Homewood, IL: Richard D. Irwin, 1965

The Managerial Grid, Blake, Robert R. and Mouton, J.S., Houston: Gulf Publishing, 1964

The Managing of Organizations, Gross, Bertram, Glencoe: The Free Press, 1962

The Measure of Management, Chapple, Eliot, and Sayles, L.R., New York: Macmillan, 1961

The Mobile Manager, Jennings, E. E., Ann Arbor: University of Michigan, 1967

The Morning After, Will, George F., New York: Macmillan, 1987

The Nature of Managerial Work, Mintzberg, Henry, New York: Harper & Row, 1973

The Perceptanalytic Executive Scale, Piotrowski, Z.A., and Rock, M.R., New York, Grune & Stratton, 1963

The Peter Principle, Peter, Lawrence J.; and Hull, Raymond, New York: William Morrow & Co. 1969

The Politics of Expertise, Benveniste, Guy, Berkeley: Glendessary, 1972

The Politics of Experience, Laing, R.D., New York: Ballantine, 1967

The Politics of Leadership, Neustadt, R., New York:: Wiley, 1976

The Power Motive, Winter, D., New York: The Free Press, 1972

The Powerholders, Kipnis, D., Chicago: University of Chicago, 1976

The Practice of Management, Drucker, Peter F., New York: Harper & Row, 1954

The Professional Fence, Klockars, Carl B., New York: Free Press, 1974

The Rational Manager, Kepner, Charles H., and Treegoe, Benjamin V., New York: McGraw-Hill Book Co., 1965

The Red Executive, Granick, D., New York: Doubleday & Co., 1960

The Renewal Factor, Waterman Jr., Robert H., New York: Bantam, 1987

The Status Seekers, Packard, Vance, New York: David McKay Co., Inc. 1959

The Twilight of the Presidency, Reedy, George E., New York: NAL, 1987

The Unconscious Conspiracy: Why Leaders Can't Lead, Bennis, Warren G., New York: AMACON, 1976

Theory Z, Ouchi, W., Reading, MA: Addison-Wesley, 1981

Time and Management, Webber, R.A., New York: Van Nostrand Reinhold, 1972

Top Management Planning, Steiner, G., New York: Macmillan, 1969

Up The Organization, Townsend, Robert, New York: Alfred A Knopf, Inc. 1970

What People Want From Business, Houser, J.D., New York: McGraw-Hill, 1938

Work and Motivation, Vroom, Victor, New York: John Wiley & Sons, 1964

Work and Authority in Industry, Bendix, R., New York: Wiley, 1976

Zen and Creative Management, Low, A., New York: Playboy Paperbacks, 1976

INNOVATION

Accelerating Innovation, Anthony, L.J., London: Urwin, 1970

Bureaucracy and Innovation, Thompson, V., University of Alabama: University of Alabama Press, 1969

Can Science Be Planned?, Brooks, Harvey, Cambridge: Harvard University Press, n.d.

Codebreakers, Kahn, David, New York: Macmillan, 1986

Communication of Innovation: A Cross-Cultural Approach, Rogers, E.M., and Shoemaker, F., New York: Free Press, 1971

Creative Experience, Follett, M. P., New York: P.Smith, 1924

Creativity, Vernon, P.E. (ed), London: Penguin, 1970

Diffusion of Innovations, Rogers, Everett, New York: Free Press, 1969

Discovering the Future, Barker, J.A., St. Paul: ILI Press, 1985

Discovery, Invention, Research, Zwicky, Fritz, New York: The Macmillan Co., 1969

Empathy and Ideology: Aspects of Administrative Innovation, Press, Charles, and Arian, Alan (eds), Chicago: Rand McNally, 1966

Heroes, MacGinnis, J., New York: Viking Press, 1976

Ideas for Social Change, Taylor, G.W., The Hague: Junk, 1966

Innovation in Organizations, Daft, R., and Becker, S., New York: Elsevier, 1978

Innovation, Organization, and Environment, Miller, R.E., Sherbrooke, Quebec:Universite de Sherbrooke, 1971

Innovations and Organizations, Zaltman, G., Duncan, R., and Holbek, J., New York: Wiley, 1973

Innovations: Scientific, Technological, and Social, Gabor, Dennis, Toronto: Oxford University Press, 1972

Intrapreneuring, Pinchot, Gifford, New York: Harper & Row, 1985

Inventors at Work, Brown, Kenneth A., New York: Tempus Books, 1987

Making of the Atomic Bomb, Rhodes, Richard, New York: Simon & Schuster, 1986

Management of Transformation, Glover, John D., and Vancil, Richard F., New York: IBM, 1968

Managing Organizational Innovation, O'Connell, J., Homewood, IL: Irwin, 1968

Motivation and Personality, Maslow, Abraham H., New York: Harper & Bros., 1954

Moving Mountains, Boettinger, Henry M., New York: The Macmillan Co., 1969

New Business Ventures and the Entrepreneur, Liles, P.R., Homewood, IL: Irwin, 1974

New Forms of Work Organization, Klein, Lisl, Cambridge: Cambridge University Press, 1976

New Venture Strategies, Vesper, Karl H., Englewood Cliffs, NJ: Prentice-Hall, 1980

Organizations and Innovation, Argyris, Chris, Homewood, IL: Irwin, 1965

Patterns of Technological Innovation, Sahal, D., Reading, MA: Addison-Wesley, 1981

Planning for Innovation Through Dissemination of Knowledge, Havelock, Ronald G., Ann Arbor: Center for Utilization of Scientific Knowledge, 1971

Radical Man, Hampden-Turner, C., New York: Anchor Books, 1971

Say It Straight or You'll Show It Crooked, Wagner, A., Englewood Cliffs, NJ: Prentice-Hall, 1981

Social Change in Complex Organizations, Hage, J., and Aiken, M., New York: Random House, 1970

Strategies for Planned Change, Zaltman, Gerald and Duncan, Robert, New York: John Wiley, 1977

Strategies for Change: Logical Incrementalism, Quinn, J.B., Homewood, IL: Irwin, 1980

Successful Industrial Innovation, Myers, J., Summer,C., and Marquis, D.G., Washington, DC: National Science Foundation, 1969

The Best and the Brightest, Halberstam, David, New York: Random House, 1969

The Diffusion of Political Innovation, Gitelman, Zvi Y., Beverly Hills: Sage, 1972

The Double Helix, Watson, J.D., New York: Atheneum, 1968

The Dynamics of Planned Change, Watson, J.; Lippitt, R.; Westley, B., New York: Harcourt, Brace & World, 1958

The Enterprising Americans, Chamberlain, John, New York: Harper & Row, 1974

The History of Invention, Williams, Trevor I., New York: Facts on File, Inc., 1987

The Human Side of Enterprise, McGregor, D., New York: McGraw-Hill, 1960

The Innovators, Shanks, Michael, New York: Penguin Books, 1967

The Management of Innovation, Burns, Tom and Stalker, G. M., London: Tavistock Publications Ltd., 1961

The Origins of the Invention, Mason, Otis T., Cambridge: The MIT Press, 1966

The Social Process of Innovation, Mulkay, M.J., London: Macmillan, 1972

The Sources of Innovation, Jewkes, John, New York: Norton, 1970

The Spirit of Enterprise, Gilder, George, New York: Simon & Schuster, 1984

The Structure of Scientific Revolutions, Kuhn, Thomas S., Chicago: University of Chicago Press, 1952

Three Steps to Victory, Watt, Robert Watson, London: Odhams, 1957

Thriving on Chaos, Peters, Tom, New York: Knopf, 1987

Work Redesign, Hackman, J. Richard, and Oldham, G.R., Reading, MA: Addison-Wesley, 1980

QUALITY ASSURANCE

Computer Effectiveness: Bridging the Management Technology Gap, Axelrod, C. Warren, Washington, DC: Information Resources Press, 1979

Computer Productivity, Axelrod, C. Warren, New York: Wiley, 1982

"On Some Statistical Aids Toward Economic Production", Deming, W. Edwards, Interfaces, Vol.5, No. 4, August 1975

Quality Assurance Programs and Controls in Nursing, Frobe, D. J., and Bain, R. J., St Louis, MO: Mosby, 1976

Quality Control Handbook, Juran, J.M. (ed), New York: McGraw-Hill, 1974

Risk: Man-made Hazards to Man, Cooper, M.G., Oxford: Clarendon Press, 1985

The Management and Maintenance of Quality Circles, Patchen, R.J., and Cunningham, R. (eds), Homewood, IL: Dow-Jones-Irwin, 1983

Total Quality Control, Feigenbaum, A.V., New York: McGraw-Hill, 1983

SYSTEMS ENGINEERING

A Guide to System Engineering, U.S. Army, TM 38-760-1, November, 1973

A Mathematical Theory of Communication, Shannon, C.E., and Weaver, W., Urbana: University of Illinois Press, 1949

A Modern Introduction to Logic, Stebbing, L.S., London: Methuen & Co., Ltd., 1930

An Introduction to Cybernetics, Ashby, W. Ross, New York: Wiley, 1966

An Introduction to Motivation, Atkinson, J.W., Princeton, NJ: D. Van Nostrand Co., 1964

Anticipatory Systems, Rosen, R., Oxford: Pergamon Press, 1985

Applied General Systems Theory, vanGigch, J. P., New York: Harper & Row, 1983

Applied Systems Engineering, Gheorghe, Adrian, London: Wiley & Sons Ltd, 1982

Architecture of Systems Problem Solving, Klir, G. J., New York: Plenum Press, 1985

Autopoiesis: A Theory of Living Organizations, Zeleny, Milan, New York: Elsevier North-Holland, 1980

Beyond Babel: New Directions in Communications, Maddox, Brenda, London: Andre Deutsch, 1972

Catastrophe Theory, Zeeman, E.C., Reading: Addison-Wesley, 1977

Challenging Strategic Planning Assumptions, Mason, R.O., and Mitroff, I.I., New York: Wiley Interscience, 1981

Characteristics of Socio-Technical Systems, Emery, F.E., London: Tavistock Publications, 1959

Collaboration in Organizations: Alternative to Hierarchy, Kraus, W.A., New York: Human Sciences Press, 1980

Communication in the Business Organization, Scholz, W., Englewood Cliffs, NJ: Prentice-Hall, 1962

Communications and Communication Systems, Thayer, Lee, Homewood, Il: Richard D. Irwin, 1968

Communications in Organizations, Rogers, E.M., and Rogers, R.A., New York: Free Press, 1976

Conceptual Blockbusting, Adams, James L., London: McLeod, 1974

Connections, Burke, J., Boston: Little/Brown, 1970

Constructive Control: Design and Use of Control Systems, Newman, W. H., Englewood Cliffs, NJ: Prentice-Hall, 1975

Creating the Corporate Future, Ackoff, Russell, New York: Wiley, 1981

Cybernetics, Wiener, Norbert, Cambridge, MA: MIT Press, 1961

Cybernetics and Management, Beer, Stafford, New York: Wiley, 1959

Cybernetics or Control and Communication in Animal and Machine, Weiner, Norbert, Boston: MIT Press, 1948

Data and Knowledge Engineering, Parrello, B.; Overbeek, R.; and Lusk, E., New York: Elsevier, 1985

Decision Analysis, Raiffa, Howard, Reading, MA: Addison-Wesley, 1968

Decision and Control, Beer, Stafford, New York: John Wiley & Sons, 1966

Decisions With Multiple Objectives, Keeney, R., and Faiffa, H., New York: Wiley, 1976

Dynamic Programming and Modern Control Theory, Bellman, R.E., and Kalaba, R., New York: Academic Press, 1965

Euphychian Management, Maslow, Abraham H., Homewood, IL: Irwin, 1965

Evolution: The Grand Synthesis, Laszlo, Ervin, Boston: Shambhala, 1987

Extraordinary Popular Delusions, Mackay, Charles, London: Richard Bentley, 1841

Fuzzy Sets, Uncertainty, and Information, Klir, G. J., and Folger, T.A., Englewood Cliffs, NJ: Prentice-Hall, 1987

General Systems Theory, VonBertalanffy, Ludwig, New York: George Braziller, 1968

Grammatical Man, Campbell, Jeremy, New York: Simon & Schuster, 1982

Great Ideas in Information Theory, Language, and Cybernetics, Singh, Jagjit, New York: Dover, 1966

Human Interaction with Computers, Rasmussen, J., New York: Academic Press, 1980

Implementation, Pressman, Jeffrey L., and Wildavsky, Aaron, Berkeley: University of California Press, 1973

Industrial Accident Prevention, Heinrich, H.W., Petersen, D., and Roos, N., New York: McGraw-Hill, 1978

Information, Organization, and Power, Zand, D.E., New York: McGraw-Hill, 1981

Intervention Theory and Method, Argyris, Chris, Reading, MA: Addison-Wesley Publishing Co., 1970

Job Design for Motivation, Conference Board, Inc., New York: Conference Board, 1971

Kinesics and Context, Birdwhistell, R., Philadelphia, PA: University of Pennsylvania Press, 1970

Knowledge and Decisions, Sowell, Thomas, New York: Basic Books, 1980

Language and Action: A Structural Model of Behavior, Clarke, D.C., New York: Pergamon Press, 1983

Language and Mind, Chomsky, Noam, New York: Harcourt, Brace, Jovanovich, 1972

Language in Thought and Action, Hayakawa, S.I., New York: Harcourt, Brace & World, 1964

Living Systems, Miller, J., New York: McGraw-Hill, 1978

Managerial Applications of Systems Dynamics, Roberts, Edward B. (ed), Cambridge, MA: MIT Press, 1978

Managerial Control Through Communication, Vardaman, G.T., and Halterman, C.C., New York: Wiley, 1968

Marketing as Social Behavior: A General Systems Theory, Sirgy, M.J., New York: Praeger, 1984

Mechanisms of Intelligence: W. Ross Ashby on Cybernetics, Conant, R. (ed), Seaside, CA: Intersystems, 1981

Metanoic Organizations, Kiefer, C.F., and Senge, P.M., Framingham, MA: Innovation Associates, 1983

Methodology for Large-Scale Systems, Sage, A. P., New York: McGraw-Hill, 1980

Modeling of Complex Systems, Vermuri, V., New York: Academic Press, 1978

Modern Systems Research for the Behavioral Scientist, Buckley, Walter (ed), Chicago: Aldine Publishing Co., 1968

Motivation Through Work Itself, Ford, Robert N., New York: American Management Association,1969

Motivational and Organizational Climate, Litwin, G., and Stringer, R, Cambridge, MA: Harvard University Press, 1968

On Purposeful Systems, Ackoff, R., and Emery, F.E., Chicago, IL: Aldine Publishing, 1972

Order Out of Chaos, Prigogine, I., and Stengers, I., New York: Bantam Books, 1984

HISTORY AND TECHNOLOGY

Max Weber: An Intellectual Portrait, Bendix, Reinhard, London: Heinemann, 1960

Mothers of Invention, Vare, Ethlie A. and Ptacek, G., New York: Morrow, 1988

National Programs and the Progress of Technological Societies, Gordon, T.S., and Shef, Arthur, Washington: The American Astronomical Society, 1968

Normal Accidents: Living with High-Risk Technologies, Perrow, C., New York: Basic Books, 1984

Previews and Premises, Toffler, Alvin, New York: Morrow, 1983

Prognostics, Polak, Fred L., New York: Elsevier Publishing Co., 1971

Silent Spring, Carson, Rachel, Boston: Houghton-Mifflin, 1962

Societal Evolution: A Study of Science and Society, Keller, A.G., New Haven, CT: Yale University Press, 1931

Software Maintenance, Martin, J., and McClure, S., Englewood Cliffs, NJ: Prentice-Hall, 1984

Technology and Man's Future, Ozbekhan, Hasan, Santa Monica: System Development Corporation, 1966

Telecommunications and the Computer, Martin, James, Englewood Cliffs, NJ: Prentice-Hall, 1969

The Existential Pleasures of Engineering, Florman, Samuel C., New York: St.Martin's Press, 1985

The Most Probable World, Chase, Stuart, New York: Pelican Books, 1969

The Poverty of Historicism, Popper, Karl, London: Routledge & Kegan Paul, 1961

The Technology Assessment Function, Mayo, Louis H., Washington: George Washington University, 1968

INDEX

A

Abstraction, two-level 136, 176, 223, 247, 249
Academia 22, 26, 31, 70, 83, 92, 123, 154, 197, 199, 204, 211-213
Adversarial relationships 47, 57, 120, 136, 171-173, 183, 184, 232, 270
Allocation 121, 136, 168, 169, 176, 191, 199, 262
Artificial intelligence 87, 257
Ashby 128, 136, 139, 150, 161-181, 189, 195, 230, 233, 257, 263, 264, 280
Assessment 135, 136, 176, 183, 220, 222, 226, 232, 234, 255, 259, 264, 282

B

Bad Seventies 17, 18, 21, 24, 26, 39, 69, 75, 83, 85, 100, 109, 134, 136, 159, 193, 221, 225, 231, 246, 255, 264
Banks 15, 16, 38, 93, 114, 142, 181, 237, 240, 252
Behavior 35, 42, 45, 55, 65, 67, 70, 71, 82, 83, 85, 87, 89, 91-93, 113, 115, 119, 121, 125, 129, 131, 134, 135, 143, 153, 168, 177, 195, 203, 209, 212, 215, 216, 222, 227, 229, 236, 241, 246, 248, 257
Boundaries 36, 53, 71, 88, 109, 132, 136, 163, 175-177, 179, 188, 220, 259
Brain 16, 17, 21, 34, 81, 85-88, 91, 97, 141, 142, 153, 154, 230, 241, 262

C

Camouflage 15, 24, 49, 54, 55, 57, 59, 63, 114, 127, 193, 241, 248
Camouflage Squared 49, 57, 248
Civilization 73, 79, 88, 92, 97, 103, 185, 192
Closure 139, 141, 177, 179, 180, 184
Cognitive dissonance 89-91, 93, 113, 125, 136, 176, 216, 234, 240-249, 253
Communications 15, 24, 55, 70, 81, 97, 99, 101, 113, 114, 117, 119, 120, 135, 136, 142, 145-149, 151, 169, 175, 179, 183-187, 248-260
Compensators 184, 185
Complex problems 2, 31, 33-35, 40, 63, 69, 70, 75-77, 79, 97, 99, 115
Compression 143, 144, 147, 183, 184
Computer 21, 26, 34, 39, 63, 65, 70, 75, 77, 87, 117, 123, 129, 131, 133, 141, 142, 145, 149, 163, 165, 171, 223, 245, 258
Connections 12, 15, 132, 135, 136, 143, 173-176, 199, 220, 234, 240, 244, 249, 253, ·255, 259, 260, 264, 280
Constraints 129, 142, 145, 148
Context 69, 71, 77, 132, 139, 151, 165, 175, 185, 225, 227, 235, 260, 268, 280
Control 22, 25, 32-35, 39, 42, 45, 47, 53, 55, 64, 69, 71, 82, 91-95, 103, 104-111, 120-131, 134, 137, 143, 146-149, 161-163, 168, 169, 173, 189, 192, 203, 205-207, 210-212, 215-217, 221-223, 225-262
Control, Cycle of 136, 139, 141, 176, 177, 179-181, 187, 221, 227
Cross-reference 114, 119. 120, 176, 136, 179, 181, 184, 244, 249, 264
Culture 22, 45, 61, 65, 88, 123, 160, 181, 205, 209, 211, 215, 236, 237, 251

D

D&D (Disconnect & Distance manoeuver) 151, 153, 164, 165, 211, 231, 243-248
Darts 136, 220, 234, 240, 243, 244, 249, 260
Deceptions 97, 132, 135, 220, 247, 255, 259, 264
Deming 49, 77, 109, 111, 114, 122, 205, 206, 244, 277, 279
Denials 21, 120-122, 135, 220, 255, 259, 264
Design for Complexity 76, 155, 166-169, 175, 179, 189-191, 225, 231, 245
Distortions 113, 115, 121-123, 135, 139, 176, 181, 229, 234, 239, 240, 245

E

Eliminations 20, 23, 27, 115, 122, 135, 176, 220, 255, 256, 260, 262, 264
Environment 16, 42, 63, 76, 83, 88, 89, 92, 93, 95, 97, 100, 103, 107, 120, 122, 127, 137, 139, 141, 148, 163, 167-169, 183, 184, 187, 189, 193, 209, 212, 217, 221, 223, 225-227, 230, 231, 239, 240, 255
EOPMD (End Of Project Mismatch Discovery) 58, 59, 63, 129, 145, 173, 189, 226, 231, 233, 248
Establishment 15, 16, 26, 40, 42, 59, 63, 73, 75, 77, 88, 92, 99-101, 103, 105, 107, 121-123, 137, 139, 157, 160, 163, 165, 192, 193, 195, 197, 199-201, 203, 206, 209, 211-229, 239, 241, 246, 251, 256, 257, 258, 260, 262-264
Expansion 88, 120, 144, 183, 184

F

F4 (The Facade of Futile Feigned Faith) 56, 57, 133, 135, 220, 259, 260, 264
Failure 12, 16, 17, 21, 24, 31, 42, 45, 47, 49, 53, 59-77, 95, 101, 105, 107, 109, 120, 121, 123, 132-135, 137, 167-179, 184, 192, 195, 209, 211, 219-222, 225, 229, 232, 234, 236, 247, 248, 252, 253, 257, 260
Feedback 27, 61, 63, 71, 73, 93, 107, 109, 111, 114, 118-128, 135-140, 149, 153, 159, 160, 176, 179, 184, 185, 193, 197, 199, 203, 209, 216, 222, 230, 244-259

Primary Working Group 55, 57, 92, 148, 149, 154, 177, 227, 240
Productivity 65, 76, 77, 123, 168, 189, 191, 206, 236, 263, 269, 270, 278, 279

Q

Quality 24, 49, 75, 77, 87, 109, 114, 121, 122, 128, 131-133, 155, 157, 163, 173, 185, 192, 203-207, 209-211, 257, 258, 263, 266, 271, 275, 279

R

RBF (Run, Break and Fix) 49, 61
Requisite variety 139, 183, see also: Variety
Resistance 47, 49, 133, 136, 169-171, 176, 181, 189, 201, 215, 223, 235, 251, 263
Risk 15, 59, 91, 109, 128, 133, 140, 168, 173, 181, 205, 206, 211, 215, 222, 225, 235, 246, 253, 259, 260
Roadblocks 113, 115, 119, 122-125, 135, 171, 176, 262
Rules 45, 53, 75, 89, 92, 93, 105, 111, 115, 119, 125, 127, 128, 131, 132, 135, 137, 139, 141, 145, 154, 171, 184, 185, 192, 200, 209, 211, 222, 223, 230, 236, 237, 244, 255, 257

S

Savannah 82, 92, 97, 99, 125, 153, 181, 185, 235, 236, 258, 286
Simple Problems 33, 51, 79, 153, 244, 250
SIPOD 176, 257
Skunkworks 136, 147, 167, 169, 171, 175, 176, 184, 186, 189, 191, 197, 231, 245
Social control 82, 91, 92, 94, 95, 128, 168, 207, 216, 223, 227, 239, 241, 248, 253
Social system 47, 59, 88, 113, 115, 136, 159, 165, 169, 175-179, 183, 185, 187, 193, 206, 213, 225, 226, 232, 235, 237, 258, 259, 261, 263
Solutions 24, 33, 34, 47, 51, 53, 55, 79, 103, 136, 157, 167, 176, 177, 209, 232, 237, 245, 250, 251, 257, 263
Status quo 12, 67, 70, 100, 111, 115, 119, 123, 125, 129, 131-133, 135, 160, 192, 197, 199, 203, 206, 209, 216, 243, 246, 262
Stress 16, 17, 24, 35, 36, 49, 55, 57, 83, 89, 93, 100, 107, 114, 125, 131, 136, 139, 146, 147, 160, 163, 217, 221-223, 227-229, 231, 233, 234, 239-241, 246, 248, 249, 252, 256, 259, 262, 265, 266, 269, 270
Stress Disposal Program 228
Structure 15, 42, 53, 69, 75, 81, 89, 99, 107, 113, 115, 131, 136, 139, 143, 145, 147, 148, 150, 151, 153, 160, 161, 163, 175-177, 179, 181, 183, 187, 188, 197, 203, 206, 212, 216, 217, 220-222, 226, 227, 230, 234, 251, 258-260, 263, 264, 266, 268, 270-273, 276, 278, 279, 281
Success 14, 27, 35, 40, 65, 67-69, 76, 77, 81, 85, 93, 95, 97, 99, 109, 111, 115, 121, 123, 134, 136, 137, 139, 141, 143, 147, 151, 153, 161, 165, 167, 171, 176, 185, 197, 199, 206, 213, 220, 221, 226, 230, 234, 236, 243, 247, 249, 252, 256, 257, 260, 262
System 2, 15, 16, 22, 42-47, 51-61, 65, 69-73, 77, 87-89, 92, 95, 99, 103-120, 132, 133, 136, 141, 143, 145, 151, 154, 155, 159-163, 165, 167, 169, 171, 173, 175-179, 181, 183-185, 187, 203, 205-207, 209, 212, 213, 215, 217, 225-227, 229-233, 235, 237, 241, 244, 246, 248, 251-253, 255-259, 261-264
Systems Engineering 75, 76, 136, 155, 168, 176, 184, 279, 280

T

Task 51, 55, 59, 71, 85, 99, 119, 128, 131, 136, 139, 141, 159, 171, 175-187
TDBD (Top Down Break Down) 136, 175, 177
Technical System 47, 136, 165, 169, 175-179, 183, 185, 206, 226, 232, 257
Territorial Imperative 136, 139, 140, 152-155, 157, 159, 171, 173, 176
Toolbox 70, 129, 159, 168, 173, 176, 220, 239, 252, 255, 260, 264
Track A 63, 93, 169, 173, 176, 191, 228, 231, 250-253, 255, 259
Track B 167, 169, 171, 173, 176, 189, 191, 228, 234, 251, 253, 255, 259
Triggers 30, 31, 42, 49, 59, 66, 67, 69, 93, 127, 131, 139, 146-148, 179-181, 211, 222, 223

U

Unfun 16-18, 21, 30-32, 34, 39, 92, 217, 219, 221, 235
Universal Scenario, The 42
Variety 27, 55, 70, 71, 75, 79, 95, 97, 103, 129, 136-153, 161-165, 173, 176, 183, 185, 195, 197, 203, 216, 221, 222, 233, 237, 252, 253, 257, 259
Voids 113-115, 117, 119, 122, 123, 135, 176, 181, 220, 243, 262
Vulnerabilities 113, 122, 135, 136, 220, 223, 229, 237, 243, 255, 260, 261, 263, 264
Workers 39, 53, 73, 77, 97, 109, 133, 148, 173, 177, 179, 180, 187, 203-213, 217, 223, 239, 249
ZOI (Zone of Indifference) 35-45, 93, 103, 135, 176, 184, 220, 259, 264

Letter from Mike

Mr. Bill Livingston
World Trade Center
New York, NY 10048

March 30, 1988

Bill:

I have gone through a lot in the last twelve months and I would not trade the experience for anything. I just spent the last week catching up on mail, books, etc. God I hate accounting - and the never ending details (mostly government prompted). I am learning (hard way) about Workman's Comp., Federal and State Unemployment, FICA, W-4, W-etc., Liability Insurance, Bonding, IRS tax payments (timely), etc. And to think - I could be screwing off somewhere in a big Corporation - making good money and benefits - if only I had a different personality. (Maybe doctors will find a transplant technique on personality - maybe an injection that causes permanent apathy). OSHA may make me wear mittens and a hardhat while working at my PC and Workman's Comp. people may force me to put up a railing on my stairs - but life is good. As the cannibals say about eating missionaries - you can't keep a good man down.

We are or have been involved with several contracts now involving many companies and corporations. Bill, it's worse than your book states. The only places I have found to be different (to some degree) are very small businesses.

My biggest customer so far is somewhat different from my old place of work, but is involved in the "Plague" to a degree that would scare the pants off of their customers. What really bothers me the most is that I need their money - enough so that I sometimes choke on telling them the truth - they do not want to hear it. They are spending multi-millions on "modernization" - over some time period. Their plans appear to be in-line with the rest of the large manufacturing concerns - short sighted - unrealistic - quite shallow. They have the exact same degree of non-cooperation between different divisions as others. They use contractors like I use disposable lighters. Every time we get requirements - they change - after coding. Our main chore is to automate a single item (interfaces with several other systems) and that much we have done. How this will play with a Master Plan (that seems absent) is anyone's guess. They like to spoon feed tasks without giving a hint at the full plan. (We don't always get along). Some of our people seem to work better in this situation and so, like any capitalist, I have backed off and am letting others put in many hours each week, at a good wage, doing what they ask of us - exactly. What a whore I have turned out to be. The hard truth is that the income we gain is what is keeping us alive. All of their people seem to be totally caught up in crisis management - responding to never ending problems caused by proceeding on new items while paying attention to old items that are now in crisis stage. I have not been able to really be a true "whore" and so I have not been the "typical" consultant. Last week I jumped their case hard about spoon feeding and lack of firm requirements and made a case where they are running up a bill far greater than need be. They didn't begin to understand what I was talking about. I did however cash their check when it came in the mail last week and our people are still putting in the hours.

Just one other note about that job. It was originally quoted as a fixed price contract job after a time and material study of the requirements. Under our first project coordinator, things were progressing - but changing. Because we design first, we were only slightly bothered by the late arrival of some details on requirements. Now with a new project coordinator, things have been changing at the speed of light - entire approaches, some philosophical changes as well. They now want coding - bottom up. I raised Hell and the contract was changed to time and material. (I was supposed to feel better?) Much more money has been spent under the T & M contract and the clock is still ticking. The item in question is now in a production status but the change requests we receive are spontaneous and quick fix in nature, sometimes undoing a fix done last week, still spoon fed with little thought towards the final objectives. So far, the status of the system has not caused finger pointing towards us - because we have been implementing exactly what was requested - but this could change, as you well know, at any time. It is my strong feeling that our ability to perform has been hampered and I have no way of knowing (yet) how all of this will come into play when we attempt to get more work from this customer. I do know that we protest more than the usual contractor and it is definitely not appreciated. Our resultant work effort efficiency has been cut in half by the constant change and the spoon feed techniques employed. Based on that, our performance can not possibly be viewed by their upper management as superior. I am depressed.

On the brighter side, the work I am doing with another customer allows me to feel professional about the effort. Hope it continues. The only difference is that the product, although (I certainly don't understand it), is totally under my control allowing it to proceed as it should - slowly and deliberately. The money is really shitty on that one however. (Oh well)

Do you know where I can buy mittens that are flexible enough to allow the wearer to type? I could also use a lead on a cheap outlet for hardhats, safety glasses and safety shoes. I got a good deal on seat belts for my secretarial chairs and will gladly give you the name of my source. Take care.

Somewhat of a Capitalistic Pig, but still CARES,

Mike

HAVE FUN AT WORK

About the author: William L. Livingston is a professional mechanical engineer with thirty years in the innovation arena. He holds over 100 patents in diverse technologies, and is the author of **The New Plague: Organizations in Complexity.**

Front Cover: Commissioned especially for this book, **Savannah Man** is by Rob Schouten, a Whidbey Island (Washington State) Visionary Artist whose "...crystalline realism shatters the perceptions and then soothes the heart." His work has been bicoastal to the United States, transoceanic to The Netherlands, and transhemispheric to the brain.

Back Cover: **On Time, Under Budget and As Planned** by Rob Schouten. One of the ART FOR ENGINEERS series from F.E.S. This particular piece makes sense in any orientation, and is available in a triangular frame so that it can be rotated to suit. Rob signed it three times.

The Cartoons: The black-line images are from the pen of Columbia, South Carolina artist Gwen Moore. She is an accomplished painter and artisan of sculpture, whose work is on public display throughout the South Eastern United States. Gwen's inestimable talent for representational symbolism has delighted fans of **The New PLAGUE**, as well as the companion posters, "ORGANIZATIONS" and "DIPTYCH."

F.E.S. LTD.

PUBLISHING

BOX 70 BAYSIDE, N.Y. 11361